LIBRARY IN A BOOK

GAY RIGHTS

Revised Edition

Rachel Kranz
Tim Cusick

Facts On File, Inc.

Facts On File, Inc.
132 West 31st Street
New York NY 10001

Library of Congress Cataloging-in-Publication Data
Kranz, Rachel.
    Gay rights / Rachel Kranz and Tim Cusick.— Rev. ed.
    p. cm.— (Library in a book)
Includes bibliographical references and index.
    ISBN 0-8160-5810-5
    1. Gay rights—United States. I. Cusick, Tim. II. Title. III. Series.
HQ76.8.U5K73 2005
323.3'264'0973—dc22   2005009832

Facts On File books are available at special discounts when purchased in bulk quantities for businesses, associations, institutions or sales promotions. Please call our Special Sales Department in New York at 212/967-8800 or 800/322-8755.

You can find Facts On File on the World Wide Web at http://www.factsonfile.com

Text design by Ron Monteleone

Printed in the United States of America

MP Hermitage 10 9 8 7 6 5 4 3 2 1

This book is printed on acid-free paper.

CONTENTS

———————————————

ACKNOWLEDGMENTS

The authors wish to thank Jeff Domoto, for his tireless and invaluable help with databases and other computer-related problems; Paula Ettelbrick, for her cogent and generous explanations; Terence Maikels, for his expert, patient work as editor on both editions; and most especially Nicole Bowen and Laura Shauger for their endless support of this project.

For his invaluable web site, www.gayrightsinfo.com, so helpful for preparing the first edition the authors thank the anonymous but thorough site author. Sadly, this site is no longer available.

Finally, Rachel Kranz wishes to thank Ellie Siegel for the conversations that began many years ago and that have borne fruit in the writing of this book.

PART I

OVERVIEW OF THE TOPIC

CHAPTER 1

INTRODUCTION TO GAY RIGHTS

One of the most astonishing social transformations of the past three decades has been the changes wrought by the gay rights movement in the United States.*

   Homosexuality, once a taboo subject that could barely be mentioned in public, has become a common topic of debate among politicians, voters, and the media. From being invisible, closeted, and fearful of persecution, gay men and lesbians have "come out" as politicians, TV stars, athletes, and "the family next door." The notion of legally recognized gay marriage, once an unthinkable concept, is now a genuine possibility in the state of Massachusetts, Canada, and several European nations—and was one of the major issues of contention in the November 2004 presidential election, when 11 states voted by significant margins to amend their state constitutions to ban it. In many states and cities around the country, gay people have won an array of court, legislative, and cultural victories: the right to receive domestic partnership benefits; antidiscrimination laws in employment and housing; positive representation in school curricula; increased penalties for antigay violence, now viewed by some as a hate crime; and an unprecedented visibility in U.S. culture. There are now openly gay musicians (k.d. lang, Elton John, George Michael), movie and TV personalities (Rosie O'Donnell, Ellen DeGeneres, the "Fab Five" on *Queer Eye for the Straight Guy*), and politicians (Massachusetts representative Barney Frank; Wisconsin

---

* Terminology for the gay rights movement has changed a great deal over the years, and at this point, no term is satisfactory for use in every situation. For convenience, this volume uses *gay*, *gay rights*, and *gay people* as umbrella terms to include gay men, lesbians, and bisexuals. In some cases transgender people are also included in the term, although many transgender people do not consider themselves gay or lesbian, and at some points in gay history, transgender rights were considered part of the gay rights movement. Nor does this volume fully cover transgender issues, although it does include some information. Occasionally, however, the term *LGBT* will be used to signify "lesbian/gay/bisexual/transgender." The authors' intention with terminology was to be respectful, inclusive, historically correct, and above all, readable.

3

representative Tammy Baldwin; New York state senator Deborah Glick; Virginia legislator Adam Ebbin; Carrboro, North Carolina, mayor Michael Nelson). Even the terminology has changed: from *homosexual, invert,* and *pervert* to *gay, queer,* and *out and proud.*

Moreover, in 2003, the U.S. Supreme Court overturned its own previous ruling and declared in *Lawrence v. Texas* that laws outlawing sodomy (a type of sexual practice associated with homosexuality) were unconstitutional. Sodomy laws had criminalized gay men and lesbians for hundreds of years; for the Supreme Court to rule that such laws violate the Constitutional rights of gay citizens was a major shift in the legal status of U.S. gay residents. The gay rights movement went on to celebrate a number of developments that seemingly hastened the possibility of legal same-sex marriage in the United States, including a 2003 ruling by the Massachusetts Supreme Court that withholding marriage licenses from same-sex couples violated the state's constitution; and the issuing of thousands of marriage licenses to same-sex couples in U.S. communities from San Francisco to New Paltz, New York. As of this writing, nine Canadian provinces (British Columbia, Ontario, Quebec, Manitoba, the Yukon, Nova Scotia, Newfoundland, and Saskatchewan) have likewise begun issuing same-sex marriage licenses, so that only three Canadian provinces remain *without* such recognition. Moreover, the Canadian Supreme Court has ruled that gay marriage does not violate the country's constitution, opening the door to a national acceptance of gay marriage—further evidence that attitudes on same-sex marriage are changing.

Yet these very victories have brought with them a backlash. Many states have amended their constitutions to explicitly ban gay marriage. In February 2004, President George W. Bush announced his support for a national effort to prohibit gay marriage through a proposed constitutional amendment that would define marriage as taking place between a man and a woman. Many nationwide religious and political groups have made antigay activity a major item on their agendas, employing a wide variety of legal and political efforts: electing antigay state and city legislators, working to repeal local gay rights ordinances, and organizing statewide referendums to overturn local antidiscrimination rules.

Nevertheless, according to a report by the American Enterprise Institute (AEI), a conservative think tank based in Washington, D.C., gay men and lesbians are more widely accepted in U.S. society than ever before. The AEI compiled 30 years' worth of public opinion polls on gay issues, revealing a significant shift in attitudes. Although about two-thirds of U.S. residents consistently oppose gay marriage, other commonly held opinions have changed:

- Approval of gays in the military rose from 51 percent in 1977 to 80 percent in 2003.
- Acceptance of gay elementary school teachers rose from 27 percent to 61 percent during the same period.
- Only 26 percent of voters in 1978 stated they would cast their ballots for a well-qualified gay presidential candidate, compared with 59 percent in 1999.

Introduction to Gay Rights

A March 20, 2004, *L.A. Times* article on the AEI findings suggested that these extraordinary shifts have resulted from a number of factors, including the African-American civil rights movement and the sexual revolution of the 1960s and 1970s. Black struggles for equality established the notion of universal civil rights, while the sexual revolution transformed Americans' notions of entitlement to sexual privacy. The AIDS epidemic from the 1980s onward has provided the public with numerous images of gay people caring for their partners, which helped transform stereotypes of homosexuals. Former president Bill Clinton's appointment of gay people to high-ranking government positions also sent the message that gay men and lesbians are full-fledged citizens. Gay images on TV and in popular culture fueled both gay visibility and public acceptance, as did inclusion of gay men and lesbians in reports on the September 11 attacks. "The whole country was undergoing collective grief and suffering," said Brad Sears, director of the Williams Project on Sexual Orientation Law at UCLA Law School, according to the *L.A. Times* article. ". . . and gay people were a part of it—the gay New York Fire Department chaplain who was killed, the gay rugby player who fought back on one of the planes. People saw those positive images." But, the article quoted Sears as saying, "The act of coming out [identifying oneself as gay] has probably been the single most important determinant in the change in public opinion polls. People learn that this isn't some kind of abstract, foreign exotic creature. This is somebody who lives down the street."

The same article stresses a newly developing generation gap when it comes to attitudes about homosexuality. According to polls, people ages 18 to 29 are far more likely to be tolerant of gay men and lesbians than are older people. A 2001 survey of high school seniors, for example, conducted by Hamilton College students in connection with the Zogby polling organization, found that 66 percent—more than double the adult ratio—supported gay marriage.

Even among older adults, however, there is a growing acceptance of gay relationships, whether as marriage or in some other legally recognized form. A November 7, 2004, *New York Times* article by Pam Belluck, analyzing the role of the antigay vote in the reelection of President George W. Bush, referred to exit polls cited by gay rights activist Mary L. Bonauto, showing that 27 percent of all voters support same-sex marriage while another 35 percent support civil unions. While anti–gay rights leaders have pointed to the electoral results as evidence of the nation's overwhelming opposition to gay marriage, gay rights activists draw the opposite conclusion: that some 62 percent of the American electorate supports some version of legal recognition for gay partnership.

Legal, political, and cultural battles bearing on gay rights are currently being fought over adoption, gay-straight alliances at public schools, the use of student fees on college campuses, the offerings of public libraries, and a host of other issues. Gay rights are hotly debated in many spheres and many contexts. Clearly, no one book can cover everything there is to know about gay rights. This book's goal is far more modest: to provide a sense of the major issues in this important movement and to offer ways of finding out more information. To that end, this chapter provides an overview of the movement and its history. The next chapter focuses on gay legal issues and mentions important court cases and major developments in government policy. Chapter 3 discusses cultural issues: what's been going on in schools, the arts, popular culture, religion, and public opinion. A chronology outlines the political evolution of gay rights. A set of brief biographies of major figures in the area and a small glossary are also available for further reference.

Part 2 of this book offers a wide variety of suggestions for researching gay rights; provides a bibliography of recent articles and major books; and lists organizations—some in favor of gay rights and some opposed. Finally, the book concludes with excerpts from laws and court decisions conveying key issues that have preoccupied the gay rights movement for the past 35 years.

It is important to remember that although there has been a powerful movement for gay and lesbian rights, there's no such thing as a single "gay rights movement." That is, while a number of people and organizations have fought many political, legal, and cultural battles, there is not necessarily widespread agreement on any side. Some gay activists have advocated working within the system; others have urged demonstrations and direct action. Some gay rights leaders argue that gay people are a distinct culture that ought to be respected; others insist that gay men and lesbians are exactly like their heterosexual counterparts except for their choice of a same-sex romantic partner. Some gay activists are deeply concerned with the rights of sexual minorities, among them transgender people and people who practice sadomasochism and other unconventional sex acts. Other gay leaders fear that "those people give the rest of us a bad name." Over the past 35 years—since the modern gay rights movement began with the Stonewall uprising of 1969—gay rights activists have argued over sexual freedom, political strategy, and the very definition of gayness and lesbianism.

Meanwhile, many gay individuals do not even see themselves as supporting "gay rights," preferring to hide their homosexuality or play down its importance. Yet these same people might be moved by a political crisis, such as the spread of AIDS or a statewide referendum calling for the firing of any teacher suspected of being gay. Or they might be moved by a more personal matter—a longtime partner being excluded from a family event, the threat of losing custody of a child, the realization that their boss or colleagues regularly exclude them from the "social" luncheons and afterwork happy hours at which company business is often discussed. To all of these people, "gay rights" means something different and the impact of "the gay rights movement" has been experienced differently as well.

As the U.S. gay rights movement has grown in influence and visibility, it has spawned an opposition movement of people and organizations who are bitterly opposed to gay rights. Like the gay rights movement to which it is responding, this "anti–gay rights" movement is not a monolithic entity, but includes a wide range of people, opinions, tactics, and concerns. Some elements of the anti–gay rights movement are religious in origin, most often citing Christian sources as evidence for the immorality of homosexuality. Jewish, Muslim, and other reli-

6

gious sources are also cited in anti–gay rights rhetoric and literature. Some elements of the anti–gay rights movement focus more on tradition, particularly where gay marriage is concerned. Thus, although many people who oppose gay marriage do so on religious grounds, many others see same-sex marriage as an unacceptable redefinition of a traditional institution. Likewise, many people, whether religious or not, view gay men and women as irresponsible, overly sexual, and/or a dangerous influence on children.

Opposition to gay rights also depends a great deal on context. Some people view homosexuality as immoral and believe that any open expression of it should be suppressed; others believe gay people deserve civil and/or political rights but should not be represented in schools or in the culture; still others are comfortable with gay cultural representations but oppose gay rights legislation.

This chapter begins by listing a broad range of topics included in the term *gay rights*. It then discusses some of the contradictions and splits within the movement and continues by offering a history of gay rights in the United States that shows some ways in which many of these contradictions and splits have played out. It also includes an overview of the anti–gay rights movement.

By the time this volume is published, the political climate may have changed yet again. Events are moving quickly, and people on all sides of the issue are continually changing their position. The resources provided by the rest of this book will enable further investigative research to track the ever-changing condition of gay rights in the United States.

GAY RIGHTS:
A BROAD RANGE OF DEMANDS

The movement for gay rights has encompassed a broad range of demands—and a great deal of conflict. The following list gives a sense of the areas that concern the modern gay rights movement. Many gay men and lesbians disagree strongly about various points on this list. However, here is a quick overview of the types of issues that currently concern many gay men and lesbians:

- *Marriage:* The effort to legalize same-sex marriage has a history that is several decades old, but progress toward winning this right for gay men and lesbians has increased dramatically in the 21st century. As of this writing, the legal status of gay marriage is far from certain, with a national debate raging over various options for the recognition of same-sex couples. The question of whether gay couples should be allowed civil marriage, civil union (a legal form of gay family recognition that differs from state to state), domestic partnership (another restricted form of family recognition), or no legal recognition at all has spurred bitter disputes both within and outside of the gay rights movement.

- ***Domestic Partnership:*** A number of civil suits recently brought by gay men and lesbians are demanding legal recognition of same-sex domestic partnership.

For example, gay men and lesbians whose partners have died have success-fully obtained standing to bring wrongful death suits. (*Standing* is a legal term indicating that a person has grounds for bringing a suit. A husband or wife has standing to sue, say, a hospital for negligent treatment that resulted in a spouse's death; a friend has no such standing.) This particular legal ac-ceptance is further indication that same-sex partnerships are gaining legal recognition.

- **Recognition of Gay Families:** Both because gay sexual practices used to be il-legal in many states, and because prevailing opinion often considered gay men and lesbians to be, by definition, "unfit parents," child custody issues have been a major focus of the gay rights movement. One of the major argu-ments gay rights activists have advanced in favor of same-sex marriage is that it would give gay and lesbian parents the same kind of legal rights to their children that straight parents enjoy. Even after 2003, when the Supreme Court struck down the sodomy laws that criminalized gay sex, gay and lesbian parents have often had difficulty winning child custody battles. Likewise, the right of gay men and lesbians to adopt children, including the right to adopt as a couple rather than as individuals, has been a focus of one aspect of the gay rights movement.

- **Employment Rights:** Although one-half of all states, hundreds of local gov-ernments, and thousands of private employers have some form of antidis-crimination law or regulation, a person can still often be fired simply because an employer dislikes gay people. Since one of the major employers in the United States is the Armed Forces, the right of gay men and lesbians to par-ticipate in the military is another concern. The gay rights movement also seeks to win recognition of same-sex partnerships from public and private employers so that a gay or lesbian partner can receive health insurance and other benefits that a married partner would enjoy. Finally, the gay rights movement seeks employment rights for gay and lesbian teachers, since many court cases have supported a school district's right to fire a teacher for being gay, while referendums in various states—so far, all defeated—have sought to make "no gay teachers" into a statewide policy. (In addition to fighting for the right to be in the classroom, many gay activists want what they call a "gay-friendly" or "gay-tolerant" curriculum: educational materials that present being gay as an acceptable way of life that deserves respect.)

- **Responses to Violence:** As numerous instances of antigay violence continue to demonstrate, it is still not physically safe to be a gay man or lesbian in the United States. Antigay violence is viewed by some as a *hate crime*—a type of crime motivated by prejudice against a certain social, ethnic, or religious group. In some parts of the country, hate crimes directed against African Americans, Jews, and other ethnic groups receive harsher penalties than crimes of violence judged not to be hate crimes. Many gay activists believe that giving hate crime status to violence directed against gay men and lesbians would send a strong message for gay rights. Other activists urge community-based responses to antigay violence, such as working to increase tolerance for gay men and lesbians and educating police officers to greater sensitivity.

- *Religious Recognition:* Groups like Dignity, a gay Catholic group, and Integrity, for gay Episcopalians, reflect the wishes of many gay people to be recognized by their religion of choice. Several Christian and Jewish denominations ordain gay and lesbian ministers and rabbis; there are also many gay and gay-friendly churches and synagogues around the country. However, most Western religions, as well as many individual congregations, are strongly resistant to the idea of accepting homosexuality, whether they view it as a sin or a psychological disorder. Hence, one part of the gay rights movement has focused on winning full religious recognition of gay men and lesbians.

- *Participation in Society:* Many gay men and lesbians point out that they enjoy the same activities as heterosexuals and share many of the same identities. Gay boys might want to be Boy Scouts or Boy Scout leaders; gay and lesbian people of Irish descent would like to march in a St. Patrick's Day parade; and gay teachers wish to pursue their careers without having to lie about their private lives. Yet, when Eagle Scout and assistant scoutmaster James Dale of New Jersey was identified in a newspaper photograph in 1990 as the leader of a gay rights group, the Boy Scouts of America expelled him. The New Jersey Supreme Court ordered the Boy Scouts to restore his membership; the organization appealed the case to the Supreme Court, which in 2000 ruled in its favor. In response, a number of communities and even the state of Connecticut have sought to withdraw their support of the Boy Scouts, on the grounds that the organization violates local antidiscrimination laws that protect gay men and lesbians. Meanwhile, St. Patrick's Day parade organizers in Boston and New York have successfully managed to forbid openly gay and lesbian groups from marching in their parades.

- *Cultural Expression:* For many years, books and visual materials that portrayed gay relationships were considered obscene, and openly gay people were virtually absent from movies, television, popular music, advertisements, and other forms of popular culture. One part of the gay rights movement has focused on creating books, movies, music, and other forms of artistic and commercial expression that portray gay life and gay concerns. In some cases this has been an alternative movement, in which gay and lesbian presses and journals, performance artists and theater companies, and music festivals and record companies have created new forms of writing, music, theater, and journalism. In other cases, cultural work takes place in the established worlds of popular and high culture, with gay novelists being published by mainstream presses and gay TV writers creating their own shows. For example, MTV Networks is launching LOGO, a gay network. Still another aspect of cultural expression has been "queer studies"—the efforts of academics of all different types of sexual orientation to challenge the very concept of gender and sexual preference and to interpret history, art, literature, and modern culture in new ways.

- **Political Power:** This term means widely different things to different people. Some gay activists focus on electing gay men and lesbians to positions of power. Others are concerned with building broad-based organizations that can lobby politicians to win gay demands. Still other gay people focus on direct action—demonstrations and other types of public protest to draw attention to urgent issues. A significant number of gay rights activists are committed to building coalitions across political movements. Of course, these activities frequently overlap.

- **Sexual Freedom:** Many gay men and lesbians became involved in various aspects of the gay rights movement because of their wish to express themselves sexually in ways that the larger society might not accept. The early gay liberation movement celebrated the freedom of gay men and lesbians to choose their partners and sexual arrangements, which often involved an interest in sexual experimentation. Some people claimed new identities: as transvestites, transsexuals, or other types of transgender individuals; as practitioners of S and M (sadomasochism); or as other types of so-called sexual minorities. Others insisted on their right to explore new types of relationships—such as various nonmonogamous arrangements or three-way relationships—or simply to enjoy the sexual opportunities available at discos, bathhouses, and clubs. For many gay men and lesbians, a commitment to sexual freedom and a respect for a variety of sexual identities is central to their vision of gay rights.

CONFLICTS AND CONTRADICTIONS

Virtually every item on the preceding list has been the cause of some controversy among those who identify themselves as supporters of gay rights. Debate and disagreement have marked the modern gay rights movement since the founding of the Mattachine Society in 1950. The following are some of the major conflicts that the movement struggles with today.

ASSIMILATIONISM VS. MAINTAINING A CULTURAL IDENTITY

Some activists, theorists, and commentators have argued that gay people are basically the same as their heterosexual counterparts. All they want is to be allowed to participate in their society on equal terms, or to be given "a place at the table," in the words of Bruce Bawer, whose 1993 book was so titled. Journalist Andrew Sullivan, former editor of the centrist journal the *New Republic*, has likewise argued in his 1995 book, *Virtually Normal*, that homosexuality is a purely personal quality, not a cultural category. In the same vein, the gay magazine *Out* has published editorials with a point of view identified as "postgay," meaning that gayness is no longer something to worry about or to be defined by.

Other gay activists and writers claim a more significant place for "gay culture," "lesbian perspectives," or a "queer outlook." Law professor and novelist

Ruthann Robson, for example, has written eloquently about the need for lesbians to resist the pressure to fit into relationships and family patterns designed by and for heterosexuals. Playwright Tony Kushner has talked about developing a "Theater of the Fabulous," informed by (though not limited to) his special perceptions and cultural style as a gay man. Kushner has also written of a "socialism of the skin," a view of politics in which sexual orientation and experience are integral to a political vision—an outlook that he likewise relates to his experiences as a gay man.

Still others argue that "gay culture" only exists because of gay oppression. Daniel Harris, for example, in his book *The Rise and Fall of Gay Culture*, analyzes gay men's historic love of divas and movie stars as a kind of cultural code. Referring to certain movies and actresses, he argues, was a way for gay men to recognize themselves and each other in a world that made a more open acknowledgment of their sexual feelings very dangerous. Likewise, attending cultural events like Judy Garland concerts was a safe way to be with other gay men, while identifying with glamorous, cosmopolitan performers was one way for gay men to feel superior to the society that seemed to hold them in contempt.

According to Harris, much of gay male culture and identity grew out of a common response to oppression. Thus, in the 1950s and 1960s, he says, there was no "generation gap" in the white gay urban culture of cities like San Francisco and New York: men from age 20 through age 70 liked the same movies, the same music, and the same style of dress. Today, he says, young gay men have far more in common with young straight men than they do with gay men in their 40s and 50s, a sign of how far the mainstream culture has expanded to include gays. As the dominant culture becomes more gay-friendly, Harris believes, assimilation—the gradual blending of gay men into the larger culture—is inevitable. (Harris's analysis is only concerned with men. Analysts of lesbian culture tend to be more skeptical about the possibilities of assimilation.)

Clearly, the conflict between the drive to assimilate and the wish to maintain an identity is less a hard-and-fast division between two distinct points of view than a kind of creative tension that shapes various debates. Do gay and lesbian politicians bring a unique and valuable perspective to the political arena, along with an important commitment to represent the interests of an ignored minority, or do they simply run as "the best candidates for the job"? Is there a way of claiming equal citizenship and of making a special cultural contribution at the same time?

The increasing visibility of the gay marriage issue has greatly affected this debate. On the one hand, many gay men and lesbians have always wanted their relationships to be granted the legitimacy and acceptance that legal marriage seems to offer; and many others have wanted the economic and practical benefits that being married confers. This pro-marriage group has been opposed by those gay men and lesbians who argue that marriage marginalizes many people in society and that gay men, lesbians, transgender people, and other queers should celebrate their differences rather than trying to fit in. A third group of gay and lesbian activists opposes marriage or is indifferent to it, but is very much opposed to efforts to ban gay marriage, which they see as part of a larger trend to undermine gay rights and civil liberties in general.

As gay men and lesbians become more visible in the larger society, winning both legal rights and cultural acceptance in some circles, all of these questions will continue to preoccupy people who identify as gay.

IS BEING GAY INHERITED, LEARNED, OR CHOSEN?

At first glance, this might appear to be a straightforward question, one that might be answered as a matter of fact by the disciplines of psychology, biology, or genetics. In fact, the question gives rise to an intensely political debate, and the search for an answer is as much driven by a particular agenda for gay politics as by an objective search for truth.

Both experts and the general public have put forth various theories of what makes people gay. Some religious traditions have viewed being gay as a choice, and therefore a sin. Other religious perspectives hold that while sexual *feelings* for people of the same sex may be inborn and therefore blameless, the choice to *act* upon those feelings is sinful. (Still other religious perspectives view homosexuality as simply another way of life and make no religious judgment on it one way or another.)

Psychological schools of thought are also contradictory. Sigmund Freud, the founder of modern psychology, held that homosexuality was not in itself a disorder but merely one of many sexual possibilities that a human being might be drawn to. Freud attributed interest in same-sex relationships to early childhood events: generally speaking, he believed that men and women who made same-sex choices later in life had become overly attached to the opposite-sex parent by age five. Thus, a boy who had a deep emotional involvement with his mother might be unable to devote himself to other women as he grew older. He might also identify with his mother, so that, feeling like a woman, he would choose men for sexual partners. However, Freud offered a parallel set of early childhood experiences to explain heterosexuality. In his view, all sexual choices were molded during these years, with a wide variety of possible results.

Psychologists and psychiatrists working in the Freudian tradition have tended to maintain Freud's analysis while discarding his tolerance. For most of its history, Freudian analysis as well as other psychological approaches have viewed male and female homosexuality as a learned pattern of behavior—and as a sickness. Attempts to "cure" the sickness have included psychoanalysis, aversion therapy (for example, showing a man pictures of naked men while administering electric shock or nausea-inducing drugs), or even electroshock therapy. Among the early testimonies heard at gay consciousness-raising sessions in the 1970s were the stories of women and men who had tried to "overcome" their same-sex feelings through therapy or who had been committed to mental hospitals by their families for months or even years.

In the early days of the gay liberation movement, gay activists were less concerned with how gayness was created and more concerned with removing the stigma that made it a sin, a sickness, or a crime. Some gay activists turned the question around, asking hostile psychiatrists, "What made *you* heterosexual?" Others took comfort from the fact that some form of same-sex activity seemed to appear in virtually every human society, as evidenced by the reports of such anthropologists as Margaret Mead. A high point for the movement came in 1973, when, after months of work by gay activists, the American Psychiatric Society took homosexuality off its official list of mental disorders. Since then, homosexuality has not been considered a mental illness.

As the 1970s ended, though, a backlash developed. Religious organizations began to promote the vision of gay men and lesbians as making sinful choices. They also portrayed gayness as something that could be imposed upon an impressionable child. When singer and former beauty queen Anita Bryant began a 1977 campaign to revoke a gay rights ordinance in Dade County, Florida, she called her movement "Save Our Children," saying, ". . . since homosexuals cannot reproduce, they must recruit, must freshen their ranks. And who qualifies as a likely recruit: a 35-year-old father or mother of two . . . or a teenage boy or girl who is surging with sexual awareness?"

Gay rights activists denied this portrait of gay men and lesbians as child molesters, but the movement still included a wide range of opinions about the true causes and nature of homosexuality. Some argued that homosexuals were just "born that way," citing the accounts of those who have claimed they "just knew" that they were "different" than other kids by the age of four or five. Generally speaking, in the 1970s and early 1980s, gay men were more likely than women to argue this position. Thus, when Congresswoman Bella Abzug began introducing a federal gay rights bill to Congress, some gay male activists wanted the bill to refer to "sexual orientation," to express their view of homosexuality as something they were born with.

On the other hand, the lesbians lobbying Abzug preferred the term *sexual preference*, to indicate that their lesbianism was an active choice. Theorist and poet Adrienne Rich wrote a famous article, "Compulsory Heterosexuality and the Lesbian Continuum," in which she argued that both men and women were more likely to prefer women's bodies, since both genders were traditionally raised by women. Thus, while it might indeed be "natural" for most men to have sexual feelings about women, most women would also probably choose female sex partners—if society did not punish this choice so severely. Rich called on women to resist society's efforts to suppress their lesbianism, inviting them to recognize what she considered the lesbian component in their female friendships and work partnerships.

Many other lesbian-feminists of the 1970s and early 1980s took a similar position, arguing that women who were true to their natures and/or genuinely committed to the liberation of women would avoid "sleeping with the enemy" and would choose lesbianism as the deepest expression of their feminism. Slogans like "Feminism is the theory, lesbianism is the practice" and "A woman needs a man like a fish needs a bicycle" expressed this view.

Gay Rights

Yet other lesbians responded to Rich with anger and dismay. They considered their erotic feelings for women as quite different from their friendships, and they accused Rich of downplaying the purely sexual component of lesbian relationships. They also argued that heterosexual feminists needed the support of the women's movement to intervene in *their* relationships; rather than being advised to sleep with women, they should be helped to change their relationships with men. Feminists who followed Rich were more likely to see lesbianism as a choice; feminists who saw lesbianism in more sexual terms were more likely to see their sexuality as inborn or determined early on. (Straight feminists had a wide range of responses to Rich, from agreeing that their relationships with women were essentially lesbian to resenting Rich's lack of concern for their own efforts to refashion their relationships with men. Some straight feminists admired what they saw as Rich's courage and clarity while still maintaining their interest in heterosexuality.)

Rich's debate with other lesbian feminists points to a larger difference between gay men and lesbians. Whereas lesbians—whether they agreed with Rich or not—tended to see their political constituency as women in general, working with the feminist movement in various ways and trying to attract a broad range of women to their events, gay men were far less interested in reaching out to straight men than in connecting with other gay men. To some extent, this was because many lesbians identified with women in general as an oppressed group, whereas many gay men did not see what they had in common with "oppressive" straight men. Likewise, many straight feminists had an interest in overcoming homophobia to reach "all women," particularly lesbians, who were often doing significant work in the women's movement, whereas straight men in general had no parallel interest in reaching out to gay men (although the straight men in the political organizations that recognized homosexuality as a category of oppression did feel such a concern and did reach out to some extent).

A new wrinkle in the debate was provided in 1991 by Simon LeVay, a biologist working at the Salk Institute for Biological Studies in La Jolla, California, who offered new support for the theory that homosexuality was somehow inborn. In the August 30, 1991, issue of *Science* magazine, LeVay published the results of a study in which he had found differences in the brains of gay and straight men. LeVay had performed autopsies on six women and 35 men. Eighteen of the men were gay men who had died of AIDS and one was a bisexual man who had also died of AIDS. According to LeVay, the hypothalamus—one tiny part of the brain—was twice as large in the gay men as in the heterosexual men he studied, while the hypothalamuses of the straight men were twice as large as those of the women.

The study provoked an immediate controversy among both scientists and activists. Initially, a spokesperson from the Lambda Legal Defense and Education Fund, the prominent gay rights legal organization, called LeVay's results "intriguing," pointing out that if homosexuality were indeed inborn, it could no longer be considered either a sin or a psychological disorder. Many activists seized on LeVay's findings with relief: now they could argue that discrimination against gay people was wrong because gayness was a biological condition that people could not control.

Other activists found this argument frightening. John DeCecco, a professor of psychology at San Francisco State University and the editor of *Journal of Homosexuality*, called LeVay's study "nineteenth-century nonsense" that could have "dangerous" political ramifications. (DeCecco's citing of the 19th century was a reference to a time when scientists sought a much more direct causal relationship between biology and behavior than is now generally accepted.) DeCecco pointed out that if people believed that gayness was inborn, they might begin trying to screen and abort "potentially homosexual" fetuses. He also argued that homosexuality was more complicated than a mere biological response: "Homosexuality is not one thing," he said. "It's had many, many different meanings over the centuries." Anne Fausto-Sterling, a professor of medical science at Brown University, agreed. LeVay's suggestion that homosexuality was somehow biological, she said, "takes a complicated, intricate gender system and reduces it to whom you want to screw."

Other people criticized LeVay from a scientific point of view. They said that a study comprised of only 41 subjects provided a sample far too small from which to draw conclusions, particularly since all the gay men in the study had died of AIDS, which is known to cause alterations in the brain.

LeVay has defended his work. He points out that he never claimed to offer a comprehensive theory of homosexuality; he was only suggesting that it might be possible to study sexual choices on a biological level.

LeVay's work seemed to find some support in the work of a team of University of Chicago scientists, headed by psychology professor emeritus (retired) Howard Moltz. His 2003 study comparing eight exclusively homosexual men and eight exclusively heterosexual men seemed to indicate that the hypothalamus, presumed to regulate sexual response and behavior, behaved differently in the two types of men. Positron emission topography (PET) scans appeared to show that in straight men, the hypothalamus indicated significantly greater neurochemical activity than in gay men.

Moltz pointed out that scientists do not yet know how to interpret these findings. The neurochemical difference might be either the cause or the effect of sexual activity, he said—or it might simply accompany the different types of sexual activity. In other words, even assuming Moltz's data are valid, they did not yet answer the question of whether homosexuality is biologically determined or caused by another factor. However, said Moltz, "it's the strongest research I know to suggest [homosexuality] . . . might be hard-wired."

Other scientists have also tried to advance biological explanations for homosexuality. In March 2003, Canadian psychologist Ray Blanchard of the Centre of Addiction and Mental Health in Toronto told the journal *New Scientist* about his study of 302 gay men and an equal number of straight men. Blanchard found that the gay men were, on average, likely to have more older brothers than the straight men, leading Blanchard to speculate that a mother's body changed in response to being pregnant with boys, perhaps exposing each subsequent male fetus to higher levels of testosterone and antibodies, which might, in turn, produce a sexual attraction to men. Blanchard further speculated that the additional hormones and antibodies (which protect the fetus against infection) may have been needed by the younger siblings in the days when children had to compete for scarce supplies of food.

Blanchard's work was supported by John Manning at the University of Central Lancashire in Preston, England. But other experts cast doubt on Blanchard's findings, pointing out that Roman Catholic and Mormon families, which tend to be larger than average, produce no greater numbers of gay men. Likewise, the trend for smaller families in the Western, industrialized world would seem to indicate fewer gay men in the population—which likewise does not seem to be true.

Finally, Joan Roughgarden, a professor of biology at Stanford University and a member of the Academy of Arts and Sciences, offers another perspective on homosexuality in her 2004 book *Evolution's Rainbow: Diversity, Gender and Sexuality in Nature and People*, in which she claims that many species—including birds, fish, reptiles, and mammals—show evidence of sexual diversity, including what might in humans be called homosexuality or bisexuality. Roughgarden points out that in traditional science, sexual diversity was considered a handicap that prevented the species from reproducing, whereas in reality, such diversity serves many different evolutionary purposes, in both nonhumans and humans.

Roughgarden's observations find support in a variety of places, including Amsterdam's Artis Zoo, where zoo education officer Dr. Charlotte Vermulen offers special tours of gay animals. Vermulen shows visitors chimpanzees that are apparently gay and lesbian, pairs of homosexual birds that raise chicks together, tropical fish that are born male and become female, and two lionesses that have developed a sexual relationship. The notion that animals can participate in same-sex relationships, even when opposite-sex partners are available, seems to indicate that there is some biological basis for homosexuality, or, at the very least, that it may not be "unnatural," as so many generations of experts have claimed.

The question of what homosexuality "really" is seemed particularly important to gay men and lesbians who saw the process of "coming out"—publicly declaring one's homosexuality—as central to the building of a gay movement. Throughout the 1970s and 1980s, gay men and lesbians emphasized the need for their brothers and sisters to claim their gay identity. The notion of remaining "in the closet"—hiding one's sexuality from others, or even failing to admit it to oneself—was seen as the ultimate betrayal, so much so that some journalists—most notably Michelangelo Signorile—established the practice of "outing," or making public the sexuality of other people against their wishes. (This practice was revived in the 2000s, as gay rights activists began outing Representatives and their staff who opposed gay marriage.)

The very notion of outing was based on the idea that coming out was a responsibility that gay people had to each other, as well as to themselves, and that it would inevitably lead both to a healthier personal life and to more political power for the gay community generally. After all, no other oppressed group—women, people of color, disabled people, people living in working-class communities or doing working-class jobs—was invisible. Only gay men and lesbians had the option of hiding their true identities. If straight people could believe they did not know any gay people, they would have a far easier time supporting discrimination; if gay people believed they were a tiny, isolated minority, they would have a far harder time standing up for their rights. In this context, the gay rights movement placed a great deal of importance on gayness or lesbianism as a *true* identity, one that a person had the responsibility to claim and even to celebrate—regardless of whether being gay was seen as learned, inborn, or too mysterious to analyze.

In the 1990s, a number of Christian antigay groups responded to the challenge posed by coming out with a challenge of their own: they called on gay men and lesbians to "convert." Whereas gay rights groups challenged people to recognize their essential homosexuality, religious organizations like Exodus International and the Christian Coalition asked people to recognize their true *heterosexuality.*

Popularized by "ex-gays" John and Anne Paulk, who met at an Exodus counseling program and were married in 1992, the idea of conversion was brought to America's attention by a series of ads appearing in mainstream magazines and newspapers in 1998. Founded in 1976, Exodus now includes more than 100 local ministries in the United States and Canada and claims to have "touched" hundred of thousands of lives.

Exodus's philosophy seems to draw on a version of classical Freudian theory: boys with absent fathers and girls with absent mothers do not progress through the "proper" developmental stages, so they turn to people of the same sex to make up for the absent parent. Their treatment includes a combination of therapy, prayer, group support, and workshops to rediscover one's "inner heterosexual." Although it has allowed no long-term studies, the group claims a 30 percent success rate, with success being defined as abstinence from homosexual activity. Some members eventually marry, while others simply abstain from sexual actions that they believe are sinful. Still other veterans of Exodus avoid homosexuality and/or maintain heterosexuality for a time, and then "slip." For example, in 1979, two of the group's founders, Michael Bussee and Gary Cooper, fell in love and left the group.

In an ironic reversal for those who remember the lengthy battle to get the American Psychiatric Association to take homosexuality off its list of disorders, the American Psychological Association has strongly advised against "reparative therapy" of the kind offered by Exodus. In 1997, the group declared that such therapy was scientifically ineffective and possibly harmful. Most mainstream psychologists and psychiatrists now view Exodus's theory of childhood development as discredited.

Some observers believe the entire debate about what causes homosexuality—indeed, about the nature of "homosexuality" itself—is based on false assumptions. Although it is true that our genes determine a great deal of who we are, the relationship between genes and human behavior remains unclear. For example, genes are generally believed to determine our height. Thus, we can assume virtually all basketball players share some genetic similarities. But although almost all basketball players have "height" genes, not all tall people become basketball players. Likewise, there is probably some genetic basis for intelligence, although there is no single gene that independently determines this quality. Moreover, childhood experiences, education, and a great many other factors go into deciding how intelligent someone may be—and intelligence is not necessarily the main factor determining how a person behaves. In the same way, even if homosexuality does have a genetic basis, the relationship between genes and homosexual behavior is extremely complicated.

Likewise, environmental factors—the conditions of a person's upbringing—may indeed affect a man's or woman's sexuality—but it is not clear how. If homosexuality were related to psychology, we ought to be able to use psychological testing to distinguish between gays and straights. Yet in blind psychological evaluations—tests in which the evaluator was not aware of the subject's sexual orientation—there was no way to tell who was gay and who was straight. No psychological pattern, problem, or tendency was associated with homosexuality; it seemed that the *only* way that gays differed from straights, as a group, was in their choice of sexual partner.

It does seem that sexuality is a great deal more mutable than the terms *homosexual* and *heterosexual* suggest. After a 12-year partnership with a woman whose child they raised together, longtime lesbian-feminist author Jan Clausen became involved with a male partner. This transition became the topic of her 1999 book, *Apples and Oranges: My Journey to Sexual Identity*. Likewise, veteran gay male activist William "Bro" Broberg, began a relationship with bisexual lawyer and activist Lisa Kaplan that was reported in *Out* magazine. "I'm not an ex-gay," Broberg told reporter Sara Miles. "I'm still basically oriented towards men . . ." In a similar vein, Clausen writes about colleagues who call her a "former lesbian," a label she rejects—as well as "bisexual"—in favor of the designation "floating woman," someone who refuses the rigid categories of "gay/straight," "masculine/feminine," "apples/oranges."

Clearly, neither Clausen nor Broberg was driven by the dislike of homosexuality that seems to motivate the "success stories" of Exodus. Nor was either reluctant to keep on living as a lesbian or gay man. On the contrary, each has eloquently described the same kind of self-questioning and fear of being condemned by their communities that have become virtual cliches for men and women who choose to be gay. "I would still like to be just gay," Broberg told *Out* magazine. "It just seems like a very bad idea to sell out true love because you don't ideologically understand how you can be feeling it."

Certainly, there are numerous examples of men and women who have considered themselves heterosexual all their lives suddenly discovering new sexual or romantic feelings for same-sex partners—or finally deciding to act upon feelings that they previously had ignored. While many gay men and lesbians tell the story of "always knowing" who they were and desperately seeking support from others like themselves, many others tell a different coming out story, in which different stages of life called for different choices. New choices might be inspired by changing life circumstances, such as parents dying or children growing up; changing social circumstances, such as a move to a more gay-friendly area; changing cultural circumstances, such as society's greater tolerance of gay men and lesbians; or simply meeting a person who suddenly makes the idea of same-sex romance seem desirable.

The idea that someone must be identified as "really" gay or straight—essentially one thing or the other—is challenged by many so-called queer theorists, who argue that our whole system of gender and sexuality is far more mutable, far more susceptible to social influences, and far more complicated than the rigid categories of "gay," "straight," "bisexual," "male," and "female" allow. Queer theory stands against the gay and lesbian movement's traditional mistrust of bisexuals (people who express sexual interest in both genders), who were often portrayed as trying to "have it both ways" or denying their true homosexual natures. (Many lesbians and gay men felt that bisexuals were untrustworthy simply because they were able to return at a moment's notice to the world of heterosexual privilege, a choice unavailable to their "purely" gay or lesbian sexual partners.)

As science, politics, and culture progress, we can expect new answers to the old questions of what makes people gay and what "gayness" is. We can also expect new ways of asking the questions.

GAY MEN AND LESBIANS: ALLIES OR ENEMIES?

The past 50 years have been marked by a certain amount of tension between lesbians and gay men. The first two modern gay rights groups were sex-segregated: the Mattachine Society, founded by three men in Los Angeles in 1950, was theoretically for both gay men and lesbians, but it had an overwhelmingly male membership; the Daughters of Bilitis, founded in San Francisco in 1955, was explicitly for women. From the beginning, lesbians and gay men faced different problems as well as common enemies. They also brought different resources and experiences to bear on their political involvement.

For many gay men in the 1950s and 1960s, a key political issue was their right to have sex. The police often raided gay bars and cruising areas (public areas such as parks, public restrooms, and the waterfront, where gay men could often go to have sex or to find sexual partners), putting men at risk of arrest, jail time, fines, and publicity that might destroy marriages, careers, and social standing.

Although there was a lesbian bar culture in many cities, women's sexual activities tended to be more private—and less visible. To this day, each gender views its own situation as a mixed blessing: While men generally feel freer to enjoy their sexuality and are recognized as sexual beings, gay men are more often targets of violence directed at their very visible sexuality. Because women in our society are generally seen as less sexual, many straight people cannot even imagine what two women could do with each other without the help of a man;

"no man, no sex," the reasoning goes. Alternately, some straight men find the idea of two women together sexually exciting. Either way, women's sexuality is suppressed or trivialized—though women who are unmistakably sexual may face severe punishment in response.

Thus, while sodomy laws—laws that made homosexual sex illegal—affected both gay men and lesbians, historically, these laws affected men and women in different ways. Gay men were most often the targets of police raids and harassment, particularly where public sexual activity was involved. Lesbians, on the other hand, suffered from sodomy laws when it came to child custody: A mother who was a lesbian or was perceived as one was by legal definition a criminal, and so could be denied the right to raise her children on those grounds alone. Even now that sodomy laws have been abolished in the United States, lesbians—and straight women—who are known to have sexual partners to whom they are not married, are often penalized by the unwritten rule that says a mother is not allowed to be sexual. (Although gay fathers may still be penalized by prejudice against homosexuality, they are in any case less likely to be awarded child custody in a society that still tends to award custody to the mother.)

Men and women faced other conflicts as they tried to work together for gay rights. The modern gay rights movement began in 1969, a time when the second wave of feminism was just getting started. Initially, feminism seemed to hold promise for both women and men as women's liberation challenged the very notion of traditional male/female sex roles. Indeed, many of the early gay liberationists were men who challenged these roles as well, asserting that men could learn to knit and sew, raise children, and engage in other traditionally "female" activities.

Yet other men who were gay longed for the prestige and recognition traditionally awarded to straight men. They saw gay activism as a way to become *more* "masculine," not less—to claim the power that society gave straight men, even if some women complained that such power was being taken at their expense.

Thus, from the first days of the earliest post-Stonewall groups, women complained that men took up "too much space," and the men had predictably mixed reactions to the charge. For example, early dances held at New York City's "Firehouse," a gay social space sponsored by the Gay Activists Alliance, were overwhelmingly dominated by gay men, who, from the women's point of view, played the music too loud and created a hypersexual atmosphere in which conversation or more low-key encounters were impossible. The men were overjoyed to have a public space where they could finally express their sexuality and meet other men; the women felt excluded from a space that they thought was supposed to be theirs too.

Certainly, there were—and are—many lesbians who celebrated their right to be sexual, enjoy multiple partners and a wide range of sexual practices, reject monogamy and marriage-like arrangements, and claim the power and freedom of an openly sexual identity that has traditionally been reserved for men. But many other lesbians were shaped by a society that viewed sex as dangerous for women, particularly young women. Then-current feminist analysis also explored the ways in which male sexuality had oppressed women, from trapping women in inequitable marriages to judging women by their appearance to terrorizing women through rape and sexual violence. For lesbian women affected by these experiences and analyses, gay men's celebration of their newfound sexual freedom seemed insensitive at best, oppressive at worst.

Many gay men, on the other hand, felt that they had spent their whole lives being asked to suppress their sexuality and play by rules that were not theirs. What did liberation mean, if not the chance to finally enjoy sex openly, to speak and write openly about it, to enjoy the new power and pleasure that the gay rights movement seemed to offer?

Out for Good, a history of the gay rights movement, cites numerous examples of early, apparently trivial conflicts between gay men and lesbians over the place of public sexuality in what was supposed to be a common movement. For example, *Come Out!*, an early newspaper of the Gay Liberation Front, one of the first post-Stonewall groups, included a detailed description of fellatio. Men felt liberated by the chance to speak openly about something they had always been made to feel ashamed of; they wanted the support of their movement in their search for sexual information and sexual pleasure. Women denounced the focus on male sex, which they felt excluded them.

Likewise, a playful representation of a giant penis, which its creators called a "Cock-a-pillar," was part of the 1971 "Christopher Street West" parade in Los Angeles (an early version of a Gay Pride parade). Many gay men loved the freedom and exuberance that the huge phallic symbol represented. But many lesbians felt that this overwhelming display of a male sex organ implicitly left them out. They did not see the gay rights movement in such overwhelmingly sexual terms, nor did they feel welcome in the presence of this reminder of male sexuality.

As both the gay rights and the women's movement continued, many lesbians came to see feminism—which called for the unity of all women—as their true political home. Why identify with gay rights, they asked, when the gay rights movement seemed to require an alliance with men who often seemed even less sympathetic to women than straight men, who at least had a built-in sexual incentive to get along with the opposite sex. As lesbian-feminism proceeded through the 1970s, an increasing number of women began to identify as *separatists*, lesbians who wished to live in exclusively female—or exclusively lesbian—communities, in which men were not allowed.

Even lesbians who had no interest in separatism felt a certain frustration in dealing with various gay rights groups, which were often dominated by men even as women did much of the organizational and clerical work. Throughout the 1970s, women frequently raised the issue of equal representation in the leadership of gay rights organizations. While some gay men were sympathetic to this demand, others resented it. If meetings attracted more men than women, they asked, whose fault was that? They believed that women need not feel excluded if they would only choose to participate. Likewise, if gay men were better fund-raisers and had more access to wealth than lesbians because of the overall social trend to pay men higher salaries than women as well as the historical pattern that offered men greater access to family wealth—why shouldn't the men continue to enjoy the political and social power that came with the money?

Then, in the 1980s, an easing of tension between male and female activists came from a most unlikely source: the AIDS epidemic. As each year brought more disastrous news of deaths within the gay male community, lesbians and gay men joined in new efforts to address the crisis. Although lesbians as a group were less affected by AIDS than either straight women or gay men, they saw the crisis as their issue, just as, in the 1970s, many of them had seen the pro-choice and battered women's movements as their issues. In the 1970s, they had identified broadly as women, and they fought for women's freedom even in areas that did not directly concern them. In the 1980s, as AIDS shaped the way mainstream America viewed homosexuality, lesbians fought for money for AIDS research, recognition of the rights of PWAs (people with AIDS), and programs of sex education and AIDS prevention.

It was not only political vision that motivated women to become involved in AIDS-related work. Many of them had always been close to gay men, whether as part of the gay rights movement or on a personal level. At the same time, AIDS raised questions for many gay men about the kind of public, no-holds-barred sexuality that they had thought was theirs by right. Many observers describe the late 1970s and early 1980s as "party time" for gay men—an era when discos and clubs were the center of gay male activity, when sex and drugs and all-night dancing were more compelling than any form of political action. The AIDS crisis both curtailed that version of sexual freedom and made politics seem more urgent.

In this new climate of political and personal urgency, gay men and lesbians were more able than before to find common ground. The new recognition of women's place in the movement was reflected in a variety of ways, both symbolic and real. For example, in 1986, the National Gay Task Force became the National Gay and Lesbian Task Force (NGLTF).

Another issue was generational. Many of the AIDS activists who started ACT UP (AIDS Coalition to Unleash Power), Queer Nation, the Lesbian Avengers, and other militant groups had grown up with mothers—and fathers—shaped by the feminist movement. While the first generation of gay activists grew up in a world in which middle-class mothers rarely worked outside the home and women politicians were virtually unknown, the ACT UP generation took it for granted that women could hold economic, social, and political power, at least to some extent. Politically active men and women in their 20s thus had different political resources than the generation that had come before.

The development of HIV and AIDS medications, especially protease inhibitors (a treatment that seems to be able to halt the disease for at least some people), seemed for a time to mitigate against the urgency of the AIDS crisis, particularly since the rates of AIDS infections among gay men had been relatively low for many years. Recently, though, infection rates have begun to rise again, particularly among gay men of color. Yet despite the renewed sense among many gay community groups that AIDS is once again a crisis, the gay community is far less defined by this issue than it was in the 1980s and 1990s—a development that has reinstated to some extent the traditional conflicts between gay men and lesbians. (Though AIDS was once viewed as primarily a gay male crisis, AIDS rates have been steadily increasing in the United States among women and youths of color, as well as worldwide, particularly in Africa, Asia, and the Caribbean. The gay rights movement has responded to the national and international AIDS crises in a range of ways, from solidarity to apathy.)

Meanwhile, the gains of the gay rights movement have tended to widen the gap between gay men and lesbians, leading to further conflicts. Gay men now have improved access to the greater economic and social power that men in general have always had. Many gay male couples fall into the privileged category known as "DINKS"—dual income, no kids. Lesbian couples are, on average, at the bottom of the economic ladder, since women's earnings average only 78 percent of men's, and since lesbians are more likely to have children, either from a previous relationship or as part of their current partnership.

CIVIL RIGHTS VS. GAY LIBERATION

As with the conflict between assimilation and maintaining a cultural identity, the tension between gay rights and gay liberation continues to shape gay and lesbian activism in profound and unexpected ways. Simply put, "gay liberation" implies the need to transform the entire society, while "civil rights" refers more narrowly to the notion of winning equal rights for gay men and lesbians within the existing society. But tempting as it is to discuss the two views as separate and distinct, in practice, they often overlap, blending into one another within a single organization—or a single individual.

In the early 1970s, *gay liberation* was a term—and an ideology—that seemed to flow naturally out of the prevailing political atmosphere of the 1960s. African Americans, women, students, antiwar activists, hippies, and members of the New Left had mounted a broad political and cultural challenge to virtually every U.S. political and social institution: capitalism, the military-industrial complex, the university system, the family, the working world of nine-to-five job, patriarchy (some feminists' term for centuries of male domination), sexual repression, and conformity. The Black Panthers were an active, viable organization whose breakfast programs for poor children accompanied their slogan of "Black Is Beautiful" and their challenge to white racism. The Vietnam War had radicalized many men and women with its view of the United States as an aggressor and of the American way of life as oppressive and dangerous to the rest of the world. The growing women's movement was challenging everything from unequal pay to the unequal use of pronouns (Why, asked some early feminists, should "he" be used generically to refer to both men and women?).

In this context, when gay patrons of the Stonewall Inn fought back against frequent police raids (see "The Stonewall Uprising" later in this chapter), their action was seen as representing a greater refusal: They had effectively declared a giant NO to the social, political, and economic system that supported only one, narrow view of human sexuality—that of monogamous, heterosexual marriage—and stood ready to violently punish anyone who transgressed. Early supporters of gay liberation could identify with the Black Panthers, New Leftists, feminists, and antiwar activists who also said "no"—not to a specific law or situation, but to what they saw as a whole system of oppression and repression. The early slogan "Gay Is Good" was a direct reference to the African-American insistence that "Black is Beautiful," while the very name "Gay Liberation Front"—an organization founded in the wake of the Stonewall uprising—drew on the National Liberation Front of the North Vietnamese.

Early manifestos of gay liberation explicitly said that without the abolition of capitalism and other repressive systems, gay people—indeed, no people—could ever be truly free. Thus early gay liberation meetings included discussion of the Vietnam War and voted to donate funds to the Black Panthers, not out of a sense of liberal guilt, but because these early activists genuinely saw their movement as part of a larger one.

Soon, though, the Gay Liberation Front was joined by a new organization more specifically focused on achieving gay legal and civil rights: the Gay Activists Alliance. Still later, gay men—and some lesbians—who saw themselves as more middle-class, more "respectable," and generally happier with mainstream society than the early "gay lib" radicals, founded the National Gay Task Force (now the National Gay and Lesbian Task Force) and the National Gay Rights Lobby (which eventually mutated into the Human Rights Campaign Fund, and then the Human Rights Campaign Foundation), organizations intended to lobby Congress and engage in other more conventional political activities.

The conflicts between conservative, liberal, and radical approaches to gay rights/liberation were also conflicts involving gender, race, and class. As we saw in the previous section, gay men and lesbians often had quite different visions of how much change was needed in the larger society to guarantee their own freedom. Middle- and upper-class gay men, who had amassed a great deal of power and privilege, were more likely to see gay rights in narrower terms. They often felt that the society as it was (the status quo) was working fine; however, *they* did not want to be excluded from it. This type of gay man tended to be white, as well, and relatively unsympathetic to demands from feminists or people of color that they broaden their approach or open their ranks. For example, the Municipal Elections Committee of Los Angeles (MECLA) was a group of wealthy gay men formed in 1977 to win more political power in Los Angeles elections. They continued for many years to raise funds with which they won electoral influence among the city's political elite. They saw no reason to include other "oppressed groups" in their ranks; their whole reason for founding the group was to take advantage of their access to money and power.

While lesbian-feminists tended to be more explicitly preoccupied with power issues, they too faced troubling conflicts over race and class, conflicts which pointed to larger disagreements over how best to achieve lesbian rights.

Initially, it seemed that the problems of power and oppression could be satisfied simply by becoming more inclusive. The history of lesbian-feminism in the 1970s is the story of one disempowered group after another challenging the leaders and members of the movement, on the grounds that women of color, Jewish women, the disabled, and working-class and poor women were being explicitly or implicitly excluded from the movement.

Lesbian-feminists often found creative ways of responding to these charges. Women's concerts, for example, an early cultural expression of the lesbian-feminist movement, frequently offered free child care, sliding-scale admissions, and signers for the hearing impaired, in their efforts to make sure that every member of the women's community was able to attend. Women's presses made efforts to include women of color and low-income women in their collectives and on their publications lists. The words *reproductive rights* were added to the term *pro-choice* or *abortion rights* to recognize that for many women on welfare, including African Americans, Latinas, and Native Americans, the problem of forced sterilization was of more concern than the legal right to terminate a pregnancy.

Despite these responses, the lesbian-feminist movement continued to struggle with the problems of social inequality, which often went beyond matters of inclusion and representation to more fundamental political issues. Many lesbian-feminists, for example, were committed to separatism, a vision of community in which only women, or only lesbians, would be allowed to participate. While these separatist communities were not by definition for whites only, many women of color, as well as many white women from poor and working-class backgrounds, found separatism problematic. These women saw their male counterparts as oppressed, too, and therefore, potential allies. While they wanted a movement that would defend their right to be lesbians, they also wanted to fight for liberation on the grounds of race, class, and the broader issues of gender. Many of them charged that separatism was inherently elitist, that only privileged white women had the resources to cut men out of their lives— and that only privileged white women would feel comfortable ignoring the problems of their fathers, brothers, and sons.

Class, race, and political vision became issues once again during the AIDS crisis. The public image of a person with AIDS was that of a middle-class white gay man who was part of the "party" culture of gay, urban communities. Gay Men's Health Crisis (GMHC), founded in 1981, was the first organization created to deal with AIDS; it was overwhelmingly dominated by white, middle-class men and remained so for some time. Throughout the 1980s, however, and with increasing urgency in the 1990s, activists raised the problems of gay men of color, who were less likely to be "out" than their white counterparts, who might not speak English as a first language, who were more likely to have sex with other men without identifying as gay, and who therefore had different needs when it came to AIDS prevention, education, and treatment.

AIDS activists—both gay and straight—also pointed out the growing problem of AIDS among women, primarily women of color, who were sexually involved with gay/bisexual men and/or with intravenous (IV) drug users. The question of how responsible an AIDS activist or support group ought to be for these other populations with AIDS speaks again to the movement's political self-definition. Is the goal specifically to improve the lives of white gay men, many of whom can now be helped by—and can afford—expensive protease inhibitors? Is the goal to help all people with AIDS, including those who cannot afford the new treatments? Would this require a simple increase in public funding or a broader challenge to the whole way health care is delivered, with a call for national health insurance or even socialized medicine? Is the movement stronger, or weaker, when it tries to speak for a broader constituency and to make more profound changes in the political and public health systems?

Differing visions of political activism also surfaced with the founding of ACT UP in 1987, a militant direct-action group that seemed to return to 1960s-style demonstrations and civil disobedience in its efforts to change the policies of corporations, the U.S. government, and the Catholic Church. Initially, at least, ACT UP seemed to represent an implicit challenge to the mainstream approaches of the more established gay rights groups. Ironically, both Gay Men's Health Crisis—the first group ever founded to respond politically to AIDS—and ACT UP were co-founded by Larry Kramer. Kramer had a radical vision for both organizations and was deeply distressed when GMHC seemed to become more interested in social services than in political action. Eventually, GMHC forced Kramer to leave the organization he had helped to found—and so, eventually, did ACT UP.

The growth of queer theory and the political activism that accompanied it raised new questions about the direction the gay rights movement should take. Queer theorists even wondered if *gay rights* was the correct term by which the movement should define itself, as some queer theorists challenged the very notion of "gay" and "straight," or even of two genders. "Why not see humanity as including many genders?" these scholars asked. "Why not see sexuality as a continuum, or as an ever-changing field of play, rather than as a set of distinct categories?"

More traditional gay rights activists responded with concern. These activists assert that many gay men and lesbians do not *want* to change the entire gender system. They simply want to be left alone to form relationships, raise children, and pursue their careers. Won't they be frightened off by an approach that purports to challenge fundamental social arrangements? And what about support from the larger society? Straight people who agree that a gay man should not be fired from his job simply for being gay might be repelled by the notion that, for instance, he has the right to wear a dress to that job.

Yet another criticism of queer theory is that on some level, it works *against* taking political action or building a movement. Many lesbians and gay men are uneasy with a theory that denies the very existence of gay men and lesbians, of men and women, in the name of an ever-changing system of multiple genders and sexualities. People who are concerned with such issues as child custody and antigay violence are puzzled or even offended by a theory that allows a heterosexual married woman such as the scholar and queer theorist Eve Kosofsky Sedgwick to proclaim that she is "really" a gay man.

Gay men and lesbians are also active participants in conservative organizations, including the Log Cabin Republicans, a group seeking both gay rights and the traditional Republican platform of "low taxes, limited government, strong defense, free markets, personal responsibility, and individual liberty," in the words of their web site statement. The very existence of that organization is a testament to the sense of security and empowerment that many gay men and lesbians feel, so that although they are openly gay and in favor of gay rights, they do not necessarily see this aspect of their politics—or their lives—as the most important factor in choosing a political affiliation. On the other hand, many Log Cabin Republicans support legalizing gay marriage, which led to a decision for the group not to endorse President George W. Bush's reelection campaign in 2004 because of his support for a Constitutional amendment banning same-sex marriage.

This discussion, which began with two clear categories—civil rights and gay liberation—has quickly dissolved into a multiplicity of political perspectives: queer theorists, lesbian-feminists, separatists, conservatives, liberals, radicals, and many others. Each of those labels contains numerous perspectives as well, the definitions of which change as political conditions change. Some observers lament that the gay rights movement is at odds with itself. Others see the very diversity of gay rights as a source of strength, in that the many different kinds of gay men and lesbians are more likely to be reached.

GAY MARRIAGE: PROBLEM OR SOLUTION?

Nowhere is this multiplicity more evident than in the current debate over gay marriage, an issue which raises virtually all of the contradictions considered so far in this chapter. Hotly debated throughout the entire history of the modern gay rights movement, the marriage issue has taken on new urgency in the 21st century, as legally recognized gay marriage became a reality in Massachusetts on May 17, 2004. Although the legal future of gay marriage remains uncertain (see "The Marriage Question" and "Legal Issues," later in this chapter), arguments within the gay rights movement about whether marriage is a desirable goal continue.

To some activists, the civil rights aspects are very clear. They believe that same-sex couples should have the same rights to enjoy the benefits of marriage that are now the exclusive property of heterosexuals—the right to be covered by a partner's health insurance, inherit property without paying an estate tax, visit a partner in a hospital or care for a partner who is disabled, and be recognized as taking part in a legitimate life partnership. They also believe that gay people should be able to adopt children as a couple, just as straight married people do, and they see gay marriage as a step toward either establishing or preserving that right.

Moreover, legalization of gay marriage would clear child custody issues. When a woman married to a man gives birth, her husband automatically assumes legal custody of the child, whether or not he is the biological father; it takes a paternity suit, custody battle, or some other legal effort to deprive him of that status. But when a woman in a lesbian partnership gives birth, her partner has no automatic legal rights. Even if the partner makes the effort to adopt the child as a second parent or to be awarded joint custody, she very often will not succeed. Likewise, in a heterosexual marriage where one partner already has children, the other partner may adopt as a second parent, if the missing parent is dead or makes no objection to giving up parental rights. This kind of second-parent adoption is far more difficult in a lesbian or gay relationship.

On one level, these are practical demands. Gay people want access to the financial benefits that go with being married, they want to be able to raise children, and, in case of medical emergency or death, they want to be sure that parents or other family members do not have the right to bar access to a gay or lesbian spouse or keep that spouse from making crucial decisions.

On another level, these are social demands. Many gay men and lesbians want the emotional satisfaction that comes from being recognized as partners, from having a relationship taken seriously, from having the same societal support that heterosexual couples do when they face difficulties and challenges, and from being recognized as married by others in their religion. (In fact, many ministers and rabbis will marry same-sex couples, although, as described in Chapter 3, this has caused a great deal of controversy within many religious denominations. However, in most states these ceremonies have no *legal* standing.)

Other gay activists have a different perspective. Some feminists—gay and straight—claim that heterosexual marriage is a property arrangement that oppresses women. Although many feminists support legalizing gay marriage—E. J. Graff eloquently argues for this position in her 1999 book, *What Is Marriage For?*—many others see it as perpetuating the notion of women and children as property. Anti-marriage feminists point out that marriage was originally a property relationship in which a man could control a woman and the children she bore—restricting the woman's sexual activities, depriving her of financial independence, even possessing the right to physically and sexually abuse her. Moreover, marriage gives the state a say in how a personal relationship should be conducted. In many states, for example, adultery is grounds for divorce. Many feminists—and other gay rights activists—object to bringing gay relationships under the rubric of state-sanctioned monogamy.

Other feminists argue that if gay marriage becomes legal, lesbian mothers who marry other women will have improved standing in child custody matters, which traditionally penalize women—gay or straight—who engage in extramarital sex. These arguments are countered by those who claim that gay marriage will only serve to further marginalize and disempower those lesbians and gay men who do not choose to marry, effectively punishing those who claim the right to less conventional sexual relationships.

Many sexual liberationists in the gay rights movement join in the anti-marriage chorus. Opponents of monogamy, for example, see marriage as an outmoded system that represses sexual freedom. They, too, argue that gay marriage will lead to even more intense discrimination against "unacceptable" unmarried gay men and lesbians. People who choose less conventional arrangements, such as three-way relationships, S and M, or transgender identities, are also concerned about being marginalized with legalization of gay marriage. Certainly, these unconventional lifestyle choices do not necessarily imply that a relationship will not be committed, longlasting, or loving—in some cases, it may even be monogamous—but it may not fit within the bounds of a legally recognized marriage. Gay people whose lives do not seem to fit mainstream ideas worry about being split off from more "socially acceptable" gay men and lesbians.

Yet another section of the gay rights movement sees gay marriage as a profoundly revolutionary step. Since many people view marriage as the foundation of mainstream society, gay people's participation in it seems to transform the nature both of marriage and of society itself. Certainly the fear that gay marriage would have this result seems to animate many religious and right-wing opponents of same-sex unions.

Lesbian marriage advocate Graff takes still a different position. Studying marriage throughout the centuries, Graff discovered that there is no single definition of marriage or the family. The idea that there is a "true" marriage that gay people could either participate in, reject, or transform is a myth, Graff argues: Marriage has meant so many different things in so many different societies that, in the larger scheme of things, enabling gay people to enter legal marriages would be just another in a long series of changes.

Writer Richard Goldstein has a related position. He argues that gay marriage will be an institution as diverse as the gay community itself. Some gay marriages will be monogamous; others will not. Some will enable the participants to live within stable partnerships that resemble the romantic ideal of heterosexual married love; others may take quite a different form. Gay marriage, moreover, will be just one choice among a spectrum that includes various forms of civil unions and domestic partnerships—arrangements that are also open to straight people who for whatever reason do not wish to marry but wish to formalize their relationship in some way. Thus gay marriage will open up new possibilities for straight people as well as gay people, softening the rigid opposition of "married—not married" as well as broadening narrow definitions of marriage. In addition, Goldstein argues, legal recognition of gay marriage would offer crucial economic benefits and child custody protection to those sectors of the gay community who most need support: women, particularly women of color.

The current interest in gay marriage takes place against the backdrop of the AIDS crisis, which has caused many gay men to reconsider their traditional attachment to sexual liberation. Gabriel Rotello, for example, in his 1997 book, *Sexual Ecology: AIDS and the Destiny of Gay Men*, has taken the position that gay men need to develop "serial monogamous" relationships (being sexual with only one partner at a time), an arrangement that resembles marriage far more than the wide-ranging promiscuity that some gay men see as synonymous with liberation. Rotello's connection of monogamy and safer sex has enraged many gay men and lesbians. Some object to his characterization of lesbians as more monogamous. The so-called pro-pleasure lesbians, for example, have pointed out that many lesbians are also seeking sexual liberation, frequently rejecting monogamy and embracing a variety of unconventional sexual practices. Others object to Rotello's association of marriage and safety, claiming that many heterosexual married couples are not monogamous either—they are just not honest about it. Still others see Rotello as retreating from the gay liberationist view; even if AIDS requires new sexual ethics and arrangements, these critics say there is no reason to adopt the outmoded and restrictive morality of the past.

In his 2004 book, *Gay Marriage*, conservative gay author Jonathan Rauch makes a pro-marriage argument based on the idea that marriage represents adulthood. Only when gay men and lesbians are allowed to marry, he writes, will they be able to aspire toward a mature vision of life, as opposed to the perpetual adolescence of current gay culture. Although Rauch has found support among some gay men and lesbians, others point out that his reasons for marriage are precisely the basis for their objection to it: the narrow-minded thinking that insists on only one form of adult, legitimate relationship, marginalizing or demonizing all others.

Thus, in *Sappho Goes to Law School* (1998), legal scholar and novelist Ruthann Robson argues that legalizing lesbian marriage will put both cultural and legal pressure on lesbians—and, by implication, on gay men. "A landlord who refused to rent to a lesbian couple because they were unmarried or not in a registered domestic partnership (either because the landlord believes in the sanctity of marriage or simply prefers to rent to a 'stable couple') does not seem to me an improvement over a landlord who refused to rent to two women because they were lesbians," she comments. Robson also cites numerous examples of cases in which unmarried heterosexual couples were denied housing by landlords who successfully claimed a religious exemption to the fair housing laws—in other words, landlords whose religion led them to believe that unmarried cohabitation was wrong.

Why, asks Robson and other analysts, should lesbians and gay men seek state-sanctioned marriage, rather than trying to make marriage-related benefits available to *all* citizens, whether married or not? Why not insure housing rights for all, rather than allowing landlords to decide who has the right to live together? Why not extend health insurance to all U.S. residents, rather than simply extending a spouse's health insurance to his or her partner? Why not allow child custody, visitation, and other similar issues to depend on a person's contractually expressed wishes, so that friends, multiple sexual partners, and others might be accorded the same status as legal spouses, if the person so wishes?

These broader questions recall the early objections of antimarriage feminists, who pointed out that if women could earn as much money as men, could depend on affordable child care, could count on affordable housing, and could rely on national health insurance, there would no longer be any *economic* reason for women and men to live together. Challenging marriage became a much deeper challenge to the prevailing social system. Lesbian and gay theorists who oppose marriage likewise ask: "Why should the state recognize any one emotional arrangement between people and reward it with legal, financial, and social benefits?"

The marriage debate raged fiercely even when it appeared that legal recognition of gay marriage was only a distant goal. When gay marriage became a more urgent issue, however, fiercely attacked by conservatives and increasingly supported by liberals, the debate took a different turn. Now even some of the gay rights activists who opposed gay marriage feel compelled to oppose as well the attacks upon it, which they see as part of a larger attack on gay rights. With gay marriage suddenly a real possibility, it became much harder to argue against it. It was one thing to insist that gay marriage was not a worthwhile goal for the gay rights movement. It was another thing to refuse the chance to win this right when receiving it seemed so near. Although there are still feminists, sexual liberationists, and others who argue that legal recognition of gay marriage will be bad for the gay rights movement and for liberation movements generally, their argument has become much harder to sustain. As events develop, the debate on gay marriage—inside and outside the gay community—is certain to continue.

A BRIEF HISTORY OF GAY RIGHTS

The following brief history is intended primarily as a reference point. Readers looking for more in-depth information on the history of the gay rights movement can look at a number of books, including John D'Emilio's *Sexual Politics, Sexual Communities: The Making of a Homosexual Minority in the United States, 1940–1970* (1983); Jonathan Katz's *Gay American History* (1976); *Gay/Lesbian Almanac: A New Documentary* (1983) and his *Love Stories: Sex Between Men Before Homosexuality* (2003); Martin Duberman's *Stonewall* (1993); Martin Duberman, Martha Vicinus, and George Chauncey, Jr.'s *Hidden from History: Reclaiming the Gay and Lesbian Past* (1989); Molly McGarry and Fred Wasserman's *Becoming Visible, An Illustrated History of Lesbian and Gay Life in Twentieth-Century America* (1998); Dudley Clendenin and Adam Nagourney's *Out for Good: The Struggle to Build a Gay Rights Movement in America* (1999); and George Chauncey's *Making of a Modern Gay World: 1935–1975* (2004).

Although this book discusses the modern gay rights movement as beginning in 1969, it is important to remember that homosexuality itself has a far more ancient history. Some form of same-sex involvement among both men and women seems to be present in virtually all societies, all eras, although, as John DeCecco, editor of *Journal of Homosexuality*, states, "Homosexuality is not one thing. It's had many, many different meanings over the centuries."

For example, the lesbian anthropologist Kendall (who uses only that name), writing in *Boy-Wives and Female Husbands: Studies of African Homosexualities*, an anthology edited by Stephen O. Murray and Will Roscoe, describes arrangements among women in the African nation of Lesotho that to her eye are lesbian: "From [university students and domestic workers] I learned of fairly common instances of tribadism or rubbing [two women rubbing their genital areas together], fondling, and cunnilingus between Bathoso women, with and without digital penetration [the penetration of fingers into the vagina]. This they initially described as 'loving each other,' 'staying together nicely,' 'holding each other,' or 'having a nice time together.'" But, Kendall stresses, because no male sexual organs were involved, the women were adamant in insisting that these relationships did not constitute "sex." Moreover, virtually all of the women who had such relationships were also married, since it was unthinkable for a woman in that society *not* to be married.

Likewise, John Boswell, in *Same-Sex Unions in Premodern Europe*, points out that modern definitions of homosexuality do not necessarily fit the lived experiences of people in other cultures and other times. Yet, he writes, "many cultures other than Western ones have recognized and institutionalized same-sex unions—Japanese warriors in early modern times, Chinese men and women under the Yuan and Ming dynasties, Native Americans from a number of tribes (mostly before white domination), many African tribes well into the twentieth century, and residents (both male and female) of the Middle East, South-East Asia, Russia, other parts of Asia, and South America." Boswell also discusses same-sex unions in ancient Greece and Rome and medieval Europe.

In one of the first history books to emerge from the modern gay rights movement, *Gay American History*, a documentary history of U.S. lesbians and gay men, author Jonathan Katz describes the difficulty of identifying same-sex activity in other historical periods: "When simply working, living, and loving, homosexuals have been condemned to invisibility." Thus, Katz points out, many of our records concern gay men and women who have "made trouble"—molesting children, committing murder, and engaging in other crimes common to both heterosexual and homosexual citizens. At the very least, however, Katz's documents—dating back to 1566 and including the account of a Frenchman in Florida charged with sodomy and murdered in 1566 by the Spanish military authorities, an execution for sodomy in Virginia in 1624, and another in New Haven, Connecticut, in 1646—indicate that homosexual activity existed in early America.

Historians and other scholars argue that although various types of same-sex *activity* have always taken place, the notion of same-sex *identity* is a relatively new one. For men and women to define themselves by their choice of sexual partner was not possible until they could live autonomous lives—that is, lives separate from the family structures that had organized the human economy from the beginning of human history until the 20th century. Not until the development of an urban culture could people afford to live apart from their families and define themselves by how they *chose* to live.

U.S. urban culture from the beginning included a gay and lesbian subculture, in the form of bars, nightlife, theatrical entertainment, and prostitution. In New York City, Greenwich Village soon became known as a center of gay nightlife. So did Harlem, reflecting the African-American community's traditional tendency to be more tolerant of gay and lesbian activity than was dominant white society.

However, if gay and lesbian life was in some sense tolerated—and certainly tolerated more in the 1920s, 1930s, and 1940s than in the 1950s and 1960s—it was also regulated. In 1933, for example, New York State's highest court upheld a regulation against gay men and lesbians congregating in bars, and the State Liquor Authority threatened to withdraw the license of anyone who served gay patrons or allowed them to congregate. Such laws drove gay and lesbian bar culture underground, into establishments run by organized crime.

Gay men, as we have seen, always had access to more public venues for their sexual activity, including such cruising areas as parks and waterfronts. Lesbians were more reluctant to engage in such public activity, and they were less likely to congregate in bars, although many predominantly working-class cities, such as Buffalo, New York, had an active lesbian bar scene. There were also some lesbian clubs in various cities. Lesbians in New York City recalled the 1930s and 1940s, when they would buy three-piece suits—jacket, skirt, and pants. They would wear the skirt on the street and change into the pants when they got to the club.

Upper-class white men had their own gay bar scene—the bars or lounges of certain aristocratic hotels. These discreet establishments included the Oak Room at the Plaza and the King Cole Room at the St. Regis in New York City, the Top of the Mark at the Mark Hopkins in San Francisco, and the Biltmore Bar in Los Angeles.

World War II produced an even more open climate for gay men and lesbians, as servicemen from out of town flocked to gay and lesbian bars. "It was as open then, from about 1944 to 1947, as it is now," recalled New York resident Leo Adams in an interview with curator and historian Fred Wasserman, coauthor of *Becoming Visible.* "Anybody in uniform seemed to be available at that time."

Even so, gay men and lesbians continued to face social isolation and legal restrictions. In 1934, for example, the Motion Picture Production Code officially banned all references to and depictions of homosexuality from Hollywood films. In the late 1940s and early 1950s, Senator Joseph McCarthy, known for his attacks upon communists—actual or suspected—in the U.S. government, was engaging in a similar attack upon homosexuals. And in the 1950s, despite a growing nightlife in cities throughout the nation—especially New York, Los Angeles, and San Francisco—police raids on gay bars and arrests of gay men rose sharply in cities as diverse as Washington, D.C.; New York; Miami; Memphis; Baltimore; Pittsburgh; Wichita, Kansas; Ann Arbor, Michigan; Minneapolis; Boise, Idaho; Seattle; and Pasadena, California. In 1959, New York City revoked the liquor licenses of virtually all gay bars.

EARLY ORGANIZING

In this climate, it was perhaps not surprising that the first gay rights organization in the United States was founded by a Communist, Henry Hay, who established the Mattachine Society in Los Angeles in 1950. (An interracial gay organization, Knights of the Clock, was also founded in Los Angeles in 1950, but its function was more social than political.) Hay called the Mattachine society a "homophile" movement, making a distinction between those who loved men and those who were explicitly sexual with them. He intended the term *homophile* to include supporters of homosexual rights as well as actual homosexuals.

Despite this apparent timidity, Hay's vision was actually quite radical, for he saw the possibility of homosexuals forming their own group to defend their own distinct culture, much as African Americans, Jews, and Mexican Americans had done. The Mattachine Society grew slowly, but, in a pattern that would be repeated throughout the 1990s, found itself energized by the very oppression it sought to end. When Mattachine Society member Dale Jennings was accused of "lewd and dissolute conduct" in a Los Angeles park, he decided to take the case to court. The first U.S. court case to raise the issue of gay rights ended in a deadlocked jury, and the case was dropped, but the Mattachine Society had made good use of the incident. Flyers distributed to various gay male venues—beaches, bars, parks, rest rooms—brought exposure, new members, and eventually, new chapters to the early gay rights group. In fact, in another common pattern of the movement, increased success led to a more conservative approach, and in 1953, the founders had to resign from the group because of their Communist ties, which made the new members uneasy. These new recruits rejected the founders' radical vision of a distinctive gay culture, claiming that they simply needed help adjusting to mainstream society. In 1954, they took up the slogan "Evolution, not Revolution," a position that would eventually lead to their demise soon after the Stonewall uprising had raised the possibility of a more militant gay liberationist approach.

The first U.S. lesbian rights group, the Daughters of Bilitis, was founded in 1955 in San Francisco. Although its political approach did not survive into the 1970s, its early membership certainly did. Founders Del Martin and Phyllis Lyon and member Barbara Gittings were gay rights activists who continued as leaders in the movement through Stonewall and for many years beyond (Martin and Lyon were among those who applied for marriage licenses in San Francisco in 2004).

From a 1970s radical perspective, though, the "DOB," as it was discreetly known ("Bilitis" was supposed to have been a lover of the allegedly lesbian poet Sappho of ancient Greece), was thoroughly middle-class, with an emphasis on respectability and no interest in the butch-femme working-class women who made up much of the lesbian bar scene. (The terms *butch* and *femme* refer to the masculine and feminine roles adopted by some men and women in gay and lesbian culture.) This ambivalent attitude toward lesbianism is reflected in the title of an article from the *Ladder*, the DOB's magazine, "Raising Children in a Deviant Relationship."

To people familiar with the gay club and bar scenes of the 1980s and 1990s, the climate of the 1950s and 1960s is almost unimaginable. Same-sex couples were not allowed to touch or even to dance together. In the gay male bars where dancing was allowed, at least one woman had to be found to get out on the dance floor—followed by two dozen or so men, all of whom could claim to be dancing with her. To avoid being harassed or even arrested, same-sex dance partners tried to dance side by side, rather than face to face. In some states, it was illegal for men to wear women's clothing and vice versa, making drag queens literally outlaws.

Novelist Leslie Feinberg recalls that in the mixed-sex gay bar she frequented in Niagara Falls, New York, lesbians and gay men danced in same-sex couples when they could—but switched to male-female couples whenever the cops appeared at the door. "We [lesbians] in our suits and ties paired off with our drag queen sisters in their dresses and pumps."

Although one middle-class gay man recalls that "few I knew were very conscious of needing liberation," for many others, the constant threat of exposure was a continual fact of life. Arrests made in gay bars might be published in the local newspaper, possibly putting an end to a person's marriage, job, and standing in the community, and bringing shame and ostracism to one's children and family. Even though gay bars became legal in New York after 1967, raids were common, and police violence was frequent, particularly against gay men. Some survivors of that time describe routine beatings inside the police wagons that took arrested gay men to the station.

THE STONEWALL UPRISING

Even before the event that simply became known as "Stonewall," there were already stirrings of a new political climate for gay men and lesbians. The *Advocate*, a gay newspaper, had been founded in Los Angeles in 1967. In New York City, Craig Rodwell had opened the Oscar Wilde Memorial Bookstore, which he intended less as a place to sell books than as a center for gay activity. Early in 1969, Carl Wittman, antiwar activist, leftist, and liberationist, had written a gay liberation manifesto that was to anticipate many of the political perspectives that marked the early 1970s.

Ironically, when the uprising finally occurred, many people failed to recognize its significance. Looking back, however, there is no denying that what began as a skirmish at a Greenwich Village bar became the harbinger of a new movement for human rights. Detailed accounts of Stonewall have taken on the quality of myth, as more people remember being there than could possibly have fit in the tiny, grimy bar. It is generally accepted that a diverse group of bar patrons, led by the drag queens who were Stonewall regulars, spontaneously began to fight back during a police raid. The resistance turned into a riot, which lasted for several days.

Something about the least accepted, most marginalized segment of the gay male community—the men who dressed as women—engaging in physical combat with New York City cops captured the imagination of both gay and straight observers. Although initial press coverage of the event ranged from scanty to contemptuous to condescending, gay/lesbian political response was immediate and strong. The Gay Liberation Front (GLF) was founded in July 1969, just weeks after the uprising. By 1970 the tiny New York group had grown to encompass 19 cells (their politically inflected word for "chapter"), 12 consciousness-raising groups, three households, a Marxist study group, several political caucuses, and a newspaper called *Come Out!*.

Two months after its founding, in September 1969, the fledgling group held its first demonstration—at the alternative weekly paper, the *Village Voice*, which had refused to print the word "gay" on the grounds that it was obscene. Although groups of women and drag queens eventually left GLF to form other groups, including the Radicalesbians and the Street Transvestite Action Revolution (STAR), the GLF continued through the early 1970s.

The next major group to form was the Gay Activists Alliance (GAA). Whereas the GLF had seen itself as part of a larger movement, the GAA defined itself as exclusively gay. The GLF had operated on New Left principles: no formal structure, open meetings, free discussion. The GAA, by contrast, operated according to *Robert's Rules of Order* (the authoritative manual for parliamentary procedure), with a formal structure and even a constitution. Founders of the GAA, while sharing many of the GLF's radical sympathies, wanted a gay-specific organization that ran more efficiently than the GLF was able to do.

Even after Stonewall, police violence and fear of the consequences of an arrest continued to haunt many gay men and lesbians. In March 1970, the same police officer who had led the raid on the Stonewall Inn began arresting people at the Snake Pit, another Greenwich Village gay bar. More than 160 people were hustled outside and brought to the police station, including patrons, management, and bartenders. All were arrested and given summonses for disorderly conduct—charges that were eventually dismissed. But Argentine national Diego Vinales was in the United States on a visa. Since the Internal Security Act of 1950 (known as the McCarran Act) had made it illegal for homosexuals to enter the United States, Vinales feared being deported once his orientation was discovered. He hurled himself out of the second-story window at the police station and impaled himself on a 14-inch spike in the wrought-iron fence below. He was brought to the hospital in critical condition and was later charged with resisting arrest. The protest at St. Vincent's Hospital, where Vinales was held, featured a GAA flyer that read, "Any way you look at it—that boy was PUSHED!! We are All being pushed."

Meanwhile, lesbian feminists were exploring their position in the larger feminist movement, particularly in the National Organization for Women (NOW), the largest and most influential national feminist group. Although feminist leader Betty Friedan had called lesbians diversionary and had even accused them of being sent by the Central Intelligence Agency (CIA) to discredit the women's movement, other NOW leaders were more sympathetic to lesbian issues. After a number of battles within the organization, a resolution supporting lesbians passed at the 1971 NOW National Conference, and in 1975 NOW declared lesbian rights to be a national priority.

ELECTORAL VICTORIES AND DEFEATS

Much of the early gay rights movement was concerned with winning political power, through electing gay candidates, passing gay rights legislation, and gaining a voice in the Democratic Party. In 1974, the first two openly gay candidates were elected: Kathy Kozachenko and Elaine Noble. Kozachenko, a University of Michigan student, won a seat on the Ann Arbor City Council. The council was a liberal body that for years had included students elected from the wards dominated by the University of Michigan. Elaine Noble's 1974 election to the Massachusetts state legislature was considered far more significant. Noble consistently stressed that she was running to represent the working people of her district, whom she intended to support through a wide variety of progressive legislation; her lesbianism was openly discussed, but was not the centerpiece of her campaign. She got a great deal of media attention for her broad-based campaign, which made her the first openly gay state representative.

Noble was soon joined by other gay legislators, including Minnesota state senator Allan Spear, who came out after he was already in office—and who then went on to win reelection in 1976. Meanwhile, for the first time in history, the 1972 Democratic Party featured five openly gay and lesbian delegates and alternates. One of them, longtime activist Jim Foster, even made a speech from the floor calling for gay rights to be added to the party platform. Though Foster's speech was made late at night, when virtually no one was listening, and though the efforts to affect the platform were not successful, gay leaders still had hopes of having a voice in the Democratic Party. Indeed, by 1980, there were 77 gay and lesbian delegates to the Democratic Convention, and in 1984, gay rights became part of official party policy.

At the same time, throughout the 1970s, more and more communities across the country were passing antidiscrimination legislation to protect gay rights in employment, housing, and public accommodation. To both opponents and supporters, it seemed that the civil rights of gay men and lesbians were fast becoming accepted.

BACKLASH

The victories of the gay and lesbian rights movement brought with them a backlash—an effort to erase the gains and return homosexuality to its former status as unspeakable sin and unpardonable crime. In 1977, singer and former beauty queen Anita Bryant led a broad-based campaign that included many religious leaders in an effort to repeal a gay rights ordinance that had recently been passed in Dade County, Florida. Bryant, whose organization was called "Save Our Children," sought to portray gay men and lesbians as child molesters, "recruiters" of innocent young people into their sinful ranks. Bryant was joined by the Reverend Jerry Falwell, who two years later would found the New Right group, the Moral Majority; the National Association of Evangelicals; the Roman Catholic Archdiocese of Miami; the president of the Miami Beach B'nai B'rith (a Jewish organization); both of Florida's senators and its liberal governor; and groups who opposed abortion rights and the Equal Rights Amendment (ERA), a proposed constitutional amendment guaranteeing equal rights to women. Bryant's referendum was successful by more than a 2-1 margin, and the measure was repealed, inspiring similar referendums in St. Paul, Minnesota; Wichita, Kansas; and Eugene, Oregon in 1978.

In what would become a familiar dialectic, defeat spurred the gay rights movement to new activism, and a record number of men and women turned out for gay rights events in the summer of 1977. Some 75,000 people marched in New York City's "Christopher Street Liberation Day March," five times as many as had marched in the previous year, while in San Francisco, 300,000 people turned out. And a nationwide orange juice boycott succeeded in convincing the Florida Citrus Commission to remove Bryant as their spokesperson.

But Bryant had also inspired California state senator John Briggs to put forward a new referendum in 1978, Proposition 6, popularly known as the Briggs Amendment, which would have banned all lesbians and gay men from working as public school teachers, while prohibiting any teacher or school employee from saying anything positive about homosexuality on school grounds. The Briggs Initiative was defeated 59 percent to 41 percent, in part because former California governor Ronald Reagan was convinced to come out against it, which influenced many voters to vote *no*. The defeat of the Briggs Amendment appeared to turn the tide of the backlash, especially since the people of Seattle also defeated an anti-gay rights referendum by a 2-1 margin.

Then, on November 27, 1978, a shocking event reminded Americans that it was still dangerous to be gay—or to support gay rights. Dan White, a right-wing former San Francisco supervisor (analogous to a city council position), enraged at what he saw as the pro-gay direction of San Francisco politics, had resigned from the board of supervisors. A few days later, he changed his mind and asked Mayor George Moscone, who was known to be gay-friendly, for his job back. When Moscone refused, White walked into city hall with a gun and assassinated first Moscone, then Harvey Milk, another supervisor, who was openly gay. White's lawyer used a strategy that became known as the "Twinkie defense," arguing that White was suffering from intense depression brought on by an overindulgence in junk food, a depression that distorted his judgment in a kind of temporary insanity. Apparently, this approach worked, for White was charged, not with murder, but with manslaughter, for which he received a sentence of only seven years and eight months. The "White Night Riots" were the result, in which gay men and lesbians in San Francisco's Castro District caused some $1 million damage in their outrage.

Just as the early, heady days of gay liberation had drawn inspiration from the liberatory climate of the 1960s and 1970s, so was the backlash of the late 1970s and the 1980s shaped by the generally right-wing trend in the United States. When Ronald Reagan was elected president in 1980, he saw his victory as a mandate to turn back the social reforms of the New Deal. New Right groups also saw his election as a signal that their time had come. Anticommunist, antiunion, antifeminist, anti–affirmative action, and antiwelfare, these new groups were also decidedly antigay. And while many Americans were uneasy about the New Right's attacks on women and people of color—at least at first—gay men and lesbians seemed a safe target.

Introduction to Gay Rights

THE AIDS CRISIS

Once again, the gay rights movement was about to witness a dialectical process, in which its greatest defeats turned into its greatest strengths. AIDS first appeared on the scene as a barely understood disease mentioned briefly as a "rare cancer" in news reports in 1981. Later, the disease was dubbed Gay-Related Immune Deficiency (GRID) since it was clear that many gay men seemed susceptible to it. By 1982, scientists realized that anyone could be infected, and that, in addition to gay men, the most common victims seemed to be users of intravenous drugs, hemophiliacs (people whose blood does not clot properly, causing them to bleed profusely from even minor cuts), and the recipients of blood transfusions. The disease was renamed Acquired Immune Deficiency Syndrome, or AIDS.

It was clear that sexual activity had something to do with the transmission of the disease, but in those early years, no one knew exactly how or why. Still, scientists understood that having multiple sexual partners increased one's chances for the disease—and multiple sexual partners were what the gay bathhouses were all about. Gradually, the call came, from both inside and outside the gay community: close the bathhouses.

For many gay men, sexual liberation was synonymous with gay rights. The idea that sexual activity—which seemed such a hard-won freedom—might prove deadly was unthinkable. The notion that bathhouses should now be closed by the state—which so many gay men remembered as the force behind humiliating arrests and raids—seemed offensive at best and oppressive at worst, particularly in a hostile political climate. Conservative commentator William F. Buckley actually wrote a *New York Times* op-ed piece calling for people with AIDS (PWAs) to be tattooed for identification. Others called for PWAs to be quarantined.

Nevertheless, some gay activists strongly believed that the bathhouses had become, not a site of sexual freedom, but a danger to public health. Others, while opposing state regulation, wanted the bathhouses to close voluntarily—or at least to police themselves, monitor group sex, conduct AIDS education, and offer free condoms. The controversy over the bathhouses continued throughout the mid-1980s. In some places, they were closed—and gay rights and civil liberties groups fought court cases to get them reopened. In other places, they closed of their own accord. Other bathhouses remained open or reopened. While some observers reported a drop in bathhouse business, others claimed that gay men continued to go to the baths—though perhaps they behaved somewhat differently once they got there.

Although the dangers of AIDS were suspected as early as 1981, President Ronald Reagan did not even mention the disease publicly until 1987 (though he did send a telegram of condolence to his old friend, movie star Rock Hudson, when it became known that Hudson had the disease in 1985). By the time Reagan addressed the issue, there were 36,000 reported AIDS cases in the United States alone (the disease was spreading even more rapidly in Africa, and cases had been reported in Europe and the Caribbean), and almost 21,000 Americans had died. A disproportionate number of the U.S. deaths were people of color.

Moreover, very little money, relatively speaking, was allocated for AIDS research. Congress did not even grant funds until 1983, when it budgeted only $33 million. A U.S. Department of Health and Human Services hotline created in 1983 was staffed with only six operators—who were expected to handle more than 10,000 calls each day. As of July 1983, some 90,000 calls had been left unanswered.

So the gay and lesbian community rallied in its own defense. In 1982, writer Larry Kramer cofounded Gay Men's Health Crisis (GMHC) in New York City. Other AIDS groups were quickly formed around the country, primarily to provide social services and support for people with AIDS. In 1987, the militant political action group, AIDS Coalition to Unleash Power (ACT UP) was formed in New York City. Soon there were ACT UP chapters elsewhere in the United States and in Paris, London, and Berlin. ACT UP protestors challenged the drug companies, the U.S. Food and Drug Administration, and the medical establishment, demanding more, better, and cheaper treatments, as well as fighting for AIDS education and prevention. In the words of sociologist Steven Epstein: ". . . the AIDS movement [was] the first in the United States to accomplish the mass conversion of disease 'victims' into activist-experts."

As we have seen, the militancy of ACT UP and the rapprochement between gay men and lesbians were two unexpected results of the epidemic, which left thousands of people dead and devastated an entire community. Yet this tragic disease also brought a new visibility and, oddly, a new acceptability to gay life in America. Ironically, people with AIDS constituted the first class of gay men (and lesbians) to receive federal protection, when the civil rights protections afforded under the 1990 Americans with Disabilities Act were extended to people with AIDS in 1998. Because people with AIDS, or people infected with HIV (the virus that causes AIDS) were considered "disabled," AIDS or HIV status could no longer be a reason to fire someone from a job or deny a person housing or public accommodation.

AIDS activism also brought the gay rights movement closer to other activist communities. The tenants' movement in New York City, for example, had traditionally resented gay men, both because of homophobia and because gay men were frequently willing to buy apartments in newly gentrifying neighborhoods, thus displacing previous tenants—poor and working-class people who were often people of color as well. Yet when landlords began evicting the surviving partners of men who had died of AIDS, the gay rights movement and tenant activists were able to unite around a common cause. (For more on AIDS and housing rights, see the discussion of *Braschi v. Stahl Associates Co.* in Chapter 2.) In New York City, this coalition led to the election of several gay leaders, including State Senator Deborah Glick, the first open lesbian to be elected to the New York State Assembly (1990), and City Councilman Tom Duane, the first openly gay man to hold that office. (Duane later became the first openly HIV-positive person to be elected to public office in New York as well. He is now a state representative.)

Introduction to Gay Rights

THE NINETIES AND THE NEW CENTURY

In the 1990s, a generation of activists appeared who had been born after Stonewall and who had a whole new set of assumptions about what being gay or lesbian in America might mean. Early in the decade, meanwhile, gay activists faced challenges in Oregon and Colorado, where statewide antigay referendums were proposed in 1992. In Oregon, the measure was defeated, although local antigay ordinances began to appear the following year. In Colorado, the infamous Amendment 2 nullified gay rights legislation elsewhere in the state and banned local governments from implementing new gay rights measures. *Romer v. Evans*, the 1996 Supreme Court ruling that overturned Amendment 2, is considered by many to be one of the most important pro-gay court rulings in U.S. history.

Throughout much of the 1990s, the Republican Party continued to position itself as deeply opposed to gay rights, particularly at its 1992 convention, where Patrick Buchanan called for "cultural war" against homosexuals. However, the 1990s were also the decade that saw the founding of the Log Cabin Republicans, a group of gay Republicans committed both to their party and to gay rights.

In 1992, Democratic presidential candidate Bill Clinton promised he would overturn the ban on gays and lesbians in the military if he were elected—and then went on to implement a far weaker policy, popularly known as "don't ask, don't tell." Ironically, more gay men and lesbians have been discharged under this policy than under the previous blanket prohibition against gay or lesbian sexual activity. (For more on military policy, see Chapter 2.)

Even in the face of escalating attacks from the religious right, gay and lesbian family arrangements received more recognition in the 1990s than in any other previous decade. By 1997, more than two dozen cities had domestic partnership registries, through which gay men and lesbians could receive some measure of legal recognition for their relationships, even if full-fledged marriage was not available. (For more on gay marriage, see Chapter 2.) More than 50 cities offered domestic partnership benefits to their municipal employees, while numerous colleges, universities, labor unions, and corporations extended such benefits as well, in a de facto recognition of gay/lesbian marriage. These figures have continued to grow, so that by 2003, according to an analysis released in 2004 by the Human Rights Campaign (HRC), 40 percent of all Fortune-listed companies offered domestic partner benefits. As this figure represents an increase of 18 percent over the previous year, it indicates a definite trend. States, cities, and counties were also increasingly likely to offer such benefits to gay couples, as well as to unmarried straight couples.

Another aspect of gay rights that has gained significance during the 1990s and the 21st century is the notion of transgender rights. *Transgender* is an umbrella term used to refer to a wide range of people and conditions, but it generally indicates people who consider that their more obvious biological gender—male or female—does not represent their true gender. Some transgender people, called transvestites, dress as members of the opposite sex (though not all transvestites are transgender; some are simply people who enjoy cross-dressing). Other transgender people seek medical help to switch genders, taking hormones and undergoing surgery so that they can more fully live out what they consider their true identity. Still others choose to live as members of the gender to which they feel they belong, without medical intervention. Many others simply endure in silence, trying to cure what they see as a psychological problem or to hide what they see as dangerous desires.

Many transgender people are not necessarily gay. They may prefer either same-sex or opposite-sex partners, before and after their transition from one gender to the other. However, since many are gay, and since their battle for rights is in some ways similar, there has been an increasing tendency to include transgender people in the gay rights movement, which indeed is often now referred to as "LGBT"—lesbian/gay/bisexual/transgender.

A comprehensive look at this issue is beyond the scope of this book, although a brief discussion of transgender rights is included under "Legal Issues" in this chapter, and a key transgender rights case is briefly described in Chapter 2. It is worth noting, however, that there is a small but significant trend in the courts to recognize transgender rights, allowing transgender people to change their birth certificates and driver's licenses, for example. The HRC report likewise notes that transgender rights are increasingly being recognized in private employers' antidiscrimination clauses.

Another key issue of the 21st century has been the role of religion in public life. President George W. Bush, who took office in 2001, announced his intention to privatize social services as far as possible, and to allocate public funds to religious agencies who might offer counseling, housing, and other assistance. These religious organizations, however, often view homosexuality as sinful or sick, and they have sometimes sought to fire or refuse to hire otherwise qualified gay personnel. Legal battles over this issue are discussed in Chapter 2, but here it is worth noting that the growing role of conservative religion in public life poses a wide range of problems for gay people.

Perhaps the most profound shift of the recent period, a transition that is discussed more fully in Chapter 3, has been the move from invisibility to visibility. When the 1990s began, gay men and lesbians were still marginalized, still invisible, still outside the frame of reference of most of American culture. Even after gay men and lesbians had won some rights, achieved political office, and created a margin of safety for their sexual and emotional lives, they were not seriously taken into account as a political or cultural force that had to be seen as part of the national life.

Now, even if religious right organizations continue to demonize gay men and lesbians, the fact that gay people exist and the assumption that they should be treated with respect has been brought to the attention of the American public in a way that cannot be ignored. Although discrimination, exclusion, and even violence against gay men and lesbians is still common, there now exists a cultural and political framework to name those problems and object to them. What use gay men, lesbians, and their allies will make of this framework in the decades to come remains to be seen.

Introduction to Gay Rights

THE MARRIAGE QUESTION

As of this writing, gay marriage has become such an important issue in the United States that the topic deserves a history of its own. In 1971, only two years after the Stonewall uprising gave birth to the modern gay rights movement, two African-American lesbians in Milwaukee went to city hall to get a marriage license. Their case eventually wound up in federal court, where they were unsuccessful. Also in 1971, the Minnesota Supreme Court ruled against Jack Baker and Mike McConnell, two men who wanted to marry each other and who argued that in the absence of a law banning gay marriage, the legislature must have intended to recognize same-sex unions. The court found that "The institution of marriage as a union of man and woman, uniquely involving the procreation and rearing of children within a family, is as old as the book of Genesis."

In 1975, a county clerk granted two men in Phoenix, Arizona, a marriage license, but the Arizona Supreme Court, likewise citing the Bible, invalidated the marriage, and the state legislature passed a bill specifically prohibiting gay marriage. Meanwhile, in Colorado, Boulder County clerk Clela Rorex asked the district attorney's office whether that state's laws allowed gay marriage. When she learned that there was no law against it, she allowed six gay couples to marry. This early effort found little response nationwide, however, as few institutions chose to recognize these marriages, despite the apparent legality of the license.

Then, in 1987, the American Civil Liberties Union (ACLU) announced its commitment to ending the legal barriers to gay marriage, while 2,000 gay couples in Washington, D.C., held a mass mock wedding in the Internal Revenue Service (IRS) building. Clearly, gay marriage was on the agenda for the movement, despite the bitter disagreements over whether it was a useful or even a desirable goal (see the more extensive discussion of this issue above). However, it was not until 1990 that a successful suit was brought. In that year, a Honolulu couple, Genora Dancel and Ninia Baehr, were likewise denied a marriage license. Despite the national ACLU's previous commitment, the group's local branch refused Dancel and Baehr's request for help. So, initially, did national gay legal groups, who thought that the issue would find too little support in mainstream society.

Nevertheless, Dancel and Baehr, later joined by other couples, took their suit to the Hawaii Supreme Court, which in 1993 upheld the couple's right to marry on the basis of the state's equal protection law. The court specified, however, that it was not speaking to the issue of gay rights but rather of gender rights. If two women wanted to marry, it seemed a failure of equal protection to say that one of them would be denied that right only because she was not a man.

The court also ruled that a ban on gay marriage might be upheld if there was a compelling reason for such a restriction. Conservative groups began pouring money into the state to prevent gay marriage, as the Supreme Court considered arguments that a compelling reason did indeed exist.

The Hawaii suit inspired concern nationwide over the prospect of gay marriage. In 1996, the U.S. Congress passed the Defense of Marriage Act (DOMA), which defined marriage as existing only between a man and a woman for purposes of federal law, affecting taxes, pensions, Social Security, and all other federal benefits. DOMA also excused states from recognizing gay marriages that might be performed elsewhere. Although the Constitution requires all other contracts to be recognized nationwide, regardless of where they are made, DOMA would seem to make gay marriage an exception to that rule.

Many observers believed that DOMA touched on such a hot-button issue that liberals had to support it regardless of their personal feelings on the issue. Significantly, President Bill Clinton signed the bill late one Friday evening, after the press corps had gone home. Although Clinton did not want to be known as the president who supported gay marriage, he evidently did not want to be known as the president who opposed it, either.

Two years after DOMA was passed, Hawaii's Supreme Court was still considering whether the state had a compelling reason to ban gay marriage. In 1998, however, Hawaii's voters passed a constitutional amendment allowing their legislature to restrict marriage to a man and a woman. In 1999, the legislature passed such a law, rendering the court case moot.

During the same period, Alaska was undergoing a similar process. On February 3, 1998, Alaska Superior Court judge Peter Michalski ruled in favor of Jay Brause and Gene Dugan, a couple who had brought yet another gay marriage suit. Like the judges in Hawaii, Michalski found that choosing a marital partner was such a fundamental right that the state needed a compelling reason to interfere with it. Nine months later, on November 3, Alaska voters also amended their constitution to define marriage as between heterosexuals only.

A similar suit had been brought in Vermont, where in late 1999 the state supreme court likewise ruled in favor of gay Vermonters' equal rights. In Vermont, however, events took a different turn. Instead of simply finding that the state needed "a compelling reason" to ban gay marriage, the court ordered the state legislature to come up with some arrangement that offered gay residents equal access to the legal and financial benefits of marriage. The result was the "civil union," a legal form that extends to committed couples (gay or straight) most benefits available under Vermont state law, such as family leave, child custody, and worker compensation. As a state institution, however, civil unions cannot extend federal marriage benefits, such as tax breaks, military pensions, Social Security, or citizenship. Moreover, unlike marriages, civil unions are not "portable"; that is, the rights they confer will not necessarily be recognized in other states.

A number of states had passed laws or amendments banning gay marriage, including California, where state senator William "Pete" Knight spearheaded a voter referendum in 2000 to amend the state constitution to define marriage as between one man and one woman. By 2005, 18 states had amended their constitutions specifically to ban same-sex marriage.

Yet the movement to legalize same-sex marriage was continuing, with the next frontier in Massachusetts. There, in April 2001, seven same-sex couples filed suit with the help of Mary Bonauto, representing Gay and Lesbian Advocates and Defenders (GLAD). As they had elsewhere, the plaintiffs claimed that their state's equal protection laws guaranteed them the right to marry. The Massachusetts Supreme Judicial Court (the state's highest court) agreed, ruling in November 2003 that same-sex couples were entitled to full legal recognition of civil marriage.

The decision set off an immediate backlash in Massachusetts in the form of a movement to amend the state constitution, redefining marriage as between one man and one woman. The proposed amendment sought to have it both ways, defining marriage as strictly heterosexual while also creating a parallel civil union form for gay couples. The move enraged gay rights activists who wanted full access to the rights and benefits of marriage, even as it dismayed conservatives who opposed civil unions. Whether the amendment will pass was not clear as of this writing. Even if it does pass, it cannot go into effect until 2006, by which time hundreds or even thousands of same-sex marriages may have been contracted. Legal questions are already being raised as to whether these marriages will be invalidated retroactively or allowed to stand.

Meanwhile, a Federal Marriage Amendment (FMA) had been introduced into the U.S. House of Representatives by Colorado representative Marilyn Musgrave, first on May 15, 2002, and then again on May 21, 2003. The FMA was an attempt to overcome objections that DOMA contravened (or violated) the U.S. Constitution by allowing states to disregard contracts that other states considered legal. A Constitutional amendment, supporters felt, would clarify the matter, defining marriage as consisting only of a male-female union and specifying that no state constitution, state law, or federal law was to be construed as requiring a state to allow same-sex marriage or to confer marital benefits on gay couples. By the early 21st century, some four-fifths of all states had already passed laws or amended their constitutions to ban same-sex marriage.

On February 24, 2004, President George W. Bush announced his support for a Constitutional amendment prohibiting gay marriage, though he did not specifically support Musgrave's FMA. Many observers believe that Bush was less interested in banning gay marriage than in proving to his right-wing and religious constituency that he stood strong on an issue that was of supreme importance to them.

At the same time, a national upsurge of gay couples seeking marital recognition was met by an unexpected wave of support from the mainstream community. In San Francisco, newly elected mayor Gavin Newsom approached Kate Kendall at the National Committee for Lesbian Rights and asked whether the time was right to push the marriage issue forward. When Kendall enthusiastically agreed, Newsom and other city officials began issuing marriage licenses, with the symbolic first marriage being performed for veteran activists Phyllis Lyon and Del Martin, founders of the Daughters of Bilitis, one of the first lesbian groups in the nation.

Between February 12 and March 11, some 4,037 same-sex marriage licenses were issued in San Francisco, resulting in 3,995 marriages. Some 90 percent of the licenses went to California couples, though gay men and lesbians came from every state in the union except Maine, Mississippi, West Virginia, and Wyoming, and from Canada, Denmark, France, Germany, the Netherlands, Switzerland, Thailand, and the United Kingdom—eloquent testimony to the deep hunger for gay marriage. News articles reported scenes of couples cheering for each other's marriages on the steps of city hall, and of longtime partners weeping with relief that they had finally been granted legal marriage.

Among those who married in San Francisco were comedian and former talk-show host Rosie O'Donnell and her partner, whose ceremony took place on February 26. O'Donnell decided to marry because her partner had been forced to testify against her in a legal dispute with the publisher of O'Donnell's magazine. Married people are exempt from testifying against one another—but O'Donnell and her partner were not afforded the same right, nor would they have been had they entered into a civil union. In response to this unequal treatment, O'Donnell felt compelled to dramatize the importance of gay marriage by joining in the San Francisco effort.

Another dramatic marriage was that of David J. Knight, son of Pete Knight, the author of the California ban on same-sex marriage. Despite his father's opposition, David married Joseph J. Lazzaro, his partner of 10 years.

Other cities in California were eager to follow San Francisco's example, including the Bay Area communities of Berkeley and Oakland. However, California marriage licenses are given out by counties, not cities. San Francisco is the only California city that is also a county.

The California Supreme Court soon issued a stay (legal proceeding that requires an activity to stop). Although the same-sex marriages were prohibited by state law, city officials argued that they were nonetheless legally binding because the law was unconstitutional. Eventually, on August 12, 2004, the state's high court found all of the San Francisco marriages invalid, ruling that Mayor Newsom had overstepped his authority. The court ordered all records of the marriages to be expunged and all license fees returned. (On March 14, 2005, a California judge ruled that the state's ban on gay marriage was unconstitutional, setting in motion a fight in the appellate courts that was expected to go to the state supreme court.)

Meanwhile in spring 2004, San Francisco's example inspired many imitators. Victoria Dunlap, the county clerk of Sandoval County, New Mexico, began issuing marriage licenses on the grounds that the state's marriage law did not mention gender. On February 20, some 26 licenses were issued to same-sex couples—until state attorney general Patricia Madrid held that the licenses were invalid under state law, halting Dunlap's effort.

Likewise, in the little New York village of New Paltz, Mayor Jason West announced that his city would also perform same-sex weddings. New Paltz had no status to issue marriage licenses, but New York state law allows married couples a six-month grace period to seek a marriage license. In any case, a New York State marriage is not necessarily invalid without a license.

West made his announcement on February 26. The next day, Nyack mayor John Shields offered to recognize same-sex marriages performed elsewhere. On

March 2, Ulster County district attorney Donald Williams charged West with 19 misdemeanor counts for performing marriages without a license, but West promised to continue performing the ceremonies. The next day, Shields announced his intention both to perform same-sex marriages and to go with his male partner to seek a marriage license.

Also on March 3, the New York attorney general's office released an informal opinion that clerks should stop issuing marriage licenses, as same-sex marriage was contrary to the intent of the state legislature. However, the opinion said, same-sex marriages legally performed elsewhere would be recognized in New York.

West continued to perform same-sex ceremonies until March 5, when New York state judge Vincent Bradley issued a temporary restraining order (another legal means of stopping someone from taking action). Although West stopped performing the same-sex marriages, two Unitarian Universalist ministers began conducting them and were then charged on March 15 by district attorney Williams with 13 counts of performing marriages without a license. On March 20, the two ministers and four other Unitarian Universalist pastors defied the law by performing another 25 same-sex marriages in New Paltz.

Other actions in support of gay marriage were taken in upstate New York, including the Rochester City Council's decision to recognize same-sex marriages performed elsewhere. Ithaca mayor Carolyn K. Peterson and her city clerk began actions to provoke a court hearing by sending marriage applications from five same-sex couples to the New York State Department of Health. If the applications were denied, Peterson planned to offer her city's legal resources to help bring suit.

Oregon state law regarding marriage is somewhat vaguely defined as a "civil contract entered into in person by males at least 17 years of age and females at least 17 years of age"—wording that leaves room for same-sex unions. Accordingly, on March 3, 2004, Multnomah County began issuing same-sex marriage licenses. Some 3,000 licenses had been issued by April 21, the date on which county circuit court judge Frank Bearden ordered the commissioners to stop issuing licenses. A study by the *Portland Oregonian* indicated that about one-third of the gay men and lesbians living in the county had received licenses, as well as couples from elsewhere in Oregon and from neighboring states. On April 14, 2005, the Oregon Supreme Court nullified the licenses. In response, Oregon governor Ted Kulongoski proposed a civil-union bill to the state legislature. As of this writing, the legislature had yet to act on the governor's proposal.

To the surprise of many observers, the judge refused to issue an injunction banning same-sex marriage. The following day, Greg Chaimov, the state legislature's attorney, issued his opinion: counties in Oregon could not prevent gay couples from getting licenses. Two days later, on March 12, state attorney general Hardy Myers issued a somewhat contradictory opinion. He found that current state law did indeed ban gay marriage, although the state supreme court would probably decide that withholding marital benefits from same-sex couples violated the state constitution. Myers stressed that he did not have the authority to order Multnomah County to stop issuing the licenses, and accordingly, the county announced on March 15 that they would continue their actions. Benton County commissioners voted to join them, having held a series of public hearings on the issue, but reversed their decision in the face of pressure from the attorney general, including a phone call threatening to arrest the county clerk. The parties decided to let three couples sue the state of Oregon in Multnomah County Court, hoping to resolve the issue.

On April 20, Justice Frank Bearden ordered the county to stop issuing same-sex licenses—but he also ordered the state to recognize the 3,022 licenses that had already been granted. And he directed the legislature to act on the issue, given that, in his opinion, the state constitution did indeed allow some form of same-sex marriage. Bearden ruled that if the legislature did not act within the first 90 days of its next session, Multnomah County could start issuing same-sex marriage licenses again. The Oregon legal battle continues, however, as both sides moved to appeal.

In nearby Washington state, Seattle mayor Greg Nickels issued a March 8 executive order recognizing same-sex marriages contracted by city employees in other jurisdictions. He proposed an ordinance requiring city contractors to offer similar recognition to their employees. On March 11, the American Family Association, a conservative group leading the attack on gay marriage, tried to block the mayor's order. Legal battles continue as of this writing.

Also on March 8, six gay couples in King County (which comprises Seattle) filed suit seeking marriage licenses. The Washington Defense of Marriage Act (DOMA) defines marriage as "a civil contract between a male and a female," but it also grants counties the authority to issue marriage licenses. In August 2004, King County superior court judge William Downing found for the couples and ruled that the state's DOMA was in violation of the state constitution. The case has been appealed to the state supreme court and is pending as of this writing.

Meanwhile, in September 2004, Thurston County superior court judge Richard Hicks made a similar ruling in a similar suit, going even further to rule that homosexuals were a protected class entitled to equal protection under the law. The Washington state supreme court is expected to rule on both cases together.

Another gay marriage battle took place in New Jersey, where on January 12, 2004, the state's domestic partnership law was signed into effect. The law was passed partly to forestall an effort to win full marital benefits for gay people. Nevertheless, on March 8 of that year, the deputy mayor of Asbury Park married a same-sex couple whose license had been quietly issued by the town clerk three days earlier. New Jersey state law requires a three-day waiting period between receiving a license and entering into marriage, and little attention had gone to the licensing procedure. The day after the marriage, however, 16 same-sex couples demanded their own licenses, rushing to avoid the injunction (court order requiring an action to stop) that state attorney general Peter C. Harvey had threatened to file. Although Harvey did not take legal action, he did send warning letters to Asbury Park officials, informing them that they might be prosecuted if they continued to act outside the law. The following day, the city council froze the

16 pending licenses and voted to sue the state for recognition of both the licenses and the marriage. On April 21, 2004, the Asbury Park City Council switched strategies. Rather than pursuing its own suit, it decided to join a Mercer County case of seven same-sex couples claiming a constitutional right to marry.

Even as some states, counties, and towns moved to support gay marriage, other jurisdictions took action against it. On March 5, 2004, for example, the Wisconsin State Assembly approved 68-27 a state constitution amendment to ban both gay marriage and civil unions. On March 12, the state senate passed the amendment 20-13. However, the 2004–05 legislature must pass the amendment as well, after which the measure will be submitted to state voters in a referendum. Action also began in Kansas for a state constitutional amendment, which subsequently was approved by voters on April 5, 2005. The Virginia house of delegates passed a law restricting same-sex marriages, as well as civil unions, partnership contracts, and any other same-sex arrangement "purporting to bestow the privileges or obligations of marriage."

Opponents of gay marriage continued to gain ground throughout the summer and fall of 2004. On July 14, the U.S. Senate failed on a procedural vote to pass a Constitutional amendment that would have outlawed same-sex marriage in the United States, while on September 30th, the House of Representatives failed to muster the necessary two-thirds majority needed to pass the Marriage Protection Amendment, a similar attempt to prohibit same-sex marriage at the constitutional level. Two states also voted overwhelmingly to amend their constitutions to ban same-sex marriage: Missouri, on August 3, by a vote of 71 percent to 29 percent, and Louisiana, on September 18, by a vote of 78 percent to 22 percent. The Louisiana amendment was thrown out 17 days later by district court judge William Morvant, who said that the law was invalid because it had two purposes, prohibiting same-sex marriage and outlawing civil unions. Both elections were seen as a sign of deep national opposition to gay marriage.

In the November 2 presidential election, voters in 11 states approved constitutional amendments to ban same-sex marriages: Arkansas, Georgia, Kentucky, Michigan, Mississippi, Montana, North Dakota, Oklahoma, Ohio, Oregon, and Utah. The smallest anti–gay marriage vote was 57 percent, in Oregon; the largest was 86 percent, in Mississippi. Observers noted that, as in the Missouri and Louisiana elections, the high number of votes against gay marriage seemed to have been achieved with relatively little effort or financial outlay on the part of the anti-gay rights movement. However, gay rights activists were also relatively disorganized and unable to muster either volunteers or financial resources to defeat the amendments. Where they were more active, they made a significant different in the voting outcomes. For example, a concerted gay rights campaign in Oregon succeeded in moving the polls by 13 points in two months, and in Kentucky, gay rights activists were able to increase opposition to the amendments by 8 points in four months. A November 14, 2004, *New York Times* article by Kate Zernike cited gay rights activists who said that in Michigan, they had won support from 80 percent of the people whom they had visited door to door, while in Kentucky, the figure was as high as 85 percent. Activists told Zernike that door-to-door canvassing and other volunteer activity could make a huge difference in building future support for gay rights generally and gay marriage in particular.

The gay marriage issue also stirred controversy among African Americans. Many African Americans, particularly those who belong to conservative churches, vehemently oppose gay marriage and deeply resent comparisons made between the African-American civil rights movement and current attempts of gay people to win new rights. Many gay activists have compared the ban on same-sex marriage to the widespread laws against interracial marriage and to the denial of marital rights to African and African-American slaves, a comparison that some African Americans find offensive.

However, other black activists support gay marriage and welcome the comparison. Coretta Scott King, the widow of civil rights leader Martin Luther King, Jr., came out against the FMA on March 24, 2004. "Gay and lesbian people have families, and their families should have legal protection," she said, "whether by marriage or civil union. A Constitutional amendment banning same-sex marriages is a form of gay bashing and it would do nothing at all to protect traditional marriages."

As of this writing, same-sex marriage is legal only in Massachusetts, where on May 17, 2004, same-sex couples began flocking to city hall to get their licenses. To some observers, the actual beginning of legal same-sex marriage in the United States came as an anticlimax. There were no riots the day the law went into effect, no raucous celebrations, no disruptions of the social order. Indeed, Massachusetts congressman and gay activist Barney Frank has predicted that once society recognizes how little difference gay marriages make to most straight people's daily lives, opposition to the issue will wither away. After all, as recently as 1961, interracial marriages were illegal in many states—a prohibition that seems inconceivable today.

The attitude of straight people toward gay marriage is difficult to measure. Clearly, many straight officials at all levels of government have offered extraordinary support for an issue that, only a few years ago, seemed to frighten even the most liberal politicians. (Many observers were surprised, for example, when the well-known, liberal U.S. senator, Paul Wellstone, joined the overwhelming congressional majority voting for the Defense of Marriage Act in 1996.) The intensity and magnitude of both gay and straight efforts to make gay marriage a reality astonished many observers on all sides of the issue.

Likewise, conservative and religious groups across the country have made opposition to gay marriage a rallying cry. They are dispensing enormous amounts of energy, money, and influence in their effort to stop what they consider the imposition of immorality upon society. Most citizens, they argue, do not approve of homosexuality, and should not be forced to implicitly condone it by allowing gay people to marry. Many conservatives also believe that allowing gay men and lesbians to marry weakens the institution for straight people.

Assessing sentiment in the center is somewhat more difficult. A nationwide poll taken in July 2003 by Pew Research revealed that 53 percent of respondents opposed making gay marriage legal while 38 percent supported the concept. In

October 2003, Pew repeated the poll, finding that opposition had risen to 59 percent and support had fallen to 32 percent. But in the same month, a poll taken in Massachusetts found that 64 percent of state voters would support a supreme judicial court ruling in favor of gay marriage, while only 34 percent would be opposed. The same poll revealed that 59 percent of state voters believed in gay people's right to marry, while 35 percent did not.

A more recent poll, taken on February 10, 2004, found contradictory evidence nationwide: although respondents declared themselves opposed to gay marriage by a 2-1 margin, 49 percent also opposed a constitutional amendment to ban gay marriage. This discrepancy in figures, though, may have more to do with opposition to allowing the federal government a control on marriage, something traditionally determined by the states. And many people may feel uncomfortable enshrining discrimination in the Constitution, even if they also oppose gay marriage or other gay rights. Potentially, opinions on the topic will continue to shift in response to both political debate and people's actual experience with the growing wave of same-sex marriages.

Meanwhile, the Netherlands, Belgium, and eight Canadian provinces permit gay marriage (Ontario, British Columbia, Quebec, the Yukon, Manitoba, Nova Scotia, Newfoundland, and Saskatchewan), and the likelihood seems great for the entire nation of Canada to follow suit, particularly given the Canadian Supreme Court ruling in January 2005 that there were no constitutional reasons to ban gay marriage. What this will mean for U.S.–Canadian relations is not yet clear, although immigration officials have already refused to recognize the marriage of one Canadian couple who sought to enter the United States on a joint tourist visa. Given the increasingly widespread support for gay marriage, and the increasing vehemence of opposition to it, the issue seems likely to continue in the public eye for some time to come.

THE ANTI–GAY RIGHTS MOVEMENT

Social, religious, and political views on homosexuality have varied widely over the centuries, with attitudes, laws, and practices shifting throughout different cultures, time periods, and circumstances. Many people—both pro– and anti–gay rights—tend to speak as though homosexuality was universally condemned until the modern gay rights movement, but a number of historians, anthropologists, and sociologists have challenged that view, presenting a much more complex and contradictory picture. Many cultures around the world have continuously or occasionally made a place for various versions of same-sex relationships; other cultures have repressed such relationships severely; still other cultures have responded to homosexuality in a range of ways. Some cultures have condoned homosexuality at some times and condemned it at others.

Therefore, this discussion of the anti–gay rights movement concerns only the contemporary United States, focusing specifically on the movement that developed in direct response to the gay rights movement. The previous sections have presented the history of that movement, including such efforts to combat the gay rights movement as Anita Bryant's "Save Our Children" campaign and the effort to pass the Briggs Amendment in California. This section will describe the anti–gay rights movement as of this writing, in an effort to make clear the various political, social, and religious arguments that have moved Americans to oppose gay rights. (For more information on specific political organizations, leaders, and positions on issues, see the anti–gay rights Web sites and organizations listed in Chapters 7 and 9, as well as many of the books and articles listed in Chapter 8.)

Like the gay rights movement it opposes, the anti–gay rights movement is varied and diverse, appealing to a wide range of people for different reasons. And, like the gay rights movement, the anti–gay rights movement is continually changing in response to a number of conditions. For example, when Vermont first recognized civil unions between same-sex partners in 2000, many conservatives and anti–gay rights leaders were bitterly opposed to such arrangements. Now, many conservatives who oppose gay marriage with equal bitterness are proposing civil unions as a more palatable or even desirable alternative. At the same time, the anti–gay rights movement in Virginia passed a sweeping law in 2004 that bans not only civil unions but also "partnership contract[s and] other arrangement[s] . . . purporting to bestow the privileges or obligations of marriage." For the first time in U.S. history, a state has explicitly outlawed child custody and guardianship arrangements between same-sex partners. Both conservative support for civil unions and conservative opposition to child custody arrangements are new developments in the anti–gay rights movement, which, like the gay rights movement it opposes, is a complex, diverse, and often contradictory collection of different ideologies and social groups.

Bearing these complexities in mind, it is still possible to delineate some basic elements of the anti–gay rights movement. One of the largest and most visible segments of this movement bases its opposition to gay rights on what it considers to be biblical authority. Although many elements of the U.S. Jewish and Muslim communities also consider homosexuality sinful, the largest and most vocal segment of the religious anti–gay rights movement in the United States identifies as Christian. Although only a few verses in either the Old or the New Testaments concern same-sex relationships, the Christian wing of the anti–gay rights movement considers homosexuality to be one of the greatest possible sins, as well as a form of corruption that is destroying families, promoting hedonism and immorality, eroding the basic moral authority of the church, and corrupting children and youth.

For the segment of the anti–gay rights movement that grounds its beliefs in Christian doctrine, homosexuality is an absolute evil with which society must not compromise. Even within this segment of the movement, opinions may vary— e.g., while all oppose gay marriage, some might agree to civil unions while others would support the Virginia legislation banning all "marriage-like" arrangements between same-sex partners. But in general, this religious opposition to gay rights focuses on the dangers of accommodating what is seen as immoral behavior and on a Christian's duty to censure such behavior wherever it is found. Thus, Robert

G. Marshall, the Virginia legislator who wrote the law banning civil unions and gay partnerships, insisted on the importance of society condemning homosexuality. "They [homosexuals] want to eradicate any institution that says what they are doing is immoral," he said in a May 22, 2004, article in the *Virginia Pilot*, implying that his law offered a clear denunciation of that immorality.

Another segment of the anti–gay rights movement, while perhaps also religious in orientation, focuses more on traditional morality and family values. Thus the supporters of the 1993 Cincinnati law that bans gay people from seeking redress against discrimination on the basis of their sexuality have called the ordinance "the grandma law." The only city-level anti–gay rights ordinance in the United States, the Cincinnati law forbids people from challenging discrimination in employment, housing, and public accommodations on the basis of sexual orientation. The term *grandma law* suggests that a grandmother—someone presumably raised with traditional values—should not be forced to hire gay people, rent rooms to them, or accommodate them in her store or restaurant if she is offended by their sexuality.

The Cincinnati law faced a challenge in the November 2004 election, and the names of the two opposing groups suggest the divergent views on this issue. The pro–gay rights group that wanted to overturn the law—to allow gay men and lesbians to seek redress for discrimination at work, in housing, or in public places—called itself "Citizens to Restore Fairness." The anti–gay rights group that wanted to retain the law—to allow people in Cincinnati to refuse employment, housing, and public accommodations to gay people without fear of legal punishment—was called "Equal Rights, No Special Rights." A spokesperson for the group, Phil Burress, quoted in a September 18, 2004, article in the *Cincinnati Post*, took issue with the notion that refusing service, housing, or employment to gay people constituted "discrimination":

"There's legal discrimination and illegal discrimination, if they want to use that word," he said. "Some call it choice." Burress also challenged the notion that gay people were facing problems because of their sexuality. "I can list 10,000 reasons why someone might lose a job or be denied housing," he said. "If there's a history of this happening, then we should talk about it. But there's no proof. Gays are an affluent and politically powerful group of people. They just don't want people speaking up who dislike their lifestyle." (The Cincinnati anti–gay rights law was defeated in November.)

The sense that gay men and lesbians are powerful people with no right to claim they are being discriminated against is shared by many African-American opponents to gay rights. While some African Americans have welcomed the notion that gay rights are linked to civil rights, others are deeply offended by what they see as an attempt to capitalize upon, co-opt, or tarnish the heritage of the civil rights movement. African-American fundamentalist churches are particularly concerned about gay rights, which they oppose deeply on religious grounds.

Whatever their position on other gay rights issues, African Americans are particularly likely to oppose gay marriage. A May 2004 poll revealed that while 59 percent of all Americans opposed gay marriage, the figure among African

Americans was 72 percent. Many African Americans, both fundamentalists and liberals, see gay marriage as eroding the two-parent family structure, part of a climate in which such families are already facing numerous threats.

Increased African-American religious opposition to gay rights made a significant difference in the November 2004 election of President George W. Bush. Although in 1996, some 65 percent of black Protestants supported equal rights for gays, in 2004, the figure had fallen to 40 percent, according to the Pew Forum on Religion and Public Life. And in the key state of Ohio, President Bush nearly doubled his support among black voters, from 9 percent in 2000 to 16 percent in 2004, according to senior analyst David Bositis of the Joint Center for Political and Economic Studies—an increase that Bositis attributed almost entirely to black Christian conservatives.

Burress articulates yet another concern of the anti–gay rights movement: The fear that people will be forced to tolerate behavior that they find intolerable and will be legally penalized for speaking out against it. Speaking of the Cincinnati law, Burress commented, "What the repeal is really about is forcing anyone who disagrees with them about homosexuality to accept it or be prosecuted. They want to file lawsuits and put people in jail who disagree with them." Similar anti–gay rights concerns include the fear that repelling homosexual advances will open the door to hate crime charges, and the worry that simply expressing religious or personal opposition to homosexuality will become illegal.

The anti–gay rights movement thus raises some pressing questions about how First Amendment rights to freedom of religion and expression can coexist with Fifth and Fourteenth Amendment rights to equal protection and due process. In the superior court cases *Pedreira v. Kentucky Baptist Homes for Children* and *Bellmore v. United Methodists Children's Home*, gay people and others, including a straight Jewish man, brought suit against their religiously based employers after being fired or refused employment as counselors. Although the plaintiffs in question had excellent work records and credentials, their employers decided that various aspects of their lifestyle—including homosexual orientation—were not acceptable to the faith-based organizations for which they worked. To what extent do these religious organizations—both of which receive public funding—have the right to refuse employment to gay men, lesbians, and others whose behavior or beliefs do not reflect Christian and/or traditional values? To what extent do gay men and lesbians have the right to insist that, if they can do the job, they should be employed; that their private choice of a sexual partner is not an appropriate grounds for refusing employment? Much of the anti–gay rights movement would hold that homosexuality is indeed appropriate grounds for refusing employment, particularly by a Christian and/or traditional organization expecting its employees to uphold religious and family values that homosexuality, by its very nature, contradicts. (For more on the *Pedreira* and *Bellmore* cases, see "Legal Issues," below.)

Finally, there is also a secular strand to the anti–gay rights movement, represented by such conservatives as the politician Alan Keyes and, interestingly, echoed to some extent by such gay conservatives as Andrew Sullivan and

Jonathan Rauch. This is the objection to "the gay lifestyle" as immature and irresponsible, focused on personal gratification as expressed through drugs, promiscuous and often dangerous sex, and a refusal to grow up and assume the adult responsibilities of marriage, family, and community participation. Some versions of this criticism—again, echoed by many in the gay community—stress what is seen as the relentless consumerism of U.S. gay culture, in which an endless search for the latest fashions and an overwhelming preoccupation with personal style and fitness replaces more altruistic and socially useful goals. (Gay rights supporters who agree with this critique stress that it applies far more to gay male culture than to lesbian lifestyles, while conservatives are more likely to view all homosexuality as leading in this direction.) Conservatives who support gay rights tend to argue that legalizing gay marriage and, perhaps, offering support for gay adoption, custody, and parenting, will help gay people "grow up" and leave behind their allegedly immature pursuit of pleasure. Anti–gay rights conservatives, on the other hand, see gay efforts to establish marriage and families as adding insult to injury. In this view, not only are gay people undermining traditional families by their immoral practices, they are mocking "real" married people and endangering children by insisting on imitating a straight lifestyle that they have refused to fully embrace.

After the November 2004 elections, anti–gay rights leaders felt heartened for a time. They saw the reelection of President George W. Bush—who supports a constitutional amendment banning gay marriage—as nationwide confirmation of their agenda. They saw a momentum against gay rights that they expected to continue. In 2003, only four state constitutions banned gay marriage. In 2004, the number had risen to 17, with an average of 67 percent of the voters in the 2004 state elections opposing gay marriage, representing some 14 million citizens. As of this writing, observers expected anti-gay marriage bans on the ballot in another 16 states in 2006: Alabama, Colorado, Florida, Idaho, Indiana, Maine, Maryland, Minnesota, North Carolina, North Dakota, Pennsylvania, South Carolina, South Dakota, Virginia, Washington, and Wisconsin.

However, gay rights activists announced their intention to develop new strategies for opposing such bans, including door-to-door canvassing and increased recruitment of volunteers in each state. And by January 2005, anti–gay rights groups were already beginning to question whether they had achieved either the national support or the presidential support that the November 2004 election seemed to indicate. In a confidential letter to White House adviser Karl Rove, conservative Christian leaders expressed their frustration with President George W. Bush's lukewarm support for a constitutional amendment banning same-sex marriage. Leading conservative people and groups who signed the letter include Reverend Jerry Falwell, Paul Weyrich, Focus on the Family, the Family Research Council, the Southern Baptist Convention, and the American Family Association.

Moreover, although many states were moving ahead with legislation and referendums to ban gay marriage, curtail gay adoption, and otherwise restrict gay rights, many other states were expanding gay rights legislation. As of this writing, there appeared to be strong momentum in favor of both the gay rights movement and the anti–gay rights movement, with no clear result in sight.

LEGAL ISSUES

Legal battles have been a major aspect of the modern gay rights movement. Yet it is important to specify the limits as well as the significance of the legal aspects of gay rights. As discussed earlier, different activists hold different visions for the gay rights movement. Some define their goal quite narrowly—no laws should exist barring gay people from having the same rights as their heterosexual counterparts.

Other activists want full participation of gay people in every aspect of society. Their vision includes total acceptance of gay men and lesbians in religious, civic, educational, and cultural institutions. Gay-friendly school curricula; the ordination of gay and lesbian ministers, priests, and rabbis; the rights of gay men and lesbians to march under their own banner in a St. Patrick's Day parade; the elimination of negative stereotyping in television, movies, and the news media—these are the kinds of goals favored by more liberal gay rights organizations.

Yet even these goals occupy an uneasy space that is sometimes within the realm of law and sometimes beyond the law's reach. The right of a teacher to be openly gay, for example, might be framed as a legal issue—but what about that teacher's right to talk openly about his or her personal life in the classroom, to take part in gay political activities in the community, or to teach a gay-friendly curriculum? Likewise, a lesbian or gay student might conceivably be able to seek legal protection if she or he is being harassed—but what about the student's opportunity to speak to a gay-friendly counselor, form a gay student group, or bring a same-sex date to a school event? It is not clear where legality ends and the place for political organizing, consciousness-raising, and other extralegal activities begins. (*Note:* An *illegal* activity is *against* the law; an *extralegal* activity is simply *outside* the law. Breaking a window on school property would be *illegal.* Convincing the principal to hold a school assembly on gay and lesbian issues might be *extralegal,* if there were no existing law to regulate the matter.) Certainly, this was the case in 1979 when Aaron Fricke, a gay high school student in Providence, Rhode Island, went to the courts and won the right to bring a male date to his school prom. If students at Fricke's school hadn't been ready to accept him and his date, his legal right would have meant very little indeed. Later, students found other ways to convince schools to change their policies than by taking them to court—though some students continue to sue their schools.

As early as 1975, gay activist John D'Emilio was warning the gay rights movement to beware of depending too heavily on either court cases or legislation. While these are important tools, he argued, they are not necessarily the most profound or lasting ways of effecting change—although they may be necessary preconditions before other kinds of work can be done. Also, the effort to win a court case, elect an official, or pass a law may itself be a larger exercise in political organizing. A campaign to elect a gay politician, change school policy, or convince a city council to pass a nondiscrimination ordinance might offer the chance to mobilize gay and lesbian supporters, speak to straight people about gay issues, work with a variety of political allies, and generally change the political and cultural climate in a community. But it can also, as D'Emilio warned, be a kind of trap: an organization's resources can become entirely focused on a few politicians or judges, while the larger community continues in ignorance or apathy.

Contrasting the case of gay men and lesbians who seek to march in their local St. Patrick's Day parades with the ability of an openly gay contingent to march in New York City's Puerto Rican Day parade reveals both the strengths and the limits of the legal approach. So far, although gay and lesbian groups in New York and Boston have sought various legal means to win their right to march under a gay Irish banner in their local parades, they have not been successful—and they have won few friends in the Irish-American community in the process. Why then have gay Puerto Ricans won more acceptance?

The answer lies not in legal rulings, but in politics. The St. Patrick's Day parade is the creation of Irish community groups in which few if any gay men or lesbians openly participate. Most mainstream Irish organizations could well believe that the role of gay people in their community is negligible, not least because Irish-American gays and lesbians who are active in political or community affairs tend not to work specifically with Irish groups. Rather, they are active with gay and lesbian organizations, or in other contexts: a multiethnic neighborhood organization, a labor union, or a women's group. As such, they have developed little credibility with the mainstream Irish community. If they want to participate in an Irish parade, their best option may indeed be a legal battle—though even a victory might serve only to convince other Irish people that gays and lesbians are truly outsiders trying to force their way in.

Puerto Rican gay men and lesbians, on the other hand, have been active in the mainland Puerto Rican community in a number of ways. Take the example of Margarita Lopez, an open lesbian who won a seat on the New York City Council representing a predominantly Latino neighborhood. Lopez is known for her commitment to gay and lesbian rights—but she has also won a reputation as a tireless fighter for tenants' rights, low-income housing, and a variety of other issues of concern to the Puerto Rican community—and to poor and working-class people generally. When she and others like her come looking for a place in the larger community's celebration, a foundation of respect and political affiliation has already been laid.

Another limit of legal approaches is the tendency to fit gay and lesbian issues into the sometimes restrictive structures already established by society and the law. Legal scholar and law professor Ruthann Robson describes this problem in her book, *Sappho Goes to Law School*, where she analyzes the contradictions between winning rights for lesbians and what she considers the distortion of lesbian lives and relationships to fit inappropriate heterosexual models. Like many other gay liberationists, Robson wonders to what extent legal battles can make more space for the gay and lesbian community, and to what extent working within the law only serves to restrict gay men and women. The rest of this chapter looks at a few of these battles. Specific laws and cases are discussed in depth in Chapter 2, while Chapter 3 discusses legal battles pertaining to culture.

SODOMY LAWS

Until 2003, nearly 20 states made homosexual sex illegal in legislation known as sodomy laws. These laws served as a constant threat in the lives of many gay men and women, posing both the literal danger of arrest and affecting such major issues as child custody battles, employment, and treatment by such civic organizations as the Boy Scouts of America. Gay rights activists also saw sodomy laws as a powerful statement equating gay men and lesbians with criminals, while anti–gay rights activists upheld sodomy laws as representing society's assertion that homosexuality is indeed immoral. The way straight people viewed gay men and lesbians, as well as the ways gay people viewed themselves, were profoundly affected by the legal climate, even if individuals were not consciously aware of specific laws.

Then, in 2003, the Supreme Court handed down *Lawrence v. Texas*, an historic ruling that found sodomy laws unconstitutional. *Lawrence* was all the more remarkable because as recently as 1986, the Court had upheld the constitutionality of sodomy laws in *Bowers v. Hardwick*. The significance of *Lawrence* (discussed in more detail in Chapter 2) is enormous. First, it changed at one stroke the legal status of gay men and lesbians in the many states that had criminalized their very existence. Then, it offered profound implications for such gay rights issues as child custody, employment, and, more dramatically, gay marriage. Although the majority decision in *Lawrence* explicitly stated that the ruling did not open the door for gay marriage, in fact, that was exactly what happened. With the highest court in the land affirming that society had no right to outlaw homosexual acts, gay rights activists felt empowered to demand full civil and legal equality, particularly with regard to marriage.

SAME-SEX MARRIAGE

As of this writing, the legal situation for same-sex marriage remains enormously complex. So far, only the state of Massachusetts has legalized gay marriage, effective May 17, 2004, and that state is in the process of considering a constitutional amendment to define marriage as between one man and one woman. The soonest the amendment could go into effect would be 2006, by which time thousands of same-sex marriages would have been contracted. It is not clear what the legal status of those marriages would be were the state to redefine marriage as heterosexual, though many legal experts have suggested that the state could not retroactively invalidate the otherwise legal unions. On a political and social level, the presence of gay and lesbian married couples might do a great deal to mitigate popular fears about the issue.

The legal situation for Massachusetts' married couples is still somewhat confusing. It is unclear what legal rights gay spouses are entitled to, given the profound opposition of many institutions to gay marriage. Will these couples have to sue to obtain the rights that straight married couples take for granted, or will their same-sex marriages be immediately accorded equal legal and civil protection? The question of federal benefits is particularly unclear. How will Massachusetts' gay married couples fare with regard to taxes, Social Security, military pensions, and immigration rights? The Defense of Marriage Act specifically denies these benefits to same-sex couples, but it seems inevitable that a challenge to this act will be brought to federal court.

The question of how Massachusetts gay marriages will fare outside the state is even more complex. As of this writing, many states have passed either legislation or constitutional amendments prohibiting same-sex marriage, and many other states are considering further bans. In some cases these prohibitions excuse the states from having to recognize gay marriages contracted elsewhere.

Some states will recognize same-sex marriages contracted elsewhere. For example, New York's attorney general has promised to honor out-of-state gay marriages, and the state comptroller has ordered the New York state pension system to recognize Canadian same-sex marriages, suggesting that the state will also honor U.S. same-sex marriages. But it is likely that at least some states will not follow suit, particularly when their state constitution prohibits it.

Yet it is not clear whether a law that explicitly refuses to recognize a contract made in another state is constitutional. Article IV of the U.S. Constitution explicitly requires states to recognize the laws and the contracts of their fellow states. Without such mutual recognition, a federal system is impossible. Getting out of a contract signed in, say, Massachusetts, would be as simple as moving to New Hampshire. No one could conduct business in such an environment—and no one could rely upon a marriage, adoption, child custody arrangement, will, divorce settlement, or any other family arrangement.

It seems inevitable that one of these bans on gay marriage will eventually be challenged in the U.S. Supreme Court. But the Court may refuse to hear such a case for many years, as it did with challenges to bans on interracial marriage, which it refused to hear for nearly 20 years. By the time the Court finally ruled on the issue in 1967, striking down all laws against such marriages in *Loving v. Virginia*, U.S. public opinion had become more tolerant. Although a 1958 Gallup poll found that only 4 percent of the public approved of interracial marriage, the civil rights movement had done a great deal to change public opinion by 1967.

Thus, the Supreme Court may decide to take a similar "wait-and-see" approach to the gay marriage issue, particularly after the controversy that has resulted from *Roe v. Wade*, the landmark 1972 decision that established a woman's right to an abortion. Given how unpopular that decision has become in some sectors, the Supreme Court may decide not to repeat the experience, withholding a judicial ruling in favor of gay marriage until an overwhelming majority of the public seems ready to accept it.

Colorado Republican representative Marilyn Musgrave proposed the Federal Marriage Amendment (FMA) to the U.S. Constitution to preclude possible acceptance of gay marriage by the high court. If passed, the FMA would specify that neither federal law, state law, or any state constitution could be construed as requiring either recognition of same-sex marriage or an equal conferral of benefits to unmarried couples or groups. A number of politicians, including President George W. Bush, have expressed support for the FMA or some similar version of the amendment. Yet passing a Constitutional amendment is extremely difficult, and the FMA, along with similar measures, has so far failed to win congressional approval. Some observers believe that many politicians, including the president, are more interested in giving lip service to the FMA than to actively working toward its passage.

Even those who disapprove of gay marriage do not necessarily agree with the notion of a Constitutional ban upon it. The only Constitutional amendment that has restricted rights rather than expanded them was the Nineteenth Amendment, which made alcohol an illegal substance. The failure of this amendment led to its repeal within two decades. People who believe strongly in individual liberty may balk at the notion of government regulation of relationships—even relationships of which they disapprove.

For others, the Constitutional ban raises states' rights issues. They see a problem with an amendment that enables states to disregard the laws passed in their fellow states. If the citizens of Massachusetts choose to allow same-sex marriage, how can the citizens of say, New Hampshire, refuse to recognize that decision? The FMA would prohibit state courts from making their own rulings on gay marriage, precluding the courts' analyses of their own state constitutions.

Supporters of the FMA, including sponsor Senator Wayne Allard, a Republican from Colorado, argue that the courts have no business deciding on such a crucial issue. Rather, the power belongs to the people and their elected representatives—power that can legitimately be expressed in the form of a Constitutional amendment. Matthew Daniels, founder and president of Alliance for Marriage, a group designed to oppose gay marriage, was quoted in a February 17, 2004, *USA Today* article as saying that lawsuits and courts were attempting to mandate a "social-policy revolution." The FMA was needed, he explained, to counter the many lawsuits by which gay men and lesbians were attempting to force the public to allow a type of relationship that most people opposed.

Marital rights continue to be an urgent issue for same-sex couples in California and elsewhere. According to an April 26, 2004, article in the *San Francisco Chronicle*, gay couple Dave and Jeff Chandler had to spend thousands of dollars to establish the legal rights that would have automatically accrued to them had they been married. They compared the cost of their effort to the approximately $100 for a marriage license that would have established their rights to share insurance, inherit each other's property, and share joint custody of their eight-month-old son.

Likewise, lesbian partners Margot McShane and Alexandria D'Amario are concerned with custody issues and parental rights. D'Amario became pregnant with twins after being implanted with McShane's fertilized eggs. The couple was forced to make a special court request to establish both partners' parental rights, so that if one parent were to die, the other would continue to maintain custody.

The court request involved enormous amounts of time and several thousand dollars—none of which would have been required of a heterosexual married couple.

Same-sex couples are not the only ones wondering about the legal and financial consequences of the gay marriage issue. According to a March 23, 2004, *USA Today* article, gay marriages in Massachusetts could affect state employers in a number of ways:

- **Health Benefits to Married Gay Couples:** Although many companies currently offer domestic-partner benefits to gay and unmarried straight couples, the companies who do not yet have such a policy might have to expand their benefits coverage.

- **Fewer Health Benefits to Unmarried Straight Couples:** Some companies that do offer domestic partner benefits may decide to abolish their domestic partnership programs and simply offer marital benefits. Indeed, in Massachusetts, many employers are already refusing to offer benefits to any unmarried couple, whether gay or straight, including such major institutions as IBM, Raytheon, Emerson College, Boston Medical Center, and the *Boston Globe.*

- **Other Benefits to Married Gay Couples:** Joint health insurance is not the only right enjoyed by married couples. Many companies allow marital partners family leave, preference for transfers in order to join a partner, and numerous other acknowledgments of their marital status. These rights and benefits would now be extended to gay married couples—though they might be withdrawn or fail to be extended to unmarried straight couples.

Companies, too, are baffled by the question of how to allocate benefits when Massachusetts gay marriages may not be recognized in other states. Suppose a Massachusetts employee moves to a neighboring state, perhaps even while continuing to work in the same office? If that employee's marriage is no longer valid, how does that affect the joint health insurance and other marital benefits to which the employee had formerly been entitled?

Meanwhile, a UCLA study prepared by the Williams Project and released in May 2004 suggested that legalizing same-sex marriage in California could net the state some $22.3 million to $25.2 million each year:

- Including same-sex partners' income when testing individuals for income-based benefit programs would render many people ineligible for state benefits.

- Tourism would increase as the state became a haven for gay couples seeking to marry.

- Increased business revenues would generate increased sales tax revenues.

Another confusing legal area is the question of how anti–gay marriage bans will affect rights and benefits previously extended to gay couples. For example, the Druid Hills Golf Club in Atlanta has filed suit against the city, which had been fining the organization for not giving partners of gay members the same benefits that went to straight members' spouses. A person married to a member of the club could visit the club without the spouse, and could inherit the membership when the spouse died. Gay members wanted the same benefits for their partners, and under Atlanta's antidiscrimination ordinance, the city had been threatening to fine the club $500 a day, up to a maximum penalty of $90,000, if the club did not comply. With the passage of Georgia's new constitutional amendment, which prohibits gay Georgians from either marrying or entering into any union that reaps "the benefits of marriage," the country club had leverage to refuse the city's threat and to sue the city in return. In fact, the club is seeking to overturn the city ordinance that offers equal protection to gay people. Observers on both sides of the issue expect the anti–gay marriage amendments to offer grounds for similar suits around the country.

Finally, same-sex marriages contracted in other countries are largely unrecognized in the United States. As of this writing, the Netherlands, Belgium, and parts of Canada recognize gay marriage, although the U.S. federal government and many state governments do not recognize the same-sex marriages that are considered legal in those countries.

CIVIL UNIONS AND DOMESTIC PARTNERSHIPS

Lesbian and gay couples have also fought for legal and economic equality through their efforts to establish domestic partnership rights. As the result of gay rights agitation, many cities and states now allow same-sex couples to register for domestic partnership, which, depending on the locale, might entitle them to some—though not all—of the rights of marriage, such as being listed as next of kin on various legal documents or enjoying visitation rights in case of medical emergencies.

Likewise, domestic partnership has been recognized by a wide variety of public and private employers, so that many same-sex couples now enjoy family health insurance and other benefits that are accorded to heterosexual married couples. In many cases, unmarried straight couples can also avail themselves of the benefits of domestic partnership.

In Vermont, domestic partnerships are recognized by the state as civil unions, a legal form that some opponents of gay marriage have suggested is more appropriate for same-sex couples than the full-fledged status of civil marriage. Civil unions were also established in New Jersey in January 2004 and went into effect in July of the same year. The proposed Massachusetts constitutional amendment banning gay marriage would also establish a form of civil union as the legally acceptable means for making marital benefits available on an equal basis to all couples.

Although most conservatives strongly opposed civil unions until very recently, many are now actually proposing civil unions as an alternative to gay marriage, even as many advocates of gay marriage consider civil unions insulting, a form of second-class citizenship that denies them the full benefits and legitimacy of marriage. However, some gay rights activists and supporters feel that civil unions are a more practical avenue toward full acceptance than an immediate demand for marriage, since more people oppose gay marriage than civil unions.

To some extent, gay marriage activists want the legitimacy and recognition that marriage seems to accord. They argue that there are also practical reasons to prefer marriage over civil unions and domestic partnership. Some 1,049 federal benefits accrue to marriage, whereas only a limited portion of those rights are associated with civil unions. For example, such federal benefits as immigration rights, tax breaks, Social Security benefits, and military pensions are not currently granted to couples with civil unions.

Moreover, civil unions and domestic partnerships are not "portable"; unlike marriage, they are only recognized within a single state. A person who marries in, say, Vermont will be considered a married person in all 50 states, whereas a person who has entered into a Vermont civil union may not be considered to have "marriage-like" rights in another state. If a gay couple travels outside of Vermont, for example, and one partner is injured in an accident, hospitals in another state may not allow the remaining partner to visit the injured party in the hospital or to make medical decisions on the partner's behalf. Indeed, a parent or sibling—even an estranged one—might be allowed to make decisions for the injured person, rather than the gay partner. Even if a hospital is willing to recognize a civil union or other legal arrangement, using legal documents to establish decision-making and visiting rights may be more difficult, stressful, and time-consuming than simply stating, "I'm the spouse."

Same-sex couples have already experienced difficulty with civil unions' lack of portability. For example, Texas, Connecticut, and Georgia courts have all refused requests to grant divorces to couples who entered into civil unions in Vermont. In Iowa, six conservative lawmakers attempted to intervene in a lesbian couple's request for a divorce from a state judge. Although the couple had received a civil union in Vermont, the state of Iowa has a law defining marriage as existing only between a man and a woman. The lawmakers argued that since the couple's union did not legally exist in Iowa, a state judge could not dissolve it.

Again, it is unclear what effect the many new state constitutional bans on gay marriage will have on civil unions and domestic partnerships. Since many state bans prohibit both gay marriage and any type of legal recognition for gay partnership, observers wonder, for example, whether employers will be prohibited from offering insurance benefits to gay partners. The first round of news stories after the November 2004 election suggests that many employers, both public and private, will continue to offer domestic partnership benefits to same-sex partners. In Ohio, for example, most public colleges will continue to offer such benefits, while the city of Cleveland Heights will proceed with its domestic partnership registry, where same-sex spouses can legally proclaim their union, though without any attached legal benefits. Likewise, on December 30, 2004, the Montana supreme court ruled that the state's public universities were obligated to provide gay employees with insurance coverage for same-sex partners.

On the other hand, cases like the suit against the city of Atlanta by the Druid Hills Golf Club (see the previous section) suggest that at least some organizations will attempt to use the new state laws to roll back the various types of recognition that gay partners had previously won.

The status of international civil unions is also unclear under U.S. law. As of this writing, civil unions are recognized in France, Denmark, Norway, Sweden, Iceland, Germany, Switzerland, the Netherlands, Belgium, and parts of Canada. However, the U.S. federal government and many state governments do not recognize these arrangements.

EMPLOYMENT ISSUES

Although workplace issues are a central concern of the gay rights movement, most of the significant activity in this regard has been in the form of employee agitation, rather than court cases or legislation. In 2000, for example, gay and lesbian groups at the Big Three automakers—General Motors, Ford, and Chrysler—were responsible for those employers extending domestic partner benefits to the same-sex partners of more than half a million gay and lesbian employees. In 2003, Wal-Mart Stores, one of the nation's largest employers, extended its antidiscrimination policies to include gay and lesbian employees. In 2004, General Electric began offering same-sex partner benefits in response to union demands during labor negotiations. These are just some of the examples of how gay rights are changing at the workplace—but in response to local and piecemeal activism rather than national, state, or other legislation.

Thus, an increasing number of public and private employers are offering domestic-partner benefits to gay couples and/or including gays and lesbians in their antidiscrimination policies. At the same time, life on the job seems to be changing for many gay people, particularly in the business world. A February 2, 2004, article in *Crain's*, a business magazine, described the welcoming climate that many gay and lesbian employees were finding in New York City companies. "Even in the most conservative industries, New York City companies have taken the lead in the past year in creating a workplace that's more welcoming to gay employees," wrote Samantha Marshall, citing domestic-partner benefits, business-supported gay networking groups, and support for gay, lesbian, bisexual, and transgender causes as part of company policy.

Some companies, for example, are offering to help gay employees' partners find jobs in New York City to facilitate the couple's move. Others are asking their gay employees to help them target the lucrative gay and lesbian consumer market. Still others are starting sensitivity training programs to help straight employees include their gay colleagues in the social life of the workplace.

According to the article, "comfort levels" for gay, lesbian, bisexual, and transgender employees rose significantly between 2002 and 2003:

- In 2002, only 32 percent of gay employees were "very comfortable" or "extremely comfortable" introducing a same-sex partner to supervisors, bosses, and colleagues, compared with 48 percent in 2003.

- In 2002, only 24 percent were "very comfortable" or "extremely comfortable" keeping a photo of their same-sex partner on their desk at work, a figure that rose to 48 percent in 2003.
- In 2002, only 35 percent were "very comfortable" or "extremely comfortable" discussing with colleagues their private social lives, including details about their gay partners, dates, and friends, compared with 54 percent in 2003.

These stories contrast sharply with the discomfort that still exists for many people in the business world. The *Crain's* article also described a woman in a large media company who sent herself a weekly bouquet of flowers, supposedly from a boyfriend, in order to hide her sexual identity. And business conditions outside of New York City are not necessarily as comfortable as within the city. Still, the *Crain's* article contrasted sharply with the late-1990s case of Joseph Daniel, who filed the first high-profile law suit on Wall Street in 1996, accusing Dresdner Bank A.G. of failing to follow through on an announced promotion and then eventually firing him after learning he was gay.

A more cloudy area of employee rights for gay men and lesbians concerns on-the-job harassment. Under federal law, sexual harassment has been illegal for a long time. Sexual harassment has traditionally been considered the creation of an unpleasant work climate for women by men who resented their presence or who wanted them to offer sexual favors. For gay men, lesbians, bisexuals, and transgender people, on-the-job harassment may not fall under this protected federal category.

Consider the case of James Quinn, a Nassau County, New York, police officer who claimed to have endured years of torment by colleagues who objected to his sexual orientation. Quinn was shown pornographic pictures and subjected to a wide variety of pranks, including colleagues putting rocks in the hubcaps of his car so that criminals could hear his car coming. Quinn's supervisors not only failed to stop the harassment, they also occasionally joined in, leading Quinn to sue for discrimination under federal civil rights law. Even though the law did not specifically apply to sexual orientation, in 1999 a jury awarded the police officer $380,000, an amount upheld on appeal by a federal judge, who found that the department's conduct had been "motivated by irrational fear and prejudice toward homosexuals."

The case of *Oncale v. Sundowner Offshore Services Inc.* shows that even straight men and women might benefit from expanded on-the-job protection for gay men and lesbians. Joseph Oncale, a roustabout (laborer) on an offshore oil drilling rig, claimed to be sexually harassed by his boss and the other men he worked with. Apparently, Oncale's coworkers believed that he was gay, even though Oncale—as well as all of his coworkers—claimed to be straight. In his suit, Oncale described mistreatment that included being pinned to the wall by fellow workers as his boss put his genitals on Oncale's head and performed a mock rape on him.

Traditionally, the courts have had difficulty dealing with same-sex harassment, and at first Oncale's case seemed to be no exception. The Fifth Circuit Court of Appeals, for example, threw out the suit on the grounds that federal law simply did not apply. Federal law has found sexual harassment to be illegal because it violates existing provisions against discrimination on the basis of sex. In other words, women have the right to be treated just as well as men. So if a man is harassing a woman by putting up pornographic images in her work space, making repeated sexual overtures, or otherwise creating a hostile climate, the woman is being discriminated against on the basis of sex—she is being asked to endure treatment that a man in her position would not have to endure. But given that both Oncale and his harassers are male, in what sense can Oncale's harassment be considered sex discrimination? And, if it's not sex discrimination, in what sense is it against the law? Oncale clearly was not being singled out on the basis of sex. He was being harassed on the basis of gender—not for being a man, but for being a *kind* of man his boss and his colleagues disapproved of.

Oncale's case led gay legal strategists to ask just how far federal provisions against discrimination on the basis of sex were supposed to go. Do they simply safeguard the right of a woman—or a man—to *be* at a particular workplace, so that a construction site must hire qualified women and a day-care center must hire qualified men? Or do the laws protect the right of people to act in ways that are traditionally reserved for the other gender—for women to wear pants, have loud voices, seem "tough"; for men to act gentle, have soft voices, seem "effeminate"? Clearly, both gay and straight people cross these gender lines, so the questions raised by *Oncale v. Sundowner* concern all people who want the freedom to choose their own behavior without being limited by rigid ideas of gender.

It therefore seemed significant that when the Supreme Court heard oral arguments in *Oncale* in 1997, the justices seemed quite receptive to discussing both same-sex harassment and the broader issues of gender. Chief Justice William Rehnquist asked whether it might be possible for a woman to sexually harass another woman, while Justice Ruth Bader Ginsburg expressed her concern about the treatment of a worker not perceived to be "made of sterner stuff."

The final decision in *Oncale*, handed down unanimously in March 1998, had somewhat mixed results for gay rights activists. On the one hand, they welcomed the part of the decision that found that sexual harassment, as outlawed under Title VII, could also include same-sex harassment. On the other hand, they were concerned about the Court's specification that federal law protected only *sexual* harassment. The decision—written by the normally conservative Justice Antonin Scalia and seconded by the conservative Justice Clarence Thomas—did not seem to open the door to using Title VII to protect gay rights on the job.

Faith-Based Initiatives and Employment Rights

Beginning in the late 1990s, a new concern emerged for gay rights activists: the question of whether gay people could be refused employment by religious agencies who considered homosexuality incompatible with their faith-based message.

Two superior court cases addressed these issues: In *Bellmore v. United Methodist Children's Home*, Aimee Bellmore, a youth counselor at the agency, brought suit against UMCH for firing her, allegedly because she did not subscribe to the agency's religious beliefs condemning homosexuality. Alan Yorker, a Jewish therapist who applied for employment to the agency, joined the suit, claiming that he was turned away because of his religion. Georgia child welfare professionals, other clergy, and the parent of a gay youth were co-plaintiffs in the complaint, arguing that tax dollars should not be used to fund a religious program that condemned homosexuality, which they argued was dangerous to LGBT young people.

Likewise, Alicia Pedreira, a lesbian social worker fired by Kentucky Baptist Homes for Children (KBHC), sued the group for her 1998 firing. Pedreira received a letter from the KBHC explaining that her "admitted homosexual lifestyle is contrary to the Kentucky Baptist Homes for Children core values." Pedreira also sued the Cabinet for Families and Children, the Kentucky state department that contracts with agencies to place children in distress. As a result, the cabinet announced its unwillingness to send children to KBHC, the largest group in the state to care for abused children, and KBHC retaliated by refusing a new state contract. Pedreira's position was that her admittedly excellent work record, not her private sexuality, should be the only factor in her employment. KBHC insisted that it had a right not to hire people whom it did not consider good role models for troubled youths. A federal court in Kentucky ruled against Pedreira in July 2001.

Gay rights advocates became even more concerned when President George W. Bush took office in 2000 and announced his support for faith-based initiatives, promoting expanded federal funding for religiously based social service agencies. Many questions remain about this issue:

1. In areas where gay men and lesbians are guaranteed protection against employment discrimination, do religious organizations nevertheless have a First Amendment right to refuse to hire them on religious grounds. (The First Amendment guarantees freedom of religious expression.)
2. Even if privately funded religious groups are allowed to refuse employment to gay men and lesbians, is that right affected by receiving public funds? Since many religiously based social service agencies do have contracts with various levels of government to provide services to needy populations, this is a significant concern for both pro– and anti–gay rights activists.
3. How will President Bush's support for faith-based initiatives shift the balance of funding, making religious organizations even more prominent in social service employment?

As the trend toward faith-based and privately funded agencies continues, these questions will continue to preoccupy people on both sides of the issue.

Federal Employment

One of the largest employers in the United States is the federal government, and civil service jobs have long represented some of the most stable and secure employment available. So the government's employment policies with regard to gay men and lesbians carry particular weight. And the decision, made at the beginning of the cold war, to prohibit gay people from any kind of federal employment, sent a clear signal to society that gay men and lesbians were not acceptable employees.

The official reason given for keeping gay people out of civil service jobs was that their homosexuality made them security risks. In an era when fear of communism and anxiety about Soviet spies was running high, antigay government officials like Senator Joseph McCarthy could argue that gay and lesbian federal employees, fearful of having their sexual activities made public, were vulnerable to blackmail by "foreign powers." The image of homosexuals and communists stealing state secrets and selling them to the Soviets was one that alarmed many Americans—though some political commentators at the time and many historians since have believed the claims of espionage and sabotage to have been exaggerated, if not entirely fabricated.

The Red Scare and the antihomosexual panic that accompanied it led the Civil Service Commission and the Federal Bureau of Investigation to develop procedures to identify homosexual job applicants and keep them from being hired, as well as to discover and fire gay people already working for the government. This antigay climate continued well into the early 1970s—but it was countered somewhat by the famous case of *Norton v. Macy*, in which the Supreme Court found that a gay man could not be fired for illegal sexual conduct if that conduct did not specifically affect the performance of his duties as a federal employee. (For more on *Norton v. Macy*, see Chapter 2.)

Another landmark for gay rights activists came in 1973, when the Civil Service Commission dropped its ban on hiring gay people. In 1978, another Supreme Court ruling suggested that openly gay federal employees had the right to keep their jobs. And in 1980, the Office of Personnel Management actively banned discrimination on the basis of sexual orientation in all federal service jobs.

FREE SPEECH AND ASSEMBLY

As discussed earlier, gays and lesbians have not only had to battle for individual liberties (i.e., the right to engage in private, consensual sexual behavior and not be discriminated against for doing so), but they have also had to fight for the right to congregate with others who share their sexual orientation. The harassment visited upon the patrons of the Stonewall Inn by the police was a way for society to discourage gays and lesbians from meeting with each other openly. In a way, the issue of open association was the spark that ignited the modern gay rights movement.

School Organizations and the Right to Assemble

The major assembly issue for gay rights activists, however, has been fought on college campuses. The landmark case is considered *Gay Students Organization of the University of New Hampshire v. Bonner*, a 1974 New Hampshire Supreme

Court case ruling that a gay student group had the same rights to a state college's facilities as any other student organization. A similar case was fought at Georgetown University, a private institution that in 1980 had expelled its gay student group from campus. Eight years later, a court case finally affirmed the right of the Georgetown gay and lesbian students to have access to campus facilities.

Controversy over gay student groups continued throughout the late 20th and early 21st centuries. In 1981, for example, Florida's legislature passed the Trask Amendment, which allowed the withholding of funds from any state institution that recognized a gay student group. Eventually, the state supreme court found that law unconstitutional. And in 1983, in an echo of *Bonner*, the Fourth Circuit Court of Appeals ordered the University of South Carolina to reinstate a gay and lesbian student group that had been prohibited from meeting on campus.

School Organizations and Free Speech

The 2000 U.S. Supreme Court case *Board of Regents of the University of Wisconsin System v. Southworth et al.* seemed to further affirm the place of gay student groups on college campuses. The issue in that case involved both speech and assembly—ironically, of conservative students who objected to being forced to support gay groups with their student activity fees.

In 1996, Scott Southworth, who described himself as a conservative Christian, filed suit with five other students objecting to the University of Wisconsin student activity fee program. Although most of the $311 fee went to such university programs as a student health clinic and day-care center, some $40 per student was allocated to a wide variety of student organizations, including a Lesbian, Gay, Bisexual and Transgender Center. Southworth and his fellow plaintiffs argued that being forced to support such "anti-Christian" programs with their student activity fees constituted a violation of their First Amendment rights by requiring them to financially support speech and assembly with which they did not agree.

Although the federal district court and appeals court found for Southworth, the U.S. Supreme Court ruled in favor of the university, holding that the fee program was a fully constitutional way for the school to promote a wide variety of student activities on campus. The decision raised some questions about the ways in which the school distributed its fees, but it also affirmed that the university could not defund gay rights groups and other organizations simply because some students objected to them. The 9-0 decision firmly upheld the university's right to charge activities fees to fund programs with which some students might not agree, an indication that the place of gay rights groups on campus was secure.

Meanwhile, a wide variety of high school gay-straight alliances were being formed. They had to call on both equal protection law and their right to free speech as they battled for their right to exist. In January 1998, for example, the Homosexual Heterosexual Alliance Reaching for Tolerance (HHART) filed the first suit claiming that a gay-straight high school club had constitutional rights. HHART, a group of some 25 students meeting at Smoky Hill High School in

Gay Rights

Aurora, Colorado (near Denver), sued the Cherry Creek School District for equal representation. The organization claimed that it had been discriminated against in various ways because it was concerned with gay issues: The club had been left out of lists of high school clubs, omitted from the "club" section of the student-parent handbook, and excluded from listings in the school's multicultural events calendar. Although the group had been permitted to put up posters at their high school, certain words and phrases had been censored from the signs: "homosexual," "lesbian," "gay," and a quote from *Hamlet*, "To thine own self be true." The suit also claimed that one student had been ordered to take a button with a gay slogan off his backpack, and that the group's adviser, teacher Linda Harmon, was refused supplemental pay for her after-hours work with the club. Moreover, the school decided to assign a counselor to the group, suggesting that members were in need of psychological help.

The month after HHART filed its suit, it won recognition by the school district as part of a federal court settlement. But other school clubs also charged school districts with discrimination. A group of students at Palmer High School in Colorado Springs, for example, charged that their gay-straight alliance was not allowed to meet on the grounds that the school did not recognize groups not directly linked to the curriculum. However, the lawsuit claimed, the school supported such clubs as Crime Stoppers, the Sci-Fi Club, the Chess Club, and the Mountain Bike Club, none of which had obvious links to school studies. The lawsuit also alleged that a coordinator of the school's anti-bullying policy had "stated that she wasn't sure that Palmer was ready to support a gay-straight alliance student group."

Likewise, in rural Kentucky, students at Boyd County High School formed a gay-straight group in October 2002. That group had the initial support of district superintendent Bill Capeheart, largely due to the 1984 Equal Access Act, which holds that public schools cannot discriminate among student clubs. Since Boyd had two Bible clubs, a service club, a 4-H club, and a chess club, it could not refuse permission to a gay-straight group.

But Reverend Tim York of the Heritage Temple Free Will Baptist Church strongly objected to the student group and organized a 2,000-person rally against it. As a result, Capeheart banned the club—along with every other high school group. When the ACLU sued to reinstate the club, Capeheart gave contradictory statements to the press, telling some reporters that he considered the club legal and a good way of teaching tolerance while agreeing with conservative TV journalist Bill O'Reilly's statement that the ACLU was "using terror to further their agenda."

Ironically, nearby Huntington High in rural West Virginia also had a gay-straight club under the auspices of principal Jerry Lake, a self-described "ultra-conservative Republican." Lake said that while he himself would never join a gay-straight group, students had the right to meet. Although Lake, too, faced some protests from his conservative community, he said, "I can't let outsiders interfere," and continued to support the club. In a January 29, 2003, *New York Times* article, reporter Michael Winerip described students in need of such a group, including 10th-grade Huntington High student Bryan Chinn. "In middle school, I was pretty much popular," Chinn told the reporter. "Then I came out. Everything changed. It was like I was someone different. It made me mad all the time." Chinn's grandmother, with whom he lived, kicked him out of the house when she discovered he was gay. Winerip suggested that students like Chinn were in desperate need of safe places where they could be accepted by their fellow students—places like the gay-straight alliance.

Although the vast majority of the nation's estimated 1,700 gay-straight high school groups continue to meet without interference, some clubs still face obstacles. In an affluent north Houston suburb in 2003, 17-year-old honor student Marla Dukler filed suit against Klein Independent School District when Klein High School refused permission for Dukler and 16 fellow students to form a gay-straight group. Klein accused the district of violating her First Amendment rights and the Equal Access Act. She also told *New York Times* reporter Steven Greenhouse about the kind of harassment that she hoped the club might address. After three boys sneaked up on her, she said, "One shoved me into a wall of lockers, and the other two called me a dyke and a faggot. My leg was really bruised. There's verbal abuse everywhere."

Some 200 of the school's 3,700 students signed a petition supporting the club, a strong show of support that helped lead the district to reach a settlement about a month after Dukler first brought suit. Although a group of parents and community leaders wanted the district to continue the fight, the settlement enabled the gay-straight group to begin meeting. It seems likely that both the number of such clubs will continue to increase and more lawsuits on the issue will be filed.

In South Orange, New Jersey, a student at Seton Hall University, a Catholic school, has sued for the university to recognize a gay rights group called TRUTH. Anthony Romeo, a gay student at Seton Hall, initially won provisional recognition for the group, but in December 2003, the university decided that "an exclusive focus on . . . sexual orientation" was counter to church teachings and thus not an appropriate basis for a student group. In response, Romeo sued, claiming that the school was violating New Jersey's antidiscrimination law, and the lawsuit is currently pending in an appellate court.

Free Speech and the U.S. Post Office

In the days before Stonewall, many gay people relied on the U.S. mail for their contact with a larger homosexual world. Men in particular sought to receive magazines, postcards, and photographs with images of male bodies in varying stages of nudity. For the many men who were terrified of revealing their gay identities in their own communities, these homoerotic images were a lifeline to a world in which their sexuality could be affirmed.

One common form of gay male erotica was the so-called physique magazines, featuring bodybuilders who were nude except for their underwear or "posing straps" (a piece of cloth that covered only the genitals). Although bodybuilding magazines were often sold in regular newsstands and were frequently available in public places such as barbershops, many gay men treated them as a mild form of pornography. Gay men also used the mail to order more explicit homoerotic materials.

However, until 1965, everything that traveled by post was regulated by the 1873 Comstock Law, which prohibited the mailing of "obscene, lewd, or lascivious" materials. The Comstock Law had been most notoriously used to prevent birth control pioneer Margaret Sanger from mailing out information about family planning. In the 1940s, it also began to be used against bodybuilding magazines, which were warned to "police their contents, even their ads" for homosexual material—or risk being unable to use the U.S. mail. In 1954, the homophile magazine *One* was seized by the Los Angeles postmaster, who refused to mail the magazine on the grounds that it was obscene and filthy. Although, like most homophile publications, *One* was more text- than image-oriented, printing mainly nonsexual articles and stories about gay life, the mere mention of homosexuality was apparently enough to qualify as obscene.

Of course, the definition of "obscene" was open to interpretation by a court, but few small publishers could afford legal battles, whether they published bodybuilding magazines, homophile publications, or actual pornography. Both the receivers and the senders of gay male images were taking enormous risks, as were those involved with homophile magazines. Many subscribers to any type of gay-related publication got their materials at post office boxes, which they held anonymously or under false names. Publishers were also creative. Because it was illegal to mail fully nude photographs, one publisher began covering male genitals with fig leaves painted in washable ink. Customers could simply rinse the ink off after they received the photos.

Despite all this caution, the first big crackdown against bodybuilding magazines occurred in 1960. Physique magazine publisher Herbert Womack was selling 40,000 copies a month when his stock was seized by the postal authorities. His case was heard by the Supreme Court in 1965, in a case known as *Manual Enterprises v. Day*. "[E]ven though the material appealed to the prurient taste of male homosexuals and was 'dismally unpleasant, uncouth, and tawdry,' it lacked 'patent offensiveness' and therefore should not be considered obscene," the Court ruled.

The sexual revolution brought further court cases that eroded the authority of the Comstock Law. In December 1965, the first full frontal male nude appeared in a publication: the homophile *Drum* magazine. *Drum* was a departure from the earlier, more staid homophile publications like *One* and the *Ladder* (published by the lesbian group Daughters of Bilitis). As Molly McGarry and Fred Wasserman explain in their book, *Becoming Visible*, "[Due to] the lead of publications like *Drum*, it became increasingly clear to many in the gay community that homosexual liberation and a larger sexual liberation could never be separated." A quote from an early ad for *Drum* makes this clear:

Introduction to Gay Rights

DRUM stands for a realistic approach to sexuality in general and homosexuality in particular. DRUM stands for sex in perspective, sex with insight and, above all, sex with humor. DRUM presents news for "queers," and fiction for "perverts." Photo essays for "fairies," and laughs for "faggots."

Free Speech and Internet Access

A major area of concern to the anti–gay rights movements and to conservatives in general is children's exposure to homosexuality and to homosexual-oriented pornography, particularly via the Internet. Conservatives of various affiliations and political positions have objected to what they see as the Internet's use as a means for making young people aware of homosexuality and helping them to locate homosexual partners. Conservatives are also concerned over youth participation in online gay rights activism. A wide variety of citizens, from many different political positions, have also become disturbed over the Internet's use as a vehicle for pornography.

As a result, many public libraries that offer Internet access have installed "pornography filters" on their services, limiting access to pornographic sites at library terminals. In many cases, the definition of "pornography" is taken to include sites with any explicit sexual information, including information about homosexuality.

Thus, in 1999, 13-year-old Emmalyn Rood logged onto the Internet at a library in Multnomah County, Oregon, seeking information about lesbianism. The teenager was trying to come to terms with her own sexual identity, and she wanted someplace away from home where she could get the information she sought. A filter screening out pornographic information at the library terminal she had previously used blocked information about homosexuality as well. So Rood used an unfiltered terminal to get the information she sought.

In 2001 Congress passed the Children's Internet Protection Act, a law tying federal funding at public libraries to the installation of filters on all public library computer terminals; Rood then became a plaintiff in a suit challenging the law. She was joined by Mark Brown, a man who found information about his mother's breast cancer at an unfiltered Philadelphia library terminal—information that also might have been blocked by commonly used filters. Library organizations were also part of the suit, which was decided by the Supreme Court in June 2003. In a 6-3 ruling, the Court upheld the federal law.

Under the statute, libraries are allowed, at their own discretion, to unblock Internet sites at adults' requests, though children seeking access to filtered sites must have their legal guardian's approval. Libraries are also allowed discretion in choosing which filters to acquire, making for a wide variety in the amount and kind of information blocked. Generally, the Supreme Court frowns on laws that can be unevenly applied. In this case, the nine justices unanimously agreed both that restricting children's access to pornography was not a First Amendment issue and Internet filters were "blunt instruments" that block more than pornography. The question on which they disagreed was the extent to which so-called overblocking was a violation of adult library users' First Amendment rights, which extend to sexually explicit materials but not to obscenity or child pornography. However, said Chief Justice William Rehnquist, who wrote the opinion for the majority, adult users could ask librarians to unblock the filters, thus guaranteeing their constitutionally protected access. Even if such a request was problematic for some adults, Rehnquist wrote, "the Constitution does not guarantee the right to acquire information at a public library without any risk of embarrassment."

Clearly, the law and the Court decision extend beyond the question of material that relates to homosexuality. Nevertheless, gay rights activists are concerned about the role of this law in blocking information on this topic to users who may indeed be embarrassed or even frightened to reveal their interest in it. They are particularly concerned about the effect on young people like Rood, for whom the question of sexual identity is often painful and even dangerous, as many gay, lesbian, bisexual, and transgender youths are abused or thrown out of the house when parents or guardians discover their sexual interests.

CHILD CUSTODY

Child custody has traditionally been an emotional issue in a country that until recently considered homosexuals criminals by definition because they were in violation of many states' sodomy laws. Even in child custody cases where sodomy laws were not invoked, gay custody cases were often ruled by the notion that "good" homosexuals should hide their relationships from their children, and that good parents should either be celibate or should be engaged in long-term monogamous relationships that resembled the ideal of heterosexual marriage. Recognition of gay and lesbian families is thus a major concern of gay marriage activists, who point out that legal same-sex marriage will make it easier for gay and lesbian parents to gain or retain custody of children they had while in heterosexual marriages or other relationships. It is not clear whether the legalization of same-sex marriage would thus make custody issues easier or more difficult for gay parents who for whatever reason could not or did not want to marry a same-sex partner. Would the increased acceptance of homosexuality that same-sex marriage implies make judges look more favorably on child custody suits by gay and lesbian parents whose heterosexual ex-spouses were seeking to terminate their custody or visitation rights? Or would an unmarried gay parent be penalized for his or her single status when compared with either a single or a married heterosexual?

The question is complicated because there is no single federal law determining how custody and visitation rights are allocated. Such issues are within the discretion of family court judges, who operate within the guidelines of state laws and regulations, but who are usually granted a great deal of latitude in making their decisions. Sometimes they are required to consider only "the best interests of the child." Sometimes they are supposed to take into account definitions of "fitness" of a parent. The extent to which homosexuality is considered contrary to a child's interests or grounds to consider a parent unfit has varied from state to state and has changed a great deal over time, particularly in times and places where sodomy laws rendered gay parents criminal by definition. At some times and in some places, even distant relatives or clearly problematic parents were considered preferable to gay or lesbian parents.

The case of *White v. Thompson* in Mississippi shows that as recently as 1990, lesbian mothers' custody of their children could be challenged not only by the children's fathers, but also by relatives further removed. In *White*, the father's parents sought custody of their grandchildren on the grounds that the mother was unfit, primarily because she was a lesbian. The Mississippi trial court agreed that the mother was "unfit, morally and otherwise, to have custody of her children."

The mother appealed the case to the Mississippi Supreme Court, arguing that the trial court had erred in basing its decision solely on the fact that she was gay. The state supreme court agreed that lesbianism could not be the *sole* issue in a judgment of fitness, but ruled that it could indeed be a major issue:

> *Although the predominant issue in this case seems to have been Mrs. White's lesbianism, and the chancellor may have relied entirely upon this, we find that a review of the entire record and circumstances present . . . shows that the chancellor's decision that Mrs. White was an unfit mother, morally and otherwise, was not against the substantial weight of the evidence.*

The circumstances also included some testimony that the children had not been properly supervised, clothed, or fed, but the extent of the problem was left vague in the final ruling. In that ruling, the judge also referred to White's class status, finding that the neglect of the children was "no more than one would expect to find in any case where a twenty-four-year-old mother with but a high school diploma and no independent means" was attempting to support her children. Yet a dissenting justice found that ". . . most of An's [the mother's] neglect is attributable to the employment she has been forced to pursue because of David's [her ex-husband and the children's father] irresponsibility." Given that Mississippi's standard practice is to automatically award custody to the biological parent, especially the mother, it seems unlikely that a heterosexual in An White's place would lose custody of her children to their father's parents without more striking evidence of her lack of fitness.

Not only did White lose custody of her children to her ex-husband's mother and stepfather (the ex-husband himself had severe financial problems, a history of alcoholism, and no interest in custody), she was also denied the opportunity to visit her children in the presence of her lover. Even if her lesbianism was not the only standard of her "unfitness," it seemed to play a key role in the custody decision.

The case of *Chicoine v. Chicoine*, a South Dakota Supreme Court ruling of 1992, also concerns restrictions of visitation for a lesbian mother. The initial case involved Lisa Chicoine, a divorced mother who sought custody of her two children, James, age 6, and Tyler, age 5. At the trial level, the children's father won custody, with Lisa being allowed unsupervised overnight visits every other weekend, as long as "no unrelated female or homosexual male [were] present during the children's visit."

The case proceeded up to the state supreme court, where an opinion written by Justice Henderson cited both Leviticus and the Egyptian Book of the Dead to justify the presumption against homosexuality:

Lesbian mother has harmed these children forever. To give her rights of reasonable visitation so that she can teach them to be homosexuals, would be the zenith of poor judgment for the judiciary of this state. Until such time as she can establish, after years of therapy and demonstrated conduct, that she is no longer living a life of abomination (see Leviticus 18:22), she should be totally estopped [sic, a legal term] from contaminating these children. After years of treatment, she could then petition for rights of visitation . . .

There appears to be a transitory phenomenon on the American scene that homosexuality is okay. Not so. The Bible decries it. Even the pagan "Egyptian Book of the Dead" bespoke against it [citation omitted]. Kings could not become heavenly beings if they had lain with men. In other words, even the pagans, centuries ago, before the birth of Jesus Christ, looked upon it as total defilement.

Although Justice Henderson's opinion was not shared by the entire court, the majority opinion did reverse the trial court's decision and terminated Lisa Chicoine's unsupervised visits. The court pointed out that "Lisa admits that it is inappropriate to hold hands, kiss and show affection to her lesbian partners in front of her children"—yet she had engaged in these open displays of affection.

Although it is usually lesbian mothers who are denied child custody, sometimes gay fathers are also deprived. In a Mississippi case, David Wiegand, a California resident, sought custody of his 15-year-old son after learning that the boy's stepfather had been arrested twice and convicted of physically assaulting the boy's mother. For eight years, Wiegand had lived in a monogamous relationship with a male partner, with whom he had entered into a domestic partnership agreement and living trust arrangement. The court agreed that the boy's father would probably offer his son a more stable home. Yet Wiegand was denied custody, a decision upheld on February 4, 1999, by the Mississippi Supreme Court. Unlike the women in *Chicoine*, Wiegand had refrained from open displays of affection in front of his son, admitting, in the words of the high court, "that an open sign of affection between homosexual partners is not proper for the child at this age . . . [Y]et despite refraining from that activity, he merely retreats behind closed and locked doors, hiding and secreting his own sexuality from [his son]." Therefore, custody was to remain with the mother (and her abusive husband), although Wiegand was granted visitation rights in the presence of his partner. As the court said:

*even if [the son] is embarrassed, or does not like the living arrangement of his fa-
ther, this is not the type of harm that rises to the level necessary to place such restrictions on [the father's] visitation with his son.*

Lisa Keen, covering the decision in the February 19, 1999, edition of the gay
newspaper, *New York Blade*, pointed out that the court discussed Wiegand's sexual practices to an extent that would probably never appear in a similar opinion
involving heterosexual parents. As the court wrote:

*According to David, [he and his male partner] regularly engage in homosexual
activities which include both oral and anal intercourse. However, they described
their sexual relations, as well as their open affections between each other, at least
in the presence of the child, to be discreet and performed only behind closed and
locked doors.*

In some cases, family recognition for gay and lesbian families cuts both ways,
for there are times when gay fathers and lesbian mothers may not wish to share
custody of their children with their former partners—yet would have to do so if
their de facto families were truly recognized. In the case of *Alison D. v. Virginia
M.* (1991), one member of a lesbian couple in New York gave birth to a child by
means of artificial insemination. When the couple separated, the biological
mother refused to let her former partner visit the child, and the New York state
court likewise refused to acknowledge the rights of the nonbiological mother.
Only one dissenting judge, feminist jurist Judith Kaye, believed that the lesbian
ex-partner had a claim to the child she had helped to raise, pointing out that
"more than 15.5 million children do not live with two biological parents, and
that as many as 8 to 10 million children are born into families with a gay or lesbian parent."

A few months after *Alison D.*, a similar case came up in Wisconsin's Supreme
Court, *In re ZJH (Sporleder v. Hermes)*. In this case, two women had lived together as lovers for about eight years. When Sporleder had tried, and failed, to
conceive a child through artificial insemination, the couple decided that Hermes would adopt a child. (As discussed below and in Chapter 2, two-parent
adoption has been extremely difficult for gay couples.) The couple separated,
the adoption was finalized, and Hermes decided not to allow her former partner to visit the child. Sporleder was then not able to win custody or visitation
rights. A number of courts in other states have made similar rulings.

A 2004 custody case between two lesbian mothers raises new legal and social
issues and indicates how much the climate for gay parenting has changed, at
least in some circles. In July 2004, the Colorado Court of Appeals upheld a 50-
50 time-sharing custody arrangement between Cheryl Clark and Elsey
McLeod, who had together raised a daughter whom Clark had legally adopted
in 1995. The couple broke up in 2001 after an 11-year relationship, and Clark
became a Christian who then sought to terminate her former partner's parental
rights because she didn't want her daughter exposed to homosexuality.

Clark wanted to restrict her daughter's access to McLeod for two years and then to end all contact. She argued that McLeod was just a "nanny." But McLeod argued that she fit the definition of a "psychological parent," a doctrine used for more than a decade in Colorado holding that a person who has had physical custody of a child for at least six months can get parenting rights, even without biological or other legal ties to the child.

Clark argued that if the court recognized McLeod as the "psychological parent," they would open the door to awarding parental rights to anyone who created a bond with a child. Nevertheless, in a ruling that would have been unimaginable only a few years ago, Denver district judge John Coughlin said that Clark, while retaining sole rights to determine her daughter's upbringing, could not teach her daughter "anything considered homophobic." Some Republican legislators tried unsuccessfully to impeach Coughlin, and Clark took the case to the Colorado Court of Appeals.

The appellate judges found that Clark's wish to restrict her daughter's relationship with McLeod contact might be harmful to the child and upheld the shared-time arrangement while returning the ruling on homophobic instruction to Denver District Court for clarification. Gay rights groups considered the decision a victory, even as Clark began an appeal to the state supreme court. As of this writing, the appeal is still pending.

Although custody fights between two gay people may at first seem like a less pressing issue to many gay rights activists than the specter of heterosexual parents denying gay biological parents their rights, all of the custody cases discussed in this section refer to the same three problems: 1) what is the definition of a gay or lesbian family? 2) what rights do the adults in those families have?— and, perhaps most importantly, 3) what is in the best interests of the child? Formerly, family courts tended to rule that being gay or lesbian itself rendered a parent unfit—much as being gay or lesbian formerly disqualified employees from the civil service. In family law as in civil service policy, the courts are coming to embrace instead the idea of a *rational nexus*—an interconnected set of reasons that determine a parent's fitness. Being gay or lesbian might or might not be part of that nexus, depending on the personal opinions of the judge. But the focus in family law is coming to be less on the specific fitness of the parent as determined by his or her sexual practices, and more on the rational nexus of factors that determine the best interests of the child.

Since the rational nexus test allows courts to take the focus off lesbianism or male homosexuality as the key criterion for fitness, advocates for gay/lesbian rights hope that this new approach will make it easier for gay and lesbian parents to keep their children. However, unless social attitudes toward homosexuality continue to change, it's likely that the rational nexus test will continue to work against homosexual parents in general and lesbian parents in particular. Besides the general prejudice against lesbian sexuality, lesbians are likely to have lower incomes than their ex-husbands, which seems to make them less desirable parents in the eyes of many courts. And if the ex-husband seeking custody is married in an apparently stable heterosexual relationship, courts may view this with more favor than either an extralegal lesbian marriage or a more unconventional lesbian relationship.

Although gay fathers are more likely to have higher incomes than lesbian mothers, they face similar types of social prejudice, as the David Wiegand case made clear. Both gay men and lesbians also face the risk that a court will favor the heterosexual parent—or even the child's grandparents.

ADOPTION

Until the late 1970s, the notion that an open lesbian or gay man might be allowed to adopt a child was virtually unthinkable—as was the idea that a single person should be allowed to adopt. However, gay rights groups in many states fought for the right of gay adoption, which gradually began to change the climate on this issue.

Although gay individuals were sometimes allowed to adopt, the concept of a gay couple adopting a child still seemed unthinkable to many people throughout the 1980s and most of the 1990s. A gay man or lesbian who was in a relationship with a biological or adoptive parent might eventually be allowed to adopt the partner's child. But for an adoption agency to grant parental rights to two same-sex parents was relatively rare.

Then, in December 1997, a New Jersey lawsuit forced that state to allow gay, lesbian, and unmarried heterosexual couples to adopt children on an equal basis with married couples. The decision came in the form of a consent decree with state authorities, the final outcome of a class-action lawsuit brought by gay and lesbian couples and by the American Civil Liberties Union. The decision did not technically affect private adoption agencies, but many observers believed that the ruling would widen the chances of gay couples adopting jointly.

The case also resulted in New Jersey residents Jon Holden and Michael Galluccio being able to adopt their foster son, Adam, in December 1997. Though the Holden-Galluccio adoption produced its share of controversy, the political climate was changing quickly. By the time the couple tried to adopt Adam's sister, two years later, they found the process, once so arduous, was now virtually routine. Although gay adoption remains out of the question in many states, other states are beginning to accept the concept of two same-sex parents who act as a couple to adopt one or more children.

Certainly the 2003 Supreme Court decision striking down sodomy laws should facilitate gay adoptions, since gay and lesbian parents will no longer be considered criminals by definition. Meanwhile, a great deal has changed since the Holden-Galluccio case of 1997. As of this writing, Florida is the only state that explicitly bans adoptions by gay people, and only Mississippi bans adoptions by gay couples. Utah bans adoption by any unmarried couple, which, in the absence of same-sex marriage, includes gay couples. In all other states, a gay couple is theoretically free to adopt.

This freedom is upheld by many U.S. adoption agencies, some 60 percent of whom accept applications from gay men and lesbians, according to a 2003 study conducted by the Evan B. Donaldson Adoption Institute. The study also found that about 40 percent of all agencies have placed children with homosexual parents. Public, private, secular, Jewish-affiliated, and Lutheran-affiliated agencies are most likely to place children with gay parents. Agencies affiliated with other religious denominations are less likely to accept applications from gay people.

In August 2003, the American Bar Association approved a recommendation that all states and courts allow gay partners and unmarried heterosexual couples to adopt children as a couple. They were speaking to a situation in many states, in which gay parents still find it easier to adopt as individuals, even if they live with a partner committed to acting as a parent.

An article by Ellen Marakowitz in the January 2004 issue of *Feminist News*, a publication of Columbia University, reviewed the current research on lesbian and gay parenting. Marakowitz cited estimates of children being raised in gay and lesbian households as ranging from one million to five million, with most experts agreeing upon a figure of about 1.5 million. These include children both from heterosexual relationships and from lesbian couples who have obtained artificial insemination or other fertility assistance. Much of the research on children's welfare, according to Marakowitz, is in the form of psychological studies seeking to compare children living in gay and straight households. The studies seem to indicate no significant differences between children raised in either type of household, including sexual orientation. In other words, children raised in gay households are no more likely to be gay than children who have only straight parents.

Although Oklahoma allows adoption by gay couples, in April 2004, Oklahoma passed a law outlawing state recognition of adoptions by out-of-state same-sex couples. As with many other state bans on recognition of gay partnership, the law is expected to be challenged as unconstitutional under Article IV, the "full faith and credit clause," which holds that states must honor each other's contracts.

A new development in recognition of gay families came on December 29, 2004, when an Arkansas judge struck down a 1999 regulation by the state Child Welfare Agency Review Board that banned gay people from becoming foster parents and prohibited placement of a child in any home in which a gay person also lived. Although the American Civil Liberties Union had brought suit against the policy on the grounds that it violated the equal protection rights of gay people, the judge overturned the policy for a different reason: The board, he said, had exceeded its responsibility to "promote the health, safety, and welfare of children" by attempting to regulate "public morality." Since there was absolutely no evidence to support the notion that foster children were less healthy, safe, or better off when they were placed in the homes of gay people, the board had overstepped its bounds.

The state intends to appeal the ruling. Their lead lawyer, Kathy Hall, argued that the state had never questioned the children's health and safety but cited the need for "normalcy" among children who had already undergone a great deal of stress.

Arkansas already allowed gay men and lesbians to adopt children, so its ban on fostering seemed unusual. Currently, no other state has such a ban in place.

TRANSGENDER RIGHTS

Although a comprehensive look at this burgeoning issue is beyond the scope of this book, it is possible to list a few of the major questions that transgender activists have raised:

- *Who Determines Gender Identity?* Traditionally, this has been considered a medical decision made by a physician at the time of a child's birth and entered on the child's birth certificate. However, some children are born with indeterminate gender characteristics—such as sex organs that are not fully visible or fully formed, or the presence of aspects of both types of sex organs. In some cases, this indeterminacy is apparent at birth; in other cases, it only becomes known later, perhaps when the child reaches puberty. Such "intersex" children have traditionally been assigned a gender by a physician, who may then perform medical intervention in support of the decision. Many adults are now challenging this approach, arguing that intersex children should be left intact and allowed to make gender decisions for themselves when they reach adulthood. Other transgender activists, including people who are not technically intersexed, are simply demanding the right to reassign their gender and to have that choice be recognized on their birth certificates and other legal documentation.

- *How Should Gender Identity Affect Marital Rights?* If a person has been assigned, say, the male gender at birth and then decides that he prefers to be considered a woman, can he, as a woman, marry a man in a heterosexual marriage? And if so, at what point does gender reassignment go into effect? Simply on the declaration of the individual involved? After a psychiatrist has certified that the person's preferred gender is genuinely more compatible with his or her personality? After medical procedures have altered the person's sexual organs? Certainly, legalizing same-sex marriages would affect this question, but given that same-sex marriages do not yet seem to have the same legal footing as heterosexual marriages, does a transgender person have the same legal rights to marry an opposite-sex partner as a person who remains within his or her gender?

- *What Rights Do Transgender People Have in the Workplace, in Public Accommodations, and in Other Spheres of Public Life?* An increasing number of public and private employers are beginning to extend antidiscrimination policies to transgender people. But activists have raised the question of how far employers and public agencies should extend themselves to recognize transgender rights. In New York State, for example, activists have objected to situations in which transgender clients of social service agencies were not allowed to use the restroom of their choice. Other issues ranging from equal access to sensitivity have been raised as well.

Gay Rights

For more on transgender rights, see a description of *In the Matter of the Estate of Marshall G. Gardiner, Deceased,* in Chapter 2, which concerns the efforts of a male-to-female transsexual who, as a woman, married Marshall Gardiner, and whose inheritance from that marriage was challenged by Gardiner's estranged son. The son argued that since the person in question had been born male, the marriage to Gardiner was a same-sex marriage and thus invalid. In a setback for transgender rights, the courts agreed.

CHAPTER 2

THE LAW OF GAY RIGHTS

LEGISLATION AND LEGAL BATTLES

This section summarizes the major legislation and legal battles in the field of gay rights, specifically with regard to sodomy; marriage; civil unions; domestic partnership; federal employment; gays in the military; AIDS and disability law; state, city, and private employment; adoption; hate crimes and violence against gay people; immigration; and transgender rights.

Those trying to arrive at a clear sense of gay legal rights must remember that these rights are often carved out in response to court cases, legislation, and custom. Anti–gay rights activists have added a new category to the list: initiatives and referendums. A major tactic of the anti–gay rights movement of the 1990s and 21st century has been to introduce statewide referendums overturning existing local antidiscrimination laws and banning news ones. Likewise, the question of gay marriage has been dealt with in the courts, in the legislatures, and via referendum, such as the numerous statewide ballot measures declaring that only marriage between a man and woman will be legally recognized. These types of initiatives often come in response to legislation or court decisions, and they are frequently challenged in the courts and worked against in the legislatures. Thus, understanding legislation and legal battles is only part of a very complicated story.

SODOMY LAWS

Although the 2003 Supreme Court decision *Lawrence v. Texas* (see below) struck down all U.S. sodomy laws, these had been a major legal issue for gay people for many years. Sodomy laws outlaw specific sexual practices, such as oral or anal sex, sometimes for all adults, sometimes for homosexuals only, sometimes for people who are not legally married.

Although at one time every state in the union had a sodomy law on the books, Illinois began the trend of decriminalizing sodomy by modernizing its penal code in 1961, legalizing all adult, private, consensual sex. (*Private sex* takes place in a private venue, such as a home, as opposed to a public place, such as a bar, park, public restroom, or street. *Consensual sex* has been freely agreed to by all parties, as opposed to rape or sexual harassment. *Adult sex* refers to all parties being above the age of consent specified in a state law.)

Significantly, the American Civil Liberties Union (ACLU), today a major defender of gay rights, did not go on record as opposing sodomy laws until 1967. Meanwhile, in 1971, the Idaho legislature first repealed and then reinstated its sodomy statute, making sodomy for both gay and straight couples a felony potentially punishable by a life sentence.

Gradually, more and more states began removing their sodomy laws from the books. The Stonewall uprising of 1969 and the gay rights movement that grew out of it were certainly important factors in this trend. So was the general loosening of sexual prohibitions that resulted from the "sexual revolution" of the 1960s and the women's movement of the 1970s. The Supreme Court also supported the trend toward eliminating laws that restricted private, consensual sex between adults. As a result, several states repealed their sodomy laws in the 1970s, so that by 1976, one-third of all U.S. gay men and lesbians were "decriminalized"—though some two-thirds of sexually active gay men and lesbians remained in implicit violation of the law.

Despite the antigay backlash of the late 1970s, states continued to take sodomy laws off the books, while court decisions vitiated (made ineffective) other sodomy laws. Nevertheless, when *Lawrence v. Texas* was handed down in 2003, more than two dozen states still considered sodomy either a misdemeanor or a felony, even though these laws were rarely enforced. Notably, several states banned sodomy among all adults—gay or straight, married or unmarried.

Thus, people on both sides of the gay rights issue consider the 2003 Supreme Court decision historic: for the first time in the United States, sexually active gay people were not by definition criminals; indeed, their equal rights under the law had been explicitly upheld. Although the majority opinion in *Lawrence* expressly stated that the decision should not be taken as offering a legal basis for gay marriage, the climate for gay rights was clearly changing.

MARRIAGE

In 1993, in *Baehr v. Lewin*, Hawaii's high court ruled that same-sex couples had the same right to marry as straight couples. The court stressed that it was referring only to the abstract principle that any two people—including two women or two men—should be able to marry; to say otherwise was to discriminate on the basis of sex. In fact, the court made an explicit distinction between "same-sex" and "homosexual," asserting that the decision had nothing to do with gay rights.

Nonetheless, many states responded by passing laws preventing the recognition of same-sex marriage: in 1995, Utah; in 1996, Arizona, Delaware, Georgia, Idaho, Illinois, Kansas, Michigan, North Carolina, Oklahoma, Pennsylvania, South Carolina, South Dakota, and Tennessee; in 1997, Arkansas, Florida, Indiana, Maine, Minnesota, Mississippi, Montana, North Dakota, and Virginia; and in 1998, Alabama, Alaska (in the form of a constitutional amendment passed by popular vote), Iowa, Kentucky, and Washington. Hawaii, the state considered most likely to legalize same-sex marriage, passed a constitutional amendment in 1998 restricting the marriage contract to heterosexual couples. Missouri attempted to pass a gay marriage recognition ban, but the state supreme court overturned it because of bad legislative procedure. However, in 2004, the state successfully amended its constitution to ban gay marriage. California passed Proposition 22, or the Knight Initiative (after Republican state senator Pete Knight, who sponsored the bill), which defined marriage as between heterosexuals and banned California from recognizing same-sex marriages contracted in any other state. Although a judge declared the law unconstitutional in March 2005, appeals courts were continuing to consider the matter as of this writing.

Meanwhile, on December 11, 1999, Hawaii's Supreme Court ruled in favor of the state's anti-marriage amendment. At the same time, a gay couple in Vermont had brought a lawsuit claiming that they had been wrongfully denied a marriage license, leading to a December 20, 1999, Vermont Supreme Court decision that distinguishing between gay and straight couples violated the state's antidiscrimination law. The state high court ordered the legislature to come up with an arrangement allowing equal legal and financial benefits to same-sex couples, leading to the category of "civil union," a legally recognized affectional partnership that offers some, but not all, of the benefits enjoyed by married couples.

The battleground moved to Massachusetts, where another gay couple had brought a lawsuit seeking marital recognition in their state. Their efforts ultimately won success with a 2003 Massachusetts Supreme Judicial Court ruling, in which justices found that denying the rights of marriage to gay citizens violated the state constitution. On May 17, 2004, the first legal gay marriages in the United States began taking place in Massachusetts. Meanwhile, thousands of gay marriages had been performed in San Francisco, and in other towns and cities across the country. As of this writing, many of these ceremonies had been nullified. (For more detail on the history of gay marriage in the United States, see "The Marriage Question," in Chapter 1. For more detail on the legal issues involved, see the section on marriage under "Legal Issues," also in Chapter 1.)

Advocates of gay marriage point out that the institution confers at least 1,049 separate rights on married people, many of which are not available with a civil union or domestic partnership. Moreover, no relationship other than marriage is "portable," enabling participants to enjoy marital rights in every state. Finally, only legally recognized marriage confers the federal benefits of marriage, including tax breaks, military pensions, Social Security, and immigration rights. The following is a partial list of some rights that accrue to U.S. married couples:

- Status as next of kin
- Eligibility for visitation privileges when spouse is in hospital or prison
- Right to consent to or disallow a spouse's autopsy
- Right to make medical decisions for spouse, including decisions about gifts of organs and body parts after death

- Right to make burial or cremation arrangements
- Right of spousal privilege, which keeps communications between spouses private, even in court testimony
- Right to cohabit on military properties and other federally controlled properties
- Automatic sharing of community property, with laws regulating its control, division, acquisition, and disposition
- Exemption from taxes when gifts, property, or other goods are conveyed to spouse
- Automatic court notice of probate proceedings
- Death benefits for the surviving spouses of government employees
- Funeral and bereavement leave in case of spouse's death
- Child custody in divorce proceedings
- Right to child support after divorce
- Joint adoptions and foster care; legal status with stepchildren
- Joint tax filing, along with deductions, credits, exemptions, and other tax breaks
- Right to share in property tax exemption for homes of completely disabled veterans
- Right to share in insurance coverage
- Eligibility for wages and worker compensation after spouse's death
- Right to a restraining order in cases of domestic violence
- Right to inherit property, particularly without a will
- Eligibility to sue on behalf of spouse, including in wrongful death suits
- Eligibility for discounts given to veterans' spouses
- Immigration benefits

On an international level, gay marriages are recognized in Belgium, the Netherlands, and eight Canadian provinces (Ontario, British Columbia, Quebec, Manitoba, the Yukon, Nova Scotia, Newfoundland, and Saskatchewan.)

CIVIL UNIONS

Civil unions provide only some state-level benefits and legal protections, without making participants eligible for the full range of benefits associated with marriage. As of this writing, civil unions are available only in Vermont and New Jersey, though many states, including Massachusetts, are considering civil union arrangements as alternatives to gay marriage.

Also as of this writing, civil unions are not necessarily recognized by other states. Some states have passed laws or added constitutional measures that specifically define marriage as taking place between a man and woman. In some cases, these measures may be interpreted as invalidating the civil union contracted in another state.

Because civil unions are such a new legal form and because civil unions—and gay partnerships in general—are such hotly contested legal categories, it is difficult to provide a complete and accurate description of all the legal rights associated with civil unions in each state. It is also unclear to what extent a state that recognizes its own civil unions might recognize the civil union arrangements of another state. Usually, any ambiguity in the law would be resolved in a suit, and indeed, gay rights groups have often deliberately sought such suits as a means of establishing legal precedents on various issues. However, since so much of the gay rights movement's attention is going to the question of gay marriage, little effort has been made so far to clarify the status of civil unions. Marriage law, on the other hand, is quite well articulated, which is part of the reason why the gay rights movement seeks the well-established protections of legal marriage for gay couples and their families.

On an international level, while only the Netherlands, Belgium, and eight Canadian provinces allowed gay marriage as of 2005, a number of countries recognized same-sex unions, including Croatia, Denmark, Finland, France, Germany, Hungary, Iceland, Norway, Portugal, Sweden, and the United Kingdom. (For more on civil unions, see the section on this issue in Chapter 1, "Legal Issues.")

DOMESTIC PARTNERSHIP

Domestic partnership is a somewhat flexible term that is generally used to indicate a relationship between two unmarried people living together who nevertheless consider themselves to be financial and/or emotional partners. The term has been used to apply to both gay and straight couples as a means for awarding unmarried partners health insurance and other benefits traditionally restricted to legal spouses. In some cases, domestic partnerships must be registered or recorded in a particular way; in other cases, it is enough for a person simply to assert that someone else is his or her domestic partner. As with civil unions, this is a hotly contested issue. As support for gay marriage increases, many conservatives who once opposed domestic partnership benefits for gay couples now argue in favor of either domestic partnerships or civil unions while objecting to gay marriage.

According to a study conducted by the Human Rights Campaign (HRC), a gay rights group, by December 31, 2003, some 7,149 private employers, colleges, and universities offered health insurance coverage to their employees' domestic partners. During the same time frame, some 200 companies in the Fortune 500—a total of 40 percent—provided domestic partner benefits. HRC stressed that the number of companies that offer such benefits is growing at an ever-increasing rate with each passing year, with the most prosperous companies being the most likely to recognize domestic partnerships. Although only 40 percent of Fortune 500 companies offer domestic partner benefits, 68 percent of the Fortune 50 do.

HRC found that by 2003, only Hawaii, Vermont, and the District of Columbia recognized same-sex couples as domestic partners. During 2003, California and New Jersey passed comprehensive domestic partnership laws that went into effect in 2004, while the Massachusetts Supreme Judicial Court supported gay couple's right to marry, a right that also went into effect in 2004.

By the end of 2003, 64 cities and countries offered domestic partnership registries that provided limited rights—primarily rights involving medical decision making and hospital visitation—to couples who registered. HRC reported that an ever-increasing number of jurisdictions are creating registries, at an ever faster rate.

Domestic partnerships are winning legal recognition in other ways. For example, after Diane Whipple was mauled to death by dogs in San Francisco in 2001, her surviving lesbian partner, Sharon Smith, won the right to bring the owners and their landlords to court in a wrongful death suit, based on the state's guarantee of equal protection under the law. In order to bring such a suit, a person must have *standing*, a legal term indicating a basis for being involved enough in the issue to have the right to sue. Typically, spouses and close relatives, such as parents, children, and siblings, have standing in wrongful death suits, but historically, gay and lesbian partners do not.

Likewise, in April 2003, a Long Island, New York, judge ruled that a gay man who had entered into a Vermont civil union with his partner had standing to bring a wrongful death suit against St. Vincent's Hospital in New York City. This case was believed to be the first in which a judge outside Vermont recognized the rights of a couple who had engaged in civil union—a significant issue, since by definition, civil unions are not "portable," and no one outside the state in which they are contracted is required to recognize them. The suit was filed by John Langan after his partner, Neal Conrad Spicehandler, died from post-surgery complications.

An even more dramatic recognition of domestic partnership came in April 6, 2004, when the September 11 Victim Compensation Fund compensated Nancy Walsh for the loss of her partner, Carol Flyzik, who had been on board American Airlines Flight 11 when it crashed into the World Trade Center in 2001. For many observers, the emotional resonance of September 11 seemed to add a special degree of legitimacy to the recognition of gay partnerships.

Again, no one is certain how the anti–gay marriage amendments to state constitutions will affect the recognition of domestic partnership. Many of the amendments explicitly ban not only gay marriage, but also any type of legally recognized same-sex union. How the amendments will be used, how they will affect public and private policy, and how they will stand up in court were all uncertain as of this writing.

On an international level, in addition to the countries that allow gay marriage or recognize same-sex partnerships in other ways, a number of countries recognize gay partnerships to a limited extent, offering some benefits to gay partners. Among these countries are Argentina, Australia, Brazil, Colombia,

The Law of Gay Rights

Costa Rica, the Czech Republic, Israel, Italy, New Zealand, South Africa, Spain, and Switzerland.

FEDERAL EMPLOYMENT

For many years, homosexuality was banned by federal civil service regulations. Due in part to the landmark case of *Norton v. Macy* (see Court Cases), homosexuality gradually became tolerated in federal employment, despite regulations in force against it.

A class action suit in 1973, *Society for Individual Rights* [a gay organization] *v. Hampton*, created a definitive change in civil service policy. A supply clerk was fired when his army discharge papers revealed his homosexuality. He brought suit against the government's antigay policy, and a federal court, using *Norton v. Macy* as its guide, ordered the Civil Service Commission to

> *forthwith cease excluding or discharging from government service any homosexual person whom the Commission would deem unfit for government employment solely because the employment of such a person in the government service might bring that service into contempt.*

In other words, the fear that having gay employees would cause the public to lose respect—to have "contempt"—for an agency was no longer a reason to fire or refuse to hire gay men and lesbians.

Accordingly, in 1975, the U.S. Civil Service Commission announced that it had dropped its ban on hiring gay people—except for the FBI and the intelligence agencies, where the fear that homosexuals could be more easily blackmailed (and were more personally unstable) continued to operate.

Then, in 1977, a federal court upheld the firing of a gay clerk who "flaunted" his homosexuality by kissing a man in public, being active in the gay rights movement, and applying for a license to marry another man. When the Supreme Court vacated the lower court's decision in 1978, it suggested that openly gay employees had the right to keep their jobs. Although the court offered no explanation in its 1978 ruling, later cases, especially *Van Ooteghem v. Gray* (1980), suggest that the free speech rights of gay civil servants are indeed protected.

So in 1980, the government took another step: The Office of Personnel Management (OPM) began to actively prohibit employment discrimination on the basis of sexual orientation in all federal civil service jobs. And throughout the 1980s and 1990s, groups such as Federal Lesbians and Gays (FLAG) and Federal GLOBE (Gay, Lesbian, Bisexual Employees) continued to push for better conditions for gay, lesbian, and bisexual civil servants.

Their efforts have been largely successful. Some 38 agencies now have nondiscrimination policies, including many cabinet departments—Agriculture, Commerce, Education, Energy, Health and Human Services, Housing and Urban Development, Interior, Justice, Labor, State, Transportation, Treasury, and Veterans Affairs—as well as the Departments of the Air Force, Army, and Navy (which supervises the U.S. Marines), though these rules apply to civilian employees only. Many other government agencies have similar antidiscrimination policies, including the offices of the president and vice president, the CIA, Environmental Protection Agency, Equal Employment Opportunity Commission (EEOC), Federal Trade Commission, Library of Congress, NASA, and the U.S. Postal Service. And on May 29, 1998, President Bill Clinton issued an executive order prohibiting discrimination against federal workers on the basis of sexual orientation. However, Clinton's order carried no enforcement measures, and it failed to include the nation's largest employer, the U.S. military—one of the last government employers with an explicit policy of antigay discrimination.

Then, in February 2004, an appointee of President George W. Bush took action that gay rights activists interpreted as a step backward in employment rights: He removed references to sexual orientation from the web site of his office. Scott J. Bloch was the newly appointed head of the Office of Special Counsel, an independent agency charged with protecting whistle-blowers and other federal employees from retribution. His office's web site had informed employees that discrimination based on sexual orientation is unlawful, and that complaints could be filed at the special counsel's office. Dating back to the 1973 suit, workers—including gay workers—could not be fired, demoted, or disciplined based on their off-duty behavior unless their actions hurt their job performance or interfered with the work of others. During President Clinton's term, antigay bias had been added to the list of banned personnel practices, pursuant to Clinton's executive order. President Bush has never rescinded that order, but Bloch's removal of all references to sexual orientation from his office's documents suggested at the very least a backing away from the commitment to oppose such discrimination.

According to a February 18, 2004, story in the *Washington Post*, Bloch asserted that discrimination against federal employees was wrong—but that it would also be wrong for him to exceed his jurisdiction. He took the information off the web site, he explained, because he was not sure how to apply the civil service law. Material that Bloch removed from the web site included a discrimination complaint form, training slides, a brochure titled "Your Rights as a Federal Employee," and other documents. Some observers wondered whether his timing related to President Bush's involvement in a battle against gay marriage, but Bloch insisted that he had not cleared his decision with the White House.

Bloch also removed an agency news release describing an investigation at the Internal Revenue Service that discovered antigay discrimination at the IRS. Colleen M. Kelley, head of the National Treasury Employees Union, expressed her concern that Bloch's removal of that information signaled a wish to muffle the Office of Special Counsel's record of fighting antigay discrimination. Bloch's action also drew fire from the HRC and from Federal GLOBE, a gay federal employee organization.

For months, congressional Democrats continued to pressure Bloch and the federal government in what they described as an effort to protect the rights of gay and lesbian employees. In early January 2005, almost a year after the controversy began, President George W. Bush joined in condemning Bloch's action. The following week, the language protecting gay and lesbian rights was restored.

GAYS IN THE MILITARY

From World War II through 1994, the military's policy on gay men and lesbians was quite clear: Homosexuality was considered "incompatible with military service." As discussed in Chapter 1, President Bill Clinton pledged during his 1992 campaign to eliminate this half-century ban and welcome gay men and lesbians as members of the U.S. Armed Forces.

Certainly, many in the gay rights movement were of two minds about welcoming gays into the military. For many, the military was seen as an evil to be avoided, particularly for those who remembered an era when the draft had brought thousands of unwilling young men to serve in a war that many regarded as unjust. On the other hand, as with gay marriage, the immediate civil rights issue seemed to many activists more pressing than the larger questions of political principle. If straight people were allowed—or drafted—into the army, then, they believed, gay people ought to have the same right. Besides the symbolic effects of military service—its suggestion that gay men and women were indeed full-fledged members of society—allowing gays into the military would give young men and women access to training, education, veterans' benefits, and other opportunities open to heterosexual youths.

Supporters of gays and lesbians in the military argued that there had always been homosexual soldiers, many of whom had received the military's highest awards. Speaking both to the gay rights movement and to society at large, they urged legal recognition for what they claimed was a long-standing situation.

Opponents of gays in the military argued that the open presence of homosexuals would weaken the morale and cohesiveness of fighting units, make straight soldiers uncomfortable about sharing quarters and showering with lesbian and gay soldiers, and run counter to the U.S. military tradition. Some opponents also said or suggested that gay men and women were less fit morally and/or physically and could not fight as well as or as bravely as their heterosexual counterparts. Many opponents of gay and lesbian soldiers did not believe that there were already many lesbians and gay men serving—with varying degrees of openness—in all branches of the military; that indeed, all fighting forces throughout history had included gay men (and, in some cases, lesbians).

In any case, Clinton's promise was not fulfilled. Georgia senator Sam Nunn, of the Armed Service Committee, and U.S. Army general Colin Powell were both strong opponents of the open participation of gay men and women in the military. Under pressure from them, losing the public relations battle, and fearful of his waning influence in Congress, Clinton retreated from his promise of an executive order lifting the ban on gays and instead instituted a policy commonly known as "don't ask, don't tell," wherein gay men and women were not allowed to make their homosexuality public, but neither could they be asked by recruiters what their sexuality was.

Gay Rights

As it turned out, Clinton's policy was probably worse for gay servicemen and women than the previous regulations had been. The new policy prohibited gay soldiers from engaging in any homosexual conduct, in or out of uniform, and actually criminalized a gay *identity:* Soldiers could be discharged just for being identified as gay or lesbian, whether or not they committed any specific acts.

As a result, more gay soldiers were discharged under "don't ask, don't tell" than under the previous ban on homosexual soldiers. According to a March 25, 2004, story in the *International Herald Tribune,* the decade between 1994 and 2004 saw some 10,000 service members discharged on the grounds that they had not concealed their sexual orientation. Meanwhile, in February 2005, a congressional study revealed that the military had spent more than $200 million to recruit and train personnel to replace troops discharged in the past decade for being openly gay.

An increase in attacks on and harassment of gay and lesbian soldiers was also noticed. Nor did the policy win Clinton any political points. The right wing attacked Clinton for being "soft on homosexuality," while gay rights activists and their allies accused him of reneging on his promise.

Reports of antigay harassment provoked such widespread concern that in August 1999 the Pentagon issued new guidelines that prohibited commanders from investigating the sexual orientation of service members who reported antigay harassment or threats. Rather, commanders were directed to investigate the threat itself.

Criticism of the policy continued, and in December 1999 Clinton finally decided to bring his policy under review, largely because of continued concern over the death of Barry Winchell, a gay soldier who had been bludgeoned to death in his Fort Campbell, Kentucky, barracks. Winchell had reportedly been harassed repeatedly by the fellow private who eventually killed him. However, because of "don't ask, don't tell," Winchell was allegedly afraid to report the harassment for fear of being discharged. Winchell's mother later sued the military for $1.8 million, a suit that the army eventually refused to accept (the army accepts suits at its own discretion).

First Lady Hillary Clinton denounced the policy, while Vice President Al Gore, in the midst of his own presidential campaign, said bluntly, "Gays and lesbians should be allowed to serve their country without discrimination." Clinton himself, in a televised weekend interview on CBS News, said that the policy he had once championed was "out of whack." On the following Monday, December 13, 1999, Defense Secretary William Cohen announced an intensive 90-day review of the policy.

Despite the review, Clinton's policy resulted in record numbers of gay-related discharges, according to a report conducted by the Servicemembers Legal Defense Network, a gay rights group. However, the group found that discharge of gay servicemembers dropped considerably in 2001, 2002, and 2003, reflecting the increased need for armed services personnel. From 1,273 discharges in 2001, figures dropped to 906 in 2002 and 787 in 2003, the lowest number since 1995. "Gay discharge numbers have dropped every time America has entered a war," the report noted, "from Korea to Vietnam to the Persian Gulf to present conflicts."

The Law of Gay Rights

In August 2004, the nation's highest military court—the armed forces court—ruled that a military ban on sodomy might nevertheless be allowed by the Constitution. Even though the Supreme Court's *Lawrence v. Texas* decision had eliminated sodomy laws as unconstitutional, the armed forces court upheld the military's right to ban sodomy. However, that decision did not speak directly to the question of whether the protections offered by *Lawrence* applied to the military. (Legally, the U.S. military operates under a separate court system, and developments in U.S. law often affect the military differently than they affect the civilian legal system.)

In November 2004, a military appeals court overturned the conviction of a soldier charged with heterosexual sodomy, a move that many observers believe will affect the treatment of gay soldiers. A male army specialist admitted that he had engaged in consensual oral sex with a female civilian in violation of Article 125 of the Uniform Code of Military Justice, which bans armed forces personnel from "unnatural carnal copulation with another person of the same or opposite sex or with an animal." When the court overturned the man's conviction, it cited *Lawrence*'s guarantees of sexual privacy. Many legal scholars believe that this represents a possible move toward abolishing the "don't ask, don't tell" policy, under which gay service members can be discharged for admitting their homosexuality.

In November 2004, the Log Cabin Republicans (an activist group of gay Republicans) filed suit in federal court in Los Angeles seeking to overturn the military's "don't ask, don't tell" policy. Their effort was followed by a Boston lawsuit filed in December 2004, in which a dozen former members of the armed forces, all of whom had been discharged for their homosexuality, claimed that both the "don't ask, don't tell" policy and the military's antisodomy statute are unconstitutional. Both suits referred to *Lawrence*'s ruling that the Texas antisodomy statute violated the constitutional right to privacy. In the December lawsuit, the discharged military personnel named the U.S. Army, Navy, Air Force, and Coast Guard and sought to be reinstated into the military.

The armed forces of some other countries do allow open homosexuality. During military activities in Iraq and Afghanistan in 2002, 2003, and 2004, Allied forces from Britain, Canada, and Australia permitted gay and bisexual soldiers to serve openly. The sight of openly gay soldiers provoked the envy of many U.S. gay and lesbian enlisted personnel, including Captain Austin Rooke, a gay army reservist interviewed in a *Herald Tribune* article. Rooke described the isolation he felt as a gay man attempting to conceal his identity as he served in Bosnia in 1997 with a NATO unit and in Qatar during the Afghanistan war. Rooke also served during the buildup to war in Iraq. "It was a stressful environment," he said, "made worse by a homophobic climate."

AIDS AND DISABILITY LAW

As stated in Chapter 1, there is one specific federal provision that protects the rights of some gay and lesbian employees: the extension of the 1990 Americans with Disabilities Act (ADA) to cover people with AIDS and HIV. (Although most gay men and lesbians do not have AIDS or HIV, and although many people with AIDS or HIV are not gay, the ruling does affect many gay men in particular and AIDS activism has often been linked with gay rights activism.) In a 1998 decision, *Bragdon v. Abbott*, the Supreme Court ruled 5-4 in favor of Sidney Abbott, an HIV-positive Maine woman filing suit against Randon Bragdon, a dentist who had refused to fill a cavity for her in his Bangor office. Bragdon had insisted on treating Abbott in a hospital, where he said he could take greater precautions against infecting himself or his staff.

Abbott argued that as a person with HIV, she was entitled to the same protection against discrimination as other disabled Americans. The Court agreed that people with AIDS or HIV did indeed come under the 1990 act's definition of the disabled—that is, people who were unable to engage in a "major life activity." Since children of people with AIDS or HIV might be born infected, people with AIDS or HIV cannot freely engage in reproduction, which the court agreed was clearly a major life activity. As a result of the 1998 decision, people with AIDS or HIV now have protection from discrimination in employment, housing, and public accommodations (i.e., restaurants, hotels, and other public places).

Gay rights groups and AIDS organizations hailed the decision, as did the American Civil Liberties Union. "It sends a message to a lot of people beyond those with HIV that they shouldn't be denied the opportunity to work or receive services because people are uncomfortable with their condition," said Gary Buseck, executive director of Gay and Lesbian Advocates and Defenders.

Another HIV-related complaint was filed with the EEOC in 2003 on behalf of Matthew Cusick, an HIV-positive gymnast fired from Cirque du Soleil. Cusick, who joined Cirque in 2002, voluntarily disclosed his HIV status to his employer and was fired in response, just three days before he was to perform in a show for which he had trained for four months. Although Cirque claimed that Cusick's status posed a health risk, Cusick challenged this notion through his representative, Lambda Legal, a gay rights group. Lambda argued that there was no medical or scientific evidence to support the notion that Cusick's HIV status created a safety hazard. Lambda also organized protests outside several Cirque shows.

Six months after the suit was filed, the EEOC ruled for Cusick. Cirque invited him back into the show, but Cusick declined, saying that he preferred not to return to a company that had fought so hard to keep him out.

Cirque, meanwhile, faced investigation from the San Francisco Human Rights Commission, since the city leased space to the performance group, and the commission believed that the company might have violated city antidiscrimination codes. Cirque eventually rewrote its own antidiscrimination policy to be consonant (in harmony) with San Francisco's code, banning discrimination on the basis of height, weight, and gender identity as well as HIV status.

"This is sending out a strong message to employers that there's a steep price to pay for discrimination," Cusick said in an April 23, 2004, article in the *San Francisco Chronicle*. "For people who are living with HIV who are being discriminated against every day, it's going to help these people to be strong to stand up to these employers."

STATE, CITY, AND PRIVATE EMPLOYMENT

Interestingly, the public's attitude toward homosexuality in general and its attitude toward antigay employment discrimination in particular, are widely divergent. A 1998 *Washington Post*/Harvard University poll found that 57 percent of the respondents thought that homosexuality itself was "unacceptable." Yet 87 percent believed that gay men and lesbians should have equal rights when it came to employment. Clearly, many people who do not approve of homosexuality per se still think gay men and lesbians should be given equal treatment at work.

According to gay rights lawyer and activist Paula Ettelbrick, that is largely because people view workplace discrimination very differently now than they used to. In her view, the civil rights movement has helped many Americans to see *any* kind of on-the-job discrimination as simply unfair. Even when an employer is not legally required to avoid antigay discrimination in particular, Ettelbrick sees a kind of cultural attitude that suggests that such discrimination is wrong. Ironically, says Ettelbrick, this very improvement makes it somewhat more difficult to pass antidiscrimination legislation. Precisely because fewer employers now feel comfortable in telling a gay man or lesbian, "I'm firing you because you're gay," it is hard to find examples of the most egregious types of discrimination. And those who do experience such treatment are often afraid to testify about it, especially if they're living fearful and closeted lives.

Incidents of discrimination still exist, however, in the subtle guise of being excessively criticized by a supervisor or excluded from key meetings, as well as in more overt forms. In 1991, for example, Robin Shahar, a lawyer, took a job in the office of Georgia attorney general Michael Bowers (the same public official involved in *Bowers v. Hardwick* [see below]). But when Shahar and her lover held a private commitment ceremony, Bowers withdrew the job offer. Bowers pointed out that according to the Supreme Court case *Bowers v. Hardwick*, then still in force, Shahar was a felon. Thus he could explain his action not as discrimination but rather as the wish to hire only law-abiding citizens. Shahar's case made it all the way to the Supreme Court—which in 1998 refused to hear it. (Ironically, that was the same year that the Georgia Supreme Court overturned the state's sodomy law. Later, in 2003, the Supreme Court decision *Lawrence v. Texas* overturned *Bowers* and declared all sodomy laws unconstitutional.)

Despite cases like Shahar's, it's clear that gay men and lesbians have won more on-the-job rights. According to the HRC, as of December 31, 2003, 14 states and the District of Columbia had laws to protect from discrimination all gay, lesbian, and bisexual workers within their borders. Another 11 states had restrictions on discrimination against gay, lesbian, and bisexual public workers. In addition, some 285 cities, counties, and government agencies offered at least some protection against discrimination based on sexual orientation, including 152 jurisdictions that extend such protection into the private sector. Also by

December 31, 2003, 10 states and the District of Columbia offered health insurance benefits to the domestic partners of public employees.

Equal benefits ordinances require contracts with a government unit to offer domestic partner benefits that parallel the benefits they offer to married couples. As of December 31, 2003, the HRC found that one state and nine cities and counties had passed such ordinances. The state law, passed in California, will go into effect in 2007. The other jurisdictions are Berkeley, Los Angeles, Oakland, and San Mateo, California; Minneapolis, Minnesota; and King County (Seattle) and Tumwater, Washington.

Portland, Maine, has an equal benefits ordinance that applies to organizations funded by the city's Housing and Community Development Program. Broward County, Florida, regulations allow the county to show preference to contractors with equal benefits programs. And Sacramento, California, requires contractors to offer the same personal and family leave benefits to domestic partners as to married employees.

As for the private employers that the HRC studied during the same period, some 2,253 employers, colleges, and universities included sexual orientation in their nondiscrimination policies, including 72 percent of all Fortune 500 companies and 98 percent of all Fortune 50 companies. As of December 31, 2003, Exxon-Mobil Corporation was the only Fortune 50 company without protection for gay people in its antidiscrimination policy. Some 400 colleges and universities had antidiscrimination policies that included gay people, as did 49 of the top 50 national four-year colleges (the University of Notre Dame was the only exception).

The number of private employers offering protection to gay workers is increasing, and so is their visibility. When Wal-Mart, one of the nation's largest employers, announced its inclusion of gay people in its antidiscrimination policy, it sent a powerful signal that gay rights efforts had reached into the American heartland. Identified as a store that appeals particularly to working-class and rural Americans, Wal-Mart might seem at first glance an unlikely company to recognize the rights of gay workers. Its action demonstrated that gay rights has become a far more mainstream issue than even five years ago.

The HRC found that private employers are offering both protection against discrimination and recognition of domestic partner benefits in ever-increasing numbers, and these voluntary actions are taking place at an ever-faster rate. Nevertheless, some employers require the additional incentive of a lawsuit, as Daniel Kline discovered in 2003. Kline had worked for United Parcel Service (UPS) for more than 20 years when his partner Frank Sories was transferred from San Francisco to Chicago. Sories and Kline had been together for almost 27 years—since Kline was 20—so Kline requested a transfer to Chicago from UPS. The company offers spousal transfers for legally married employees, but as gay men, Sories and Kline could not marry. Kline's request was approved at district and regional levels, then denied by corporate headquarters on the grounds that he was not legally married.

Kline and Sories were registered domestic partners in California, where they owned a home together. They had also designated one another as beneficiaries of each other's wills. They held power of attorney for each other and were empowered to make health-care decisions for one another. Kline had been able to designate Sories as the beneficiary of his UPS employee benefits, including retirement savings, stock plans, and life insurance. But, only nine years away from his pension, he could not move to Chicago to join his partner. The couple were separated for eight months as Kline struggled with his employer.

The couple sued UPS on August 19, 2003, on the grounds that the company's action violated California's Fair Employment and Housing Act's prohibition against discriminating against employees on the basis of their marital status. UPS offered Kline a transfer a month later, and the couple was reunited in Chicago. The suit continued, however, as Kline and Sories sought damages for the suffering and expenses they had incurred. A settlement was announced on February 19, 2004. UPS spokesperson Peggy Gardner stressed that the company had already begun including domestic partners in its transfer policy before the lawsuit was filed. "The policy had been changed earlier in the year but had not been fully communicated to all employees yet," she said.

GAY ADOPTION

New Jersey made U.S. history in December 1997 by becoming the first state in the nation to allow both gay and heterosexual unmarried couples to adopt children on the same basis as married couples. Lawyers had argued that state policy against gay adoptions violated the equal protection rights of lesbian and gay couples. Moreover, the lawyers claimed, as in custody cases, the best interests of the child should take precedence.

Conservative groups decried the decision, but the precedent had been set. Gay couples had won another form of legal recognition.

The New Jersey couple in question was Jon Holden and Michael Galluccio, who adopted their son, Adam, when he was two years old. The couple had begun caring for Adam when he was three months old, a drug-addicted baby who had been exposed to—but not infected with—HIV. Under previous policy, Holden or Galluccio might have been able to adopt separately—as in the cases discussed in the custody section of this book. By adopting as a couple, however, they were assured that both would have rights to the child.

A December 20, 1997, editorial in the *Washington Post* pointed out that the New Jersey decision was actually only "an incremental development in the debate" over gay adoption. As the editorial explained, many states already permitted gay men and lesbians in relationships to adopt children, and many others allowed a gay man or lesbian to adopt a partner's child later on. Some gay couples had even adopted children *as* couples—but only because of court decisions. The new achievement in the New Jersey case was to "remove as a matter of state policy the fiction that the state is dealing with individuals rather than with a couple. More than anything else, the settlement is an acknowledgment of the current reality."

Although the *Washington Post* editorial urged caution in the matter of adoption policy, Holden and Galluccio found quite a different reception when they adopted a second child in 1999. Their first adoption effort "took a battery of lawyers, a court ruling, and a landmark change in New Jersey policy," according to an article by Joan Biskupic in the November 5, 1999, edition of the *Washington Post*. Yet when the two men adopted their second child, "it took them only a few months of the usual paperwork that any couple might face." Galluccio says that it is not just the rules that are changing. "In 1997, when we finally got Adam, our family was an oddity to people," he told Biskupic. "There was a look of bewilderment in people's eyes. But now, we've become more ordinary."

Like many gay activists who fall into the "gay liberationist" rather than the "civil rights" camps, legal scholar and professor Ruthann Robson supports the growing acceptance of lesbian families—but cautions against too great an eagerness to fit lesbian (and, by implication, gay male) arrangements into the traditional patterns of heterosexual family life. Like many gay liberationists, she wonders why only two lesbians are allowed to coadopt a child, and why they must be involved in a monogamous, long-term relationship that looks as much as possible like heterosexual marriage. Why, she wonders, could not three or more people agree to raise a child? Why could not people who engage in a variety of sexual arrangements still not offer a stable, loving home to a child? Moreover, like others who hold her view, Robson worries that the kinds of lesbian (and, by extension, gay male) families that are accepted by the courts are the ones in which upper-class incomes and trust funds help to erase the courts' traditional reluctance to recognize same-sex couples. In their gratitude for court approval, Robson warns, lesbians (and gay men) risk reinforcing the oppressive restrictions of class and heterosexual marriage.

Meanwhile, gay adoption has reached a level of acceptance in the United States unimaginable only a few years ago. In 2002 and 2003, for example, as many as 20,000 adoptions were completed by gay and lesbian couples. Adoption by gay couples is now protected by either law or appellate court rulings in 11 states and the District of Columbia.

Gay adoption cases continue to set new precedents. On August 4, 2003, for example, the California Supreme Court upheld second-parent adoptions, a form of adoption in which a second parent can gain parental rights without the first parent terminating his or hers. Second-parent adoption is a strategy employed by many gay men and lesbians: When one partner gives birth or has prior custody of a child, a second-parent adoption can win parental rights for the partner, provided the custodial parent agrees. When heterosexuals marry, the husband or stepparent automatically shares parental rights in the other partner's child, but gay couples have no such legal resource unless same-sex marriage becomes legal. (Second-parent adoption can also be undertaken by two people who are not partners, such as a mother and daughter who might share custody of the daughter's fatherless child or two relatives who agree to raise a child together.)

The California second-parent adoption case involved Annette Friskopp and Sharon Silverstein, a San Diego couple who had been together for 11 years before separating. While they were together, however, Silverstein gave birth to two sons through artificial insemination. Friskopp adopted the older boy and was in the process of adopting the younger child when the couple split up in 2000. Silverstein challenged Friskopp's right to adopt, but Friskopp argued successfully that she could adopt as a second parent if Silverstein agreed to allow it. The supreme court then sent the case back to the lower courts to find out whether Silverstein had given her consent.

The California case offered important support to second-parent adoption. As of January 2004, some 10,000 second-parent adoptions have taken place in the United States (many, but not all, to gay parents) and have been approved by appellate courts in California, the District of Columbia, Illinois, Indiana, Massachusetts, Pennsylvania, New York, and New Jersey. California, Connecticut, and Vermont have laws expressly permitting second-parent adoptions. Trial court judges have granted second-parent adoptions in Alabama, Alaska, Delaware, Hawaii, Indiana, Iowa, Louisiana, Maryland, Minnesota, New Mexico, Oregon, Rhode Island, Texas, and Washington. On the other hand, Colorado, Nebraska, Ohio, and Wisconsin expressly ban second-parent adoptions. Although Nebraska does not allow second-parent adoptions under its own laws, a 2002 decision by the Nebraska Court of Appeals found that the state had to recognize a second-parent adoption that had been granted in Pennsylvania.

Florida is currently the only state in the union to ban gay adoptions by law but the 1977 law was recently challenged by two gay couples, all licensed foster parents. Steven Lofton and Douglas Houghton were seeking to adopt a child they had fostered since the 1990s. Wayne Smith and Daniel Skahen had together fostered several Florida children since receiving their foster licenses in 2000. A federal judge upheld the law in 2001, and an appeals court twice affirmed the decision in 2004. Judge Stanley Birch, writing the unanimous opinion for a three-judge panel, explained that the law had been passed because the legislature had not considered gay adoption to be in the best interests of displaced children (although the state does permit gay people to be foster parents). The legislature was therefore the place in which further debate should continue, not the courts. The decision is expected to influence opinion in the neighboring states of Georgia and Alabama.

In Oklahoma, the threat of a lawsuit led the state to recognize homosexual couples on a child's birth certificate. Gregory Hampel and Edmund Swaya were a Washington State couple who in 2003 adopted two-year-old Vivian, born in Oklahoma. Vivian's birth state does not permit gay couples to adopt, so Oklahoma issued a birth certificate listing Hampel as the sole father. Swaya sought to join his partner on Vivian's birth certificate so he would be equally entitled to make medical decisions for her and to take her on international flights.

In March 2004, the state attorney general ruled that if a local child was adopted by a couple in another state, the Oklahoma birth certificate had to list both gay partners as parents. But by May, the legislature had passed a law overturning the decision, holding that other states could not force Oklahoma to list two same-sex names on a birth certificate. "The radical homosexual agenda includes trying to be recognized both as married couples and as a . . . family union," said state senator James A. Williamson, the Republican who sponsored the legislation, as quoted in the May 7, 2004, *Washington Times*. "That's their agenda and they're going to continue pushing the envelope. . . . The whole concept of family . . . is being challenged across the nation." Currently, gay rights activists are considering challenging the Oklahoma law on the grounds that the U.S. Constitution's full faith and credit laws require states to recognize and respect each other's laws.

On December 29, 2004, an Arkansas judge struck down a 1999 regulation by the state Child Welfare Agency Review Board banning gay people from becoming foster parents and prohibiting placement of a child in any home in which a gay person also lived. The judge was responding to a suit brought by the American Civil Liberties Union, who claimed the policy violated the equal protection rights of gay people.

However, the judge overturned the policy on different grounds: He said that the board was charged only to "promote the health, safety, and welfare of children," whereas the ban on gay foster parents or family members was actually an effort to regulate "public morality." The judge relied upon evidence introduced at trial that children thrive just as much with gay as with straight parents and guardians.

The state intends to appeal the ruling on the grounds that children in foster care are undergoing unusual amounts of stress and need the "normalcy" that a straight family would provide. Despite the ban on gay fostering, however, Arkansas continues to allow gay men and lesbians to adopt children. Currently, no other state has a similar ban on gay fostering in place.

HATE CRIMES AND VIOLENCE AGAINST GAY PEOPLE

The notion of "hate crimes"—crimes that include an element of bias, or hate, against a particular group—became widely understood in the 1990s, as gays and lesbians, people of color, and other oppressed groups sought to increase the penalties for bias crimes and bias-related violence. The first instance of gay men and lesbians receiving any kind of federal protection was their inclusion in the 1990 Hate Crime Statistics Act, which requires the U.S. Department of Justice to collect, maintain, and report statistics on criminal acts that are motivated by race, religion, national origin, or sexual orientation. Although Senator Jesse Helms of North Carolina called the act part of a conspiracy by "the radical elements of the homosexual movement," the Senate passed the law by a 92-4 vote, and the bill passed the House by a similar margin.

The federal law does not allow for any specific actions to be taken by the federal government, nor does it increase criminal penalties for any type of crime. Moreover, in order to win the sexual orientation provision of the law, the following text had to be included:

the American family life is the foundation of American society; federal policy should encourage the well-being, financial security, and health of the American family; and schools should not de-emphasize the critical value of American fam-

ily life. . . . Nothing in this Act shall be construed, nor shall any funds be appropriated to carry out the purpose of the Act be used, to promote or encourage homosexuality. . . . Nothing in this section creates a right to bring action, including an action based on discrimination due to sexual orientation.

Indeed, during the first few months after the Hate Crimes Statistics Act was enacted, the justice department refused to accept complaints of violence against gay men and lesbians on its Hate Crimes Hotline.

On October 6, 1999, President Clinton signed an executive order amending the U.S. military's criminal code to impose harsher penalties when bias against sexual orientation was involved in violent crime. The executive order also allowed for confidentiality for soldiers and officers who consulted privately with therapists, in an apparent effort to allow the victims of antigay crime to receive therapy without opening themselves to nonconfidential administrative proceedings that would dismiss them from the service on the basis of their homosexuality.

Federal hate crime laws protect only religion, race, and national origin and apply only if the victims were engaged in one of six specific protected activities; thus, gay men, lesbians, bisexuals, and transgender people are not offered hate crime protection. Although in June 2004 the U.S. Senate passed a hate crime bill that would have included crimes committed on the basis of sexual orientation, the House defeated the bill in October 2004—the second time in four years that House Republicans have come out against such legislation.

Twenty-four states and the District of Columbia offer extra penalties for crimes that include bias on the basis of sexual orientation (Arizona, California, Connecticut, Delaware, Florida, Illinois, Iowa, Kentucky, Louisiana, Maine, Massachusetts, Minnesota, Nebraska, Nevada, New Hampshire, New Jersey, New York, Oregon, Rhode Island, Tennessee, Vermont, Washington, and Wisconsin), while 20 states have hate crime laws that do not include sexual orientation (Alaska, Arizona, Colorado, Georgia, Idaho, Maryland, Michigan, Mississippi, Missouri, Montana, North Carolina, North Dakota, Ohio, Oklahoma, Pennsylvania, South Dakota, Texas, Utah, Virginia, and West Virginia), and seven states have no hate crime laws.

A number of questions have arisen as to the usefulness of hate crimes law to gay rights activism. The Gay and Lesbian Alliance Against Defamation (GLAAD), the Human Rights Campaign (HRC), the National Gay and Lesbian Task Force (NGLTF), and Parents, Families and Friends of Lesbians and Gays (PFLAG), along with many other religious, ethnic, feminist, and civil rights groups, have all supported the notion of hate crimes legislation. But many observers have questioned whether such laws will in fact reduce the amount of bias crime that actually takes place, or whether it will simply add to the current climate of fighting crime with harsher sentencing rather than education and organizing.

The National Coalition of Anti-Violence Programs (NCAVP) and its parent organization, the New York City Gay and Lesbian Anti-Violence Project, released a report on antigay violence in 2004. Although the groups urged governmental jurisdictions at all levels to add sexual orientation and gender identity/expression to existing anti–hate crime legislation, they also recommended community-based solutions: creating a climate of increased tolerance; funding programs to serve victims; supporting research into antigay and other hate-based violence; offering rehabilitation and alternatives to prison; funding local efforts to diminish violence; improving the training of police officers and other officials; and banning the "gay panic defense," in which someone who has attacked a gay person is allowed to claim that fear of being propositioned drove him or her to violence.

Some observers consider it ironic if not problematic that hate crime legislation relies so heavily upon police protection and FBI support, when officers from all levels have often been unsympathetic to gay people. The NCAVP released a statement in October 2003 excoriating the FBI for undercounting gay-related hate crimes in its annual Uniform Crime Report (mandated by the Hate Crimes Statistics Act). Although the FBI found only 1,244 victims targeted because of their actual or perceived sexual orientation, the NCAVP's 2002 report discovered 1,968 incidents in only 12 regions across the country, implying that the national total must be even higher.

NCAVP executive director Clarence Patton remarked that the FBI routinely undercounted antigay hate crimes because local agencies often were not required to report them—and so did not. Even in areas that were required to inform the FBI of such incidents, jurisdictions often failed to do so. In New York, for example, only 12 percent of all state agencies submitted data. "Though we'd love to believe that there were no hate crimes in 442 of 505 jurisdictions in New York State, experience unfortunately tells a different story," Patton commented.

Other opponents of hate crime laws—both inside and outside the gay rights movement—object to them on civil liberties grounds. They argue that violent actions should be punished but without extra penalties based on what the attacker might have thought. Nevertheless, many gay rights advocates continue to push for hate crime laws as a way to communicate to society that antigay violence is not acceptable.

Meanwhile, hate crimes like the one committed against 15-year-old Newark resident Sakia Gunn continue as a reminder that gay men, lesbians, bisexuals, and transgender people are not yet fully safe in the United States. In 2003, Gunn was killed while waiting for a bus with friends after allegedly refusing the advances of Richard McCullough. Charged in Gunn's murder, McCullough also became one of the first residents of New Jersey charged with a bias-related crime for his actions against the young lesbian. Gunn's death resulted in community-wide efforts to prevent future violence, including the founding of a chapter of PFLAG and the establishment of a scholarship in her name. The first scholarship recipient was the charter president of her school's Gay/Straight Alliance and a member of Students Against Violence Everywhere (SAVE).

IMMIGRATION

Immigration law for gay men and lesbians has been influenced by three legal situations: sodomy law, which until 2003 criminalized homosexual sex in many states, anticommunist hysteria of the 1940s and 1950s, which led to the passage of the McCarran-Walters Act of 1950, banning both communists and "sexual deviates" from entering the United States (in 1967, the Supreme Court ruled that this definition applied to lesbians and gay men); and lastly, gay relationships' lack of legal standing which means that foreign-born gay and lesbian partners of U.S. citizens cannot obtain visas and other immigration assistance as they could if they were legally married.

Congress's 1990 Immigration Act removed sexual orientation as a basis for denying citizenship. But U.S. Immigration and Naturalization Service (INS) regulations are still in place denying citizenship, visas, and any other permission for entry into the United States to anyone who is HIV positive under the division as reorganized into the U.S. Citizenship and Immigration Services (USCIS). Opponents of gay rights feel strongly that HIV-positive people should not be allowed into the United States, where they might spread the infection and place an increased burden on the public health system. Gay rights activists argue that such policies are discriminatory, particularly for binational couples in which the foreign partner is HIV positive.

Unlike heterosexual couples, gay couples cannot use their marital status as leverage to obtain green cards, permanent residence status, or other benefits for their partners. Again, the anti–gay rights movement feels strongly that gay people should be denied marital benefits, even as gay rights activists argue that gay partnerships should be recognized. The Permanent Partners Immigration Act (PPIA), developed in response to the Defense of Marriage Act (DOMA), would enable gay couples to claim the same immigration rights for their partners to which heterosexuals are currently entitled—that is, preferential treatment helping the foreign partner enter and remain in the United States. Although gay rights activists have said they will not introduce this act in a Republican-controlled Congress, they have received bipartisan support for the measure in both houses and are optimistic that it may one day pass.

Ironically, any state-level gay marriage, civil union, or other type of partnership arrangement works against foreign nationals who are trying to obtain U.S. residency. These arrangements make the foreign citizen's sexual preference visible to an immigration officer, who might respond negatively on that account. Also, if a foreign national is staying in the United States on a visa that indicates only "temporary intent" to remain in the country, a marriage-like arrangement—viewed as "permanent intent" to stay—could result in the denial of any permission to reside in the United States. According to the Human Rights Campaign, some 35,000 LGBT binational couples in the United States are currently facing these and other types of legal difficulties.

Another category of immigration is political asylum. According to the 1980 Refugee Act, permission to reside in the United States is granted to foreign nationals if return to their native country would endanger their lives, liberty, or safety. In 1993, the INS granted its first political asylum on the grounds of endangerment due to sexual orientation in the case of a gay Mexican citizen who claimed that returning to his native Mexico would jeopardize his life. Granting political asylum to LGBT people is rare—not least because a person must apply for asylum within one year of his or her entry into the United States, a requirement of which most foreign nationals are not aware. But the 1993 case has opened the door to other LGBT foreigners, as evidenced by the September 2004 case of Louise Reyes-Reyes. A preoperative transsexual from El Salvador who had dressed and acted as a woman for the past 16 years, Reyes was able to evade deportation when the Ninth Circuit Court of Appeals ruled in her favor. She claimed to have been kidnaped, raped, and beaten at the age of 13 by a group of men in San Salvador, leading her to flee to the United States at age 17. Her case has returned to immigration court, which may deport her on the grounds of having failed to apply for asylum within the required one-year period. But the fact that her deportation was stayed indicates a growing sympathy for cases like hers in at least some parts of the legal system.

In October 2004, Lambda Legal Defense and Education Fund filed suit with the ninth U.S. Circuit Court of Appeals in San Francisco in the case of Jorge Soto Vega, a gay man who sought asylum from his native Mexico after having been beaten and threatened by police. Soto filed for asylum in 2002, claiming that his sexuality put him at risk of injury or death. In January 2003, immigration judge John D. Taylor ruled against him, claiming that Soto Vega's deportation did not put the man at risk because he could not be readily identified by "the stereotypical things that society assigns to gays . . . it would not be obvious that he would be homosexual unless he made that obvious himself." Soto Vega's lawyer argued that such reasoning should not be part of an asylum decision, comparing the judge's ruling to the refusal of asylum to a European Jew on the grounds that he or she could have escaped the Nazis by passing as a Christian. As of this writing, the case is pending.

TRANSGENDER RIGHTS

Although a complete discussion of transgender rights is beyond the scope of this book, a brief summary of law relating to transgender people is included here. As the acronym "LGBT" implies, many gay rights activists consider transgender people part of their movement, even though some gay rights activists—and many transgender activists—do not. It is important to note that the category "transgender" includes people along the spectrum of medical intervention—from those who simply dress and live as a gender that does not match their biology, to those who take hormones or use other nonsurgical means to alter their bodies, through those who rely on surgery to transform their primary and secondary sex characteristics. Sexual preferences of transgender people vary as well, with transgender people making both same-sex and opposite-sex choices for their new gender.

The Human Rights Campaign found that as of December 31, 2003, some 79 private employers, colleges, and universities include the terms *gender identity* and/or *gender expression* in their written nondiscrimination policies, including 26 Fortune 500 companies—up from three in 2000 and 15 in 2002. Although no federal law bans employment discrimination for transgender people, several states and the District of Columbia do have laws on the matter. In Kentucky and Pennsylvania, executive orders have banned transgender discrimination in the public sector. In Maine, Minnesota, Rhode Island, New Mexico, and California, both public and private transgender discrimination are prohibited by law. And in Connecticut, Florida, Illinois, Hawaii, Massachusetts, New Jersey, and New York, state court, commission, or agency rulings have interpreted existing state law to include at least some protection against discrimination for transgender employees. Also by the end of 2003, some 61 cities and counties had banned transgender discrimination in the workplace.

U.S. court cases on transgender issues have mainly focused on the rights of transgender people to change their name and sex on their birth certificate. In 1976, a New Jersey case was the first U.S. decision to assert the right of post-operative transsexuals to marry in their new sex. However, marital rights of transgender people remain a highly contested issue, as expressed in a 2000 Texas case—allowed to stand by the U.S. Supreme Court—in which the court declined to hear a transsexual's claim about her husband's wrongful death, on the grounds that the transsexual was not really a woman and therefore could not legally have married a man. Likewise, in the case known as *In the matter of the estate of Marshall G. Gardiner*, a 2002 ruling by the supreme court of Kansas found that J'Noel Gardiner, a male-to-female transsexual, could not legally inherit half the estate of late husband, Marshall Gardiner. The Kansas high court overturned an appeals court ruling that had recognized J'Noel's marital status, saying that the crucial issue was J'Noel's gender at the time of her marriage. But the state supreme court found instead that J'Noel was "really" a man and so could not legally marry Marshall. The case resulted from a suit brought by Marshall's son, Joe, who challenged the legality of his father's marriage after discovering J'Noel's sex change.

A landmark ruling for transgender rights came in February 2003, when a Florida state judge awarded custody of two children to Michael Kantaras, a female-to-male transsexual who had married his wife, Linda, in 1989. Kantaras had had a sex-change operation in 1987, a fact of which his wife was aware when they married. He went on to adopt his wife's infant son from a previous marriage. When his wife conceived a child through artificial insemination, Kantaras, as the legally married husband of the mother, was automatically granted legal paternity. But when the couple began a bitter divorce proceeding in 1998, Linda Kantaras claimed that their marriage—and thus her ex-husband's rights—were invalid because he was, legally, a woman, and same-sex marriage is illegal in Florida.

Prior to the dispute, an independent custody evaluator had ruled that Michael Kantaras was the better parent. Linda Kantaras challenged the ruling and, a year later, Judge Gerard O'Brien awarded Michael Kantaras custody of the two children, affirming that he was the legal parent of both children. Legal observers believe that the ruling could provide nonbiological parents and step-parents grounds to seek visitation or custody.

INTRODUCTION TO MAJOR COURT CASES

The rest of this chapter summarizes the landmark court cases in the field of gay rights that currently have the most relevance for the legal battles likely to occur over the next several decades. Key federal and state cases in the area of sodomy law, legal protection, federal employment, free speech and assembly, family recognition, housing rights, and transgender rights are summarized, and their impact on the gay rights movement is explained.

Although each of the cases profiled remains extremely important for both pro– and anti–gay rights activists, it is important to note that none of these cases stands as the last word on any issue. *Bowers v. Hardwick*, for example, the 1986 U.S. Supreme Court ruling that upheld Georgia's sodomy law, would seem to have established the principle that the highest court in the land looked kindly on state laws prohibiting certain types of sexual activity. Yet several states—including Georgia—went on to overturn their own sodomy laws, either via legislative action or through court decisions, and the Supreme Court itself overturned *Bowers* in 2003 with its ruling in *Lawrence v. Texas*. Likewise, in *Braschi v. Stahl Associates Co.*, the New York Supreme Court found that a long-standing domestic partnership of two men constituted a de facto family that ought to receive the same recognition in housing matters as a legally married heterosexual couple. Yet the same court later ruled against a lesbian who sued her former partner for visitation rights to a child the two had long cared for together, seeming to contradict its earlier recognition of lesbian and gay families. Students of the legal side of gay rights, then, must know about relevant court decisions but should not mistake them for absolute guides to future trends in either legislative or legal arenas.

SUPREME COURT CASES

BOWERS V. HARDWICK (1986)

Background

Michael Hardwick, a 29-year-old man, had been issued a summons for drinking a can of beer from a paper bag outside the Atlanta gay bar where he worked. Since he had not yet paid his fine for "public drunkenness," a police officer went to his home to serve him a warrant. A houseguest answered the door and allowed the officer in to see whether Hardwick was home. The officer found Hardwick's bedroom, opened the door, and saw Hardwick and another man having oral sex on the bed. "What are you doing in my bedroom?" asked Hardwick when he saw the officer, who eventually arrested Hardwick under an 1816 statute prohibiting oral and anal sex by either homosexuals or heterosexuals, punishable by one to 20 years in prison.

The Law of Gay Rights

Legal Issues

If it had been up to the state of Georgia, Michael Hardwick would only have spent one night in jail, for the prosecutor declined to press charges after that. But Hardwick decided to challenge the law by bringing suit against state attorney general Michael J. Bowers. Hardwick and his supporters hoped to bring into question the entire notion of sodomy laws. Hardwick and his partner were both consenting adults having sex in the privacy of their bedroom. The law under which they were convicted would have applied equally to a married heterosexual couple and suggested a degree of invaded privacy that gay rights activists believed would horrify the American public.

Indeed, the U.S. Court of Appeals for the Eleventh Circuit upheld Hardwick's position with enthusiasm, "The activity [Hardwick] hopes to engage in is quintessentially private and lies at the heart of an intimate association beyond the proper reach of state regulation," ruled the lower court. If the state wanted to regulate such private activity, it would have to prove a "compelling interest" to do so, an interest that Hardwick and his lawyer, Harvard law professor Laurence Tribe, believed did not exist.

The Georgia state attorneys saw it differently. For them, what was at stake was the legality of homosexuality itself. As Bowers wrote in his brief:

> In Georgia it is the very act of homosexual sodomy that epitomizes moral delinquency. . . . [Homosexuality] leads to other deviate practices, such as sadomasochism, group orgies, or transvestitism, to name only a few. . . . [Homosexual sodomy is often committed in] parks, rest rooms, "gay baths," and "gay bars," and is marked by the multiplicity and anonymity of sexual partners, a disproportionate involvement with adolescents and indeed, a possible relationship to crimes of violence. Similarly, the legislature should be permitted to draw conclusions concerning the relationship of homosexual sodomy in the transmission of AIDS. But perhaps the most profound legislative finding that can be made is that homosexual sodomy is the anathema of the basic units of our society—marriage and the family. To decriminalize or artificially withdraw the public's expression of its disdain for this conduct does not uplift sodomy, but rather demotes those sacred institutions to merely other alternative lifestyles.

Decision

On June 30, 1986, the Supreme Court handed down its ruling, upholding the sodomy law. The law actually referred only to, "any sexual act involving the sex organs of one person and the mouth or anus of another." But the justices ignored the heterosexual implications of that language and noted particularly that gay men and lesbians had no right to engage in *homosexual* sodomy.

"The issue presented is whether the Federal Constitution confers a fundamental right upon homosexuals to engage in sodomy and hence invalidates the laws of the many states that still make such conduct illegal and have done so for a very long time," wrote Justice Byron R. White in the majority opinion.

Gay Rights

Michael Hardwick was asking the Court to establish "a fundamental right to engage in homosexual sodomy. This we are quite unwilling to do." As for the argument that the privacy of one's home should offer some protection, White wrote, that would be like saying that it would be permissible to harbor stolen goods or narcotics at home.

The Court's dissenting opinion, written by Justice Harry A. Blackmun, was more supportive of gay rights: "I can only hope," Blackmun wrote, "that the court will reconsider its analysis and conclude that depriving individuals of the right to choose for themselves how to conduct their intimate relationships poses a far greater threat to the values most deeply rooted in our nation's history than the tolerance of nonconformity could ever do."

Impact

Both gay rights activists and those who opposed gay rights noted the significance of the date that *Hardwick* was handed down: the day after the 17th anniversary of the Stonewall uprising. Yet "[i]t was not the ruling itself that angered [gay legal activists] so much," wrote Dave Walter in the August 5, 1986, issue of the *Advocate*, a gay paper. "[R]ather, it was the blatantly homophobic opinion that accompanied the decision."

To gay rights activists, singling out gay sex was bad enough. The justices in the majority had gone further, comparing gay sex to "adultery, incest, and other sexual crimes," and citing the biblical roots of social prohibitions against same-sex practices.

There was another important legal implication to the ruling. Previously, U.S. law had referred only to particular acts. But in the *Hardwick* case, "homosexuals" were defined as people who performed certain acts. Gay men and lesbians had become a criminal class under a decision that supported the right of heterosexuals to perform the very same acts.

The decision provoked immediate protest. Thousands of gay men and lesbians in New York City took to the streets in two demonstrations that were the biggest in New York since the 1970s: One thousand men and women sat in at Sheridan Square in Greenwich Village, stopping traffic at several intersections. And a protest march disrupted the July Fourth "Liberty Weekend" at the Statue of Liberty that was being attended by President Ronald Reagan and Chief Justice Warren Burger. The news also sparked protests in Washington, D.C., San Francisco, Cincinnati, and Dallas.

But, perhaps ironically, *Hardwick* turned out to have little actual impact on U.S. sodomy laws. Although the door seemed wide open to do so, no state ever reinstated a sodomy law in response to the decision, and several other states and the District of Columbia later took their sodomy laws off the books: Nevada (1993), District of Columbia (1995), Rhode Island (1998), and Arizona (2001). Moreover, courts in Kentucky (1993), Tennessee (1996), Montana (1997), Maryland (1999), Georgia (1998), and Minnesota (2001) overturned their sodomy laws.

Indeed, a Gallup poll conducted on July 1 and 2, 1986, for *Newsweek* found that Americans disapproved of the Supreme Court decision by 47 percent to 41 percent and opposed by 57 percent to 34 percent the decision's logical conclusion: that "states should have the right to prohibit sexual practices conducted in private between consenting homosexual adults." (The poll was conducted by telephone with 611 adults, with a 5 percent margin of error.)

In any event, *Bowers*'s life as a Supreme Court decision was brief. In 2003, the Supreme Court overturned its previous finding with its ruling in *Lawrence v. Texas*, which struck down sodomy laws of all types—both those that outlawed the practice generally and those that banned it only between same-sex partners. (For more on *Lawrence v. Texas*, see below.) It is extremely unusual for a Supreme Court to invalidate an earlier decision, particularly after such a relatively short period of time, indicating perhaps that *Bowers*'s primary impact was ultimately to illuminate the contradiction between sodomy laws and the generally permissive and egalitarian direction of U.S. society.

HURLEY V. IRISH-AMERICAN GAY GROUP OF BOSTON (1995)

Background

The city of Boston had celebrated St. Patrick's Day on March 17 for more than two centuries. Over the years, a parade through the streets of Boston had become an important component of the celebration, which was sponsored by the city until 1947. In that year, however, Mayor James Michael Curley granted authority to organize and conduct the parade to the South Boston Allied War Veterans Council, a volunteer group of people elected from various South Boston veterans groups. (South Boston was a predominantly Irish-American neighborhood with a strong sense of Irish heritage.) Ever since 1947, the council had been granted the permit and organized the parade.

In 1992, a group of gay, lesbian, and bisexual Irish Americans, along with other supporters, formed a group known as GLIB (referred to in the Supreme Court decision both by those initials and as "Irish-American Gay Group of Boston"). GLIB applied to the council for permission to march in the parade behind a banner reading "Irish-American Gay, Lesbian and Bisexual Group of Boston." The council denied GLIB permission to join the parade, so GLIB got a court order allowing it to march, which it did, apparently without incident.

In 1993, GLIB applied again for a permit, and again was turned down. In response, GLIB filed a suit against the council and its leader, John J. "Wacko" Hurley, as well as the City of Boston. GLIB charged that to deny the group a permit was to violate the state and federal constitutions, as well as the state's public accommodations law, which outlawed discrimination on the basis of sexual orientation in a public place.

The state trial court took GLIB's side. Refusing to let the group march in the parade was discrimination, the court ruled, and it ordered the council to allow the group to march "on the same terms and conditions as other participants." The council appealed the issue to the Massachusetts Supreme Judicial Court, which agreed that not letting GLIB march constituted discrimination. The council then took the matter to the U.S. Supreme Court.

Legal Issues

Each side in *Hurley* sought to frame the legal issues differently. According to GLIB, this was a matter of discrimination in a public place. Since the parade was a public event taking place on the streets of Boston, it fell under the same category as, say, a restaurant or theater. Just as the state's antidiscrimination law prohibited a restaurant from refusing service to gay, lesbian, or bisexual customers simply because of their sexual orientation, so did that law prevent the South Boston Allied War Veterans Council from keeping GLIB out of the parade.

Hurley and the council claimed that the issue was not one of discrimination, but rather free speech as guaranteed under the First Amendment. Just as the First Amendment guarantees each citizen's right to speak, so it guarantees his or her right *not* to speak. By forcing the council to include a gay rights group in the parade, the state courts were abridging the council's right to control its own message. And if Massachusetts's antidiscrimination law could be used to abridge the council's free speech, then that law was unconstitutionally vague.

In support of its argument, the council pointed out that GLIB was not the only group that had been denied a permit to march. The council had previously excluded the Ku Klux Klan (a group that explicitly promoted white superiority) and ROAR (a group that opposed busing African-American students to predominantly white schools—a major issue in South Boston for many years). Presumably, permission was refused because the council did not like the groups' messages and did not want to associate them with an expression of Irish-American pride. If the council could forbid participation to these groups, why could it not exclude groups "with sexual themes" at odds with the parade's "traditional religious and social values"?

The state courts were not persuaded by these arguments. They felt that the state's antidiscrimination law mandated the inclusion of any group that wished to join the parade, particularly since "a proper celebration of St. Patrick's . . . Day requires diversity and inclusiveness." The First Amendment did not apply, according to the Massachusetts Supreme Judicial Court, since the parade was not focused "on a specific message, theme, or group." In other words, if the parade had promoted one particular idea, the council could have refused entry to groups with opposing ideas. But in fact, the council had let virtually any group join the parade, exercising no editorial control over the many different kinds of banners that the marchers brought. The parade was therefore not an exercise of free speech but rather a public recreational event. And to refuse accommodation to GLIB and its banner was not an exercise of free speech but simple discrimination.

Notably, supreme judicial court justice Joseph R. Nolan dissented. Nolan argued that the parade did not need "a narrow or distinct theme or message . . . to be protected under the First Amendment." Moreover, he wrote, the parade was not simply a recreational event, but rather an expression of particular views being held by the council. There had been overwhelming evidence that the council had not sought to ban gay men, lesbians, and bisexuals *per se*. It had only refused to let them carry a banner proclaiming a message with which the council did not agree.

Decision

The Supreme Court ruled unanimously in favor of Hurley and the council. Parades, according to the Supreme Court, were not public recreational events. Rather, they were expressions of particular points of view, and as such, they were entitled to First Amendment protection.

The Court acknowledged that the "point of view" expressed by the St. Patrick's Day parade could not be boiled down into a single message. The council, wrote Justice David Souter for the Court, was like a composer selecting many different themes to make up a complicated presentation. But just because the message was complicated did not mean it was not protected. The First Amendment gave the council the right to exclude any theme from its parade, just as it protected an artist or any other speaker from being required to express a message with which the speaker did not agree.

Souter granted that the council had not been particularly selective about most of the other messages in the parade. Nevertheless, it still had the right to be selective whenever it wished to do so. He also agreed that neither the message of the parade itself nor GLIB's message was "wholly articulate"—that is, they were not directly stated. Nevertheless, Souter wrote, a contingent marching behind GLIB's banner

> *would at least bear witness to the fact that some Irish are gay, lesbian, or bisexual, and the presence of the organized marchers would suggest their view that people of their sexual orientations have as much claim to unqualified social acceptance as heterosexuals.*

If the people organizing the parade did not believe "these facts about Irish sexuality," or if they objected to "unqualified social acceptance of gays and lesbians," or if they had any other reason whatsoever to object to GLIB's message, they had the right under the First Amendment to refuse to allow GLIB to march. Government, in the form of courts or legislation, could not force the council to make a statement against its will.

At the same time, the Court ruled that Massachusetts's antidiscrimination law was constitutional. It simply did not apply to the question of which banners should be included in a parade.

Impact

The conditions that gave rise to the original suit in *Hurley* are still in force: As of this writing, gay men, lesbians, and bisexuals cannot march in either the Boston or the New York City St. Patrick's Day parade under a banner proclaiming their

111

sexuality. *Hurley* speaks to the cultural divide that often characterizes gay rights issues: progress for gay rights activists on some fronts; setbacks for them on others. In addition, many gay rights activists do not agree with the strategy of using the courts to force organizations or events to include them, fearing that even pro-gay rulings might establish legal precedents that could be used against gay groups or events.

Hurley was also the major precedent cited in *Boy Scouts v. Dale* (2000, see below), in which the Court would rule that the Boy Scouts of America (BSA) had the right to exclude an openly gay man, on the grounds that his mere presence in the organization constituted a message that the BSA had the right not to express. The principle in both cases was the same: simply by making their identities public, gay men, lesbians, and other sexual minorities were conveying a message with which an organization might disagree—a disagreement that could be legally expressed by excluding openly gay people from participating in the organization. This principle has been invoked by religious organizations seeking to ban openly gay men and lesbians from employment, on the grounds that employing, say, gay and lesbian counselors in a social service agency "sends a message" to clients that contradicts the group's religious beliefs. Although *Hurley* is not necessarily cited in such cases, the decision has become part of the legal and political climate.

The controversy over a group's right to ban gay men and lesbians from jobs for which they are otherwise qualified is particularly intense when religious groups receive government funding to provide social services. This trend increased under President George W. Bush's push for faith-based initiatives—and so has the incidence of gay men and lesbians being fired not because of anything they have said or done, but simply because of who they are. (For more on this issues, see *Pedreira v. Baptist Children's Homes of Kentucky*, below.) If the trend to privatize social services continues, and if these services continue to be provided by religious groups who consider homosexuality immoral, *Hurley* might be used to trump other antidiscrimination laws. If a religious school receives federal money through a voucher program, for example, could it fire or refuse to hire a teacher for being openly gay, on the grounds that the teacher's very identity violates the school's religious principles? Could it fire or refuse to hire a teacher for having another faith, or for openly holding other ideas that the church does not condone?

Hurley raises the question of whether gay identity itself is a form of speech, one that can legitimately be curtailed under certain circumstances. The only statement made by the GLIB banner at issue in the case was that Irish gay men, lesbians, and bisexuals existed, and—implicit in their presence in the parade—that they sought the "unqualified social acceptance" that Souter had cited in his opinion. They made no other statement about politics or the Irish community. Under what circumstances does antidiscrimination law protect groups who seek such acceptance, and under what circumstances does the law consider that gay people's mere public presence constitutes speech that another group has the right to curtail? While *Hurley* does not give a definitive answer to this question, it certainly raises the issue.

The Law of Gay Rights

ROMER V. EVANS (1996)

Background

The story of *Romer v. Evans* begins in Colorado in 1992. The right-wing backlash that had swept the nation throughout the late 1970s and 1980s made itself felt in statewide referendums in Oregon and Colorado. Each vote would have overturned all local gay rights legislation in their respective states while prohibiting the further passage of antidiscrimination laws.

The Oregon measure, known as Proposition 9, called gay people "abnormal" and "perverse." It was defeated 57 percent to 43 percent. The following year, however, antigay activists took the fight to a local level and passed more than a dozen antigay initiatives in cities, towns, and counties.

Meanwhile, in Colorado, the antigay Amendment 2 passed 53 percent to 47 percent. The measure, which nullified existing gay rights laws in Denver, Boulder, and Aspen, provided that

> *Neither the State of Colorado . . . nor any of its agencies, political subdivisions, municipalities, or school districts, shall enact, adopt, or enforce any statute, regulation, ordinance or policy whereby homosexual, lesbian or bisexual orientation, conduct, practices or relationships shall constitute or otherwise be the basis of, or entitle any person or class or persons to have or claim any minority status, quota preferences, protected status or claim of discrimination. . . .*

After Colorado voters approved the referendum, a coalition of gay rights activists sued the state in 1996 in an effort to block the referendum from taking effect. The title of the case *(Romer v. Evans)* is actually misleading. Richard G. Evans, a civil servant in the Denver mayor's office, was a member of the gay rights coalition. Colorado governor Richard Romer was named as the defendant in the case as he was the chief executive of the state even though he personally opposed the referendum. After the initial court case ruled to overturn the referendum, the state appealed the case to the Supreme Court, thus making Romer the plaintiff in the Supreme Court case by name only.

Legal Issues

Were gay people a privileged group using the law to win special rights, or were they a persecuted minority that had the right to seek necessary protection under the law? Right-wing organizations took the former position, which led them to sponsor Colorado's Amendment 2 as well as Oregon's Proposition 9. Under the Colorado amendment, gay men, lesbians, and bisexuals were a priori prevented from claiming discrimination or seeking protection under the law.

Gay rights groups took the second position—and objected strongly to a law that prevented them from seeking legal protection anywhere in the state of

Colorado. NGLTF family policy director Paula Ettelbrick called the law "particularly vicious."

Decision

The U.S. Supreme Court struck Amendment 2 down. In his majority opinion, Justice Anthony M. Kennedy wrote a ringing denunciation of the amendment:

> *Amendment 2 classifies homosexuals not to further a proper legislative end but to make them unequal to everyone else. This Colorado cannot do. A state cannot so deem a class of person a stranger to its laws.*

In other words, the Court found that no state can simply rule against a group of people, denying them equal protection under the law. If *anyone* was allowed to seek legislative protection against discrimination under Colorado state law, gay men, lesbians, and bisexuals ought to be able to do so as well. For the first time, the highest court in the land had explicitly ruled that gay men and lesbians were entitled to the right of "equal protection under the law," which is guaranteed under the Fourteenth Amendment to the Constitution.

Justices Antonin Scalia, Clarence Thomas, and William Rehnquist dissented, in a minority opinion written by Scalia. First, Scalia took issue with the majority's opinion that "homosexuals" were a politically unpopular group that required the Court's protection. He found that notion "nothing short of preposterous" given their "enormous influence in American politics" and the fact that they composed "no more than 4% of the population [yet] had the support of 46% of the voters on Amendment 2."

Scalia also berated the Court for "tak[ing] sides in the culture wars":

> *When the Court takes sides in the culture wars, it tends to . . . [reflect] the views and values of the lawyer class from which the Court's Members are drawn. How that class feels about homosexuality will be evident to anyone who wishes to interview applicants at virtually any of the Nation's law schools. The interviewer may refuse to offer a job because the applicant is a Republican; because he [sic] is an adulterer; because he went to the wrong prep school or belongs to the wrong country club; because he eats snails; because he is a womanizer; because she wears real-animal fur; or even because he hates the Chicago Cubs. But if the interviewer should wish not to be an associate or partner of an applicant because he disapproves of the applicant's homosexuality; then he will have violated the pledge which the Association of American Law Schools requires all its member-schools to exact from job interviewers: "assurance of the employer's willingness" to hire homosexuals.*

In other words, Scalia did see "homosexuals" as a protected class with special rights—rights presumably not available to people who ate snails, wore real fur, had gone to the wrong prep school, or belonged to the Republican Party. He and his fellow signers of the minority opinion partook of the conservative view that sees gay rights not as "leveling the playing field" but rather as giving special protection to people who do not really need it.

Impact

Despite the minority opinion, most observers saw *Romer v. Evans* as a victory for the gay rights movement, although it is only in retrospect that the full impact of *Romer* has become clear. Although *Romer* extended the Constitution's equal protection to people targeted on hostile grounds, activists in the late 1990s and early 21st century pointed out that it did not necessarily wipe out long-standing refusals of state and federal governments to recognize gay and lesbian rights, particularly in the areas of marriage, child custody, and civil participation in such organizations as the Boy Scouts. Nor did it necessarily prevent future anti–gay rights legislation from passing. Perhaps most importantly, activists said, the case did not necessarily have an impact upon the growing power of antigay religious and political organizations or upon the widely held perception among some segments of society that homosexuality was "evil" or "a sickness."

Yet when the Supreme Court decided *Lawrence v. Texas* in 2003, striking down all sodomy laws and specifically overturning its own 1986 decision of *Bowers v. Hardwick*, it was *Romer* that the majority cited as justification. (For more on *Bowers*, see above. For more on *Lawrence*, see below.) *Romer*'s ringing denunciation of any laws specifically designed to discriminate against homosexuals seemed to imply the unconstitutionality of sodomy laws, which historically had been used to criminalize both homosexual behavior and homosexual identities. Using *Romer* as a foundation for *Lawrence*, the Court went on to insist upon the full citizenship of gay men and lesbians—a decision that has in turn opened the door for gay activists' claims to legal recognition of same-sex marriage.

BOARD OF REGENTS OF THE UNIVERSITY OF WISCONSIN SYSTEM V. SOUTHWORTH ET AL. (2000)

Background

In 1995, law student Scott Southworth was attending the University of Wisconsin at Madison, where student activity fees—levied in addition to tuition, room, and board—then totaled $331.50. Most of the fees went to such student facilities as the student union, a health clinic, and a day-care center. Less than one-third of each student's fee went to support a wide variety of campus organizations that were supposed to enrich the quality of student life by providing diverse activities and opportunities for students to express themselves.

With the help of his attorney, Southworth wrote a letter to the Board of Regents, the state organization that supervises the university system. Southworth, who described himself as "a conservative Christian," considered many of the organizations to be "violently partisan, anti-Christian hate groups," and he asked if he could "opt out" of some of the fees, particularly fees earmarked for the

Gay Rights

Lesbian, Gay, Bisexual and Transgender Center. For one semester, Southworth calculated, he was entitled to a refund of $7.99.

The board did not agree, responding that Southworth either paid the full activity fee or left the university. So Southworth brought suit in federal district court with the aid of the Alliance Defense Fund, a conservative legal group whose mission is to "de-fund the Left." He was joined in his suit by five other students, all of whom claimed that being forced to support groups offensive to their own personal beliefs was a violation of their First Amendment rights of free speech and association. As the case was discussed in the media, observers noted that socialist, feminist, and gay rights groups were among those supported by student activity fees.

Legal Issues

District court judge John Shabaz, a former Republican leader in the Wisconsin State Assembly, agreed with Southworth and his co-plaintiffs, finding that the fee program forced students "to support political and ideological activity with which they disagree"—a clear violation of First Amendment rights. The district court relied on such precedents as a 1977 Supreme Court ruling that teachers could not be forced to pay for the lobbying and political activities of their union and a 1990 Supreme Court decision that lawyers belonging to the California Bar Association could not be forced to pay for the lobbying activities of that group.

The University of Wisconsin appealed the decision, but the appeals court reaffirmed most of the district court's findings. Although the courts disagreed to some extent on the exact legal arguments to be used and on some aspects of how the university's student fees were distributed, the appeals court basically held that the current program violated students' First Amendment rights. Just as all citizens are guaranteed the right to speak freely and to associate with any group they choose, the appeals court ruled, so must all citizens be free *not* to say certain things or to associate with groups with whom they disagree.

Decision

The Supreme Court overturned the previous decisions, finding unanimously that the fee program was potentially constitutional. All nine justices agreed that the university had every right to charge student activity fees and to disburse them to a wide variety of groups, including organizations that some students might find objectionable.

Then the justices' opinions diverged. Six justices signed on to the majority opinion written by Justice Anthony M. Kennedy, which raised questions about how the university chose which groups were to receive funds.

First, though, Kennedy stressed that charging a fee over which students had no direct control was not in itself a violation of First Amendment rights. The fee, he wrote, was charged simply to allow "the free and open exchange of ideas by, and among, [university] students." By definition, such an exchange might include speech that some students found objectionable, creating the grounds for possible First Amendment violations. The solution, however, was not to allow each student to decide which university-funded organizations he or she was willing to support. Rather, the university must be allowed to fund student activities while maintaining "viewpoint neutrality." The university needed a fair and balanced way to decide which student groups received the money, and it might also be required to ensure that a broad spectrum of different views were funded by the activity fee. If the university met those requirements, students' First Amendment rights had been protected.

Consequently, Kennedy sent the case back to the appeals court to make sure that a "viewpoint-neutral" procedure was being used to allocate funds, while affirming the university's right to continue the student activities program.

Justice David H. Souter wrote a concurring opinion, joined by Justices John Paul Stevens and Stephen Breyer, affirming the university's program but taking issue with the notion that "viewpoint neutrality" had to be further determined. In the minority's view, the university had already established its viewpoint neutrality; the only question remaining was whether Southworth and his co-plaintiffs' rights had been violated. Souter and his colleagues believed they had not.

Souter specifically cited *Hurley v. Irish-American Gay, Lesbian and Bisexual Group of Boston* (1995, see above) as an example of a situation in which the government had inappropriately forced someone to express opinions. When the state court ordered the South Boston Allied Veterans Council to include an Irish gay rights group in its St. Patrick's Day parade, it was violating the council's rights by compelling it to certain types of speech and association with which it did not agree. The situation at the University of Wisconsin was entirely different, however. In the free and open exchange of ideas that characterized a university, it was inevitable that students would subsidize some ideas with which they did not agree. Certainly some student groups would express views that other students found offensive, just as some college courses would include speech to which some students objected. Yet students were not free to "opt out" of tuition payments nor were universities required "to offer a spectrum of courses to satisfy a viewpoint neutrality requirement." In exactly the same way, Souter wrote, the University of Wisconsin had the right to charge an activity fee without guaranteeing a broad spectrum of student groups.

Impact

When lower courts ruled in favor of Southworth and his co-plaintiffs, gay rights activists and others viewed the decision with alarm. They considered it part of a trend in which conservatives and the Religious Right would continue to silence gay voices. Many gay rights activists feared that the events in Wisconsin would open the door for similar actions around the country, in which right-wing and conservative students—often backed by well-funded legal institutes—would attempt to eliminate gay rights activity on campus. Since the University of Wisconsin's Madison campus is known as one of the most liberal, activist, gay-friendly campuses in the nation, threats to the existence of gay rights groups there had seemed particularly dangerous to gay rights leaders. By the same token, conservatives hailed the lower court decisions as helping to erode what they viewed as liberal and/or left-wing dominance of colleges and universities.

Then, in 2000, the Supreme Court declared its unanimous support for the university's program, which seemed to offer support for gay rights groups and their presence on campus. At the same time, though, the Supreme Court remanded the program itself to the lower courts for review, allowing district court judge Shabaz to rule a second time that the university's fees were unconstitutional, this time because they had not been distributed according to the Supreme Court's standard of "viewpoint neutrality." Once again, it seemed as though conservative and religious efforts had been successful in discouraging an active gay presence on a liberal campus.

But in 2002, the appeals court overturned Shabaz's decision to find for the university, which had adjusted some of its funding guidelines since the case had been brought. The university, student leaders, and gay rights activists all considered the appeals court decision a major victory. Gay rights leaders in particular hailed the decision, which seemed to put to rest fears that gay student groups could be defunded or thrown off campuses.

However, some gay rights activists were concerned about what they saw as the continuing use of the First Amendment as a cover for attacking gay rights. As the organizers of the St. Patrick's Day parade had done in *Hurley* and as the Boy Scouts of America would do in *Boy Scouts of America v. Dale* (2000, see below), Southworth and his fellow conservatives had cited the First Amendment as supporting their right to disassociate themselves from gay men and lesbians. A number of religious organizations, including social service agencies receiving government funds under a variety of auspices, likewise used the First Amendment to justify firing or refusing to hire gay men and lesbians for positions for which they were otherwise qualified. Moreover, churches have often sought exemptions to laws banning discrimination on the basis of sexual orientation, claiming that First Amendment guarantees of freedom of religion include the right to refuse employment to gay men and lesbians on religious grounds.

As of this writing, *Southworth*-style challenges to on-campus gay rights organizations appear to have died down, and the clear precedent set in *Southworth* would certainly seem to have a discouraging effect on future such actions. The use of the First Amendment to object to gay rights, however, seems to be a legal strategy that conservatives and religious groups will continue to employ.

BOY SCOUTS OF AMERICA ET AL. V. DALE (2000)

Background

In 1978, eight-year-old James Dale joined a New Jersey Cub Scout pack and began his rise through the ranks of Scouting to reach one of its highest honors, the rank of Eagle Scout, which he achieved in 1988. As the Supreme Court decision notes, "By all accounts, Dale was an exemplary Scout."

The Law of Gay Rights

In 1989, Dale became an adult member of the Boy Scouts of America and was made assistant scoutmaster of a troop. He also went off to attend Rutgers University, where he came out as a gay man and became copresident of the Rutgers University Lesbian/Gay Alliance. In 1990, he spoke at a seminar about psychological and health issues for gay and lesbian teenagers, where he was interviewed by a local newspaper. When the paper published the interview and Dale's photograph, identifying his presidency of the Lesbian/Gay Alliance, he was stripped of his membership in the Scouts and his position as assistant Scoutmaster on the grounds that the Boy Scouts "specifically forbid membership to homosexuals."

In 1992, Dale filed a complaint in New Jersey Superior Court, citing the same type of public accommodations statute that GLIB, the Irish gay, lesbian, and bisexual group of Boston, had filed in *Hurley v. Irish-American Gay Group of Boston* (see above).

Legal Issues

Like Massachusetts, New Jersey has a state law that prohibits discrimination in public places on the basis of sexual orientation. Dale was in effect arguing that the Boy Scouts's decision was the equivalent of a restaurant or a theater forbidding him entrance simply because he was gay. New Jersey law forbids that type of discrimination, and Dale charged that the Boy Scouts had violated that law.

New Jersey Superior Court held that the public accommodations law did not apply. The Boy Scouts were far from being a public place; rather, they were a private group that under the First Amendment had the right to associate with whom they pleased and to express whatever messages they wished. The court found that the Boy Scouts had made their opposition to homosexuality very clear, and that the government had no business forcing them to make a statement that implicitly contradicted that position.

The appellate division did not agree. It ruled that the public accommodations law did indeed apply to the Boy Scouts. Although the Boy Scouts were arguing that the First Amendment protected their right to refuse Dale's membership, the appellate court found that the Scouts were simply discriminating against Dale on the basis of his sexual orientation, a type of discrimination that violated the law.

The New Jersey Supreme Court likewise held that the Boy Scouts were a place of public accommodation. True, private clubs are allowed to exclude members, on the grounds that people have a right to "intimate association" (to make personal choices about the people with whom they want to associate). But the Boy Scouts were a large enough group to accommodate a wide range of people. They were not sufficiently "personal or private" for protections of intimate association to apply.

Moreover, the state supreme court said that while the Boy Scouts did have a general belief in moral values, Dale's membership in the group would not "affect in any significant way [the Boy Scouts'] existing members' ability to carry out their various purposes." In other words, if the Boy Scouts had a specific goal of opposing homosexuality, then obviously it would be contrary to their First Amendment rights to force them to include someone whose membership made it harder for them to work toward that goal. But the Boy Scouts had only general goals concerning morality, and there was no reason to believe that Dale's membership would interfere with their pursuit.

In matters of law, the term *compelling interest* is often used. The phrase indicates that there is a very strong reason to permit the government to do something that otherwise would not be allowed. The Boy Scouts were arguing that New Jersey's antidiscrimination law was unconstitutional because it limited people's free speech. But that limitation, the court said, was justified by the state's compelling interest in eliminating "the destructive consequences of discrimination from our society."

Finally, the court addressed the Boy Scouts' use of *Hurley*, which they had cited in support of their First Amendment right to exclude Dale. The *Hurley* decision had held that the organizers of Boston's St. Patrick's Day parade were not legally obligated to include a group of gay men, lesbians, and bisexuals marching under a banner announcing their presence if the organizers felt that by including this group, they were being forced to send a message with which they did not agree. However, the state supreme court said that simply reinstating Dale back into the Boy Scouts "does not compel the Boy Scouts to express any message." The Boy Scouts' free speech was not in danger here. Dale's right to belong to a public organization without being discriminated against was the main issue.

Decision

When this case was taken to the Supreme Court, the Court ruled 5-4 in favor of the Boy Scouts. Chief Justice William Rehnquist wrote the majority opinion, joined by Justices Sandra Day O'Connor, Antonin Scalia, Anthony M. Kennedy, and Clarence Thomas.

The question, Rehnquist wrote, was what kind of message the Scouts wanted to send, and whether including Dale in the group interfered with their ability to send that message. If including Dale did not interfere with the Scouts sending their message, then under the antidiscrimination law, the Scouts had no right to exclude him. If, however, Dale's presence in the group sent a message that the Scouts did not want to send, then their First Amendment rights enabled them to throw him out.

Rehnquist quoted Scout Oath and the Scout Law as the mission statements of the organization. The Scout Oath reads:

On my honor I will do my best
To do my duty to God and my country
and to obey the Scout Law;
To help other people at all times;

The Law of Gay Rights

To keep myself physically strong,
mentally awake, and morally straight.

The Scout Law reads:

A Scout is
Trustworthy Obedient
Loyal Cheerful
Helpful Thrifty
Friendly Brave
Courteous Clean
Kind Reverent.

"Thus," wrote Rehnquist, "the general mission of the Boy Scouts is clear: '[T]o instill values in young people.'" The Boy Scouts had asserted that homosexual conduct was inconsistent with those values, "particularly with the values represented by the terms *morally straight* and *clean.*" True, the Scouts did not expressly mention sexuality or sexual orientation. "And the terms *morally straight* and *clean* are by no means self-defining." Different people would interpret those ideas in different ways, but the Boy Scouts had a right to interpret their own rules as they wished.

The question then became, were the Boy Scouts twisting their interpretation of these rules simply to exclude Dale—which would be discrimination—or had they already interpreted their rules to mean that homosexuality was unacceptable, which would be free speech. Rehnquist quoted a 1978 position statement in which the Boy Scouts' president and Chief Scout Executive had explicitly said that homosexuals could not be Scout leaders and cited other statements that had been made after Dale's membership had been revoked, repeating the notion that "homosexual conduct" was "inconsistent" with the Scout Law. Thus, Rehnquist wrote, the Boy Scouts were not discriminating against homosexuals. They were simply asserting that Dale's presence in the group as assistant scoutmaster interfered with their ability to send the message they wanted to send.

Of course, Rehnquist acknowledged, the Court had to be very careful in how it interpreted "expressive association." Once the Court agreed that someone's mere presence in the group was sending a message, antidiscrimination laws would lose their force. Any group could "erect a shield against antidiscrimination laws simply by asserting that mere acceptance of a member from a particular group would impair its message."

But Dale, by his own admission, was not simply a gay man; he had become the copresident of a gay rights group "and remains a gay rights activist." Thus, Rehnquist wrote, "Dale's presence in the Boy Scouts would, at the very least, force the organization to send a message, both to the youth members and the world, that the Boy Scouts accepts homosexual conduct as a legitimate form of behavior." As *Dale's* precedent, the *Hurley* decision had not supported the parade organizers' right to exclude gay people from marching in the parade but

121

did allow them to exclude gay people carrying a banner asserting that they were Irish gays, lesbians, and bisexuals. It was the banner, not the presence of gay people, that the parade organizers had the right to exclude. In Dale's case, it was the openness of his gay activism that made it all right to exclude him. This was true even if the main purpose of the Boy Scouts was not to express a particular message on homosexuality, and it was true even if they wanted to express their messages on homosexuality by example rather than in words. It was true even if they allowed other scout leaders to disagree with their policy while not allowing the same latitude to Dale. Thus,

> The presence of an avowed homosexual and gay rights activist in assistant scout-master's uniform sends a distinctly different message from the presence of a het-erosexual assistant scoutmaster who is on record as disagreeing with Boy Scouts policy. The Boy Scouts has a First Amendment right to choose to send one mes-sage but not the other. The fact that the organization does not trumpet its views from the housetops, or that it tolerates dissent within its ranks, does not mean that its views receive no First Amendment protection.

Justice John Paul Stevens wrote a dissenting opinion for the four-person mi-nority in the Boy Scouts decision, which consisted of himself along with Justices David Souter, Ruth Bader Ginsburg, and Stephen Breyer. Since the Boy Scouts were excluding Dale on the grounds that his presence was inconsistent with their values, what, Stevens asked, were those values?

First, according to the Boy Scouts' own statements, "[n]either the charter nor the bylaws of the Boy Scouts of America permits the exclusion of any boy." More-over, the group had said that "our membership shall be representative of all the population in every community, district, and council" [emphasis in original]. The Boy Scouts had even provided their own definition, in the Boy Scout Handbook, of "morally straight" and "clean," definitions that made no mention of homosexu-ality or indeed of sexual behavior of any kind. In fact, Stevens wrote, Scout policy directed Scoutmasters to avoid discussing sexual matters with Scouts whenever possible, suggesting that the boys talk about these matters with parents, religious leaders, teachers, doctors, and other professionals. Finally, Stevens pointed out, while the Scouts did support religion in a general way, the group's bylaws stressed that the Boy Scouts were "absolutely nonsectarian." Surely, Stevens wrote, the Scouts were aware "that some religions do not teach that homosexuality is wrong."

Stevens acknowledged that the 1978 memo cited by Rehnquist did indeed declare that homosexuality and Scouting were incompatible. But, he wrote, "simply adopting such a policy, has never been considered sufficient, by itself, to prevail on a right to associate claim." In other words, a group could not simply declare that it had a policy that excluded members of a particular group and then exclude them. That was discrimination, and antidiscrimination laws were able to trump such policies.

Stevens quoted several more statements made by the Scouts and analyzed them in detail. Using the Boy Scouts' own words against them, he attempted to show both that the Boy Scouts' policy did not inherently forbid homosexual membership and that the policy itself had shifted over time in response to criticism. Although the Scouts had initially attempted to show that homosexuality was inconsistent with the main purposes of Scouting, they had given up that effort by 1993 (after Dale's suit had begun), saying instead that including gays would be contrary to "the expectations that Scouting families have had. . ." In other words, the 1993 policy statement did not assert that including gay men would violate the group's purpose, only that it would challenge the expectations of its members. This, wrote Stevens, was simply a form of discrimination, similar to other types of discrimination that the Court had forbidden in the past.

In the *Hurley* case, the gay/lesbian/bisexual group was actually conveying a message by participating in the parade. But Dale's membership in the Scouts was not intended to convey any message. He simply wanted to be a Boy Scout:

> *His participation sends no . . . message to the Scouts or the world . . . [He] did not carry a banner or a sign; he did not distribute any fact sheet; and he expressed no intent to send any message . . . Indeed . . . there is no evidence that the young Scouts in Dale's troop, or members of their families, were even aware of his sexual orientation, either before or after his public statements at Rutgers University.*

Finally, Stevens compared prejudice against homosexuals to racial prejudice and to prejudice against women. All types of prejudice were supported by isolation. However,

> *interaction with real people, rather than mere adherence to traditional ways of thinking about members of unfamiliar classes, have modified these opinions . . . If we would guide by the light of reason, we must let our minds be bold. I respectfully dissent.*

Justice Souter, joined by Justices Ginsburg and Breyer, wrote a brief additional dissenting opinion. The purpose of this second opinion was to stress that support of gay people or opposition to prejudice was not the main issue. Rather, the issue was that no one had shown that Dale's mere membership in the Scouts sent any message that interfered with the Boy Scouts' pursuit of its goals. Hypothetically, some individual might be so identified with a particular position that his or her mere presence did indeed send a message that might interfere with the message that a group wished to express. If such a case were ever to come before the Court, the Court's opinions about stereotypes and prejudice would be irrelevant; only the First Amendment would matter.

Impact

Although the Boy Scouts of America won their case, their apparent victory set off a nationwide backlash, leading to numerous lawsuits against the group, withdrawal of funding from at least 60 United Way chapters, and efforts by government officials across the country to withhold public land, facilities, and funding from the Scouts.

For example, in 2000, a lesbian couple and an agnostic couple, each with a Scouting-age son, filed suit through the American Civil Liberties Union (ACLU) against the Boy Scouts' residence in Balboa Park in San Diego, California, which the Scouts were renting from the city for $1 per year, a $2,500 administrative fee, and an agreement to spend $1.7 million to upgrade the park. The suit charged that Scout policies favoring religion and banning homosexuals made the couples feel unwelcome in the public facility and that by renting city land to a religious group like the Scouts, the city was violating the separation of church and state.

The Scouts insisted that they were not a religious organization, but in July 2003, a U.S. district judge ruled that they were. Thus, the city could not lease them public land. The city, which had also been named in the suit, dropped out of the case in January 2004 by settling with the ACLU. The Scouts continue to appeal, along with filing suit against the city council for breaking the lease. They are also charging discrimination, on the grounds that the city should make the land available to the Scouts on the same terms as to other groups. On February 24, 2004, they added a charge that city employees were harassing Scouts by photographing their vehicles and levying huge parking fines against them.

The conservative group, the American Civil Rights Union (ACRU), spoke out in favor of the Scouts in the *Weekly Standard*, a conservative journal. "The San Diego case represents an ominous metamorphosis in the gay rights movement," wrote ACRU executive director Peter Ferrara. "Gay rights used to represent the freedom for adults to do what they want with their sex lives behind closed doors . . . But . . . the ACLU . . . now . . . seeks . . . the vilification and marginalization of those who hold to traditional morality." The ACLU argued that the Boy Scouts cannot violate antidiscrimination laws by excluding whole categories of people from membership and then expect public subsidies.

Meanwhile, the Scouts also brought suit against the Connecticut state government, which in 2000 removed the Scouts from a list of groups to which state employees could contribute through an office charity drive. The Scouts were removed on the grounds that their participation in the drive would violate the state's gay rights law, a move that government officials said was based on a state supreme court ruling that barred the military from recruiting at the University of Connecticut law school. Just as their "don't ask, don't tell" policy violated the state's antidiscrimination law, so did the Scouts' policy of excluding homosexuals.

Although in California the Scouts had insisted that they were not a religious organization, in Connecticut, they asked for a religious exemption to remain on the charity-drive list. Connecticut's law against antigay discrimination allows religious groups to treat gays differently if their religious teachings require it. But Connecticut denied the exemption on the grounds that the Scouts were not a religious organization.

The U.S. Supreme Court refused to hear the Connecticut case in March 2004, a decision that was widely regarded as a defeat for the Scouts. Implicitly, the Court's refusal to hear the case opened the door for other bodies to ban the Scouts from public facilities.

A number of other public and private groups have taken action against the Scouts, leading to incidents such as the following:

- As of July 2004, the United Way in Portland, Oregon, began cutting off some $150,000 per year that it had given to the Scouts for inner-city youth programs, in response to complaints from gay rights groups.

- In June 2003, the California Supreme Court ordered that any state judges who volunteered with the Scouts must remove themselves from any cases involving gay people.

- In 2000, the National Education Association adopted a resolution asking school boards to require that any private organization using school facilities must have a nondiscriminatory membership policy. In response, Congress voted in 2002 to deny federal education funding to any district that discriminated against the Scouts.

In March 2005, a bipartisan group of senators introduced legislation that would require all levels of government to make facilities available to the Scouts if other groups are allowed to use them.

Another type of impact of the *Boy Scouts* decision was reported in a May 11, 2001, article in the *Providence Journal*. In that year, the Rhode Island Medical Society adopted a resolution saying that the Scouts' ban on gay membership greatly increased the risk of depression and suicide among gay youths whom the medical society said were already more prone to those problems than their straight counterparts. Although a doctor associated with the conservative Massachusetts Family Institute accused the Rhode Island group of "pursuing a political agenda rather than a real desire to help people stay healthy," the medical society pointed out that they had reviewed numerous studies about the links between gay youth suicide, and depression before coming to their decision.

The *Providence Journal* article also cited the example of Scott Pusillo, then a 21-year-old gay senior at Johnson and Wales University. When the Scouts kicked out James Dale, Pusillo was 15, struggling with his sexual identity and with his parents' divorce. He considered the Scouts a place of refuge and was devastated by their judgment that Dale, otherwise a model Scout, had been considered unfit.

"Here was this organization that I'd given my life to, in essence saying that something was wrong with you if you were gay," Pusillo told the *Providence Journal*. "When you're put down and told that you're worthless . . . and that you don't belong in an organization like the Boy Scouts, you start to believe it."

Pusillo went on to make two suicide attempts. He also became an Eagle Scout, then a troop leader, then an activist in Scouting for All, a group that is pressuring the Scouts to include gay people. In April 2001 the Scouts kicked him out as well. He continued to work with Scouting for All, hoping to help young men who felt the confusion he once experienced.

The ultimate impact of *Boy Scouts v. Dale* is still unclear. On the one hand, the Court has firmly upheld the notion that a gay person's mere presence in an organization sends a message, a line of reasoning that might be used to support other types of antigay discrimination. Although Dale was a gay rights activist, it was his openness as a gay man, not any particular activity he undertook, that was deemed to send the message. On the other hand, public outcry against the Scouts was widespread and mainstream to an extent that neither the Scouts nor the gay rights movement anticipated. How this response will ultimately affect the Scouts remains to be seen.

JOHN GEDDES LAWRENCE AND TYRON GARNER, PETITIONERS V. TEXAS (2003)

Background

In Houston, Texas, in 1998, officers of the Harris County Police Department got a call about a disturbance involving a weapon that sent them to the home of John Geddes Lawrence, who was engaging in a sexual act with Tyron Garner. The police, entering to investigate the disturbance, witnessed the act, which violated a Texas law that prohibited same-sex sodomy. Although many states' sodomy laws simply prohibited one or more types of sexual acts, Texas's law explicitly said that these acts were illegal only when committed between people of the same sex.

Accordingly, the police arrested Lawrence and Garner. They spent the night in jail and were ultimately convicted by a Justice of the Peace. The two men demanded a trial in Harris County Court. They did not contest the fact that they had violated the Texas law—but they challenged the constitutionality of the law itself.

Legal Issues

Lawrence and Garner held that the Texas law against homosexual sodomy violated the Equal Protection and Due Process clauses of the Fourteenth Amendment:

> . . . *no state shall make or enforce any law which shall abridge the privileges or immunities of citizens of the United States; nor shall any state deprive any person of life, liberty, or property, without due process of law; nor deny to any person within its jurisdiction the equal protection of the laws.*

The court of appeals upheld the men's conviction, based on the U.S. Supreme Court's earlier ruling in *Bowers v. Hardwick* (see above). In *Bowers*, the Court had ruled that a Georgia sodomy law was constitutional, which seemed to give grounds for the Texas law as well. When the men appealed their case to the Supreme Court, the high court agreed to consider three questions:

1. The Fourteenth Amendment's Equal Protection Clause guarantees every citizen equal protection under the law. But the Texas sodomy statute only applied to sexual acts committed by same-sex couples, leaving heterosexual couples free to behave as they pleased. Did the Texas statute violate the Equal Protection Clause?
2. The Fourteenth Amendment's Due Process Clause has long been interpreted to guarantee citizens liberty and privacy. Did the men's conviction for an adult consensual act in a private home violate their rights under the Due Process Clause?
3. Should *Bowers v. Hardwick*, which had upheld a Georgia sodomy law, be overruled?

This last question was particularly significant, as it is very rare for the Supreme Court to overturn one of its own decisions. The Court has a strong interest in stability. When it hands down a decision, courts, lawyers, legislators, and private citizens must all regulate their conduct accordingly. True, the Court does sometimes overrule itself, but usually after a much longer period of time has elapsed and social attitudes have changed. To overrule a decision that was less than 20 years old would be a very strong statement.

Decision

The Court ruled 6-3 that adults were indeed entitled to engage in private consensual sexual acts under the Due Process Clause. Moreover, wrote Justice Anthony M. Kennedy in a majority opinion joined by Justices John Paul Stevens, David Souter, Ruth Beder Ginsburg, and Stephen Breyer, to come to that conclusion, it was indeed necessary to overturn *Bowers*. Because overturning a previous Supreme Court decision is such a momentous act, Kennedy spent most of his opinion justifying that aspect of the ruling.

First, he wrote, the *Bowers* court had asked "whether the Federal Constitution confers a fundamental right upon homosexuals to engage in sodomy." But formulating the question in this way revealed the Court's "failure to appreciate the extent of the liberty at stake." The issue for homosexuals was not simply the right to have sex, and to phrase it that way was demeaning,

> *just as it would demean a married couple were it said that marriage is just about the right to have sexual intercourse. . . . When sexuality finds overt expression in intimate conduct with another person, the conduct can be but one element in a personal bond that is more enduring.*

The laws in *Bowers* had further-reaching consequences than merely prohibiting a specific sexual act. It touched upon "the most private human conduct, sexual behavior, and in the most private of places, the home." Whether or not the law ever recognized same-sex relationships, Kennedy wrote in an obvious allusion to gay marriage, homosexuals had the right to engage in personal relationships with one another without being punished as criminals.

Moreover, wrote Kennedy, the *Bowers* Court had justified its ruling by citing the "ancient roots" against homosexuality. Yet there was no specifically American legal tradition against homosexuals. Although sodomy laws had a long history in the United States, they were part of a larger body of laws against non-procreative sex (sex that did not lead to the creation of children), without mention of sexual orientation. Nor were early sodomy laws generally enforced against consenting adults acting in private. Instead, they usually involved "predatory" acts against those who could not or did not consent: between men and minor girls or boys; between adults involving force; between adults of different statuses, in which the lower-status person might have trouble saying no; and between men and animals. "Far from possessing 'ancient roots,'" Kennedy wrote, "American laws targeting same-sex couples did not develop until the last third of the 20th century." Strikingly, Kennedy relied in this part of his opinion upon works by gay rights activists and scholars Jonathan Katz (*The Invention of Heterosexuality*, 1995) and John D'Emilio and E. Freedman (*Intimate Matters: A History of Sexuality in America*, 2nd edition, 1997).

Although in the year that *Bowers* was handed down, sodomy remained illegal in 25 states, only nine states had singled out same-sex relations. And in the years after *Bowers* was handed down, 12 states dropped their sodomy laws, leaving only 13 states with sodomy laws, just four of which restricted their proscription to same-sex sodomy. Even those states—of which Texas was one—tended not to enforce the laws with regard to consenting adults acting in private.

Meanwhile, Kennedy wrote, the Supreme Court had handed down two significant decisions since *Bowers* that cast further aspersions upon that decision. In *Planned Parenthood v. Casey* (1992), the Court had not only ruled that "this Court's obligation is to define the liberty of all, not to mandate its own moral code," but also that the Due Process Clause "protects personal decisions relating to marriage, procreation, contraception, family relationships, childrearing, and education." In *Romer v. Evans* (1996), the Court had struck down laws that singled out homosexuals. Both decisions suggested problems with *Bowers*, which had supported a law criminalizing private sexual conduct of a kind generally associated with homosexuals.

Furthermore, Kennedy continued, the stigma inherent in the Texas anti-sodomy law was not "trivial." Even though same-sex sodomy was only a misdemeanor in Texas, the consequences of criminalizing homosexual sex had serious consequences for the dignity of the persons involved, "including notation of convictions on their records and on job application forms, and registration as sex offenders under state law."

Normally, a Supreme Court case relies only upon U.S. law and precedent. But when a case is weak for other reasons, Kennedy wrote, it was legitimate to look at criticism from other sources. The *Bowers* decision had called upon the tradition in Western civilization that had condemned homosexuality for thousands of years. But prejudice against homosexuals was no longer consistent with the values of a wider civilization. The European Court of Human Rights, for example, had rejected same-sex sodomy laws, and many other nations had protected the rights of homosexual adults to engage in private, consensual sex. Nor had anyone shown that there was some urgent governmental reason for circumscribing personal choice. Although it was generally better to let Supreme Court decisions stand, overturning *Bowers* would actually be more consistent with other decisions made before and after it.

Finally, Kennedy wrote, *Bowers's* rationale did not withstand careful analysis. Justice Stevens had written a dissenting opinion in *Bowers*, pointing out that even if a majority considered a particular practice immoral, that was not reason enough to uphold a law banning that practice. Stevens had also written that individual decisions about sexual conduct, even when not intended to produce children, were nevertheless a form of liberty protected by due process. "That analysis should have controlled *Bowers*," Kennedy concluded, "and it controls here. *Bowers* was not correct when it was decided, is not correct today, and is hereby overruled."

At least twice in his decision, Kennedy made a point of saying that *Lawrence* did not involve government recognition for same-sex relationships—that is, it did not concern the question of gay marriage. Rather, *Lawrence* was about respect for the private lives of gay people, whose right to liberty under the due process clause included "the full right to engage in their conduct without intervention of the government."

Kennedy ended his decision with an acknowledgment that times change. In an apparent criticism of the "strict constructionism" of Justice Antonin Scalia and other conservatives, who tended to justify their decisions by referring to the original intentions of the Constitution's authors, Kennedy put himself on the side of historical change:

> *Had those who drew and ratified the Due Process Clauses of the Fifth Amendment or the Fourteenth Amendment known the components of liberty in its manifold possibilities, they might have been more specific. They did not presume to have this insight. They knew times can blind us to certain truths and later generations can see that laws once thought necessary and proper in fact serve only to oppress. As the Constitution endures, persons in every generation can invoke its principles in their own search for greater freedom.*

Justice Sandra Day O'Connor wrote a separate opinion supporting the majority decision to overturn the Texas anti-sodomy law. However, she explicitly did not join the Court in overturning *Bowers*, a decision for which she had voted in 1986. In her opinion, *Lawrence* was not a matter of the due process clause, concerning individual liberty and privacy. Rather, it was a matter of the equal protection clause. The Texas anti-sodomy law had singled out homosexuals, so it violated equal protection and was unconstitutional. The Georgia law at issue in *Bowers* had outlawed sodomy in general, and so, in O'Connor's opinion, it was absolutely constitutional.

O'Connor agreed with Kennedy that the Texas law "brands all homosexuals as criminals, thereby making it more difficult for homosexuals to be treated in the same manner as everyone else." But that had not been the issue in *Bowers*. The *Bowers* decision rested upon the notion that it was permissible for the government to make a law that promoted morality, and that homosexual sodomy was not a right so fundamental that outlawing it violated the due process clause. O'Connor still believed that this analysis was correct. *Lawrence*, by contrast, raised the issue of whether a law that singled out homosexuals violated the Equal Protection Clause. O'Connor believed that it did.

O'Connor went on to make an interesting point, one that resembled the arguments of many gay rights scholars. By outlawing homosexual sodomy, she wrote, the Texas law created a situation in which "*being* homosexual carries the presumption of being a criminal" (emphasis in original). In a sense, the Texas law criminalized not behavior, but identity. It singled out a whole group of people and called them criminals. Indeed, to label someone a homosexual in Texas was literally to call that person a criminal. Thus the Texas sodomy statute subjected homosexuals to "a lifelong penalty and stigma." As *Romer* had shown, such singling out of homosexuals was a clear violation of the Equal Protection Clause.

Some might argue that a law that banned sodomy—a sexual practice upon which most homosexuals had by definition to rely—could never be neutral. But, O'Connor wrote, that was not the question before the Court in this decision. Nor could Texas assert any legitimate state interest that might override gay people's rights as citizens, such as national security (the rationale used for discriminating against gays in the military) or preserving the traditional institution of marriage. Therefore, there was no constitutional basis for the Texas law.

Justice Scalia wrote a dissenting opinion, joined by Chief Justice Rehnquist and Justice Thomas. He spent most of his opinion criticizing the Court's willingness to overturn *Bowers*, a decision taken "a mere 17 years ago." Kennedy had used widespread opposition to *Bowers* as a reason to overrule it, but then, Scalia asked, why should that not be the same basis for overturning *Roe v. Wade*, the landmark decision guaranteeing women's right to an abortion? Certainly there was enormous opposition to that decision, yet in *Planned Parenthood v. Casey*, a case concerning abortion rights, the liberal justices who had voted to overturn *Bowers* were just as staunch in their defense of *Roe*: "To overrule under fire in the absence of the most compelling reason . . . would subvert the Court's legitimacy beyond any serious question." If that was how they had felt in the 1992 *Casey* decision, Scalia wrote, why would they not maintain the same position now?

Scalia agreed that the *Romer* decision (which he had opposed) eroded the foundations of *Bowers*. But again, he turned to abortion-related decisions to show that various Supreme Court rulings had eroded *Roe* and others. Moreover, many subsequent decisions had relied upon *Bowers*, including a decision upholding federal bans on gays from the military; laws against sex outside of marriage and against adultery; and an Indiana public indecency statute. *Bowers* asserted that the government had the right to uphold traditional morality—a right that was behind "state laws against bigamy, same-sex marriage, adult incest, prostitution, masturbation, adultery, fornication, bestiality, and obscenity. . ." These laws, Scalia wrote, could only be sustained by the same principles that upheld *Bowers*, and "Every single one of these laws" had been called into question by the *Lawrence* decision. "The law," wrote Scalia, quoting *Bowers*, "is constantly based on notions of morality, and if all laws representing essentially moral choices are to be invalidated under the due process clause, the courts will be very busy indeed."

Although the majority defended the rights of homosexuals to engage in sodomy, Scalia wrote, they did not go so far as to say that sodomy was such a fundamental right that it was protected by the Fourteenth Amendment. In that case, the only question was the extent to which the government had a "rational basis"—good reason—to abridge citizens' liberty. In Scalia's opinion, the government had very good reason indeed: "to further the belief of its citizens that certain forms of sexual behavior are 'immoral and unacceptable'—the same interest furthered by criminal laws against fornication, bigamy, adultery, adult incest, bestiality, and obscenity." *Bowers* had held that this *was* a legitimate state interest, and Scalia saw no reason to change that opinion now. Instead, with *Lawrence*, the Court had taken a decision that "effectively decrees the end of all morals legislation."

Finally, Scalia took up his disagreements with O'Connor, focusing on her point that the Texas law criminalized not behavior but identity. "Of course the same could be said of any law," he wrote. A law against public nudity, for example, stigmatized nudists. Was that necessarily unconstitutional? Even if the Texas sodomy law *did* discriminate against homosexuals, such discrimination could be justified by the government's interest in "the enforcement of traditional notions of sexual morality."

Scalia stressed that the decision left "on pretty shaky grounds" the state laws against gay marriage. O'Connor had tried to support those laws by mentioning the preservation of traditional marriage as a legitimate state interest. But, Scalia wrote in a statement with which many gay rights activists would ironically agree, "'preserving the traditional institution of marriage' is just a kinder way of describing the State's *moral disapproval* of same-sex couples" (emphasis in original). By not maintaining the courage of her convictions, O'Connor was simply twisting the law to suit herself:

> In the jurisprudence Justice O'Connor *has seemingly created, judges can validate laws by characterizing them as "preserving the traditions of society" (good); or invalidate them as "expressing moral disapproval" (bad). [emphasis in original]*

Finally, Scalia took on what he called the "law-profession culture, that has largely signed on to the so-called homosexual agenda." Scalia cited Kennedy's "grim warning" that outlawing gay sex was "an invitation to subject homosexual persons to discrimination in both the public and in the private spheres." This statement made clear, Scalia wrote, "the Court has taken sides in the culture war." But the Court's job was not to make public policy or to protect homosexuals from discrimination. Rather, it was to make sure "that the democratic rules of engagement are observed," in a role of neutral observer. What about all those many Americans who did not want openly gay people "as partners in their business, as scoutmasters for their children, as teachers in their children's schools, or as boarders in their home?" From their point of view, they were "protecting themselves and their families from a lifestyle that they believe to be immoral and destructive." By viewing their actions as "discrimination" that the Court was supposed to prevent, the Court was isolating itself from these mainstream Americans:

> *So imbued is the Court with the law profession's anti-anti-homosexual culture, that it is seemingly unaware that the attitudes of that culture are not obviously "mainstream," that in most States what the Court calls "discrimination" against those who engage in homosexual acts is perfectly legal; that proposals to ban such "discrimination" under Title VII have repeatedly been rejected by Congress . . . that in some cases such "discrimination" is mandated by federal statute [i.e., the law] mandating discharge from the armed forces of any service member who engages in or intends to engage in homosexual acts); and that in some cases such "discrimination is a constitutional right [(see Boy Scouts of America v. Dale)].*

Scalia stressed that he himself had no objection to homosexuals "or any other group" promoting their agenda in a democratic fashion. "But persuading one's fellow citizens is one thing, and imposing one's views in absence of democratic majority will is something else." Scalia concluded by warning that the Court had opened the door not only to laws in support of same-sex marriage but to court rulings that same-sex marriage must be permitted, even against the clear wishes of the majority of citizens in a state.

> *Today's opinion dismantles the structure of constitutional law that has permitted a distinction to be made between heterosexual and homosexual unions, insofar as formal recognition in marriage is concerned. If moral and disapprobation of homosexual conduct is "no legitimate state interest"; . . . and if, as the Court coos (casting aside all pretense of neutrality), "[w]hen sexuality finds overt expression in intimate conduct with another person, the conduct can be but one element in a personal bond that is more enduring," what justification could there possibly be for denying the benefits of marriage to homosexual couples exercising "[the] liberty protected by the Constitution?"*

Justice Thomas joined Scalia's dissenting opinion and wrote an extremely brief opinion of his own. He wrote that the Texas anti-sodomy law was "uncommonly silly," and that if he were a member of the Texas legislature,

I would vote to repeal it. Punishing someone for expressing his sexual preference through noncommercial consensual conduct with another adult does not appear to be a worthy way to expend valuable law enforcement resources.

Nevertheless, Thomas wrote, he could not find any basis in the Constitution for overturning the law.

Impact

Justice Scalia was correct in his predictions. Legalizing sodomy did indeed open the door to gay marriage, and only a few months after *Lawrence* was handed down, the Massachusetts Supreme Judicial Court ruled that to deny marriage to the state's gay citizens was to violate the state constitution's guarantees of equal protection under the law. As described elsewhere in this book (see Chapters 1 and 4), the *Lawrence* decision was followed by a flurry of activity around same-sex marriage. Indeed, straight government officials like San Francisco mayor Gavin Newsom were willing—even eager—to contravene the laws of their jurisdiction in order to marry same-sex couples. Across the country, city councils, county clerks, mayors, and other officials were suddenly willing to take huge risks to help gay couples marry, while the urgency and intensity of the issue incited a new militancy within the gay rights movement.

Yet the "mainstream Americans" whom Scalia had cited were not necessarily won over to support the gay marriage issue or even to increase their support of gay equality. A July 30, 2003, story in the *Houston Chronicle* noted "a backlash after the Supreme Court decision," citing polls showing a decline in public support of gay rights. A CNN–*USA Today* Gallup poll taken in July 2003 showed that 48 percent of respondents believed that gay relationships should be legal, while 46 percent believed they should not. However, in early May of the same year, 60 percent supported legalizing gay relationships, with only 35 percent opposed.

According to Frank Newport, executive editor of the Gallup poll, "The trends had clearly been moving up in terms of public acceptance of the legality of homosexual relations and also on other gay and lesbian measures in the polls." But in two separate polls taken in July 2003, Gallup surveys found a shift against gay rights, mainly among conservatives, moderates, and churchgoers. Although in May 2003, 54 percent of those polled held that homosexuality should be considered an acceptable lifestyle, only 46 percent held that opinion in July, with the percentage of those opposing homosexuality rising by six points to about half.

The six months after *Lawrence* also saw an increase in violence directed against lesbians, gay men, bisexuals, and transgender people, according to the National Coalition of Anti-Violence Programs (NCAVP), a gay rights group. The NCAVP found a 24 percent increase in the half-year after *Lawrence*, with particularly sharp rises in certain areas: 120 percent in Chicago, 133 percent in Colorado, and 43 percent in New York. San Francisco saw a slightly lower increase in violence—14 percent—but an increase nonetheless. The NCAVP pointed out that in many areas, "significant downward trends reversed themselves," according to NCAVP acting executive director Clarence Patton.

"At the end of the day, the fact is that those who hate us are running scared because we have made progress in this society, in the Supreme Court, in the nation's media and culture wars," Patton suggested. "The message being sent is, 'Stay in your closets; and don't you dare ask to be treated as human beings,' but that message will continue to be ignored by this community."

Perhaps ironically, Patton's analysis was echoed by many leaders of the Christian Right, as described in an August 1, 2003, *Houston Chronicle* article. According to reporter Alan Cooperman, such leaders attributed the drop in support for gay rights to the new realization by many Americans "that the legalization of gay marriage, which once seemed remote, is suddenly a real possibility."

Some observers believe that *Lawrence* is a decision of landmark status comparable to *Brown v. Board of Education*, constituting such a profound change in the legal climate that it will take years to evaluate its full impact. For the first time in U.S. history, the highest law in the land had recognized homosexuals' right to full protection of the law. No longer criminals by definition, gay people were now legally recognized as full citizens. What this legal shift portends for the future has yet to be determined.

FEDERAL COURT CASES

NORTON V. MACY (1969)

Background

Early on the morning of October 22, 1963, a budget analyst at the National Aeronautics and Space Administration (NASA) was driving his car around Lafayette Square, a well-known gay cruising area in Washington, D.C. The driver picked up another man, drove once around the square, and dropped his passenger off where he had found him. This behavior was observed by two police officers in the morals squad, a special unit charged with watching out for acts considered immoral, such as prostitution, drug dealing, and homosexual behavior. The driver was arrested, as was the passenger, Madison Monroe Proctor, who said that the driver had felt his leg and invited him up for a drink. The men were taken to the morals office, while the head of the morals squad called the driver's boss, NASA's chief of security. The employee, Clifford Norton, was fired, because, in the words of the eventual federal court ruling:

> *NASA concluded that appellant [Norton] did in fact make a homosexual advance on October 22, and that this act amounted to "immoral, indecent, and disgraceful conduct." It also determined that, on the basis of his own admissions to [the NASA Security Chief] . . . appellant possesses "traits of character and personality which render [him] unsuitable for further Government employment."*

This judgment was upheld by various levels of the civil service, so Norton appealed his case to the Supreme Court.

Legal Issues

At stake in *Norton v. Macy* was the extent to which immoral or illegal behavior should disqualify a person from holding a federal job. At the time of the case, there was no question that Norton had admitted to certain acts that were illegal in the District of Columbia—and generally regarded as immoral by mainstream society. Yet should such illegal and apparently immoral behavior constitute a reason for firing a federal employee?

Decision

The court took no exception to Norton's arrest or to the law under which he was arrested. But, the court ruled, even if Norton *had* been guilty of "immoral, indecent, and disgraceful conduct," it was not the government's business to police the private behavior of its employees:

> *. . . the notion that it could be an appropriate function of the federal bureaucracy to enforce the majority's conventional codes of conduct in the private lives of its employees is at war with elementary concepts of liberty, privacy, and diversity.*

The only way a person's immorality could be of concern to a federal employer, said the court, was if that immorality specifically impinged upon the person's ability to perform his or her duties.

The court was at pains to specify that homosexuality might indeed be an impediment to performing some federal jobs. The risk of blackmail, the possibility of personal instability, the prospect of offensive overtures to others in the workplace, and the dangers of conduct that might bring embarrassment to the agency were all acceptable reasons to fire a gay person or to refuse to hire one. However, to fire someone for being gay, a federal employer had to establish the connection between being gay and being unfit for a particular job. It could not justify a firing "merely by turning its head and crying 'shame,'" to quote the circuit court ruling.

Impact

Norton v. Macy established what came to be known as the "rational nexus" test—the notion that being gay did not per se make a person unfit for employment. Rather, there had to be a *rational nexus* (a set of interconnected reasons) to believe that the person would be unfit. Since Norton was a competent employee, did not have access to classified documents, had kept his coworkers unaware of his conduct, and did not have contact with the public, there were no rational grounds for firing him.

Although in later cases the courts were able to find a rational nexus between homosexuality and unfitness based on what gay rights advocates considered extremely weak criteria, the changing attitudes of the 1970s began to have their effect. Moreover, the fact that so many gay men and lesbians were now open about their sexuality meant that their sexual lives could no longer be a cause for blackmail. In 1971, in a kind of legacy of *Norton v. Macy*, the *Washington Post* actually criticized the Civil Service Commission for its blanket prohibition against homosexuals, claiming that gay employees' "private sexual behavior is their own business."

STATE COURT CASES

GAY STUDENTS ORGANIZATION OF THE UNIVERSITY OF NEW HAMPSHIRE V. BONNER (1974)

Background

This case involved the Gay Students Organization (GSO), which on November 9, 1973, sponsored a dance on the University of New Hampshire campus. "After the dance," according to the state supreme court's ruling, "there was criticism by the Governor of New Hampshire, who complained to the University about the propriety of allowing such a 'spectacle.'"

Then the GSO sponsored a play, which was presented on December 7, 1973. "Although the play itself caused little comment," the court decision explained, "there was some reaction to 'Fag Rag Five' and 'Fag Rag VI,' two 'extremist homosexual' publications which were distributed sometime during the evening." (*Fag Rag* was a Boston-based gay newspaper, known for its provocative writing on sexuality.) As a result, the governor of New Hampshire wrote an open letter to the university's board of trustees, in which he stated that "indecency and moral filth will no longer be allowed on our campuses. Either you take firm, fair and positive action to rid your campuses of socially abhorrent activities or I, as governor, will stand solidly against the expenditure of one more cent of taxpayers' money for your institutions." In other words, stop gay activity on campus or risk losing funding.

Legal Issues

From the point of view of gay rights supporters, the issue was the right of gay students to assemble freely, as guaranteed under the First Amendment. From the point of view of gay rights opponents, the matter concerned the right of a public university to determine what kinds of activities were appropriate for its campus.

Decision

The supreme court found for the GSO. "[T]his case is quite simple," the decision read. "The First Amendment guarantees all individuals, including university students, the right to organize and associate 'to further their personal beliefs.'" Unless the university could show compelling reason not to do so, it was required to recognize any "bona fide student organization and grant to that organization the rights and privileges which normally flow from such recognition."

Impact

Bonner established the right of gay students to form organizations at public universities and colleges. The case was important to gay student groups fighting for the right to form clubs at private universities in the 1980s and at high schools in the 1990s.

BRASCHI V. STAHL ASSOCIATES CO. (1989)

Background

Miguel Braschi and Leslie Blanchard were two men who had lived together in a rent-controlled Manhattan apartment for nearly a decade. When Blanchard died, the building owner threatened to evict Braschi, since only Blanchard's name was on the lease. Had Blanchard and Braschi been a heterosexual married couple, Braschi would have had the right to retain the lease; as the survivor in a gay couple, Braschi seemed to have no rights. He took the landlord to the highest court in the state of New York, referring to the New York City rent-control regulation forbidding eviction of "either the surviving spouse of the deceased tenant or some other member of the deceased tenant's family."

Legal Issues

At stake in *Braschi* was the legal recognition of a gay domestic partnership. Since U.S. lesbians and gay men cannot get married, gay rights activists and opponents are both keenly interested in the various ways in which legal recognition can be accorded to their de facto arrangements.

Decision

The court found for Braschi, ruling that he was a surviving spouse or member of Blanchard's family and therefore entitled to a share in Blanchard's lease:

> . . . *we conclude that the term family, as used in [the regulation], should not be rigidly restricted to those people who have formalized their relationship by obtaining, for instance, a marriage certificate or an adoption order. The intended protection against sudden eviction should not rest on fictitious legal distinctions or genetic history, but instead should find its foundation in the reality of family life. In the context of eviction, a more realistic, and certainly equally valid, view of a family includes two adult lifetime partners whose relationship is long-term and*

characterized by an emotional and financial commitment and interdependence. This view comports both with our society's traditional concept of "family" and with the expectations of individuals who live in such nuclear units. . . .

In its consideration of Braschi and Blanchard's family life, the court noted approvingly that the two men had lived together as permanent life partners for more than 10 years, regarding each other and being regarded by others, as spouses:

The two men's families were aware of the nature of the relationship, and they regularly visited each other's families and attended family functions together, as a couple. Even today, appellant [Braschi] continues to maintain a relationship with Blanchard's niece, who considers him an uncle.

The court went on to cite the financial involvement of the two men—Blanchard had given Braschi power of attorney, left him his estate, and named him beneficiary of his life insurance policy; the two men shared checking and savings accounts and credit cards. "Hence," the ruling concluded, "a court examining these facts could reasonably conclude that these men were much more than mere roommates."

Impact

As the result of the *Braschi* ruling, the New York State Housing Agency announced a broader definition of family that explicitly included same-sex couples. In a community decimated by AIDS, in which many surviving partners were not named on the leases of their own homes, this had enormous significance for both the gay rights and the tenants movements.

CHAPTER 3

——————————————

GAY RIGHTS AND U.S. CULTURE

As discussed in previous chapters, the term *gay rights* may indicate a political movement or legal status. *Gay rights* may also be used in a more general sense, to express the place of gay men and lesbians in U.S. culture. Students of the issue might ask whether gay rights has progressed to the point where Americans take for granted the representation of gay men and lesbians in popular culture, as characters on TV shows and in movies, as figures in advertising, and as popular musicians. Or they might look at the extent to which gay people feel safe coming out in various occupations. They could look at the way gay issues are represented in the news media. Or they could examine the extent to which gay men and lesbians have or have not won full participation in religion, education, and civic organizations, such as the Boy Scouts of America. All of these areas of inquiry would reveal something about the kinds of rights enjoyed by gay men and lesbians in the United States at this point in history.

As with the study of other aspects of gay rights, examining gay people's place in the culture is rife with contradiction. A lesbian mother in Mississippi may lose custody of her child to her husband's parents even as the TV shows *Will & Grace* or *Queer Eye for the Straight Guy* win millions of viewers and are routinely referred to elsewhere in mainstream culture. A gay high school student faces harassment, bullying, even physical violence, while gay-straight high school clubs are winning recognition as never before. The Boy Scouts of America announce that openly gay members are not welcome—and a number of communities across America then withdraw public support for the Scouts. In some churches, gay men and lesbians can become ministers and in some cases enjoy the church's recognition of their marriage; in others, homosexuality is viewed as the ultimate immorality. On the one hand, gay men and lesbians are visible and empowered in our culture as never before; on the other hand, gay people still face physical, emotional, and economic abuse that ranges from losing a job to being denied membership in a church to being attacked or even murdered for their sexual orientation.

A comprehensive assessment of gay men and lesbians in U.S. culture is clearly beyond the scope of this book. This chapter highlights some of the key areas for gay rights that seem to go beyond strictly legal rights (although courts and legislatures may be involved), specifically discussing gay activity in culture, education, and religion.

FREE SPEECH AND COMMERCIAL
SUCCESS: GAY CULTURE IN THE 1990s
AND THE TWENTY-FIRST CENTURY

The 1990s began in the wake of a major cultural battle for supporters of gay rights. In 1989, the work of the late gay photographer Robert Mapplethorpe, which included homoerotic images of nude men, was featured in a traveling exhibit that appeared in a number of museums around the country, including the Contemporary Arts Center of Cincinnati. Mapplethorpe's more controversial images featured sadomasochistic imagery, including a self-portrait of himself naked except for a leather cap and jacket with a bullwhip inserted in his anus. Also in the exhibit was a photograph of a man's torso in a three-piece suit, with a large black penis sticking out of the unzipped pants.

Recognizing the potentially volatile nature of the exhibition, officials restricted access to the museum to those over the age of 18, and even removed images felt to be disturbing or explicit to a special, isolated room. Nevertheless, a local sheriff raided the exhibit and eventually obtained a grand jury indictment against museum director Dennis Barrie on obscenity charges. Although he was eventually acquitted, Barrie left the museum.

Meanwhile, the exhibit had been funded by the National Endowment for the Arts (NEA) to travel around the country and was slated to go on to a museum in Washington, D.C. In response, Senator Jesse Helms and the Religious Right charged that public funds should not be used to support "pornography," particularly in the nation's capital.

Attacks on the NEA continued. In 1990, NEA head John Frohnmayer, fearing further obscenity charges, withdrew grants that had been made to four performance artists—Karen Finley, Holly Hughes, Tim Miller, and John Fleck. Hughes, Miller, and Fleck were leading figures in gay culture, while Finley, publicly identified as straight, was known for the way her work challenged narrow ideas of gender and criticized the sexual and social repression of women. Each of the "NEA Four" had already been approved by an independent panel of artists, so Frohnmayer's action struck many as, if not outright censorship, a high-handed government intervention to curtail artistic freedom. Moreover, under pressure from the Religious Right, the NEA went on to include a "decency clause" in all of its grants: to get public money, recipients had to promise not to do "obscene" work.

Public outrage at gay culture continued in various forms throughout the 1990s. In Charlotte, North Carolina, for example, a progressive city known as "the showplace of the South," the Mecklenburg County Commission voted to stop funding organizations that exposed the public to "perverted forms of sexuality." The commission's action was inspired by a local production of *Angels in America*, a Pulitzer Prize–winning play by Tony Kushner featuring several gay characters. *Angels* had won several awards on Broadway, where it had played for several months, and the show soon became a favorite of regional theaters around the United States. Since the local production was presented by the Charlotte Repertory Theater, which received some funding from the county, county commissioners felt justified in cutting funds to the arts council that had funded the theater, to prevent further support for images of "deviant sex." Although to gay rights supporters, the play merely presented recognizable portraits of gay men, opponents were outraged by the play's matter-of-fact acceptance of homosexuality and its images of (fully clothed) men embracing as a prelude to having sex.

The commission's action drew fire from local gay and lesbian activists—and from the local business community, which feared that the antigay and anti-art activity would make Charlotte look provincial and unfit to host the many banks and corporate headquarters it was courting. A mere week after the county commissioners voted, executives from a wide variety of groups—including the Charlotte-based NationsBank Corporation, First Union Corporation, Duke Power Company, and the local Urban League—announced a campaign directed against the offending politicians, who were facing reelection the following year.

The leader of the county commission's action was Hoyle Martin, an African American originally from New York City who voted with socially conservative white Republicans to get his measure passed. Martin admitted that these politicians did not usually represent the interests of his inner-city constituents. But he was willing to make common cause with them against the more liberal elements on the commission in order to discourage homosexuality, which he considered one of America's greatest threats.

The actions of Helms, Frohnmayer, and Martin took place against a growing visibility of gay culture in America, most notably on television, but also in movies, theater, popular music, and the literary world. When both TV comedian Ellen DeGeneres and her character on the sitcom *Ellen* came out as lesbians in spring 1997, the move caused both more and less furor than anyone expected. On the one hand, advertisers such as the Chrysler Corporation pulled their commercials from *Ellen*'s "coming out" episode, and individual stations, like one in Birmingham, Alabama, refused to air the April 30 episode. When a Birmingham gay comedian tried to rent a theater to show the episode, the theater owner refused, saying that the issue was "too controversial." (The comedian was eventually able to rent a city-owned theater.)

Yet millions of people watched Ellen come out on Disney-owned ABC-TV, and the show was renewed for the following season. When *Ellen* was finally pulled from the air, it was not due to any political controversy, but rather because of low ratings. The openly gay DeGeneres has gone on to appear in mainstream movies and to host her own talk show.

In March 1999, the conservative Christian Action Network tried to stem the tide of gay themes and characters on television by calling for an "HC"—"homosexual content"—rating to be attached to every TV show with a gay character. Max Mutchnick, openly gay cocreator of the sitcom *Will & Grace*, which features two openly gay characters responded calmly: "[HC is] totally offensive, but it adds up to nothing. The numbers are telling us everything." Indeed, according to Scott Seomin, entertainment media director of the Gay and Lesbian Alliance Against Defamation (GLAAD), the spring 1999 TV season featured more than 25 gay or bisexual characters on network series, with more new gay characters featured on shows the following fall. Despite various right-wing and Christian right efforts to boycott TV programs, networks, and advertisers associated with gay-themed shows, the trend has been for an increasing number of openly gay characters to populate the small screen.

On broadcast TV, gay characters have begun to appear on shows whose theme is not specifically gay or lesbian. The medical show *E.R.*, for example, features a major character named Dr. Kerry Weaver, whose storylines sometimes revolve around her lesbian identity and sometimes deal with other issues. Over the past several years, viewers have seen the middle-aged Kerry go through a number of emblematic lesbian experiences: first sexual relationship with a woman, fear of becoming known as a lesbian (which cost her several relationships with partners who were ultimately unwilling to hide their identities), an eventual willingness to come out at work, having a baby with her partner, and engaging in a custody battle for her son when her partner died and her partner's family took temporary custody of the child. Gay and lesbian characters have also shown up on the teen cult hit *Buffy, the Vampire Slayer* (currently off the air but frequently seen in syndication), and on a number of other comic and dramatic programs.

Cable TV has always enjoyed more latitude than broadcast programming, enabling the premier Showtime network to feature an American version of the sexually explicit British hit, *Queer as Folk*. Over the years, *Queer as Folk* has taken on a number of gay and lesbian political issues, including antigay violence, homophobic police and politicians, AIDS, and antigay discrimination at work. It has also portrayed social and cultural themes in urban gay life from a gay perspective as its characters struggle with monogamy, unrealistic standards for body and appearance, pornography, childrearing, the lack of gay images in popular culture, and the sometimes puritanical restrictions of "official" gay culture. Although lesbians have traditionally been less visible than gay men on television and elsewhere, *The L Word* is an hour-long Showtime drama focusing on a diverse group of gay women who, like the *Queer as Folk* characters, struggle with both personal and political issues.

Meanwhile, the premier network HBO also includes gay characters on its hit show, *Six Feet Under*. Unlike the characters in the Showtime programs, whose relationship to gay and lesbian issues is a primary part of their TV identities, the primary gay character on *Six Feet Under* is simply a man who happens to be gay. This casual treatment suggests that at some point, gay and lesbian identity will be viewed as just one more characteristic, like being from the South or working as a lawyer—not irrelevant, but hardly all-encompassing.

The big screen has not been nearly as inclusive. Although big-budget Hollywood movies like *In and Out* and *The Birdcage* have drawn a certain amount of attention, most of the increased attention to gay culture in the movies have come from such independent filmmakers as Rose Troche (*Go Fish*, 1994; *Bed-*

rooms and Hallways, 1999), Don Roos (*The Opposite of Sex*, 1997), and Todd Haynes (*Velvet Goldmine*, 1998; *Far from Heaven*, 2002). Yet even in the movies, gay and lesbian characters are showing up as part of the social landscape. The mainstream 2004 teen movie *Mean Girls*, for example, which focuses on teenage girls, features a gay male best friend whose sexual identity is well-known to others in the school, as well as a straight girl falsely assumed to be lesbian. Although these characters face a certain amount of bullying and harassment, so do all the kids who are considered "different" or who have displeased the popular "Queen Bee" girls who run the school by being meaner than anyone else.

Another American movie featuring gay characters is *The Hours*, a 2002 film directed by British director Stephen Daldry that included popular actresses Meryl Streep and Julianne Moore playing characters erotically involved with other women, and actor Ed Harris as a gay male poet dying of AIDS. The movie was adapted from Michael Cunningham's Pulitzer Prize–winning novel—another sign of the increasing visibility of gay and lesbian artists in mainstream culture.

Certainly gay and lesbian artists, themes, and characters have played a significant role in recent New York theater seasons. In 2003, composer Marc Shaiman won a Tony Award, Broadway's highest honor, for his work on the musical *Hairspray* and made awards-ceremony history by kissing his male partner on the TV broadcast. In 2004, the Pulitzer Prize for drama was awarded to *I Am My Own Wife*, a play about a gay transvestite under the Nazi and Communist regimes in Germany. When Harvey Fierstein's *Torch Song Trilogy* opened on Broadway in 1982, the openly gay characters were considered a revolutionary addition to the Broadway stage. Twenty years later, such gay-themed shows as *Avenue Q, Take Me Out,* and a sexually explicit production of *Cabaret* take their place without comment alongside other mainstream entertainment.

The publishing world has also displayed a kind of casual openness to gay and lesbian books, authors, and photographers that would have been unthinkable only five years ago. Mainstream commercial presses feature political analyses of gay marriage and gay culture, as well as gay self-help books, memoirs, and humor. For anyone who remembers the time when homophile magazines had to be sent to anonymous post office boxes in brown paper wrappers, the number, range, and variety of commercial gay titles is truly remarkable.

On the other hand, gay men are still more visible than lesbians in mainstream culture, and the world of publishing is no exception. Although such writers as Dorothy Allison, Sarah Schulman, Sapphire, and Adrienne Rich have gained a certain amount of fame, lesbian writers and poets have generally had more difficulty than their gay male counterparts.

In response to the extreme difficulty of being accepted into the mainstream, as well as from a genuine commitment to alternatives, lesbian cultural institutions flourished in the 1970s. Kitchen Table Press, for women of color; Crossing Press's feminist series; Spinsters Ink; Firebrand; Aunt Lute; and Diana Press were only some of the women's publishers that released lesbian novels and poetry, self-help books, anthologies, and political analyses, publishing authors like

Gay Rights

Jewelle Gomez, Sally Gearheart, Adrienne Rich, Audre Lorde, Jane Rule, Cherrie Moraga, and Barbara Smith. Yet, the same cultural acceptance that has enabled novelist Dorothy Allison (*Bastard Out of Carolina, Cavedweller*) to find a home with a commercial press, has also helped drive many alternative publishers out of business.

The 1970s and 1980s were also a time of "women's music," with events like the annual Michigan Womyn's Festival and performers like Holly Near, Meg Christian, Cris Williamson, Margie Adam, and Alix Dobkin as regular fixtures on the women's concert circuit. Many of these women recorded with Olivia, a women's record company that for a time expanded into a virtual network of women's businesses, including a travel agency. Partly driven by a separatist ideal and partly inspired by a utopian image of women's community, lesbian feminists and other women ran a wide range of businesses, from bookstores to coffeehouses to vegetarian restaurants. This commodification of lesbian culture reached a peak in May 1993 with a *New York* magazine cover article declaring the advent of "lesbian chic," which presented female same-sex relationships as glamorous, slightly exotic alternatives to heterosexual relationships. For many lesbians, this image of them as sexy, urbane women was a welcome relief from the popular stereotype that portrays them as mannish, unattractive asexuals. Many others, though, were disturbed by the implication that lesbianism was merely a set of lifestyle poses that could be put on and discarded at will.

Nowadays, gay and lesbian voices are heard in the mainstream music world to an extent unimaginable only 25 years ago. Throughout the 1990s, many world-famous musicians openly declared their homosexuality, with little or no impact on their commercial popularity. One of the first to do so was 1970s British rock star and now Broadway composer, Elton John, who has gone on to be a major celebrity advocate for gay rights and AIDS research and prevention. Other British pop stars to come out of the closet include Boy George, who had early in his career used his sexual ambiguity as a way to distinguish himself from other singers, and George Michael, who was unwillingly outed when he was arrested in April 1998 for indecently exposing himself to a male undercover police officer in a Beverly Hills, California, public restroom. Both have since become vocal supporters of gay rights.

As of this writing Rufus Wainwright is the only significant American male pop star who has openly identified himself as gay; however, several prominent North American women musicians have chosen to make their sexuality public. Among them are k.d. lang who, in 1992, became the first major lesbian singer to come out. She chose to make her announcement in the pages of *Vanity Fair* magazine, which posed her and model Cindy Crawford in a very provocative cover photo: lang in a barber chair, her face lathered in shaving cream, while Crawford pretends to shave her—a scenario that lang describes in the article as a fantasy of hers. Such an unambiguous representation of lesbian sexual fantasy in a mainstream publication had been unheard of until then and was an indication of how far the culture had come in tolerating depictions of same-sex desire. On the other hand, the Indigo Girls (Amy Ray and Emily Saliers), also

144

openly lesbian, faced discrimination in May 1998, when they gave a series of free concerts at high schools in three southern states. Parents in South Carolina and Tennessee objected to their presence at the schools because of their sexual orientation, forcing the duo to cancel three concerts. Another prominent lesbian entertainer, Melissa Etheridge, along with her then partner Julie Cypher, has become a vocal spokesperson for gay parents. When Cypher was pregnant with their first child, she and Etheridge posed for the cover of *Newsweek* magazine because, as they told *Rolling Stone* in February 2000, they felt "it meant something to the [gay and lesbian] community." Given how little coming out has hurt these musicians' careers, it is likely that this trend will continue into the future.

Meanwhile, in the world of alternative music, gay and lesbian musicians are strikingly prominent. Such artists as Bob Mould (head of the alternative group Magnetic Fields) and Ani di Franco have brought new voices into the independent music scene. And gay issues in the mainstream music world were highlighted by white rapper Eminem, who drew criticism from both gay and straight listeners when he made a homophobic slur against the (straight) musician Moby. Eminem surprised both the gay and straight communities when he sang a much-publicized duet with openly gay musician Elton John at the Grammy Awards, signaling at the very least that the situation for gay and lesbian musicians remains as contradictory as the position of gay culture in the rest of the society.

The gay and lesbian magazine world faces many of the same issues as the alternative press. Many of the early gay and lesbian publications identified deeply with gay rights, feminism, sexual liberation, and/or gay liberation. Journals like *Fag Rag, Gay Sunshine,* and *Come Out!* celebrated the exciting new post-Stonewall gay identity, while newspapers like the *New York Native* and the California-based the *Advocate* were considered political vehicles as much as sources of information. One short-lived but extremely influential publication was *Outweek,* which was produced in New York from June 1989 to June 1991. Among other things, *Outweek* served as an important voice of the AIDS activist community; was instrumental in the promotion of the term *queer* as a replacement for the words "gay" and "lesbian"; and introduced the concept of "outing" (the practice of publically disclosing a celebrity's or politician's sexual orientation, usually against his or her wishes) through the weekly column of staff writer Michelangelo Signorile. Many members of the gay and lesbian community, though, found *Outweek's* politics to be too radical and its attitude toward straight people too hostile. As a result, it never found a wide, national readership or large companies willing to buy ad space in its pages. Today, glossy publications like *Out* and *POZ* (for people with HIV/AIDS) feature ads from Fortune 500 companies and profiles of heterosexual movie stars along with their coverage of gay politics and culture. Furthering the trend to a more mainstream, "corporate" model of gay and lesbian publishing, in February 2000 *Out* announced that it had been acquired by Liberation Publications, the company that publishes the *Advocate*. Liberation Publications went on to create or acquire other publications and presses and, as of this writing, also owns *Out Traveler*, *HIV Plus*, and Alyson Books (a lesbian press)—further evidence of the increasingly corporate nature of gay publishing. As gay men have become established as a niche group, several commercial publications have targeted them, including *Genre*, an upscale publication for professional men, and *Instinct*, described as a gay male version of *Cosmopolitan*. Lesbians have been targeted to a lesser extent by such magazines as *Curve* and *Girlfriends*. The existence of such publications as *Alternative Family Magazine*; *A&U (Art & Understanding)*; *Cybersocket Web Magazine*; *Gay Parent*; and *QV*, for gay male Latinos, attests to the role of niche marketing in the gay publishing world, as does *XY*, which targets young gay men (and men who like to read about them).

The proliferation of magazines targeted at gay men is due in part to the notion that this demographic is a particularly affluent sector of the population. Men earn more money than women, the reasoning goes, and when two men live together without children (a more common configuration for gay men than for straight couples or lesbians), their "dual-income no kids," or DINKS, household will naturally have more to spend on consumer goods than its straight or lesbian counterpart.

As a result, advertisers are increasingly developing strategies to reach gay men. According to an August 15, 2003, article in the *Dallas Morning News*, the companies behind Ford vehicles, Miller beer, Absolut vodka, Tylenol PM medication, Mitchell Gold furniture, and John Hancock financial services are creating gay-specific ads showing or referring to same-sex couples, occasionally also including children in their portrayal of gay households. The Avis rental car company has an ad campaign that identifies the company as gay-friendly and almost apologizes for taking so long to publicize a company policy that allows domestic partners to be automatically included as additional drivers on all rentals. American Airlines sponsors a float in the Dallas gay pride parade and seeks "official airline" status for many gay and lesbian conferences. And Miller beer, known for its "guy-oriented" ads focusing on men trying to pick up women, developed a TV commercial in which women try to pick up first one man, then another—until they notice the two men holding hands. According to Howard Buford, an executive at the marketing and advertising company that created the ads, "Straight men really enjoyed [the ad]," as well as straight women and gay men.

According to a study conducted by Prime Access Inc. and Rivendell Marketing Company, gay- and lesbian-targeted ad spending, as measured through the gay and lesbian press, had grown to $208 million by 2001—a fourfold increase in less than 10 years. With estimates of self-identified U.S. gays and lesbians ranging from 14 million (5 percent of the U.S. population) to 28 million (10 percent), the gay and lesbian market is clearly significant, especially when you consider that even the lower figure is slightly bigger than the Asian-American market. The public relations and marketing firm Witeck-Combs Communications Inc. estimates that gay men, lesbians, and bisexuals command $450 million worth of buying power, as compared to an estimated $300 million for Asian

Americans (a figure determined by the Selig Center for Economic Research at the University of Georgia).

Yet a 2001 book by University of Massachusetts at Amherst professor M.V. Lee Badgett claims that "Gay men's and lesbians' lives are characterized by economic disadvantage—not economic privilege." In *Money, Myths, and Change: The Economic Lives of Lesbians and Gay Men*, Badgett explains that gay and bisexual men earn 17 percent to 28 percent less than their straight male counterparts, although straight women, lesbians, and bisexual women seem to earn about the same amount. Since lesbians and bisexual women are less likely to interrupt their careers to raise children, however, their economic discrimination may be read in the fact that they do not earn *more* than straight women. Still, Badgett says, "The biggest economic issue for lesbians is being women, and for gay men it's being gay." She suggests that antigay groups and gay marketing groups have inadvertently collaborated to portray the gay and lesbian community as privileged and affluent, whereas in fact, being gay or bisexual is an economic disadvantage, at least for men.

However the gay community compares to mainstream society, a significant number of gay people do have disposable income to spend, and advertisers' trend toward targeting gay men (and, to a lesser extent, lesbians) seems bound to continue. For some gay rights activists, this is good news, signaling greater acceptance; for others, it indicates a problematic increase in corporate dominance over gay culture. Thus, the dilemma in gay and lesbian culture parallels the larger tensions in gay and lesbian politics: accessibility versus political clarity; assimilation versus the maintenance of a unique identity; commercialization versus an alternative vision. Some might find a mainstream publisher's release of a gay male self-help book revolutionary or at least a sign that gay men have finally been accepted into the culture at large. Others see the event as symbolic of co-optation, the loss of a uniquely gay perspective in the face of mass cultural homogenization. Lesbian culture remains more marginalized and less commercial than gay male culture, but to some extent it, too, is making its way into the mainstream.

EDUCATION

There are two major issues in education for gay men and lesbians: the rights of gay and lesbian teachers and the rights—and safety—of gay and lesbian students. As with other issues we have examined, there is quite a bit of overlap between legal issues—court cases, referendums, legislation—and cultural issues—the general level of acceptance for lesbians and gay men in our society.

GAY TEACHERS' RIGHTS

One of the first incidents involving a gay teacher's right to be politically active was the case of John Gish, a high school teacher in Paramus, New Jersey, who was fired in 1972 for accepting the presidency of the local Gay Activists Alliance. The case continued through 1980, when Gish's firing was upheld by New Jersey State Education Commissioner Fred G. Burke, who called Gish's activism "conduct unbecoming to a teacher."

Another turning point for gay teachers' rights came in 1977, when the Oklahoma state legislature unanimously passed a law requiring gay and lesbian teachers to be dismissed and banning the favorable mention of homosexuality in the public schools. The legislation was challenged in a case that went to the Supreme Court in 1985. The Court invalidated the law by a tie vote of 4-4, giving many unwarranted optimism when *Bowers v. Hardwick* came before the Court the following year.

As discussed in Chapter 1, the 1978 Briggs Initiative sought to achieve a similar goal via referendum in the state of California. Proposition 6 would also have removed all gay teachers from the school system, as well as banned positive references to "homosexual" behavior. The initiative, however, was defeated, which seemed to many to be an affirmation, albeit back-handed, of gay and lesbian teachers' right to teach.

From the 1970s into the 21st-century, gay and lesbian teachers continued to fight a number of battles across the nation. In 1993, for example, the Tenth Circuit Court of Appeals ruled that school officials in Kansas could legally refuse to hire a teacher who was suspected of being gay. Even though the applicant in question was heterosexual, the court upheld the district's right not to hire him.

In the more gay-positive atmosphere of the 1990s and the early 21st-century, teachers have tended to fight back more often than before—and, occasionally, they win. Wendy Weaver, for example, was a teacher and volleyball coach in Spanish Fork, Utah. After acknowledging to a student in 1997 that she was a lesbian, she was fired from the coaching part of her job and put under a gag order: She was told that if she discussed her sexual orientation with "students, staff members or parents of students," she would be fired.

Weaver thought that the gag order was wrong and that she would be unable to comply with it. Since the seven children that she and her partner were raising together were students at the school, the gag order would have banned her from talking about her sexuality with either her partner or her children. Accordingly, she brought a federal lawsuit against the school district, which she won in 1998. Parents and students continued to complain to the school board about Weaver, but the district remained supportive. Weaver's opponents tried to bring suit in federal district court, but a judge dismissed the lawsuit in 1999. Then her opponents sought to have the state supreme court declare her unfit to teach, on the grounds that her lesbian identity meant that she was breaking the state's sodomy laws, then in force. Weaver's opponents wanted her fired, but the school district continued to support her, and the Utah high court eventually ruled in April 2003 that those bringing suit lacked "a legally protectible interest in this controversy." The court said that parents or students with a complaint against a teacher were obliged to bring their grievances to the local school district (which had already refused to act), the Professional Practices Advisory

Commission (a division of the state board of education), or the state board of education itself. (Ironically, the state's sodomy laws—part of the basis for complaining about Weaver's lack of fitness—would be struck down by the U.S. Supreme Court a few months later.)

Weaver attributed her opponents' hostility to her own popularity and evident happiness with her life. "That doesn't go with their perception that gay people are evil or unhealthy," a news story quoted her as saying.

Weaver's story exemplifies both the hostility that gay and lesbian educators can face, and the support that they can receive from their communities, even in conservative states like Utah. Other gay and lesbian teachers have also been able to turn to their communities or their unions. The California Teachers Association (CTA), for example, took up the case of Jim Merrick, a 40-year classroom veteran and winner of the 1996 Chamber of Commerce Teacher of the Year Award in a rural district outside Bakersfield, California. Merrick spoke out anonymously against a local politician who called gay people "sick." Somehow, his own sexuality became known to parents, who began to remove their children from his classroom. Merrick and his union fought the administration's concession to the transfer requests, which they claimed violated the state labor code's provisions against job discrimination on the basis of "actual or perceived sexual orientation." Merrick also filed a complaint with the state and took medical leave due to job-related stress.

But Merrick was deeply committed to the fight he had begun. Alluding to the 1998 case in Wyoming in which a gay college student was murdered, Merrick said, "I don't want another Matthew Shepard to happen, if I can help in any way. I've got lots of gay and lesbian kids in that school who are . . . getting the wrong message. We need to send them a different message."

In March 1999, Merrick settled the lawsuit he had filed, with the district agreeing to apologize for removing students from his classes and committing to a stronger nondiscrimination policy. Merrick returned to work as a curriculum specialist for the few months remaining until the retirement he had planned for June 1999. He considered the settlement a model, however, for how to overcome bigotry in public institutions, a sentiment seconded by CTA staff counsel Scott McVarish, who said the settlement would be "the blueprint for how all school districts in California must protect the rights of gay teachers."

The stories of Weaver (who now goes by her unmarried name, Chandler) and Merrick indicate that teaching is still a difficult profession in which to be gay. On the one hand, gay men, lesbians, and bisexuals are experiencing increasing acceptance by many sectors of the public. On the other hand, the Religious Right and other conservatives are willing to fight to remove gay teachers from their positions. These stories raise particularly difficult questions: Do teachers have rights that outweigh a parent's right to have a child moved to another classroom? Should groups that protect the rights of teachers also show regard for parents' legitimate concerns about what kind of classroom environment they want for their children? Some teachers argue that their districts would oppose a parent's move to transfer a child to avoid a teacher on the grounds of race, age, or physical handicap, while allowing parents to transfer students away from lesbian and gay teachers. But what about a parent's wish to have a teacher that is simply "more compatible" with the child or who shares the parent's own political, philosophic, or moral views? How should parents' rights be balanced with a school district's commitment to diversity and tolerance? These are questions that may be raised more often as gay and lesbian educators receive more recognition.

STUDENT RIGHTS

In 1980, a Providence, Rhode Island, gay teenager named Aaron Fricke sued for the right to bring a male date to his high school prom. Fricke's 1995 memoir of the incident, *Reflections of a Rock Lobster*, introduced much of the United States to the existence of "out and proud" gay teenagers.

The 1982 establishment of Philadelphia's Byton High, the nation's first high school for gays and lesbians, also affirmed that young gay men and women had the right to receive support as they claimed their identities. In 1985, the New York City Board of Education followed suit by helping to establish the Harvey Milk School for gays and lesbians. More than ever before, gay and straight students are now working together to overcome homophobia and promote awareness of gay issues.

Aaron Fricke described a remarkably tolerant climate for himself and his date in 1980. Many other gay and lesbian teenagers, however, have suffered from teasing, harassment, and outright physical danger in school districts across the nation. In 1996 Wisconsin teenager Jamie Nobozny became the first student to bring a successful suit against the school authorities that had failed to protect him from harassment that occurred beginning in the seventh grade and continuing through eleventh grade, including beatings that required hospitalization. Similar suits have been brought in states across the country.

In Doug Ireland's January 31, 2000, *Nation* article, "Gay Teens Fight Back," California student Jared Nayfack described an incident on a trip sponsored by his Catholic high school, during which he was beaten to "a bloody mess" by a bigger student who, he said, "could have killed [him]." The other student was not punished; instead, Jared was put on academic and behavioral probation and was told by the dean that "I was at fault because I'd 'threatened the masculinity' of the kid who'd beat me up."

"Five or ten years ago, kids would go to a youth service agency and say, 'I need help because I think I'm gay,'" says Rea Carey, quoted in the same article. Carey is the executive director of the National Youth Advocacy Coalition (NYAC), a coalition of various service agencies that supports gay youths. "Today, more and more they say, 'I'm gay and so what?. . .' Being gay is not their problem, it's their strength. These kids are coming out at 13, 14, 15. . . . But they are experiencing more violence because of that."

A number of studies support the perception that gay, lesbian, and bisexual youths are at risk of violence, particularly at school. Human Rights Watch

Gay Rights and U.S. Culture

(HRW), a New York–based group that has monitored violence and human rights abuses in such troubled locations as Kosovo, also studied the plight of young people in the United States, concluding in 2001 that some two million U.S. students are bullied each year because they are—or are believed to be—homosexual. Moreover, HRW found that teachers often ignored, condoned, or even encouraged the harassment. Their report, "Hatred in the Hallways: Discrimination and Violence Against Lesbian, Gay, Bisexual and Transgender Youth in U.S. Public Schools," was based on interviews with 140 youths and 130 school employees and parents in California, Georgia, Kansas, Massachusetts, New York, Texas, and Utah. According to the HRW report, students spent a great deal of time and energy trying to be "invisible"—avoiding other students in school and on the way to and from school, skipping gym classes, and finding other strategies to avoid being harassed or beaten.

Also in 2001, researchers at the University of California at Davis reported that young people with same-sex attraction were more likely to have been attacked, to have been in fights requiring medical treatment, and perhaps even to have perpetrated violence.

In 2002, more than one-half of teens surveyed by the National Mental Health Association (NMHA) reported that classmates used such slurs as "fag" and "dyke" nearly every day. Ironically, the NMHA also found that some three-fourths of the students who were harassed and targeted were in fact straight.

These studies were supported by the 2003 investigation conducted by the Gay, Lesbian, and Straight Education Network (GLSEN). In a study based on a survey of 887 middle and high school students from 48 states and the District of Columbia, GLSEN found that some 84 percent of lesbian, gay, bisexual, and transgender students reported being verbally harassed because of their sexual orientation, with 82.9 percent of the students stressing that faculty rarely intervened, even when they witnessed the incident.

The GLSEN study also found a connection between school violence, poor performance, and lowered goals. The youths who reported being significantly harassed averaged a 2.9 grade point average (GPA), as opposed to a 3.3 average for students who had not been harassed. They were also twice as likely to indicate that they did not intend to go to college.

With the right school atmosphere, however, students' aspirations remained high. Only 10.1 percent of students who could identify supportive faculty at their school reported that they did not intend to go to college, as opposed to the 24.1 percent of those who could not identify supportive faculty and did not plan to continue their education. Likewise, students who believed there were no policies intended to protect them were nearly 40 percent more likely to skip school because of being too afraid to go.

Nevertheless, few states have laws protecting gay youth. The 1999 Columbine school shootings inspired a wave of anti-bullying workshops, laws, regulations, and programs, many of which were specifically intended to help gay students. But, as reported in a February 21, 2003, article in the *Wall Street Journal*, many tolerance and diversity programs were attacked by antigay conservatives, causing the programs to be either abolished or modified so as not to target gay youth. Gay students, along with their parents and supporters, viewed the efforts to eliminate these programs as yet another attempt to erode gay rights. Conservatives saw the gay elements of the anti-bullying programs as gay rights' groups covert efforts to smuggle in their own agenda under the guise of a program with a different intention.

The *Wall Street Journal* article included poignant accounts of gay youths who reported being targeted. Justen Deal, for example, an 18-year-old college freshman, described harassment so intense that he first changed high schools and then dropped out for a while. In a January 2, 2003, story in the *Missoula Independent*, a high school freshman known as Sam related an incident in which a female classmate said, "Quit looking at me, you stupid f------ faggot." Other classmates called Sam "fag" and "queer," and one student pretended to vomit on Sam while the class laughed and the teacher looked on, as though merely observing student high spirits. Eventually, Sam's mother came to fear that her son was in physical danger and she pulled him from the school, although he later had to return.

Sam's school district made an effort to create a more welcoming environment. But, as the GLSEN and HRW studies showed, many school districts do not. Although the number of gay-straight alliances is growing, many gay youths experience schools as isolating, hostile, and even physically dangerous places. In such environments, it is difficult to determine the impact of such legal milestones as the *Lawrence v. Texas* decision or the growing popularity of gay-themed TV.

RELIGION

Ever since a United Church of Christ congregation in Northern California ordained the first openly gay minister in 1972, faith communities in the United States have grappled with the issue of how best to serve the spiritual needs of their gay and lesbian congregants, while attempting to maintain traditional church teachings on homosexuality. Throughout the 1990s and continuing into the present, gays and lesbians have sought a reevaluation of many of these teachings, which have traditionally considered same-sex relationships sinful. Activists seeking a place in their churches have demanded instead to be given full recognition, including the rights to marry and be ordained. These demands have been posed in various ways—gay Catholics have formed Dignity; gay Episcopalians, Integrity; many gay Jews and Christians have founded their own synagogues and churches. And churches have responded in various ways. Some denominations or movements have fully welcomed gay men and lesbians, some have allowed gay members but not gay religious leaders, and some have welcomed gay people while condemning the practice of homosexuality.

However they have responded, it is safe to say that no religious group in the United States has remained entirely untouched by the new religious presence of gay men and lesbians. The most significant gay rights development of the early part of the 21st century, the partial legalization of same-sex marriage, is particularly significant in that, for many citizens, marriage is both a civil and a spiritual institution. Although gay activism has focused only on *civil* marriages, most marriages in the United States are solemnized within the context of a religious ceremony. For many religious traditionalists, therefore, the push for legal recognition of same-sex marriage represents an assault on what they view as a sacred institution that is the cornerstone of civilized life. In a statement released to the press in support of President George W. Bush's call for passage of a Constitutional amendment outlawing gay marriage, Catholic archbishop Charles Chaput of Denver succinctly stated the position of many conservative religious leaders: "Social science, the wisdom of our religious traditions and the simple common sense of our lived experience, all point in one direction—that marriage is the union of one man and one woman for the sake of raising children in a stable family, and it's vital for the well-being of society."

Gay activists counter that marriage does not necessarily have to involve the care of children. They point out that many people get married who either can't have children, don't want to have children, or are too old to have children. Some argue that there is another, equally valid, spiritual tradition that holds marriage to be the ultimate expression of love between two people, regardless of whether or not they choose to reproduce. Others argue that the concept of marriage as existing only between one man and one woman is a uniquely Western concept, one which would be foreign to the traditional religious teachings of many African, Middle Eastern, and Asian cultures.

There is every reason to believe that gays and lesbians will continue to confront religious institutions with these kinds of issues into the foreseeable future. As the Reverend Harold Brockus, a Presbyterian minister who was one of the first in that denomination to bless the commitment ceremonies of same-sex couples, told Sharon Tubbs when she interviewed him for her article, "Do Gays Have a Prayer in Churches?" in the February 8, 2004, edition of the *St. Petersburg (Florida) Times*, "At the local church level, things are going to continue evolving, and more and more gays are going to continue coming into the local churches . . . the more that happens, the more hearts [will] continue to change."

However, there is a significant and vocal group of religious leaders who have no interest in accommodating gay people, either in the pews or in society. From their perspective, homosexuality is a dangerous, unhealthy lifestyle that under no circumstances should be promoted or even tolerated. The Supreme Court's overturning of the Texas sodomy statute in 2003 and the Massachusetts high court ruling legalizing same-sex marriage, also in 2003, were viewed by many religious conservatives as an affront to their traditional values, spurring a backlash throughout 2003 and 2004. Black ministers in Georgia, traditionally aligned with liberal social causes, lobbied their legislature to ratify an amendment to that state's constitution that would outlaw gay marriage; the Vatican issued a document instructing Catholic politicians worldwide that they had a "moral duty" to publicly oppose any legislation favoring gay marriage or adoption rights; and Christian activist groups, such as Focus on the Family and the

Christian Coalition, have been among the most active supporters of a proposed amendment to the U.S. Constitution that would restrict marriage to one man and one woman.

But for many gay activists, the low point in their community's relationship with religious conservatives came following the tragedy of September 11, 2001. Two days after the terrorist attacks on the World Trade Center and the Pentagon, Pat Robertson, the president of the Christian Coalition, invited fellow religious conservative Jerry Falwell to appear on Robertson's *700 Club* television program. Robertson asked Falwell to offer his opinions on why the attacks had occurred, and Falwell stated his belief that God had allowed "the enemies of America to give us probably what we deserve." While Falwell was responding to Robertson's concern about the separation of church and state in America, he went further by blaming specific American groups for the worst terrorist attack in U.S. history. Along with liberal organizations, such as the ACLU and People for the American Way, Falwell singled out "the gays and the lesbians who are actively trying to make that an alternative lifestyle."

Reaction to Falwell's remarks from both liberals and conservatives was swift and condemnatory. The White House issued a statement from President Bush calling the remarks "inappropriate," and both Falwell and Robertson eventually apologized for the incident. However, they continued to insist that what they perceived as a moral drift in American values had contributed to the circumstances surrounding the attacks. (It should be noted that Falwell's statements represented an extreme in conservative religious views. Many religious leaders derided Falwell within days of his comments.)

CATHOLIC CHURCH

The Catholic Church has long held that homosexual orientation is not in and of itself morally wrong but is instead an "inclination" that is "disordered." Therefore, homosexual persons are expected to live a celibate life. Recently, however, Catholic leaders have increased the rhetorical heat against what they deem "deviant behavior." On August 1, 2003, the Vatican's agency in charge of church doctrine, the Congregation for the Propagation of the Faith, issued a 12-page guideline to Catholic bishops entitled "Considerations Regarding Proposals to Give Legal Recognition to Unions Between Homosexual Persons." While condemning "unjust discrimination against homosexual persons," the document clearly reiterated the church's opposition to any legislation that would grant gay and lesbian couples the same civil benefits as heterosexual married couples: "There are absolutely no grounds for considering homosexual unions to be in any way similar or even remotely analogous to God's plan for marriage and family. Marriage is holy, while homosexual acts go against the natural moral law." The paper went on to say that allowing children to be adopted by gay and lesbian couples "would actually mean doing violence to these children" because it would be placing them in an unhealthy home environment.

Observers pointed out that the document comes at a time when many traditionally Catholic countries or countries with sizable Catholic minorities, such as Canada, France, and Germany, have enacted legislation either granting gay and lesbian citizens full marriage rights or extending many of the benefits associated with marriage to same-sex couples. They also note that the document was released just two months after the U.S. Supreme Court ruled sodomy laws unconstitutional. Some people question the impact the document will have on public policy at a time when many Catholics, both in the United States and in Europe, routinely ignore church teaching on a variety of issues, from reproduction to divorce. A survey by the Pew Forum on Religion and Public Life, released around the same time as the Vatican statement, found that only 41 percent of white Catholics in the United States were opposed to gay marriage.

For some Catholics in the United States, though, the Vatican pronouncement was a welcome and necessary moral directive. William Donahue, spokesman for the conservative Catholic League said in a press release that his group was "particularly delighted" that the Vatican made the "strong statement in favor of marriage" after a widespread pedophilia scandal. He continued, "It sends an unmistakable message that just because a tiny few in the priesthood have embarrassed the church by having sex—mostly with men—this does not mean that the church will silence its voice on matters that are sexual." Donahue was referring to a sexual abuse scandal in the Catholic Church that consumed much of the attention of U.S. Catholics throughout 2002, during which a number of priests had been revealed to have engaged in unlawful sexual transgressions including child molestation. More shocking was the news that some church leaders knew of these transgressions and covered them up by moving priests to new parishes, often causing sexual abuse to spread to these new parishes.

The sex abuse scandal forced the Catholic Church to confront the reality of gay people on the altar and in the congregation, especially as most of the transgressions were same-sex. A report commissioned by the United States Conference of Catholic Bishops (USCCB), prepared by researchers at John Jay College in New York and released in February 2004, found that 81 percent of sex crimes against children and adolescents committed by Catholic priests were homosexual in nature, a reversal of the statistics that apply to the general population, in which heterosexual child abuse, primarily involving adult men and young girls, overwhelmingly outweighs same-sex abuse. However, the study did not go so far as to blame homosexuality itself, instead calling upon the church to understand it better. It urged that homosexual candidates to the seminary be more closely screened and provided with specialized instruction to help them maintain celibacy, and denounced the ordination of what it termed "sexually dysfunctional and psychosexually immature men" by a church desperate to fill the ranks of a dwindling priesthood. Some bishops, though, pointed to the scandal as proof that homosexuality was incompatible with priestly life. Cardinal Anthony Bevilacqua of Philadelphia summed up this position when he was quoted as saying, "we feel a person who is homosexually oriented is not a suitable candidate for the priesthood, even if he did not commit an act."

This was not the resolution of the issue that most gay activists were seeking. Matthew Gallagher, executive director of the gay Catholic group Dignity, called the findings "discrimination in the name of God." He added, "Bishops are not using modern thinking when they say a gay man is more prone to having sex than a straight man." To counter what they perceive as dishonesty on the part of the church, some Catholic gay men, lesbians, and supportive straight people have joined the Rainbow Sash Movement. Founded in 1997 by an Australian man, Nick Holloway, members wear rainbow-colored sashes to Catholic gatherings as a visible reminder of the presence of gays in the church. In addition, each year on the church holiday Pentecost, participants around the world wear the sashes to cathedrals as a form of protest. Reactions to these actions have varied widely. Cardinal Francis George of Chicago refused to give communion to protesters. In St. Paul, Minnesota, parishioners blocked access to the altar for any person wearing a sash. This was in contrast to Los Angeles, where the archbishop extended an invitation to the group to attend services. For some the rainbow sash represents the conflict they experience as gay Catholics: proud of their identity but aware of how far they are from gaining full acceptance by their religion.

EPISCOPAL CHURCH

Although there is no official policy banning gay unions, the church does believe that homosexuality is incompatible with church teachings. In 1996, however, a church court ruled that there was "no core doctrine prohibiting the ordination of a noncelibate homosexual person living in a faithful and committed relationship with a person of the same sex." Some 2.4 million people belong to the Episcopal Church USA.

Recently, though, the Episcopal Church was fiercely divided over the consecration of Gene Robinson as bishop of New Hampshire in a ceremony on November 2, 2003. Robinson became the first openly gay bishop in the modern history of any Christian denomination. Even more offensive to some traditionalists was the fact that he lives with his male partner, who joined him in the bishop's residence.

Since the Episcopal Church is the American branch of England's Anglican Communion, the move had worldwide implications. Rowan Williams, the archbishop of Canterbury and head of the Anglican Communion, issued a statement denouncing the event. Bishops around the globe, particularly those in Africa and Asia, said they would refuse to recognize Robinson as a fellow church official. And a number of U.S. parishes announced plans to splinter from the church and regroup under a new name. Some even went so far as to withhold contributions to their diocese's operational funds to protest what they viewed as an immoral act.

Even within Bishop Robinson's diocese, reactions were polarized. Many New Hampshire residents were proud that their state was breaking new religious ground, while others, such as Bill Hamilton from an Episcopal church in Laconia, were appalled. In an interview with Stephen Bates for the *Guardian* newspaper he stated his deep discomfort with the new bishop, "This man is putting his sexuality ahead of Christianity, ahead of everything. I have nothing against homosexuals, but don't talk, don't tell, don't flaunt it in my face."

As of this writing, no individual parish or diocese has formally left the Episcopal Church or the Anglican Communion over the issue, but three parishes in Los Angeles announced they were breaking with the diocese there and putting their churches under the authority of the archbishop of Uganda, a move that other dioceses have since imitated. However, church officials, deeply concerned about this possibility, convened a 17-member international commission of scholars—the Lambeth Commission—in October 2003 to study ways to prevent a schism.

In October 2004, the report was released. Its chief recommendation was that the U.S. Episcopal Church should express regret for the turmoil that arose from Robinson's consecration as bishop and that there should be a moratorium on bishops "living in a same-gender union" until the church was ready to accept such relationships. The report stopped short of saying that Robinson should step down. Nor did it say that gay bishops per se were prohibited; only those actually living in "same-gender unions," as Robinson is. In response, the Episcopal Church declared a moratorium on the appointment of *any* bishop for one year, as of March 15, 2005.

The report also criticized the bishops from abroad who agreed to minister to U.S. churches distressed by the growing acceptance of homosexuality within the United States. At the same time, the report found problematic a decision by the Canadian branch of the church, known as New Westminster, to approve blessings for same-sex unions.

Although initially, the report was viewed by most observers as a blow to gay rights within the Episcopal Church, Robinson expressed more optimism in an October 21, 2004, *New York Times* article by Laurie Goodstein. Although Robinson was initially disappointed by the report, he said that it left "wiggle room" for sympathetic clergy to continue blessing same-sex unions. And he pointed out that those who made him bishop were not asked to express regret for their decision but only for the turmoil that the decision caused.

Conservatives in the church, opposed to gay rights, were in turn frustrated by the decision, which they saw as too liberal. In the same *New York Times* article, Archbishop Peter Akinola, primate of Nigeria, expressed his outrage that the report did not rebuke Robinson or those who had elevated him to bishop and claimed that "a small, economically privileged group of people" were trying to "subvert the Christian faith," imposing a "new and false doctrine."

Although many U.S. Episcopalians oppose their church's acceptance of homosexuality and were deeply upset by Robinson's elevation to bishop, liberal, pro-gay rights sentiment is most common in that church and elsewhere in the developed world. But the Episcopal Church has only 2.3 million members, as opposed to the more conservative Anglican Church of Nigeria, which has 17 million members. Whether the church will be able to avoid a schism continues to be unclear. However, as Barbara Harris pointed out to *Guardian* reporter Stephen Gates, she faced similar dismay when she became the first woman bishop, an appointment made even more controversial because she was a divorced African American. The church survived that controversy intact. It remains to be seen whether it will survive this one.

Not all denominations have faced such dramatic internal debate as the Episcopalians or such explicit challenges as the Catholics. But none has remained untouched by gay and lesbian activism.

UNITED METHODIST CHURCH

The United Methodist Church is also facing a potential split over the issue of gay people in its midst. Partly in response to the ordination of Gene Robinson in the Episcopal Church, attendees at the General Conference in May 2004 affirmed their stand barring sexually active gay clergy and declaring homosexual behavior to be incompatible with Christian teaching. Three hundred demonstrators from the gay interfaith activist group Soulforce briefly shut down the conference by marching through the assembly hall to protest the church's treatment of gays.

In response to the protests, Reverend Bill Hinson, president of the Confessing Movement, a group of conservative Methodists, said the continuing struggle between those in the church who support gay rights and traditional groups like his had become "more than the church can bear." He issued a proposal that stated, "The time has come when we must begin to explore an amicable and just separation that will free us both from our cycle of pain and conflict." The proposal went on to say that liberal churches could keep their existing property and clergy could keep their pensions.

While Hinson's proposal to splinter the denomination into conservative and liberal congregations never made it to the floor for a vote, his recommendation was indicative of how deeply divided church members are over gay issues. As with the Anglican Church, some of the most vocal opposition to making any accommodation for gays and lesbians came from delegates belonging to branches of the church in African and Asian countries. It remains to be seen how the church, traditionally viewed as one of the most "American," will be able to reconcile these differing cultural perspectives.

At the same national meeting, the church's Judicial Council reviewed the case of Reverend Karen Dammann of Ellensburg, Washington. Dammann had been accused of violating the church's policy against ordaining gays and lesbians after she revealed to the head of the Methodist Pacific Northwest Conference that she was in a committed relationship with another woman. She was subsequently acquitted in a church trial by a jury of 13 fellow Methodist pastors, a move that outraged many conservatives. They appealed her case to the Judicial Council, despite church rules stating that not-guilty verdicts cannot be appealed. The council agreed that it had no jurisdiction to review the case; however, it issued a companion decision stating that a bishop cannot legally appoint someone who was found by a church trial to be a "self-avowed, practicing homosexual." So while Dammann was able to maintain her position as pastor, her case has made it more difficult in the foreseeable future for other lesbians or gay men to do the same.

Indeed, in December 2004, a jury of 13 clergy members in eastern Pennsylvania convicted Reverend Irene Elizabeth Stroud of homosexuality by a vote of 12-1 and then voted 7-6 to remove her from the ministry. Stroud had come out to her congregation in 2003, saying that she lived in a committed relationship with her partner. She said before her trial that she expected to be convicted. Afterward, she predicted that the struggle over gay and lesbian ministers would continue.

LUTHERANS

The largest Lutheran denomination in the United States is the Evangelical Lutheran Church in America (ECLA), with more than five million members. As with the Methodist Church, the Lutherans have had to confront the events taking place in the Episcopal Church. Gene Robinson's appointment as an Episcopal bishop is especially problematic for Lutherans because clergy of either denomination can be ministers at each other's churches. However, Lutheran policy forbids the ordination of openly gay or lesbian clergy, and a similar prohibition applies to bishops. A vote to sever the ties between the two denominations was defeated at the Lutheran synod in August 2003, and there is no indication that Robinson's ordination will seriously damage the relationship. The church plans to decide in 2005 whether or not to ordain openly gay people and to bless same-sex unions.

JUDAISM

Within modern Judaism, there are four major movements. *Reconstructionist*, the most liberal strand, allows gay men and lesbians both to marry within the religion and to become ordained as rabbis. *Reform Judaism*, historically known for its liberal views, supports gay people's legal right to marry and on March 29, 2000, its governing body, the Central Conference of American Rabbis, voted to allow members to officiate at same-sex commitment ceremonies. Among *Conservative Jews*, the ordination of Episcopalian Gene Robinson is having an impact. His appointment as bishop of New Hampshire is prompting the Committee on Jewish Law and Standards to reexamine the movement's long-standing ban against same-sex unions and gay and lesbian rabbis. As Ami Eden points out in an August 29, 2003, article for the Jewish newspaper *Forward*, Anglicans and Conservative Jews "occupy similar spots on the denominational spectrum within their respective religious traditions"—both value preserving traditions, but both also want to be fully engaged in the modern world. As of this writing, the committee was still debating these issues. Regardless, the Conservative movement no longer considers homosexuality an "abomination" and continues to debate whether it is a "sin." *Orthodox Judaism* stands firmly against homosexuality, based on the Book of Leviticus; however, Orthodox Jews also believe in upholding the other 612 commandments on other matters specified for Jews in the Torah (Old Testament).

ISLAM

Islam, like Christianity, is an international religion with a wide spectrum of beliefs, practices, and institutions. Tolerance of homosexuality in Muslim countries has varied widely from place to place and from time to time, as has been true in Christian countries.

One of the major Muslim organizations in the United States is the Islamic Society of North America, which condemns homosexuality on its web site, calling it "a moral disease, a sin, and corruption." It also contends that people are not born gay or lesbian but rather acquire these "evil habits due to a lack of proper guidance or instruction."

In countries with substantial Muslim populations, treatment of gay people varies. In strict Islamic cultures, such as those of Saudi Arabia, Iran, and Afghanistan when it was under the Taliban, homosexual acts between men are punishable by death. In January 2002, three men were beheaded in the southern Saudi Arabian city of Abha for homosexuality, although according to one source, their execution was for raping boys. In more moderate nations, such as Turkey, Indonesia, and Lebanon, gay men and lesbians are usually left alone, while in liberal Muslim countries in sub-Saharan Africa, homosexuality is widely accepted, with varying legal status.

However, it is important to keep in mind that cultural realities are always changing. In some countries, the influence of fundamentalist Islamic teaching is making itself felt, as previously liberal societies have grown more conservative. Egypt, which at one time was one of the centers of gay life in the Middle East, has in recent years had incidents of harassment in gay bars and clubs. International attention focused on this country in May 2001 when Egyptian officials arrested 52 men for attending a party on the Queen Boat, a floating disco on the Nile River known as a gay hangout. Eventually 21 of them would be given the maximum sentence of three years for "habitual debauchery" (there is no law specifically against sodomy in Egypt).

While life has become more difficult for gays and lesbians in Egypt, in other countries it has become easier. In recent years, Saudi Arabia has relaxed its enforcement of laws against gay people. Some of this liberalization can be attributed to the large numbers of young Saudis who have recently returned from the United States because of stricter immigration policy here. Newspapers are now allowed to discuss gay issues, and Saudis have recently gained access to gay-themed web sites, which used to be blocked.

In the United States, many gay and lesbian Muslims face the additional challenge of being immigrants or the children of immigrants. Some are rejected by their traditional-minded families when they come out while others lead "double lives" to prevent their families from learning about their sexuality. In 1998, Pakistani immigrant Faisal Alam founded *Al-Fatiha* (a term for "the Beginning" in the Islamic holy book, the Qu'ran [Koran]), a group for gay, lesbian, bisexual, transgender, and "questioning" Muslims. According to Alam, traditional Muslim parents often blame Americans for "brainwashing" their children, in some instances going so far as to kidnap them and return them to their native countries to try to change their sexuality. Alam himself tried to hide his gay identity from his parents under the guise of being a Muslim rights activist. In a June 17, 2002, interview with the *Miami Herald*, he described the results of his dual life: "I had a nervous breakdown. I was hospitalized for a couple of weeks . . . And I promised it would never happen to anyone else."

Much like Christians, Muslims in the United States and worldwide are struggling with the contrary trends of fundamentalism and modernism. How this will affect the religion's approach to gay rights is unclear.

CHURCH OF JESUS CHRIST OF LATTER-DAY SAINTS (MORMONS)

Mormons not only consider homosexuality a sin, but they have also consistently urged church members to oppose gay rights. The church also has harassed gay members who try to leave. Owen Edwards, a California gay man who was born into the church, tried to resign his membership in March 2000 after Mormons were instructed to support the passage of Proposition 22. The anti–gay marriage amendment eventually was approved, and the church was widely criticized for its political activities connected to the law's passage. Edwards sent a letter to his bishop asking to have his name removed from the membership rolls. In return, he was informed that his request had triggered a "bishop's court" disciplinary hearing. The church eventually backed down and allowed Edwards to leave on his own, but gay Mormons in Utah have not been able to sever their ties to the church as easily. Members there who have tried to leave because of their sexuality have been subjected to church trials, home visitations by church officials, and shunning by members of their family. As Loyd Bulkley, a gay Mormon, told the *San Francisco Examiner* on July 17, 2000, ". . . you can quit going and they can harass and torment you, they send teachers over and people to visit you and call you and invite you to functions. They want you back into the church . . . then if you do something wrong, they'll kick you out."

SOUTHERN BAPTIST CONVENTION

The nearly 16 million Southern Baptists in the United States make the Southern Baptist Convention (SBC), the largest U.S. Protestant denomination—and one of the most antigay, so much so that the leadership amended the SBC's constitution in early 2000 to make support for homosexuality the sole disqualifier for membership. And on June 14, 2000, the church made its antigay stance part of its faith and message statement, which is considered second only to Scripture by the SBC.

More recently, at its annual national gathering in June 2003, the SBC announced a new initiative to encourage church members to minister to gay people. It urged its 42,000 congregations to develop programs that would expose gays and lesbians to ex-gays and has developed a Bible study web site that includes testimonials from gay people who say they've become heterosexuals through their religious faith. At the same meeting, the church reaffirmed its opposition to gay marriage through the passage of a resolution asking all Southern Baptists to "continue to oppose steadfastly all efforts by any court or state legislature to validate or legalize same-sex marriage or other equivalent unions. . ."

The SBC's antigay position has often led to activism. In 2003, they threatened to cancel their 2005 meeting scheduled for Nashville if that city passed a gay nondiscrimination measure. And the SBC's own medical and retirement fund for pastors has been criticized by church members for investing in Carnival Cruise Lines because the travel company allows gay groups to book all-gay cruises on its ships.

One of the group's most publicized acts was its boycott of the movies, television shows, and theme parks associated with the Walt Disney Corporation. For many years, Disney had found allies, and therefore loyal consumers, within the ranks of religious conservatives, who viewed the company as producing "profamily" entertainment products. However, several changes within the corporation in the 1990s led many on the Religious Right to view the company with increased hostility. Disney's decision to extend medical benefits to the same-sex partners of employees and its tolerance of an annual "Gay Day" staged at Walt Disney World, in Florida, were cause for concern among many Southern Baptists and led the SBC to threaten a boycott of the company in June 1996. But it was the Disney-affiliated ABC network sitcom *Ellen* that most rankled the conservative members of the church and pushed them to take action. When Ellen DeGeneres chose to come out of the closet, both as a celebrity and as a character on the show, in April 1997, the SBC's response was swift and unambiguous. In June of that year, the membership voted to boycott all Disney-related merchandise and entertainment. As of 2005, the SBC boycott against Disney is officially still in effect; however, it has had little effect on the company's profits.

UNITED CHURCH OF CHRIST

One of the smallest (1.4 million members) and newest (founded in 1957) Protestant denominations in the United States, the United Church of Christ (UCC) is also one of the most progay. The church has ordained openly gay ministers since 1972 and remains the only Christian denomination to recognize same-sex marriages. The church has spoken out against sodomy laws and for equal gay participation in the military. Moreover, the UCC's highest body, the General

Synod, has actively called on its congregations to study homosexuality and declare that they are "open and affirming."

In December 2004, the United Church of Christ found itself at the center of a controversy as TV networks CBS and NBC refused to air a commercial it had produced. The commercial made explicit the UCC policy of accepting everyone, including same-sex couples, and implicitly accused other Christian denominations of violating Jesus' message by excluding certain categories of worshippers. Although the ad aired on many other network and cable stations, CBS and NBC considered the commercial too controversial.

PRESBYTERIAN CHURCH

Like the Catholic Church, Presbyterians make a distinction between homosexual identity and homosexual acts. The general assembly of this 2.6 million–member denomination has allowed non-celibate gay men and lesbians to apply for the ministry but insists that ordained ministers be celibate. A 2002 proposal to change the celibacy requirement was defeated. In 2000, the church voted that its doctrine does not forbid same-sex "holy unions," thereby giving pastors the authority to perform them with the stipulation that they cannot be called marriages. If a pastor performs a "marriage" ceremony, he or she can be sanctioned.

THE RELIGIOUS SOCIETY OF FRIENDS (QUAKERS)

The Religious Society of Friends is a loosely organized denomination with no church hierarchy. Questions of policy are decided by each meeting house, or church, and there are no ministers among Friends, so ordination is not an issue. Thus, the Quakers as a body cannot be said to have any particular stance on gay rights. However, traditionally, Quakers have tended to be supportive of movements for social change, such as civil rights and gay rights, and many Quaker meeting houses do recognize gay and lesbian marriages.

UNITARIAN UNIVERSALIST ASSOCIATION

Unitarians have always been one of the most liberal of all denominations—they do not even consider themselves Christian, strictly speaking, favoring a more eclectic theology to go with their humanist views. Known for its support of gay rights, the Unitarian Universalist Association (UUA) incurred the wrath of the Boy Scouts of America (BSA) in 1998, when the BSA ordered the Unitarians to stop giving out religious awards to Unitarian scouts.

Unitarian ministers have also been very active in the same-sex marriage actions that took place throughout the United States in the first months of 2004. Ministers from the denomination presided at gay weddings in San Francisco, and the church's web site offers a "Same Sex Wedding Planning Guide." Julie and Hillary Goodridge, the lead plaintiffs in the Massachusetts case that established gay marriage in that state, were married by a Unitarian minister. Two of the more significant Unitarian figures to emerge from the marriage debate are Dawn Sangrey and Kay Greenleaf. Along with Mayor Jason West, the two women, one straight and the other gay, officiated at weddings of same-sex couples in New Paltz, New York, in March 2004. They were later charged with solemnizing marriages without a license, making them the first clergy members nationwide to be prosecuted for marrying gay couples. While Unitarian ministers have been performing religious marriages for same-sex couples for decades, Sangrey and Greenleaf broke the law when they signed affidavits stating the couples were married under state law. Their case is still pending, but their actions have gained them the respect and support of Unitarians nationwide. With 250,000 members, the UUA is hardly a widespread organization, but it has long been known for taking the lead on civil rights and related issues.

GAY RIGHTS IN THE FUTURE?

What has the gay rights movement accomplished in the past 30 years, and what might be expected in the future? Not surprisingly, the answers are contradictory.

For example, despite the enormous changes made in the treatment of gay and lesbian youth—programs at lesbian and gay community centers, gay and lesbian high schools, even some group homes for gay youth—disproportionate numbers of young gay people continue to commit suicide, as do a very high number of gay male adults. A study in the April 2000 issue of the *American Journal of Public Health*, coauthored by psychologists Vickie Mays and Susan Cochran, found that 19 percent of men who reported having sex with other men had attempted suicide at least once in their lives versus only 3.6 percent of exclusively heterosexual men out of a sampling of 3,503 men. An article by B. Bower in *Science News* on October 23, 1999, reported on a study of 103 pairs of male/male twins aged 35 to 53. In each set of twins, one man had had sex only with females, while the other reported at least one male sex partner after age 18. (The men were taken from a larger study of 3,400 twin pairs who had served in the U.S. military between 1965 and 1975.) Nearly 15 percent of the participants with male sex partners had tried to commit suicide, compared with only 4 percent of the strictly heterosexual twins. Bower reports that "Homosexual twins also reported substantially more periods of contemplating their own death or the demise of others, wanting to die, and thinking about committing suicide."

The same article cites a study by psychologist David M. Fergusson of New Zealand's Christchurch School of Medicine, in which 1,265 New Zealand children were tracked from birth to age 21. Fergusson found that "suicide attempts and a variety of mental disorders—including major depression and substance abuse—occur particularly frequently in homosexual and bisexual young adults."

"Taken together with earlier studies, there can be little doubt . . . that homosexual orientation is associated with suicidality, at least among young men," said Gary Remafedi, a psychiatrist with the University of Minnesota Youth and AIDS Projects in Minneapolis, who published comments on the two studies.

For another indication of problems facing the gay community, we might look at the increasing rates of HIV infection among young men. According to a New York City Department of Health study, 18 percent of all African-American gay men aged 15 to 22 are infected with HIV, along with some 9 percent of young Latinos and 3 percent of young whites. The same study found that nearly 46 percent of all young gay men had engaged in unprotected anal sex in the past six months, according to a February 19, 1999, article by Mark Sullivan in the *New York Blade*. "Activists said the study confirms what they already suspected," Sullivan wrote, "that prevention messages haven't gotten through to minorities. Officials at Gay Men's Health Crisis said that anecdotal information prompted that organization to put programs in place—programs such as Peer 2000 and Soul Food, which are specifically geared toward young Black and Latino men."

Sullivan cited a San Francisco study that found similar results: for gay men aged 26 to 29, only 58 percent reported consistent condom use in 1997, down from 62.2 percent in 1994; the proportion of gay men who said they never use a condom during anal sex rose from 30 percent in 1994 to 38 percent in 1997. And of that latter figure, 68 percent said they did not know the HIV status of all of their sex partners of the past six months. Although these studies were conducted in the 1990s, experts say that little has changed in the early part of the 21st century. Gay youths are more likely than their elders to have unprotected sex, and the problem is particularly acute among young men of color who have sex with men, who often do not identify as gay and so believe they do not need to take the precautions recommended by predominantly white gay men's groups.

Yet despite the continued setbacks and the issues on which very little progress has been made, "the gay rights movement continually passes small mileposts even when more major markers aren't in sight," as journalist Deb Price contends:

> *Much like driving across a prairie state, there's a sameness to the gay rights landscape now that creates the illusion of standing still. . . . In reality, we're part of the fastest-moving civil rights struggle in U.S. history, as attorney Evan Wolfson of Lambda Legal Defense and Education Fund always enjoys pointing out. "Compared to the past great struggles for equality," he notes, "ours is moving at Internet speed."*

Those who oppose gay rights present an oddly similar view: On the one hand, they contend that the majority of Americans opposes "the immoral lifestyle" of homosexuality; on the other hand, they find ever more arenas in which lesbian and gay cultural and political power can be felt. From images on television to elected public officials, from state supreme courts' recognition of same-sex marriage rights to churches that perform gay marriages, from antidiscrimination laws to corporate benefits for same-sex couples, the landscape for gay rights has markedly changed—even while some things apparently remain the same. What kinds of changes may take place in even the near future, and how quickly these changes will be felt, remains to be seen.

CHAPTER 4

CHRONOLOGY

1869

- The word *homosexual* is created by Hungarian physician Karoly Maria Benkert (writing under the pseudonym K. M. Kertbeny).

1896

- The world's first periodical dealing with homosexuality—*Der Eigene* ("The Community of the Special")—is published in Germany.

1897

- Perhaps the first homosexual rights group, the Scientific Humanitarian Committee, is formed in Germany by Magnus Hirschfeld, Max Sporh, and Erick Oberg.
- British sexologist Havelock Ellis publishes *Sexual Inversion*, which is considered the first book in English to treat homosexual behavior as neither illness, sin, nor crime.

1924

- The first U.S. gay rights group, the Society for Human Rights, is founded in Chicago but soon disbanded when the wife of one of the members reports the group to the police.

1948

- U.S. sexologist Alfred Kinsey publishes his report *Sexual Behavior in the Human Male*, in which he puts forth the famous figure that 10 percent of all U.S. males may be homosexual.

1950

- The McCarran Act is passed, excluding both Communists and "sexual deviates" from immigrating to the United States.

Gay Rights

1950–1954

- The nationwide hunt to expose homosexuals in U.S. government, the military, and other public realms, led by Senator Joseph McCarthy, leads to thousands of men and women losing their jobs for being either actual or suspected homosexuals. This political development is closely linked to McCarthy's hunt for actual or suspected Communists.

1951

- *The Homosexual in America*—one of the earliest arguments for tolerance of gay life—is published by Edward Sagarin, under the pseudonym of Donald Webster Cory.
- In Los Angeles, the Mattachine Society is founded by Harry Hay, Bob Hull, and Chuck Rowland to support gay men and lesbians and to educate the public on gay issues.

1955

- The first U.S. lesbian organization, Daughters of Bilitis (DOB), is founded in San Francisco by Del Martin and Phyllis Lyon, who also publish DOB's journal, the *Ladder*, until 1972.

1961

- Illinois becomes the first state to decriminalize private homosexual acts between consenting adults.

1964

- The Society for Individual Rights, a social and political club for gay men and lesbians, is founded in San Francisco.

1965

- Seven gay men and three lesbians picket the White House in the first gay rights protest in U.S. history. However, the protest is dwarfed by the 20,000 antiwar protestors gathered that same day at the Washington Monument.

1966

- The North American Conference of Homophile Organizations (NACHO) is founded to coordinate protests against antigay actions by the federal government.

1967

- The Supreme Court rules that the McCarran Act's ban on "sexual deviates" applies to lesbians and gay men.

Chronology

1968

- Reverend Troy Perry founds the Metropolitan Community Church in Los Angeles. It is the first "gay church" in the United States and will go on to found branches in many other U.S. cities.

1969

- Carl Wittman's pre-Stonewall "Gay Manifesto" anticipates many of the goals of the early gay liberation movement.
- *June 27:* The day of entertainer Judy Garland's funeral also marks the beginning of the riots at the Stonewall Inn. Today these riots are generally understood as the beginning of the modern gay liberation/gay rights movement.

1970

- The Lutheran Church comes out against state sodomy laws and for antidiscrimination legislation to protect gay men and lesbians—although it maintains the right to exclude gay people from its own clergy.
- *June 28:* In a forerunner of modern gay pride events, 10,000 people commemorate the Stonewall uprising by marching in "Christopher Street Liberation Day" in New York City.

1971

- The National Organization for Women, perhaps the largest and best-known U.S. feminist group, adopts a policy making the oppression of lesbians "a legitimate concern for feminism."
- A recommendation for the repeal of all sodomy laws is adopted by President Richard Nixon's National Commission on Reform of Federal Criminal Laws.
- Idaho first repeals, then reinstates, the state's sodomy laws, which make homosexual acts a felony carrying a sentence of five years in prison.

1972

- East Lansing, Michigan, adopts the first ordinance outlawing discrimination against gay men and lesbians in city hiring.

1973

- Rita Mae Brown's *Rubyfruit Jungle*, a groundbreaking autobiographical novel about growing up lesbian, is published.
- The American Psychiatric Association removes homosexuality from its list of mental disorders in the *Diagnostic and Statistical Manual II*, its official catalog of mental and psychological problems.

- Lambda Legal Defense and Education Fund—one of the first organizations devoted specifically to gay legal rights—is founded in New York City.

1974

- New York City congresswoman Bella Abzug introduces the first federal Gay and Lesbian Civil Rights Bill.
- *January:* The Combahee River Collective, a feminist group led by African-American lesbians, holds its first meeting, in Roxbury, Massachusetts. Their publications would become pioneering documents in the development of lesbian feminism, bringing together an antiracist and a gay liberation critique.
- *November:* Openly gay candidates win their first U.S. elections: Kathy Kozachenko to the Ann Arbor, Michigan, City Council, and Elaine Noble to the Massachusetts house of representatives.

1975

- Despite his consistently superior ratings, the U.S. Air Force discharges Sergeant Leonard Matlovich on the grounds of his sexual orientation, as armed forces regulations require. Matlovich begins a long court battle to protest his discharge. On September 8, Matlovich becomes the first openly gay man to appear on the cover of *Time* magazine.

1976

- The U.S. Supreme Court upholds the state of Virginia's sodomy laws by a 6-3 vote.

1977

- Billy Crystal plays the first gay character on a successful TV series: Jodie Dallas on the sitcom *Soap.*
- The State Department ends a decades-long policy when it announces that it will no longer consider sexual orientation as a reason to deny employment.
- *January:* Florida's Dade County passes an ordinance forbidding discrimination based on sexual identity. The official who introduces the ordinance, Ruth Shack, had featured a commercial sung by Anita Bryant as part of her campaign.
- *June:* In a campaign led by Anita Bryant, voters repeal Dade County's ordinance, setting off a nationwide backlash against gay rights. Following the Dade County repeal, gay rights ordinances are overturned by referendums in St. Paul, Minnesota; Eugene, Oregon; and Wichita, Kansas. A gay rights ordinance in Seattle is upheld.
- *November:* After many unsuccessful campaigns, San Francisco activist Harvey Milk finally wins a seat on the San Francisco Board of Supervisors, becoming the first openly gay person to be elected to the government of a large U.S. city.

Chronology

1978

- California voters defeat the Briggs Initiative, which would have allowed for the firing of all gay and lesbian teachers and of all teachers who refer positively to homosexuals in the classroom.
- San Francisco adopts its first gay rights ordinance.
- San Francisco has the largest Gay Pride parade in history—250,000 to 300,000 marchers—at least partly in response to the Briggs Initiative.
- *November 27:* Former San Francisco supervisor Dan White kills his fellow supervisor, the openly gay Harvey Milk, along with San Francisco mayor George Moscone in their city hall offices.

1979

- The Moral Majority, a right-wing group opposed to gay rights, among other causes, is founded by Reverend Jerry Falwell.
- Stephen M. Lachs, the nation's first openly gay judge, is appointed to the bench by California governor Jerry Brown.
- *May 2:* A San Francisco jury convicts Dan White of the lesser charge of manslaughter. The verdict enrages that city's gay population, which erupts in what has come to be known as the White Night riots.
- *October:* The first national gay and lesbian civil rights march on Washington, D.C., draws more than 100,000 participants.

1980

- The Human Rights Campaign Fund, a gay lobbying organization, is founded.
- Six blind lesbians found the Womyn's Braille Press, dedicated to making lesbian and feminist literature available on tape and in Braille.
- A federal judge orders the U.S. Air Force to allow Sergeant Leonard Matlovich—who was discharged for being gay—to reenlist. Instead, the air force offers Matlovich a $160,000 settlement, which he accepts.
- Gay teenager Aaron Fricke wins a lawsuit in Providence, Rhode Island, that enables him to bring a male date to his high school prom.
- Director William Friedkin's efforts to make *Cruising*, a movie about the "underside" of New York City gay life that starred Al Pacino, are frustrated by local gay protests, which object to the movie as homophobic and as encouraging violence against gays. Nonetheless, the film is completed and released.

1981

- Congressman Roger Jepsen introduces the "Family Protection Act," which, among other issues, would deny Social Security, welfare, and veterans' benefits to gay people as well as to those who propose that homosexuality is acceptable.

171

- *June:* The Centers for Disease Control report a rare form of pneumonia contracted by five gay men in Los Angeles; they believe the disease is linked to "some aspect of homosexual lifestyle." The disease, then called GRID (gay-related immune deficiency), will later be known as AIDS.
- *August:* Larry Kramer and a group of activists begin meetings that will lead to the founding of Gay Men's Health Crisis (GMHC), the first group to respond to AIDS.

1982

- The first statewide gay and lesbian civil rights bill, with provisions for employment, housing, and public accommodations, goes into effect in Wisconsin.
- Philadelphia's Board of Education establishes the nation's first high school for gays and lesbians, Byton High. In 1985, New York City will establish the Harvey Milk School for gay and lesbian students.
- *August:* The first Gay Games are held in San Francisco after a battle with the U.S. Olympic Committee, which will not allow the event to be called the "Gay Olympics."

1983

- *Torch Song Trilogy*, Harvey Fierstein's play about gay identity, wins the Tony Award for Best Play on Broadway; Fierstein wins the Best Actor award for starring in his own work.

1984

- Scientists at the Pasteur Institute in France, led by Luc Montagnier, announce the discovery of the virus that causes AIDS.
- The city of Berkeley, California, extends domestic partnership benefits to gay and lesbian employees—the first time gay and lesbian partners have been recognized for benefits.
- *Labor Day:* Wigstock—an annual drag festival—is first held in New York City.
- *Election Day:* The 20,000 voters of West Hollywood, a Los Angeles neighborhood, vote to establish themselves as a new city; the five-person city council of this famously gay area includes a homosexual majority of two gay men and a lesbian.

1985

- Former city supervisor Dan White, released from jail after the murder of Mayor George Moscone and fellow supervisor Harvey Milk, commits suicide.
- Fourteen years after it is first introduced, a gay rights bill passes in New York City.

Chronology

- *October 2:* Movie star Rock Hudson dies of AIDS, helping to raise the national consciousness of how widespread and deadly the disease is.

1986

- New Right spokesman Terry Dolan, who has long opposed "homosexual lifestyles," dies of HIV-related illness; after his death, many acquaintances assert that he was gay.
- *June:* In *Bowers v. Hardwick*, the U.S. Supreme Court upholds the right of states to make laws prohibiting sodomy and other private sexual acts between consenting adults. Meanwhile, the supreme court of Nevada—the only state where heterosexual prostitution is legal—upholds that state's sodomy law.

1987

- U.S. congressman Barney Frank announces that he is gay, the first congressman to do so voluntarily (Representative Gerry Studds had earlier admitted he was gay in response to a scandal involving an alleged affair with a page).
- *March 24:* ACT UP (the AIDS Coalition to Unleash Power) protests against the cost of AIDS drugs by shutting down Wall Street; 17 people are arrested for civil disobedience. This is the beginning of a new, more militant approach in AIDS activism that will also energize the gay rights movement.
- *July 15:* For the first time, the *New York Times* uses the word "gay," rather than "homosexual."
- *October 11:* Almost 650,000 lesbians and gay men participate in the second March on Washington, where the quilt of the Names Project—memorializing people who have died of AIDS—is displayed for the first time.

1988

- Oregon voters repeal an executive order of the state's governor prohibiting discrimination in the employment of gay men and lesbians.
- Although the District of Columbia has passed a gay rights ordinance, the U.S. Congress votes to deny the district funding unless the measure is revoked.
- Raleigh, North Carolina, adopts a gay rights ordinance.

1989

- In *Braschi v. Stahl Associates Co.*, a New York court of appeals rules that a gay male couple can be considered a "family" where housing rules are concerned, allowing surviving spouse Miguel Braschi to continue to enjoy his partner's lease.
- A Cincinnati jury trial rules that homoerotic portraits of men by the late gay photographer Robert Mapplethorpe violate a local obscenity law and shuts down the Mapplethorpe show at a local museum. Senator Jesse Helms and

173

others use the controversy to attack the National Endowment for the Arts, which they claim supports "obscene" work with public funds.

- *spring:* The first university or college department of lesbian and gay studies in the United States is established at San Francisco City College.

1990

- Largely as a result of the Mapplethorpe controversy, the National Endowment for the Arts (NEA) withdraws funds from performance artists Karen Finley, John Fleck, Holly Hughes, and Tim Miller. Three of the so-called NEA 4 are gay; all four speak out against the action as a homophobic infringement of free speech.
- A new generation of activists forms Queer Nation in New York City.
- In Polk County, Florida, officials agree to cease requiring gay prisoners to wear pink bracelets, a practice supposedly intended to reduce the spread of HIV, the virus that causes AIDS, by helping to distinguish gay from nongay prisoners.
- Congress ends a decades-long policy of using sexual orientation as a basis for denying immigration; however, a visitor's HIV-positive status is still grounds for denying a visa.
- President George H. W. Bush signs the Hate Crime Statistics Act, which requires the U.S. Department of Justice to collect statistics on criminal acts motivated by race, religion, national origin, or sexual orientation—the first time sexual orientation is included as a protected category in federal legislation.
- The Americans with Disabilities Act extends civil rights protection to disabled Americans—including people with AIDS. (Since 1998 it is no longer legal to discriminate against people with AIDS in housing, employment, or public accommodations.)

1991

- In Dallas, the First International Deaf Gay and Lesbian Conference is held.
- Amnesty International, a group that protects political prisoners, decides to extend its campaigns to include gay men and lesbians imprisoned on account of their sexual orientation or activities.
- Washington, D.C., and Baltimore each hold their first Black Gay Pride Day.

1992

- Navy airman apprentice Terry Helvey is sentenced to life imprisonment for the deadly beating of fellow sailor Allen Schindler, who is so badly disfigured that his mother has difficulty identifying him; Helvey is quoted as saying, "I'd do it again."

- Colorado passes Amendment 2, a referendum prohibiting gay rights legislation statewide and overturning gay rights ordinances in Boulder, Denver, and Aspen. A similar referendum in Oregon, Proposition 9, is defeated.
- *May 28:* The Lesbian Avengers, a direct action activist group of mainly young women, holds its first meeting in New York City; the group will later be instrumental in preventing an antigay referendum from being passed in Idaho.

1993

- Although one of President Bill Clinton's election promises was to lift the ban on gays in the military, his executive order instead establishes the policy known as "don't ask, don't tell," a policy that will lead to an increased rate of gay and lesbian discharges from the armed forces.
- A group of gay Republicans known as Log Cabin Republicans is founded in Washington, D.C.
- The *New York Times* reports that some 1,100,000 participants join in the March on Washington for Lesbian, Gay, and Bi [bisexual] Equal Rights and Liberation—while President Clinton and most legislators leave town for the weekend.
- The supreme court of Hawaii reverses a lower court's decision against same-sex marriage, raising the possibility that gay marriage might become legal in Hawaii.
- The Oregon Citizens Alliance—responsible for the defeated Proposition 9—joins with other antigay groups to target 11 states for antigay referendums over the next two years: California, Georgia, Idaho, Iowa, Maine, Minnesota, Missouri, Montana, and Washington.
- Although New York City public schools have adopted "Children of the Rainbow," an inclusive curriculum focusing on cultural diversity and including some gay-positive materials, five of 32 local school boards refuse to teach the curriculum, largely because of its tolerance for "gay lifestyles."
- *April 25:* Some 20,000 women march in the Dyke March on Washington, D.C.

1994

- At the fourth annual Gay Games in New York City, Olympic gold medalist Greg Louganis announces that he is gay.
- Massachusetts becomes the first state to outlaw discrimination against gay and lesbian students in the public schools.
- The Hawaii state senate adopts a bill outlawing same-sex marriage in an effort to preclude the possibility of court decisions allowing for such marriage.

Gay Rights

- The U.S. Congress passes the Defense of Marriage Act (DOMA), which defines marriage as taking place only between a man and a woman. DOMA, which passes overwhelmingly, represents the first federal effort to define marriage, which had previously been a state matter.
- The Employment Non-Discrimination Act (ENDA) is introduced in Congress. ENDA would add sexual orientation as a category in the Title VII protections against workplace discrimination. As of early, 2000, the bill has still not been passed.

1995

- A court ruling holds that gays and lesbians who want to march together under a gay-themed banner cannot join in the St. Patrick's Day parade in Boston if the parade committee wishes to keep them out.

1996

- *January:* Protease inhibitors—a new treatment for AIDS—are introduced, and AIDS deaths fall by 47 percent.
- *May:* In *Romer v. Evans*, the U.S. Supreme Court overturns Colorado's Amendment 2, ruling that states may not target specific groups, including lesbians, gay men, and bisexuals, and forbid them from seeking civil rights.

1997

- *April 14:* Ellen DeGeneres, star of the ABC sitcom *Ellen*, announces that she is a lesbian and appears on the cover of *Time* magazine; her TV character comes out later that spring, making *Ellen* the first successful network sitcom whose main character is openly gay.
- *December:* The New Jersey Supreme Court rules that gay couples must be treated with the same procedures as straight couples when it comes to adopting a child; they are responding to efforts by Jon Holden and Michael Galluccio to adopt a child as a couple.

1998

- *February:* In a statewide referendum, Maine becomes the first state to nullify a statewide gay rights law. Activists claim that part of the problem was the timing of the election, an off-season when no other matters were on the ballot, prompting voters in 1999 to approve a constitutional amendment ensuring that referendums are introduced as part of general elections.
- *June 25:* The protections of the Americans with Disabilities Act are extended to include people with AIDS/HIV.
- *September:* State senator William J. "Pete" Knight introduces Proposition 22, popularly known as the Knight Initiative, a statewide referendum that

would keep same-sex marriage from being recognized in California, including gay marriages recognized by other states.

- *October 6:* College student Matthew Shepard is brutally beaten and left to die in Laramie, Wyoming; his death galvanizes gay protest and mainstream media outrage across the nation.

- *Election Day:* Hawaii adopts a provision in its state constitution forbidding same-sex marriage.

- *Election Day:* The first openly lesbian member of Congress—Tammy Baldwin, of Madison, Wisconsin—is elected.

- *November 22:* The sodomy law contested in *Bowers v. Hardwick* is struck down by Georgia's own supreme court.

- *December:* Dade County, Florida, the area where the backlash against gay rights began in 1977, passes another gay rights ordinance.

1999

- *Memorial Day weekend:* President Bill Clinton appoints James Hormel ambassador to Luxembourg. Hormel is the first openly gay ambassador to represent the United States. Clinton makes the appointment on a holiday weekend, when Congress is not in session, to circumvent Mississippi senator Trent Lott's determination not to let Hormel's nomination come to the Senate floor for a vote.

- *August:* The New Jersey Supreme Court rules that James Dale, an Eagle Scout and assistant scoutmaster expelled from the Boy Scouts of America (BSA) in 1990, must be reinstated. Dale was expelled after the BSA had learned he was gay.

- *December:* Hawaii's Supreme Court rules that the state's new constitutional amendment now precludes same-sex marriage; meanwhile, Vermont's Supreme Court orders the state legislature to find a way to offer same-sex couples the same legal and financial benefits as heterosexual couples, whether via marriage or some other arrangement.

- In the wake of the murder of U.S. Army private Barry Winchell, who was killed by associates who suspected him of being gay, President Clinton asks defense secretary William Cohen to review the "don't ask, don't tell" policy. Vice President—and presidential candidate—Al Gore comments that gay people should be able to serve in the military without discrimination.

2000

- *March 7:* California voters overwhelmingly approve Proposition 22 (the Knight Initiative), which defines marriage as exclusively between one man and one woman, and which forbids the state from extending legal recognition to same-sex marriages contracted outside of its borders.

Gay Rights

- **March 29:** The Central Conference of American Rabbis, the governing body of Reform Judaism, votes to allow its members to officiate at same-sex commitment rituals.
- **April:** Vermont's house of representatives passes a law granting homosexual couples all of the legal rights accorded to heterosexual couples. Nationwide debates on the so-called civil union begin.
- **June:** New York's state legislature passes a hate crimes bill that includes sexual orientation among its protected categories. The vote comes after an 11-year effort by Republicans in the state senate to block passage of the bill.
- **June:** A Texas appeals court strikes down a law making homosexual sodomy illegal, on the grounds that since heterosexual sodomy has been legal since 1973, the law violates the state's Equal Rights Amendment.
- **June 28:** The U.S. Supreme Court supports the Boy Scouts of America's right to ban gay scoutmasters, on the grounds that First Amendment protection of freedom of association outweighs New Jersey's law against discrimination in public accommodations.
- **July 1:** The Vermont law on civil unions, having passed the state senate and been signed by the governor, goes into effect.

2001

- **April:** Same-sex marriage becomes legal in the Netherlands, the first country in the world to grant full marriage rights to same-sex couples.
- **September 11:** Mark Bingham, a 21-year-old member of the Log Cabin Republicans, a gay Republican group, is one of the passengers who dies on United Airlines Flight 93. His heroic actions on the flight inspire numerous media reports that provide an image of a gay hero in a time of extreme crisis.
- **September:** Conservative ministers Jerry Falwell and Pat Robertson make remarks implying that the September 11 tragedy is divine retribution for American permissiveness toward homosexuality, among other things; they later apologize for the remarks.
- **November:** The city council of Fort Wayne, Indiana, passes an ordinance that extends its antidiscrimination law to include sexual orientation.

2002

- Colorado Republican representative Marilyn Musgrave introduces a draft of the Federal Marriage Amendment, which would amend the Constitution to define marriage as between one man and one woman and which would preclude courts from interpreting either state or federal constitutions as requiring states to recognize same-sex marriage.
- **July:** The Big Brothers Big Sisters of America, a group that pairs adult men and women with fatherless and motherless children, begins to require all 500 of

its local affiliates to allow gay men and lesbians to participate in the program. The American Family Association urges its members to contact businesses that sponsor the organization and press them to have the group change its policy.

- *October 24:* Harry Hay, cofounder of the Mattachine Society, dies.

2003

- *January:* Belgium becomes the second country in the world to legalize same-sex marriage.

- *March:* The U.S. Census Bureau releases figures revealing that 34.3 percent of households headed by lesbians and 22.3 percent of households headed by gay men are raising children, and that 99.3 percent of all U.S. counties include at least some gay residents.

- *March 24:* New Mexico governor Bill Richardson, a Democrat, signs the New Mexico Hate Crime Act, mandating higher penalties for hate crimes, including those resulting from homophobia.

- *May:* Colorado Republican representative Marilyn Musgrave reintroduces the Federal Marriage Amendment.

- *May 28:* Texas Republican governor Rick Perry signs the Texas Defense of Marriage Act, permitting Texas to withhold recognition of same-sex marriages or civil unions conducted in other states.

- *May 30:* Kentucky Democratic governor Paul Patton signs an executive order prohibiting employment discrimination based on sexual orientation, making Kentucky the 10th state with such a law. Kentucky also becomes the first state to prohibit discrimination based on gender identity.

- *June 10:* The U.S. Department of Justice, which had banned its annual employee gay pride celebration, reverses that order to permit the event.

- *June 18:* The Ontario Court of Appeals makes Canada the first country in the Western Hemisphere to honor same-sex marriage by ruling that same-sex marriages will be recognized in the province.

- *June 26:* The U.S. Supreme Court delivers *Lawrence v. Texas*, striking down U.S. state sodomy laws.

- *July:* Wal-Mart extends its antidiscrimination policy to include sexual orientation.

- *October:* FBI statistics reveal that 16.7 percent of U.S. hate crimes in 2002 were due to bias against the victim's perceived sexual orientation, the highest rate in the 12 years during which federal records were kept.

- *November 18:* The Massachusetts Supreme Judicial Court rules that prohibiting same-sex marriage violates the state constitution.

- *November 20:* The U.S. Congress passes a resolution condemning all violations of internationally recognized human rights standards based on real or perceived sexual orientation or gender identity.

Gay Rights

- **November:** Senator Wayne Allard and Republican colleagues introduce the Federal Marriage Amendment in the U.S. Senate.
- **December 23:** Michigan governor Jennifer Granholm signs an executive order that extends the state's antidiscrimination law to include sexual orientation.

2004

- **January 1:** Tasmania becomes the first Australian state to recognize same-sex civil unions.
- **January 8:** The New Jersey state legislature creates domestic partnership status for same-sex couples, to go into effect in July. The move is viewed as the state's effort to preclude gay marriage.
- **January 26:** The first voter-approved domestic partnership registry in the nation begins operating in Cleveland Heights, Ohio.
- **January 28:** The 11th U.S. Circuit Court of Appeals upholds Florida's ban on adoption by gay people.
- **January 30:** The Kansas court of appeals rules that the state can punish Matthew Limon more severely for having sex with a minor because the minor was someone of the same sex—despite the defense's argument that the *Lawrence v. Texas* decision of 2003 abolished sodomy laws.
- **February 2:** Officials in Boyd County, Kansas, end a long legal battle by allowing a gay-straight alliance club to meet at the local high school.
- **February 4:** The Massachusetts Supreme Judicial Court responds to a state senate inquiry by affirming that civil unions are not an adequate substitute for marriage as they still indicate an inferiority of same-sex couples.
- **February 6:** Ohio Republican governor Bob Taft signs the state's Defense of Marriage Act, which outlaws same-sex marriage, bans state benefits from going to same-sex couples, and denies recognition of same-sex marriages, civil unions, or domestic partnerships performed in other states.
- **February 12:** Under the leadership of Mayor Gavin Newsom, San Francisco city officials start issuing marriage licenses to same-sex couples, despite a California law prohibiting such marriages. The first couple to be married are Del Martin and Phyllis Lyon, founders of one of the United States' first lesbian groups a half-century earlier. Conservatives and so-called pro-family groups intend to sue Newsom for violating California law.
- **February 20:** In response to seeing the same-sex weddings in San Francisco, Cambodia's king Norodom Sihanouk says that Cambodia should also allow same-sex marriage and should treat transvestites well.
- **February 24:** After some contradictory statements from the White House, President George W. Bush announces his support for a Constitutional amendment that would ban same-sex marriage, though he does not actually endorse the Federal Marriage Amendment.
- **February 26:** New Paltz Green Party mayor Jason West announces that his town will perform marriages for same-sex couples. The town will not try to

issue marriage licenses, but in New York lack of license is not sufficient grounds to void a marriage; and in any case, couples have six months to obtain a licence from the time they are married.

- *March 2:* New Paltz mayor Jason West is charged with 19 criminal counts of "solemnizing" marriages without a license.

- *March 5:* The Wisconsin State Assembly approves a state constitution amendment to ban same-sex marriage or civil unions.

- *March 5:* The Kansas house of representatives passes a proposed amendment to prohibit same-sex marriage.

- *March 8:* The U.S. Supreme Court refuses to hear an appeal from the Boy Scouts of America (BSA) to a Connecticut court ruling that allows the state to refuse funds to the BSA because of the Scouts' antigay policies. By refusing to hear the appeal, the court in effect upholds the state rulings, giving license to other states and municipalities to continue their exclusion of the Scouts for similar reasons.

- *March 10:* Indianapolis mayor Bart Peterson uses an executive order to extend to gay men and lesbians the city's antidiscrimination protection.

- *March 11:* Michael Heath, a lobbyist for Maine's Christian Civic League, which opposes gay rights, threatens to out closeted politicians who do not vote to ban same-sex marriage in the state.

- *March 11:* The California state supreme court orders all gay marriages to stop in San Francisco, after almost 4,000 such marriages have already been performed.

- *March 12:* Wisconsin's state senate approves a state constitutional amendment that would ban same-sex marriages and civil unions in the state.

- *March 14:* Maine legislators and government officials are so angry at Michael Heath's threat that the lobbyist is forced to resign, while Maine politicians begin to look with new sympathy at gay rights efforts.

- *March 15:* Commissioners in Multnomah County, Oregon, promise to continue issuing same-sex marriage licenses.

- *March 19:* Quebec joins British Columbia and Ontario in making same-sex marriage legal. The move means that more than two-thirds of all Canadians live in provinces where gay marriage is legal.

- *March 20:* The Reverend Karen Dammann is acquitted for having allegedly violated the Methodist Church's prohibition against lesbian and gay ministers.

- *March 29:* The Massachusetts legislature passes a proposed amendment to the state constitution banning same-sex marriage while legalizing civil unions. The vote must be affirmed during the next two-year session and then face a referendum in fall 2006.

- *April 20:* Oregon judge Frank Bearden orders that Multnomah County stop performing same-sex marriages, after more than 3,000 such marriages had been performed.

Gay Rights

- *April 21:* The Virginia General Assembly passes the Affirmation of Marriage Act. The legislation, an amendment to the state's anti–gay marriage law, goes beyond merely outlawing same-sex marriage and states that "a civil union, partnership contract or other arrangement between persons of the same sex purporting to bestow the privileges or obligations of marriage is prohibited."

- *May 17:* Massachusetts becomes the first state in the history of the United States to issue marriage licenses to same-sex couples.

- *May 25:* Viacom, one of the largest entertainment conglomerates in the United States, announces the launch of LOGO on its MTV networks. LOGO will be the first cable channel aimed at gays, lesbians, bisexuals, and transgender people and is scheduled to debut in June 2005.

- *June 29:* The First U.S. Circuit Court of Appeals upholds the Massachusetts Supreme Judicial Court decision that required the state to begin issuing marriage licenses to same-sex couples who applied for them. In its ruling, the court contends that the only proper way to contest the ruling is to change the state constitution.

- *July 14:* The U.S. Senate fails to pass a Constitutional amendment that would outlaw same-sex marriage in the United States.

- *July 21:* The 11th Circuit Court of Appeals in Atlanta lets stand a decision upholding Florida's law banning adoption of children by gays and lesbians. At the same time, one of the judges states in an addendum to the ruling that he is personally in favor of considering same-sex couples for adoptive parenthood.

- *August 3:* By a margin of 71 percent to 29 percent, Missouri voters overwhelmingly approve a measure to amend their state constitution to ban same-sex marriage.

- *August 12:* The California Supreme Court rules that San Francisco mayor Gavin Newsom overstepped his authority by issuing marriage licenses to same-sex couples and declares the 4,000 civil weddings that he and his aides performed to be "void and of no legal effect." The court orders all records of the marriages to be expunged and the license fees returned to the parties in question.

- *August 12:* New Jersey governor James E. McGreevey announces his resignation after disclosing that he is gay and has had an affair with his former aide, Golan Cipel. McGreevey makes the announcement with his wife Dina by his side. He will step down on November 15.

- *August 16:* A bankruptcy judge in Tacoma, Washington, rules that the federal Defense of Marriage Act (DOMA) is Constitutional, the first decision of its kind since the law was passed in 1996. The case involved Ann and Lee Kandu, who had legally wed in British Columbia and who were trying to file for bankruptcy protection as a married couple.

- *August 30:* U.S. representative Edward L. Shrock, of Virginia, announces that he will not seek another term in Congress after a Web blog posting asserts that he is gay. While in Congress, Rep. Shrock, who is married, voted for legislation outlawing same-sex marriage.

Chronology

- *September 7:* The board of the Log Cabin Republicans, the party's largest political organization for gay men and lesbians, votes not to endorse George W. Bush for reelection because of his support for a Constitutional amendment to ban same-sex marriage.

- *September 7:* A superior court judge in Thurston County, Washington, rules that gays and lesbians are part of a protected class and so the state's Defense of Marriage Act (DOMA) is unconstitutional. The ruling is the second in four weeks to strike down the state DOMA; a King County superior court judge had also ruled that the state's constitution does not support the denial of same-sex marriage rights, though that judge stopped short of finding homosexuals to be a protected class.

- *September 18:* Voters in Louisiana approve an amendment to their state's constitution outlawing same-sex marriage. As in Missouri, the margin of victory is huge: 78 percent to 22 percent.

- *September 30:* The federal Marriage Protection Amendment fails to garner the necessary two-thirds majority in the U.S. House of Representatives that would have ensured its passage. The measure would have amended the U.S. Constitution to prohibit same-sex marriage.

- *October 18:* The Anglican Church's Lambeth Commission issues its report on homosexuality within the church, ordering those who appointed gay bishop V. Gene Robinson to express regret for the turmoil they caused and calling a moratorium on the elevation to bishop of anyone living in a "same-gender union."

- *October 26:* In a television interview, President George W. Bush repeats his support for a national ban on same-sex marriage but says he would not object to individual states establishing civil unions.

- *November 2:* Voters in 11 states approve Constitutional amendments banning same-sex marriage and in some cases prohibiting gay people from establishing any form of legally recognized partnership. The states are Arkansas, Georgia, Kentucky, Michigan, Mississippi, Montana, North Dakota, Oklahoma, Ohio, Oregon, and Utah.

- *November 29:* The Supreme Court refuses to hear a challenge to the 2003 Massachusetts high court ruling establishing gay marriage in that state. In effect, by not hearing the challenge, the Supreme Court voted to let gay marriage stand.

- *November 29:* The third U.S. circuit court of appeals strikes down on free speech grounds a law that would have allowed the Defense Department to withhold funding from colleges and universities that denied access to military recruiters because of the armed forces' antigay policies.

- *December 2:* Lesbian Methodist minister Irene Elizabeth Stroud is defrocked for homosexuality by the United Methodist Church.

- *December 9:* Canada's Supreme Court holds that there is no constitutional reason to ban gay marriage in Canada, opening the door to a nationwide legal recognition of gay marriage in that country.

- **December 29:** A judge strikes down Arkansas's 1999 ban on children being placed into foster care with gay parents or in any family where a gay member is living, saying that the policy is irrelevant to the health, safety, and welfare of the state's children.
- **December 30:** The Montana Supreme Court rules that the state's public universities must provide gay employees with insurance coverage for their domestic partners, despite the new anti–gay marriage amendment to the state constitution.

2005

- **February 5:** Manhattan justice Doris Ling-Cohan rules that gay and lesbian couples in New York State should have the right to marry.
- **February 6:** New York City mayor Michael Bloomberg promises to appeal Ling-Cohan's ruling, saying that while he personally supports gay marriage, he wants to spare gay and lesbian couples the anguish of the California experience, in which illegal marriages were eventually overturned. Gay activists and political leaders take strong exception to the mayor's statement.
- **March 14:** New York City health officials announce the discovery of a new "supervirus"—a strain of HIV that seems to be resistant to most drugs used to prevent the virus from spurring a full-blown case of AIDS. The announcement was prompted by two HIV-positive men who proceed rapidly to develop AIDS despite a variety of drug treatments.
- **March 14:** A California judge rules that the state's ban on gay marriage is unconstitutional, setting in motion a fight in the appellate courts that is expected to go to the state supreme court. The ruling is used by anti–gay rights activists as evidence of the need for a constitutional amendment that would preempt state judges from making such rulings.
- **March 21:** Some research scientists and gay activists take issue with the New York City announcement of the "supervirus," condemning it as a scare tactic and claiming that many factors might have been responsible for the two men's rapid progression from being HIV positive to having AIDS.
- **March 30:** Maine becomes the 16th U.S. state to pass gay rights legislation and the sixth state to ban bias based on gender identity. Maine governor John Baldacci signs into law a bill that adds sexual orientation and gender identity to an existing statewide law banning discrimination in employment, housing, public accommodations, education, and credit. Anti–gay rights activists immediately begin mobilizing for a referendum to overturn the law, as they did when a similar gay rights law passed in 1998.
- **April 5:** Kansas voters approve an amendment to the state constitution that bans gay marriage as well as civil unions, possibly preventing same-sex couples from receiving family health insurance and other "marriage-like" benefits. Although gay marriage is already illegal under Kansas state law, the amendment raises the prohibition to the level of the state constitution, in an effort to preclude judges from finding anti-gay-marriage laws unconstitutional, as occurred in California and Massachusetts.

CHAPTER 5

BIOGRAPHICAL LISTING

Sidney Abbot and **Barbara Love,** partners and pioneering lesbians in the early feminist movement. They were among the organizers of a group of lesbians who attended the Second Congress to Unite Women in May 1970, arranged for the lights to be turned off, and then appeared on stage in lavender T-shirts stenciled with the slogan Lavender Menace, the phrase that feminist leader Betty Friedan had used to describe the "lesbian threat" to the women's movement. They were also early founders of the Radicalesbians, an offshoot of the Gay Liberation Front, and together coedited *Sappho Was a Right-On Woman* (1972), one of the first U.S. collections of lesbian literature.

Bella Abzug, New York congresswoman who introduced the first gay rights legislation in 1974—and continued to campaign for legislation for many years thereafter. She was known for her devotion to gay rights, particularly after she campaigned in gay male bathhouses.

Wayne Allard, Republican senator from Colorado who helped rewrite and then introduced an amendment to the U.S. Constitution that would define marriage as only taking place between a man and a woman.

Dorothy Allison, writer and activist. Allison is the author of *The Women Who Hate Me* (a collection of poems), *Trash* (a collection of short stories), *Bastard Out of Carolina* (a novel that was a finalist for the National Book Award), *Two or Three Things I Know for Sure* (a memoir), *Skin* (a collection of essays), and *Cavedweller* (a novel).

Sheldon Andelson, major fund-raiser behind the Municipal Elections Committee of Los Angeles (MECLA), one of the first gay efforts to use fund-raising as a way to attain behind-the-scenes political power. Andelson was influential in California and national politics for many years and was appointed to the California Board of Regents by Governor Jerry Brown in the late 1970s.

Gloria Anzaldúa, coeditor, with Cherríe Moraga, of *This Bridge Called My Back: Writings by Radical Women of Color,* a pioneering anthology of works by African-American, Latina, and other feminists. Moraga and Anzaldúa were also coeditors of *Compañeras.* When *This Bridge* was published in 1981, very few works by women of color had appeared, and Anzaldúa and Moraga helped to establish that lesbian-feminism could be a multiracial movement representing women from a wide range of economic back-grounds. Anzaldúa is also the author of *Borderland/La Frontera*, among other works.

Virginia Apuzzo, activist and politician. At the 1980 Democratic National Convention, Apuzzo coauthored the first lesbian and gay civil rights plank ever adopted by a major U.S. political party. She is the former executive deputy commissioner of the New York State Division of Housing and Community Renewal, former commissioner of the New York State Civil Service, and a former executive director of the National Gay Task Force (since renamed the National Lesbian and Gay Task Force).

Ninia Baehr and **Genora Dancel,** Hawaii couple whose 1990 lawsuit kicked off the modern gay marriage movement when the Hawaii Supreme Court ruled that the state constitution required the state to offer gay couples equal access to the rights and benefits of marriage. The final decision in the case came to be known as *Baehr v. Lewin*, after John C. Lewin, director of Hawaii's department of health.

Jack Baker, the first openly gay person to be elected president of the University of Minnesota student body. This pioneering gay activist was featured in *Life* magazine with his lover, Mike McConnell, whom he married in a public (extralegal) ceremony.

Tammy Baldwin, Madison, Wisconsin, woman who in 1998 became the nation's first lesbian congresswoman.

Robert Bauman, former Republican U.S. representative from Maryland who was known for his antigay role in Congress in the 1970s—and for the 1980 scandal surrounding the revelation that he had been buying sex from male prostitutes in Washington, D.C. After the incident, Bauman, who was married, apologized publicly to his wife and stepped down; the revelations hurt the conservative cause by making antigay leaders seem like hypocrites.

Arthur Bell, former *Village Voice* columnist, now deceased. His position at the radical New York City newspaper enabled him to play a prominent role in the early gay rights movement of the 1970s. Bell was also an early member of the Gay Activists Alliance.

Lisa Ben, activist, singer, and writer who published the first known U.S. publication by and for lesbians, *Vice Versa*, a hand-typed and privately circulated periodical of the late 1940s.

Elizabeth Birch, executive director of the Human Rights Campaign (HRC). She held the position when HRC became the first gay rights organization to host a sitting U.S. president—Bill Clinton, who attended an HRC awards dinner in 1997. Birch also gained a certain notoriety when HRC endorsed right-wing New York senator Al D'Amato over liberal opponent Charles Schumer, in gratitude for D'Amato's votes on certain key congressional issues.

Mary Bonauto, lawyer who brought the suit known as *Baker v. State of Vermont*, which resulted in Vermont creating the civil union, an institution designed to offer same-sex couples equal access to the marital benefits enjoyed by straight couples. She was also lead counsel in *Goodridge v. Department of Public Health*, which resulted in November 2003 in the Massachusetts Supreme Judicial Court decision requiring the state to recognize civil marriage.

Melvin Boozer, the first openly gay person to be among the nominees for vice president; Boozer was nominated at the 1980 Democratic convention, which eventually chose Walter Mondale as its vice presidential nominee. In his convention speech, Boozer spoke of the similarities between the oppression he had experienced as an African American and as a gay man. President of the District of Columbia's Gay Activists Alliance, Boozer served for a short time as the Washington representative of the National Gay Task Force (which has since been renamed the National Gay and Lesbian Task Force).

Ivy Bottini, activist who helped found the first local (New York) chapter of the National Organization for Women (NOW) but was forced out of NOW in 1970, as part of that organization's internal fight over the extent to which lesbians should be part of the women's movement. Bottini is widely credited with having developed the idea of feminist consciousness-raising, in which women shared personal stories in a noncritical, supportive environment in an effort to discover the political dimensions of their lives—a technique that has been widely used by feminist and lesbian-feminist groups, as well as by early gay liberation groups.

Michael J. Bowers, Georgia attorney general. Bowers is noted for prosecuting Michael Hardwick in the 1986 Supreme Court case that became known as *Bowers v. Hardwick* and for withdrawing a job in his office promised to lawyer Robin Shahar when he discovered she was a lesbian.

John Briggs, California state senator who introduced the 1978 referendum, Proposition 6, which is also known as the Briggs Initiative and which would have banned gay and lesbian teachers from public schools and prohibited any positive mention of homosexuality on school grounds.

Howard Brown, former head of the Health Services Administration. Appointed in 1965 by New York City mayor John V. Lindsay, Brown was used to working behind the scenes for gay causes—but caused quite a stir when he came out as gay in a front-page *New York Times* story on October 3, 1973. Brown's prominence led him to be chosen first chair of the National Gay Task Force (later renamed the National Gay and Lesbian Task Force).

Rita Mae Brown, writer. Her 1973 autobiographical novel, *Rubyfruit Jungle*, is known as a classic lesbian coming-of-age story and was one of the first lesbian novels to achieve commercial success. Brown's other novels include *Six of One, In Her Day, Venus Envy, High Hearts,* and several series of mysteries one of which she "coauthored" with her cat, Sneaky Pie Brown. She also won notoriety for her affair with the then-closeted tennis champion Martina Navratilova, on which *Six of One* was based.

Anita Bryant, singer and former beauty queen who led the first successful antigay backlash, the 1977 effort to repeal the Dade County, Florida, gay rights ordinance. Bryant rose to fame very quickly with her organization, "Save Our Children," as she charged that lesbians and gay men were looking to "recruit" young people since, she contended, they could not "reproduce." Bryant's successful campaign against the Dade County ordinance galvanized a response from the gay community—but it also inspired more successful anti–gay rights activity throughout the nation. Her popularity dropped sharply in the 1980s, however, and she ceased to be a symbol of the anti–gay rights movement.

Phil Burress, head of the Equal Rights, No Special Rights, an anti–gay rights group that led the fight against the repeal of the anti–gay rights ordinance in Cincinnati, Ohio. He is also head of the Cincinnati antipornography group Citizens for Community Values. Burress won national recognition as an anti–gay rights leader when in 1996 he organized a group of Christian conservatives that went on to the strategy for a state-by-state attack on gay marriage, which has resulted in some 40 states having passed legislation and/or constitutional amendments banning same-sex unions.

Patrick Califia, formerly Pat Califia, transgender writer and former columnist for *Out* magazine. Califia is known for his commitment to working-class issues, his activism on behalf of the transgender movement, and his open championing of sadomasochistic relationships as deserving of inclusion in a larger gay and lesbian community. As Pat Califia, she was the author of *Sapphistry, The Lesbian S/M Safety Manual, The Advocate Advisor, Doc and Fluff* (a novel), *Macho Sluts* (a novel), *Public Sex*, and *Sex Changes.*

Michael Callen, one of the earliest AIDS activists, who caused a stir in 1982 when he publicly made a connection between his sexually promiscuous life and his infection with the disease. Previously, leaders who called for gay men to change their sexual habits had been seen as suspect, but Callen had been known for championing sexual freedom, so his call for restraint had enormous impact during the early days of the crisis.

Margarethe Cammermeyer, recipient of the Bronze Star, a medal awarded for meritorious achievement, who was discharged from the Army National Guard after coming out as a lesbian. She went on to become an activist for lesbian and gay rights.

Jack Campbell, the first major financial supporter of the gay rights movement and the founder of Club Baths, a chain of gay male bathhouses.

Jimmy Carter, president of the United States (1977–81). The first U.S. presidential candidate to acknowledge gay rights as an issue. Thanks to his aide, Midge Costanza, gay rights activists met with government officials in the White House for the first time.

Madolin Cervantes, heterosexual woman who served as treasurer of the Mattachine Society at the time of the 1969 Stonewall uprising. Her presence was yet another cause of dissension between the old-line homophile group and the new militant gay activism.

Mary Cheney, openly gay daughter of Vice President Dick Cheney, and the target of pressure from gay rights groups around the country after her father endorsed a Constitutional amendment that would define marriage as taking place only between a man and a woman. She helped run her father's reelection campaign for the 2004 election, and Cheney publicly distanced himself from the Republican Party plank on gay marriage, saying that marriage should be a state issue.

Jean Joseph Jacques Chrétien, prime minister of Canada. After two Canadian provinces legalized gay marriage, Chrétien announced that he would not oppose efforts to legalize gay marriage throughout Canada.

Karen Clark, a Minnesota state representative who was elected in 1980. She is the longest-serving openly gay public official in the United States.

Michelle Cliff, Jamaican-born writer and editor who, with poet/activist and partner Adrienne Rich, was coeditor of *Sinister Wisdom,* one of the most influential feminist magazines of the 1980s. Her books include a volume of poetry, *Claiming an Identity They Taught Me to Despise,* and the novels *Abeng, No Telephone to Heaven,* and *Free Enterprise.*

Bill Clinton, president of the United States (1993–2001). Clinton is noted for his 1992 campaign pledge to end the ban on gays in the military and for his 1993 executive order establishing "don't ask, don't tell," a policy whereby gay servicemen and women would be dishonorably discharged for disclosing their sexual orientation—but whereby recruiters and superiors were forbidden to ask whether someone was gay as a means of keeping or getting them out of the service. Clinton was also the first sitting U.S. president to attend a gay rights event, a fund-raiser held by the Human Rights Campaign in 1997, and he has consistently supported various gay rights bills, including the Employment Non-Discrimination Act (ENDA), the 1994 measure (which remains unpassed) to outlaw employment discrimination on the basis of sexual orientation. He is further known for signing the Defense of Marriage Act (DOMA), the first federal attempt to regulate marriage contracts in an effort to prevent same-sex marriage nationwide, and for being the first president to appoint an openly gay ambassador.

Roy Cohn, lawyer known for his involvement in the right-wing, anticommunist activities of the 1950s, particularly in the trial that led to the execution of Julius and Ethel Rosenberg. In the 1970s, he was a leading figure in the Republican Party and spoke out frequently against gay rights. He was later revealed to be gay and died of an AIDS-related illness, an irony that playwright Tony Kushner explored in his Broadway hit, *Angels in America,* which features Cohn as a major character.

Matt Coles, head of the Lesbian and Gay Rights Project of the American Civil Liberties Union (ACLU). Coles was one of the main architects of the ACLU's challenge to Colorado's Amendment 2, which resulted in the Supreme Court decision *Romer v. Evans,* upholding the legality of gay rights ordinances. He has led numerous other campaigns on such issues as gay adoption, gays in the military, and gay civil rights.

Jeanne Cordova, well-known leader in 1970s and 1980s gay politics in Los Angeles. She was also hired for a time to write a column for the *Advocate.* Cordova was one of the organizers of the 1973 West Coast Lesbian Conference and a member of the collective that published *Lesbian Tide,* a lesbian newspaper.

Gay Rights

James Dale, openly gay assistant scoutmaster and Eagle Scout who was expelled from the Boy Scouts of America when his sexual orientation was revealed via a photograph showing him as the leader of a Rutgers University gay rights group. Dale's lawsuit over his expulsion from the Boy Scouts reached the New Jersey Supreme Court in 1999, when the state high court ruled unanimously that the Boy Scouts' ban on gay and bisexual men was unconstitutional under New Jersey's antidiscrimination law. The U.S. Supreme Court overturned the state decision in 2000.

Jo Daly, an early organizer of the Alice B. Toklas Club, an influential lesbian and gay Democratic club in San Francisco. Daly was one of the few openly gay delegates to the 1976 Democratic convention and was the first full-time paid liaison between San Francisco's Human Rights Commission and the gay community.

Matt Daniels, founder of Alliance for Marriage, a leading national organization formed to oppose same-sex marriage.

Gray Davis, California governor, 1999–2003. In his first two years of his governorship, he signed three new gay rights bills: one establishing an antidiscrimination provision, another outlawing discrimination against gay/lesbian students and teachers, and the third criminalizing housing and job discrimination against gay men and lesbians. Davis was thrown out of office in a recall election that replaced him with conservative Republican and former movie star Arnold Schwarzenegger. He signed additional gay rights legislation just before leaving office. Some observers believed that his support of gay rights was one of the factors leading to his recall.

Madeline Davis, with Jim Foster, the first openly gay person to address a national political convention—the Democratic Convention of 1972.

Ellen DeGeneres, lesbian comedian and actress who came out publicly in 1997 and whose character on the network sitcom *Ellen* also came out. DeGeneres was featured on the cover of *Time* magazine, saying "Yep, I'm Gay!"—an indication of how much national attention the event had drawn.

Terry Dolan, a New Right activist known for his pioneering use of direct mail to raise funds for the right wing. Although Dolan lobbied strongly against gay rights, it was discovered that he himself was gay when he died of an AIDS-related illness.

Tom Duane, first openly gay New York City Council member; first openly HIV-positive elected official in the United States (New York state senator, 1999–   ). Duane is known both for his gay rights leadership and for his strong ties to the tenants and community movements of his district.

Martin Duberman, scholar and historian; professor of history at the Lehman Graduate Center of the City University of New York, where he directs the Center for Lesbian and Gay Studies, and a founder of the Gay Academic Union. His pioneering work on gay history includes *About Time: Exploring the Gay Past*; *Cures: A Gay Man's Odyssey*; and *Stonewall*. With Martha Vicinus and George Chauncey, he is the coeditor of *Hidden from History: Reclaiming the Gay and Lesbian Past*. He has also written eloquently on race, notably *In White*

America, and is the author of *Paul Robeson*, considered the definitive biography of the singer and activist. He is also the author of *Left Out: The Politics of Exclusion: Essays, 1964–1999*, and *Haymarket: A Novel.*

Eminem, white rap artist whose apparently homophobic songs and actions drew fire from the gay community, particularly after he used a homophobic slur against the straight singer Moby. However, when Eminem invited prominent gay spokesperson and singer Elton John, to join him on stage at the 2001 Grammys, he confounded many of his critics by his apparently fraternal gesture to an openly gay artist.

Stephen Endean, executive director of the Gay Rights National Lobby and a national lobbyist for gay rights; founder of the Human Rights Campaign Fund, considered by many to be the major U.S. gay lobbying group. Endean's background was as a Minneapolis activist who lobbied his state legislature to pass a gay rights bill; although his efforts during the 1970s were unsuccessful, a statewide bill finally passed in 1993.

Lillian Faderman, scholar and teacher whose book, *Surpassing the Love of Men: Romantic Friendship and Love Between Women from the Renaissance to the Present*, established the existence of protolesbian "romantic friendships" among many women previously believed to be heterosexual; Faderman is especially well-known for her thesis that 19th-century poet Emily Dickinson could be said to be in love with her sister-in-law, Sue Gilbert. Faderman's work established the widespread existence of romantic friendship, suggesting that some version of lesbianism was far more widespread than previously believed. She is also the author of *Scotch Verdict; Odd Girls and Twilight Lovers: A History of Lesbian Life in Twentieth-Century America; To Believe in Women: What Lesbians Have Done for America—A History*; and *Naked in the Promised Land: A Memoir.*

Nathan Fain, one of the founders of Gay Men's Health Crisis (GMHC) and a pioneering journalist who covered the AIDS epidemic for the *Advocate* during the early years of the crisis.

Reverend Jerry Falwell, minister, televangelist, and founder of the Moral Majority, one of the nation's first and most powerful New Right/Religious Right organizations and renamed the Liberty Federation in 1999. Falwell is also the founder of Liberty University, in Lynchburg, Virginia, and is the host of the religious TV program *Old-Time Gospel Hour.* He is the author of *Listen, America!, The Fundamentalist Phenomenon, Champions of God*, and an autobiography, *Strength for the Journey.* Falwell won further notoriety among gay rights groups and their supporters when after September 11, 2001, he suggested that the tragedy was God's punishment for America's permissiveness toward homosexuality, among other sins—remarks for which he later apologized.

Matt Foreman, longtime gay rights activist; as of this writing, head of the National Gay and Lesbian Task Force (NGLTF). He was formerly executive director of Empire State Pride Agenda in New York, the nation's largest statewide gay rights group. He also served as head of the New York City Anti-Violence Project, a gay rights group that focuses attention on antigay violence, including violence within gay and lesbian relationships.

Jim Foster, founder of the Alice B. Toklas Club, the first gay Democratic political club in the nation. He and Madeleine Davis were the first openly gay people to address a national political convention—the Democratic Convention of 1972.

Jim Fouratt, founder of the Gay Liberation Front and a major gay leader in the post-Stonewall period. Fouratt was an early member of the Gay Activists Alliance and ACT UP.

Barney Frank, Democratic representative from Massachusetts; first U.S. member of Congress to voluntarily announce that he is gay. Frank has been a staunch supporter of gay rights and other progressive causes during his many years of service in the House.

Betty Friedan, feminist leader of the 1970s, notorious for claiming that lesbians were being sent by the CIA to discredit the feminist movement and for calling lesbians "the lavender menace." Friedan is also known for helping to inspire the second wave of U.S. feminism with her book *The Feminine Mystique*, in which she identified "the problem that has no name"—the unnamed but powerful malaise of middle-class American women who were restricted to domestic lives, a condition that Friedan considered unfulfilling.

Barbara Gittings, with her partner, Kay Tobin Lahusen, a leading spirit in the homophile and modern gay rights movement, leader in the Daughters of Bilitis, and a key figure in the efforts to convince the American Psychiatric Association to remove homosexuality from its list of disorders.

Barry Goldwater, right-wing Republican who surprised many by coming out strongly in favor of gay rights, not least because he had a gay grandson. Goldwater was also an explicit supporter of lifting the ban on gays in the military.

Jewelle Gomez, poet, novelist, essayist, and a former editor of *conditions*, a feminist magazine. *Conditions* was part of the widespread efforts of the early lesbian-feminist movement to establish a forum where women—especially lesbians—could express themselves, which was especially important in a time when mainstream magazines and book publishers all but ignored both lesbians and radical feminists. Poetry was an important aspect of the cultural battle of lesbian-feminism, and writing poetry was seen as a political act, especially for women of color like Gomez. Her poetry collections include *Flamingoes and Bears* and *The Lipstick Papers*. She is also the author of the novel *The Gilda Stories* and the essay collection *Forty-Three Septembers*.

David Goodstein, the controversial publisher of the influential Los Angeles–based gay newspaper the *Advocate* (January 1, 1975–June 22, 1985). In addition to running one of the two major U.S. gay newspapers for over a decade (the other paper was the *New York Native*), Goodstein played a key role in gay politics, helping to found the National Gay Rights Lobby (although he then refused to give the group his financial support) and influencing popular responses to many issues through his editorial policy. He is also somewhat notorious for having been extremely slow to recognize the AIDS crisis in the early 1980s, as his commitment to sexual freedom led him to see the dangers of the sexually transmitted disease as overrated; for some time, he viewed those who advised sexual restraint as homophobic.

Jeannine Gramick, a Catholic nun, who, with Robert Nugent, traveled around the United States, trying to get Catholic parishes to fully accept homosexuals in the church. Her ongoing battle with the Vatican has been featured in news stories and documentaries, and she continues as a spokesperson for Catholic gay and lesbian issues through her Washington, D.C.–based organization, New Ways Ministry.

Barbara Grier, cofounder, with Donna McBride, of Naiad Press, the oldest existing lesbian publishing company in the United States.

Harry Hay, cofounder of the first U.S. gay rights group, the Mattachine Society. Hay was forced out of his own group in 1953 by new, more conservative members who feared repercussions of his Communist past. Hay later went on to form the gay spiritual group, the Radical Faeries.

Jesse Helms, former right-wing U.S. senator from North Carolina. He is a leading figure in antigay legislation and is noted for his attempts to strip funding from the National Endowment of the Arts for its alleged support of obscene material as well as homosexuality. Helms is also known for his opposition to affirmative action, feminism, and a host of other progressive causes. Helms was instrumental in the Senate's opposition to James Hormel, whom President Bill Clinton appointed as the nation's first gay ambassador. He has recently become known for advocating increased U.S. aid to Africa to combat the transmission of AIDS from pregnant mothers to their children, although he continues to oppose other types of foreign aid and funding for AIDS services in the United States.

Jon Holden and **Michael Galluccio,** New Jersey couple who sought to adopt a son *as* a couple. Their suit led to the New Jersey Supreme Court ruling that stated gay couples had to be accorded the same rights in an adoption procedure as heterosexual couples.

Amber Hollibaugh, writer, filmmaker, and activist. She is known for her theoretical writings defending lesbian butch-femme culture and for her film *The Heart of the Matter,* about women and AIDS. Hollibaugh is also the former head of the Lesbian AIDS project of the GMHC.

James Hormel, businessman who became the first gay ambassador when President Clinton nominated him in 1998 to serve in Luxembourg. Because of Senator Trent Lott's unwillingness to let the vote on Hormel come to the Senate floor, Hormel's ambassadorship (awarded in 1999) relied solely on Clinton's appointment.

Reverend Jesse Jackson, the first U.S. presidential candidate to make support for gay rights a central part of his campaign (in 1984). Although Jackson and gay rights groups have quarreled over various issues, he is generally considered a strong supporter who has done much to link gay and lesbian issues with civil rights for people of color. However, in 2004, Jackson drew the line between gay rights and civil rights, particularly when it came to gay marriage.

Although Jackson said he supported gay rights, he made a point of saying that in his culture, marriage meant a union between a man and a woman.

Elton John, prominent British pop-rock singer and composer who was one of the first major singing stars to come out as gay. The singer caused controversy when he appeared with Eminem at the 2001 Grammys after the rapper had angered the gay community with apparently homophobic remarks on his albums and in his public statements.

Jill Johnston, former *Village Voice* columnist who wrote the classic books *Lesbian Nation* and *Marmalade Me. Lesbian Nation* was one of the first books by a mainstream publisher—or indeed, by any publisher—to acknowledge the existence of lesbian-feminism and to explain its significance to a wider world beyond the political circles within which the movement had begun.

Dr. Franklin Kameny, a Harvard-trained astronomer who was the first openly gay person to bring suit against the federal government. In 1953, he was arrested for stopping to watch the arrest of another gay man, and he took the matter to court. Kameny was also the first openly gay person to run for federal office—he ran for Congress from the District of Columbia in 1972. He was the founder of the Washington chapter of the Mattachine Society and a leader in organizing repeated demonstrations for gay rights.

Morris Kight, Los Angeles leader who helped found the Gay Liberation Front and the Los Angeles Gay Community Services Center.

Pete Knight, California state senator who spearheaded California's Proposition 22, also known as the Knight Amendment, which defined marriage as taking place between a man and a woman. Knight's son, David, married his longtime male partner in February 2004 during the flurry of gay marriages in San Francisco. Knight did not attend his son's marriage and continued in his opposition to gay marriage until his death in the spring of 2004.

Edward Koch, controversial former New York City mayor and congressman, with a long and complicated relationship to gay rights. As a congressman, Koch helped fellow New York representative Bella Abzug sponsor gay rights legislation in the mid-1970s; as mayor, he tried to extend civil rights protections to lesbians and gay men but faced opposition from the Catholic Church that ultimately defeated him. He was accused of being unresponsive to AIDS activists, not least because he had been insulted by Larry Kramer, founder of Gay Men's Health Crisis, the major AIDS activist group of the 1980s.

Larry Kramer, screenwriter, novelist, playwright, and activist. Kramer cofounded—but then was expelled from—the Gay Men's Health Crisis (GMHC), the first major AIDS activist group. He later cofounded—and was also expelled from—ACT UP, a major AIDS activist group of the 1990s. Kramer also won notoriety with *Faggots*, his 1978 novel decrying promiscuity in the gay community, and with *The Normal Heart*, a successful off-Broadway play about the founding of GMHC. In 2004, he became a vocal critic of the increasing use of crystal methamphetamine in the gay community.

Tony Kushner, Pulitzer Prize–winning and Tony Award–winning playwright whose major work, *Angels in America: A Gay Fantasia on National Themes*, brought gay issues into mainstream American theater. The movie version of this play, broadcast on HBO, won several Emmys. Kushner followed the two-part, six-hour play (dubbed separately as *Millennium Approaches* and *Perestroika*) with *Slavs*, an exploration of the former Soviet Union, and *A Dybbuk*, an adaptation of an earlier play set in Russia at the dawn of the 20th century (in Kushner's version, the Holocaust is also evoked). He has taken an active role in speaking out on gay issues and on politics in general, publishing most frequently in *The Nation*. One of his most controversial statements was made after the death of Matthew Shepard, when Kushner accused any church that had expressed antigay bias of being responsible for Shepard's murder. (He also accused himself and others who had not worked hard enough for gay rights of being similarly to blame.)

Dick Leitsch, leader of the New York Mattachine Society during the days of Stonewall. To the new generation of gay activists, he quickly became a symbol of what they viewed as the ineffectual old homophile movement.

Audre Lorde, poet and writer who cofounded Kitchen Table: Women of Color Press with Barbara Smith; a strikingly important act at a time when much of the visible work of the lesbian-feminist movement was dominated by white women. Lorde also published numerous volumes of poetry, including *The Marvelous Arithmetic of Distance;* memoirs, including *The Cancer Journals* and *Zami: A New Spelling of My Name* (which she called a "mythobiography"); and essays, including *Sister Outsider.* Whether she was writing poems about racism, discussing her journeys through racial and sexual politics, or sharing the intimate details of her battle with breast cancer, Lorde raised new political issues and made new connections between areas of life that had previously been seen as separate. Thus she helped make the fight against breast cancer into a feminist issue, and she raised the importance of the lesbian/gay rights movement in fighting racism and sexism as well as homophobia.

Trent Lott, Republican senator from Mississippi. Lott compared homosexuality to kleptomania during a 1999 congressional debate and refused to let the ambassadorial nomination of gay businessman James Hormel come to the Senate floor for a vote.

Phyllis Lyon and **Del Martin,** cofounders in 1953 of the first U.S. lesbian organization, Daughters of Bilitis. The couple also coauthored *Lesbian/Woman*, a classic memoir about growing up lesbian and beginning their partnership. Lyon and Martin continued as leading lesbian activists well into the 1970s and 1980s, and in 2004 they were the first gay couple to be married at San Francisco city hall.

Robert Mapplethorpe, openly gay photographer. His homoerotic work was the subject of a great deal of controversy, particularly after a posthumous exhibit of his pictures led a local sheriff to obtain a grand jury indictment for obscenity against the director of the Contemporary Arts Center of Cincinnati. The Mapplethorpe exhibit featured sadomasochistic imagery, including a self-portrait of Mapplethorpe naked in a leather jacket and cap with a bullwhip inserted in his anus; there was also a photo of a man's torso in a three-piece suit, with a large black penis sticking out of the unzipped pants. The director was eventually acquitted, but Mapplethorpe's name has come to symbolize allegedly obscene, homoerotic, and publicly funded art (money for the exhibit to tour had come partly from the National Endowment for the Arts [NEA]), and the controversial artist was invoked by right-wing senator Jesse Helms and others in their battle to eliminate funding for the NEA.

Leonard Matlovich, U.S. Air Force sergeant discharged in 1975 after admitting his homosexuality. Although Matlovich had consistently been awarded high ratings for his service, armed forces regulations required that he be discharged once his sexual orientation was discovered. Matlovich considered his discharge unfair and continued to fight it for five years, until finally, in 1980, a federal judge ordered the air force to allow him to reenlist. The air force also offered Matlovich another choice—a $160,000 settlement—which the former sergeant accepted. Because Matlovich had been seen as such an outstanding soldier, he helped to raise the issue of gays in the military, particularly after he became the first openly gay man to appear on the cover of *Time* magazine in 1975.

Joseph McCarthy, right-wing U.S. senator who won political fame by crusading against communists and homosexuals, both of whom he claimed were corrupting the U.S. government. He is largely responsible for the U.S. Civil Service's ban on gay men and lesbians, maintained from the late 1940s through the mid-1970s.

James Michael "Mike" McConnell, gay rights activist. McConnell is also the lover of Jack Baker, whom he married in a public—though extralegal—ceremony in the early days of gay liberation. McConnell was fired from his job with the University of Minnesota when his homosexuality—and his activism—became public; he brought an unsuccessful suit claiming discrimination.

Norma McCorvey, gay, pseudonymous plaintiff in *Roe v. Wade*, the 1973 Supreme Court case that led to the legalization of abortion. She is the author of *I Am Roe*, a memoir about that experience. Later, McCorvey became disillusioned with feminists, whom she said "used" her, and she turned to antiabortion religious right groups, for whom she became a spokeswoman.

James E. McGreevey, New Jersey governor who announced his resignation in August 2004 after disclosing that he was gay and had been having an affair with former aide Golan Cipel. McGreevey's "I am a gay American" speech, in which he disclosed his sexuality and apologized to his wife for infidelity, was temporarily a topic that won national attention, as commentators noted that McGreevey had just become the highest openly gay elected official in the nation, until his resignation on November 15 of that year. McGreevey was criticized for the evidence and rumors of scandal that had plagued his administration, including his hiring of Cipel, whom many believed was not qualified for the positions he had held. A Democrat, McGreevey was also criticized for choosing to step down after the general election, when a Democrat would be appointed to take his place, rather than vacating office before the election, when a Republican candidate might have won an electoral victory.

Harvey Milk, the first openly gay San Francisco supervisor, known for his tireless dedication to gay rights—and for his assassination, along with gay-friendly mayor George Moscone, at the hand of fellow supervisor Dan White. Many gay rights advocates see him as a martyr to the movement. He is the subject of a famous biography, *The Mayor of Castro Street,* by well-known, openly gay reporter Randy Shilts. The biography was later adopted into a film documentary as well as an opera.

Kate Millett, feminist theorist, writer, and sculptor whose gradual admission of bisexuality in the early 1970s helped raise the issue within the feminist movement. Some leaders of the National Organization for Women, including Gloria Steinem, rallied around her; others, notably Betty Friedan, felt that open lesbians would discredit the feminist cause.

David Mixner, Los Angeles gay rights leader who helped found the Municipal Elections Committee of Los Angeles (MECLA), a group of wealthy gay men (later joined by some gay women) who became extremely influential in local and national politics. Mixner also had a certain amount of influence as a friend and early supporter of President Bill Clinton.

Cherríe Moraga, coeditor with Gloria Anzaldúa of *This Bridge Called My Back: Writings by Radical Women of Color,* a pioneering anthology of political works by African-American, Latina, and other feminists. When this collection first came out, very few works by women of color had appeared, and the two editors helped to establish that lesbian-feminism could be a multiracial movement representing women from a wide range of economic backgrounds. Moraga is also a playwright and essayist whose work includes *Loving in the War Zone.*

Robin Morgan, editor of the pioneering anthology *Sisterhood Is Powerful,* as well as a collection of essays entitled *Sisterhood Is Global.* Until 1993, she was the longtime editor of *Ms.* magazine, the first feminist publication to reach a broad, nationwide audience. In the 1970s, Morgan was known for helping to establish connections between lesbianism and feminism.

George Moscone, gay-friendly mayor of San Francisco who was assassinated along with supervisor Harvey Milk at the hands of ex-supervisor Dan White. White had resigned from the board of supervisors because it seemed to him too liberal and too supportive of gay rights; when he changed his mind and asked Moscone to reinstate him, Moscone refused. White then shot and killed Moscone and Milk in their offices at city hall.

Marilyn Musgrave, Colorado Republican representative who introduced the Federal Marriage Amendment in 2002 and again in 2003. The amendment would define marriage as between one man and one woman, as well as prevent court decisions from establishing same-sex marriage in any state.

Jamie Nabozny, gay Wisconsin teenager who, in November 1996, became the first student to successfully bring a suit against a school and school district for failure to protect him from antigay violence and harassment. A federal jury found that school officials had violated his Constitutional right to equal protection when they dismissed his requests for help during five years of escalating attacks from other students that eventually led to injuries requiring surgery.

Holly Near, singer and songwriter who alerted many women to the links between feminism and lesbianism when she came out as a lesbian in the 1970s. She is also known for her musical partnership with folksinger Ronnie Gilbert of the Weavers. Near's pioneering lesbian-feminist album was *Imagine My Surprise*. Her other albums include *Hang in There, Fire in the Rain*, and *Don't Hold Back*.

Joan Nestle, cofounder, with Deborah Edel, of the Lesbian Herstory Archives in New York City and prominent editor whose anthologies include *The Persistent Desire: A Butch-Femme Reader,* the *Women on Women* series (with Naomi Holoch), and *Sister and Brother* (with John Preston). She is also the author of *A Restricted Country*.

Gavin Newsom, San Francisco mayor whose support of gay marriage led him to defy California's statewide ban on gay marriage in February 2004. He told the city clerk to issue same-sex marriage licenses, which resulted in more than 4,000 gay marriages being performed in San Francisco before legal action forced Newsom to call a halt and the California Supreme Court eventually invalidated the marriages.

Elaine Noble, Massachusetts state representative and the first openly gay candidate elected to state office in the United States. She was an important grassroots leader in Boston politics who established that gay candidates could offer leadership on a broad range of issues.

Sam Nunn, former Georgia senator and head of the Armed Services Committee who strongly opposed President Clinton's efforts to lift the ban on gay men and lesbians in the military. As a result of his pressure, Clinton instituted the famous "don't ask, don't tell" policy.

John J. Cardinal O'Connor, Catholic leader who presided over the archdiocese of New York during the height of gay activism. O'Connor was known for his opposition to homosexuality and for his concern about sex education and the distribution of condoms, which gay rights activists saw as a necessary measure to combat the spread of HIV/AIDS. As a result, the militant gay rights group ACT UP sponsored a controversial protest in St. Patrick's Cathedral during a Sunday mass as a way of bringing its opposition to the cardinal's home ground. In 1995 on Gay Pride Day, O'Connor made a strong statement condemning antigay violence and opposing those who believed that Christianity required hatred of homosexuals. However, to many in the gay rights and AIDS activist communities, he remained a symbol of the institutional power wielded by those who oppose gay rights.

Rosie O'Donnell, popular talk-show personality and actress who married her partner, Kelli Carpenter, in San Francisco in February 2004, despite a statewide ban on gay marriage. O'Donnell was moved to the action because, in a recent legal dispute, her partner had been forced to testify against her.

O'Donnell realized that if she had been entitled to spousal privilege, she and her partner would have been protected. The parent of several children, she was as of this writing considering founding a magazine that would focus on gay parenting issues.

Jean O'Leary, leading figure in lesbian-feminist separatist politics in New York and Los Angeles. She was also a cochair of the National Gay Task Force (NGTF) and a close friend of Midge Costanza, former aide to President Jimmy Carter. With Bruce Voeller, she established the importance of female leadership of the NGTF, which has since changed its name to the National Gay and Lesbian Task Force.

Reverend Troy Perry, founder of the Metropolitan Community Church. Begun in Los Angeles in 1968 and dedicated to supporting gay and lesbian members, the church how has branches all over the United States. Perry had been an ordained charismatic preacher but was thrown out of his own church for homosexuality.

Reverend Fred Phelps, Southern Baptist minister and pastor of the Westboro Baptist Church in Topeka, Kansas, whose opposition to gay rights and homosexuality in general led him to found the "God Hates Fags" web site and to organize protests against homosexuality at the funerals of those who have died from AIDS. Phelps gained national attention when he organized a demonstration at the funeral of Matthew Shepard, a gay youth murdered in Laramie, Wyoming, in 1998. Phelps's militant antigay stance prompted another anti–gay rights leader, Reverend Jerry Falwell, to condemn him and other Christians who, in Falwell's view, preached hate rather than love. Phelps has also been active in protesting same-sex marriage. On September 8, 2003, he showed up to protest the first day of school at the Harvey Milk High School, a New York City public school for lesbian, gay, bisexual, and transgender youths. He and his followers have recently gone around the country protesting the play, *The Laramie Project*, which negatively portrays him and them.

Jonathan Rauch, writer for the *National Journal* and *Atlantic Monthly* and author of *Gay Marriage: Why It Is Good for Gays, Good for Straights, and Good for America*. In that book, Rauch argues that without the option of marriage, gay men and lesbians are doomed to perpetual adolescence.

Ronald Reagan, president of the United States from 1980–88. Under his presidency, most of the New Deal federal programs established by Franklin D. Roosevelt in the 1930s were abolished. Reagan's presidency coincided with the AIDS crisis; AIDS activists see him as failing to address the issue early enough and never being willing to allocate sufficient funds for it. He was also seen as creating a climate under which the New Right and Religious Right could flourish.

Adrienne Rich, lesbian-feminist poet, essayist, and theorist. She wrote the influential essay, "Compulsory Heterosexuality and the Lesbian Continuum," arguing for the notion that there was a continuum between female friendship and lesbian relationships and that most women would probably choose lesbian relationships if society would not violently punish them for it and/or propagandize against them. Her feminist essay collections, *Of Woman Born* and *On Lies, Secrets, and Silences*, have been widely read and cited by other feminists; her volumes of poetry include *A Change of the World, Diving into the Wreck, Dream of a Common Language*, and *A Wild Patience Has Taken Me This Far.* She has received the National Book Award and many other awards.

Sylvia Rivera, militant drag queen who broke away from the Gay Activists Alliance (GAA) to found Street Transvestites Action Revolution (STAR). A participant in the Stonewall riot, she gained notoriety within the gay community in 1970 while working as a prostitute; she simultaneously circulated a GAA petition demanding a New York City Council bill barring antigay discrimination.

Craig Rodwell, founder of the Oscar Wilde Memorial Bookstore in New York City, a pre-Stonewall center for gay culture. He was also the organizer of the first New York City Gay Rights parade.

Mitt Romney, Massachusetts governor who opposed the state's move toward same-sex marriage. Although the Massachusetts Supreme Judicial Court ruled in 2003 that the state's constitution required that gay men and lesbians be given equal access to civil marriage, Romney helped spearhead a movement to amend the state constitution to read otherwise. He also ordered city and town clerks to make sure that same-sex couples who received marriage licenses were not residents of other states, pursuant to a 1913 state law, even though no such interrogation is commonly conducted for straight couples.

Rick Santorum, Republican senator from Pennsylvania who in 2003 drew fire from gay rights groups when he compared homosexuality to incest, bigamy, and adultery. His remarks particularly angered gay columnist Dan Savage, who began a campaign to associate Santorum's name with an unpleasant byproduct of anal sex.

Jose Sarria, the first openly gay person in the United States to run for public office. Sarria, a waiter and cabaret performer at San Francisco's Black Cat, ran for the office of city supervisor in 1961.

Antonin Scalia, Supreme Court justice known for his deep opposition to gay rights, particularly as expressed in his minority opinion in *Romer v. Evans*, the decision that overturned Colorado's Amendment 2. The Colorado law, passed by referendum, itself overturned all gay rights measures in the state while banning any future legislation that would have outlawed discrimination on the basis of sexual preference. Scalia's minority opinion defended Amendment 2, arguing that gay men and women were not a minority that needed the Supreme Court's protection, but a powerful political lobby that could legitimately be restrained by a law like the one passed in Colorado. Scalia also dissented in *Lawrence v. Texas*, the Supreme Court decision striking down U.S. sodomy laws.

Walter Schubert, first openly gay member of the New York Stock Exchange and the founder of Gay Financial Network, a web site focusing on news items of special interest to gay investors.

Robin Shahar, lawyer who had been offered a job in the office of Georgia attorney general Michael J. Bowers. When Shahar had a private commitment ceremony with her lover, Bowers discovered her sexual orientation and withdrew the job offer, citing the Georgia sodomy law then in effect that technically made Shahar a felon.

Father Paul Shanley, Catholic priest known during the 1970s and 1980s for his support of gay liberation but who was later revealed to be preying on the teenagers and young men who came to him for help. His story came out as part of the revelations connected to the Catholic Church's sex abuse scandals of the early 21st century.

Judy Shepard, mother of murdered youth Matthew Shepard who gained national attention in the wake of her son's death. Although Judy Shepard had been relatively obscure and apolitical before the murder, she gradually became a spokesperson for gay rights and continues to fight for legislation that would increase the penalties for hate crimes against lesbians and gay men.

Matthew Shepard, college student whose brutal murder in Laramie, Wyoming, provoked a nationwide outcry over antigay violence and led to support for hate crimes legislation around the nation.

Randy Shilts, influential author and journalist who covered many gay rights issues, most notably the AIDS crisis. He is the author of *And the Band Played On*, an important account of that crisis; *The Mayor of Castro Street: The Life and Times of Harvey Milk*; and *Conduct Unbecoming: Gays and Lesbians in the U.S. Military*.

Edward L. Shrock, U.S. representative from Virginia and an outspoken opponent of same-sex marriage. In August 2004, Shrock announced he would not seek reelection after a web log posting asserted he was gay. Shrock was married at the time the posting appeared.

Michelangelo Signorile, former writer for *Outweek* and inventor of the strategy of "outing" in the early 1990s, in which Signorile would reveal the true sexuality of prominent gay men who were passing as straight. Signorile was widely criticized for this approach, but he insisted that prominent gay figures had a duty to help the gay community by making their presence known, particularly during the AIDS crisis, when people with AIDS or HIV were getting little attention or support from government or private institutions. Signorile continues to write and speak on gay issues.

Barbara Smith, editor, theorist, writer, and publisher. Smith has been one of the major voices to articulate an African-American lesbian-feminist-socialist position and has long been recognized as one of the major African-American theorists and activists in the gay rights movement. With the Combahee River Collective, a group formed in 1973 as the Boston chapter of the National Black Feminist Organization, Smith helped write "The Black Feminist Statement," which was deeply influential in the feminist movement and beyond. Smith also wrote and coedited several books that were central in articulating an African-American viewpoint in the feminist and lesbian movements. With Gloria T. Hull and Patricia B. Scott, she edited *All the Women Are White, All* *the Blacks Are Men, But Some of Us Are Brave*, the first black women's studies anthology. With Lorraine Bethal, she edited *Conditions: Five, The Black Women's Issue*, a highly influential issue of a major lesbian-feminist magazine. She also edited *Home Girls, A Black Feminist Anthology* and, with Elly Bulkin and Minnie Bruce Pratt, wrote *Yours in Struggle: Three Feminist Perspectives on Anti-Semitism and Racism*, which played a significant role in the lesbian-feminist and feminist movements' debates on anti-Semitism and racism in the late 1970s. Her 1974 essay, "Towards a Black Feminist Criticism," was one of the first to argue that a black women's literary tradition existed and should be studied. With Audre Lorde, she was cofounder of Kitchen Table: Women of Color Press, which insured that women of color would have a voice in the feminist movement of the 1970s and 1980. *The Truth That Never Hurts: Writings on Race, Gender and Freedom* (1998) is a collection of her essays and speeches.

Charles Socarides, psychiatrist who held the theory that homosexuality was a disease therapy could cure. He was a major opponent of gay objectives in the 1973 fight to remove homosexuality from the American Psychiatric Association's list of disorders. Ironically, his son proved to be gay and became a gay rights activist.

Gerry Studds, first openly gay U.S. congressman, though not willingly—Studds came out when a scandal involving sex with congressional pages revealed his homosexuality. He was otherwise known as a liberal congressman active on a variety of issues.

Andrew Sullivan, one of the best-known gay conservatives. Sullivan is the former editor of the *New Republic* who became known for his books *Virtually Normal: An Argument About Homosexuality; Love Undetectable: Notes on Friendship, Sex, and Survival;* and *Same-Sex Marriage: Pro and Con*, which he edited. Sullivan has argued vehemently for same-sex marriage and for the rights of gays to serve in the military, both of which he sees as basic acknowledgment of gay people's citizenship and humanity. However, he opposes the more liberal and radical segments of the gay rights movement, which in his view constrain the liberties of other segments of society by imposing upon them an acceptance of gay men and women that is not their own choice.

Brandon Teena, transgender victim of a fatal gay bashing. Born Teena Brandon but able to pass successfully as a young man, Brandon Teena achieved notoriety when he was brutally murdered in a small Nebraska town. His story was later told in a documentary, *The Brandon Teena Story*, and in an award-winning feature film, *Boys Don't Cry*.

Jamiel Terry, openly gay son of Randall Terry, head of the antiabortion group Operation Rescue and an antigay activist. When Jamiel came out, Randall announced that his son was no longer welcome in his home. Jamiel made his sexuality public in an article he wrote for *Out* magazine. Both Terrys then gave interviews to Belief Net explaining their divergent positions.

Robin Tyler, lesbian-feminist comedian and speaker who conceived the idea of the first National March on Washington for Lesbian and Gay Rights. The

1979 event grew out of a joking remark that Tyler had made in response to a local defeat for gay rights in St. Paul.

Urvashi Vaid, former executive director of the National Gay and Lesbian Task Force, one of the major national gay rights groups in the United States. Her 1995 book, *Virtual Equality: The Mainstreaming of Gay and Lesbian Liberation,* is a major document of the transformation of the gay/lesbian rights movement from invisibility to political prominence. However, Vaid points out, "virtual" equality means that in many ways gay and lesbian rights are illusory, for while gay people have become more visible and politically active, they are still subject to violence and discrimination. Vaid was formerly a member of the feminist collective that published the journal *Sister Courage* in Boston.

Bruce Voeller, founder of the National Gay Task Force, an organization he went on to create after his experience as third president of the Gay Activists Alliance. Voeller wanted to create a more middle-class, middle-of-the-road organization that would focus on lobbying and achieving concrete results rather than on seeking a broader definition of gay rights.

Jason West, mayor of New Paltz, New York, who gained national fame when he announced that he would perform same-sex marriages in spring 2004 despite the apparent illegality of the action. Eventually, West was forced to stop performing the ceremonies, but not before he inspired other mayors in upstate New York to take similar actions, including the gay mayor of nearby Nyack.

Byron White, Supreme Court justice who wrote the *Bowers v. Hardwick* decision, reaffirming states' rights to pass sodomy laws, including versions of such laws that were specifically antigay.

Dan White, former San Francisco supervisor who assassinated Supervisor Harvey Milk and Mayor George Moscone. At his trial, White claimed that he was suffering from depression brought on by eating too much junk food, a gambit that became known as the "Twinkie defense." White received less than eight years for voluntary manslaughter but was released from prison early. He killed himself in 1985.

Mel White, gay evangelist and former speechwriter for Jerry Falwell, who broke away from Falwell to found Soulforce, a gay evangelical group.

Barry Winchell, U.S. Army private first class who was killed at Fort Campbell, Kentucky. His death eventually caused President Clinton to order a review of his "don't ask, don't tell" policy, which many believe contributed to the murder. Winchell had apparently been harassed by his assailant before the murder but was afraid to report it for fear of revealing his sexual orientation.

CHAPTER 6

GLOSSARY

a priori A legal term, meaning "before the fact." A lawyer might say, for example, that in a state where sodomy is illegal, a sexually active lesbian seeking custody of her child is a priori a criminal; that is, she has been established as a criminal before the custody proceedings have even begun.

ACT UP (AIDS Coalition to Unleash Power) A militant group founded in New York City in 1987 that favored demonstrations and direct action to protest inadequate AIDS research and discrimination against people with AIDS; chapters soon spread all over the United States. Frequent targets included drug companies that refused to make treatments available at reasonable prices; the Food and Drug Administration, for refusing to speed up the availability of new treatments; the federal government, for allocating insufficient funds and attention to the epidemic; and the Catholic Church, for opposing widespread AIDS education and the distribution of condoms, which were known to help prevent the spread of the disease.

age of consent The age at which state law considers a person old enough to consent to a sexual act, usually age 16 or 18. Sex with a person below the age of consent is considered *statutory rape*, that is, rape by definition. In many countries, the age of consent is older for homosexual than for heterosexual sex.

AIDS (acquired immune deficiency syndrome) A term used to describe the many diseases caused by HIV, the human immunodeficiency virus. AIDS was formerly known as GRID (Gay-Related Immune Deficiency) because the syndrome was first identified among gay men in the United States. Gay activists Bruce Voeller and Virginia Apuzzo pressed the U.S. Centers for Disease Control for a name change as it became clear that anyone, gay or straight, could succumb to the disease.

Amendment 2 Successful 1992 statewide referendum that outlawed gay rights legislation in Colorado. Until Amendment 2 was overturned by the U.S. Supreme Court in *Romer v. Evans* (1996), this law superseded the antidiscrimination ordinances in the Colorado cities of Aspen, Boulder, and Denver.

American Center for Law and Justice (ACLJ) A conservative legal group affiliated with the right-wing Christian Coalition that has recently brought suit against several cities who offer domestic partnership benefits to same-sex couples.

American Civil Liberties Union (ACLU)   An organization devoted to *civil liberties*, the rights and freedoms guaranteed under the Constitution. In recent years, the ACLU has worked with many gay rights groups to support the right to sexual privacy and the abolishment of sodomy laws; same-sex marriage; and gay people's right to freedom of speech and free expression.

bisexual   A term that describes sexual actions or feelings that involve people of either sex; people who call themselves bisexual are expressing their ability to be sexually interested in either men or women, though not necessarily to the same extent.

bottom   A slang term used to refer to the submissive or more passive partner in a lesbian/gay relationship or in a sadomasochistic relationship. It also refers to the receptive partner in specific sexual acts.

Briggs Initiative   A referendum unsuccessfully introduced to California voters in 1978 by State Senator John V. Briggs that would have barred gay men and women from teaching in the public schools.

butch   A slang term meaning "masculine" or "the masculine one" that can be used to refer to either gay men or lesbians. In gay and lesbian relationships, gender roles are sometimes divided, with one partner being the "butch" and the other the "femme."

Christian right (Religious Right)   A term used to refer to the portion of the right wing that specifically identifies itself with Christianity, basing its politics on a fundamentalist reading of the Bible and a wish to enforce Christian morality in the political arena. More specifically, the term refers to such leaders as Reverends Jerry Falwell and Pat Robertson and their hundreds of thousands of followers in Falwell's Liberty Alliance and Robertson's 700 Club.

circuit   An informal national network of gay male dance parties catering to the affluent segment of gay society and associated with drug use and unprotected sex.

civil union   A legally recognized version of domestic partnership, instituted in 2000 by the state of Vermont when the state's supreme court ordered the legislature to come up with an institution whereby the state's gay citizens could have equal access to the marital benefits that straight people enjoyed.

coming out   The process by which a gay man or lesbian declares his or her sexual orientation to himself/herself and/or others. People may speak of being "out" to their parents but not "out" at work, for example.

consenting adults   A term used to describe people whom state law recognizes as old enough to consent to sexual acts.

crystal methamphetamine   A highly addictive drug that is currently associated with increased rates of addiction and unprotected sex in the gay male community. The drug, also known as crystal meth, Tina, crank, ice, and speed, causes heightened sex drive, stamina, and euphoria.

custody   The right and responsibility to care for a child, often in dispute after a divorce when parents go to live in separate households. Historically, lesbian mothers (and, less frequently, gay fathers) have been denied custody of their children on the grounds of their homosexuality.

de facto   A legal term meaning "in fact." Legal advocates of gay rights often speak of de facto recognition of same-sex relationships; that is, even though a relationship is not recognized in law by a marriage contract, it may be recognized in fact, by the extension of domestic partnership benefits, custody rights, and so on. Another example of a de facto relationship is the parental status of a same-sex partner who helps to raise a child; such a person might have no legal standing but might be recognized as "in fact" acting as the child's parent.

The Defense of Marriage Act (DOMA)   A 1994 bill passed overwhelmingly by Congress in response to the possibility that same-sex marriage might be recognized in Hawaii. Because our federal system requires each state to recognize contracts—including marriage contracts—established by one another, in the absence of specific contravening policy, conservatives pushed for a federal policy that would prohibit same-sex marriage in all 50 states. Many gay rights advocates believe that DOMA is an unconstitutional usurpation by the federal government of power that has traditionally belonged to the states.

de jure   A legal term meaning "in law," to be contrasted with de facto, which means "in fact." Legal advocates of gay rights often contrast the de facto recognition of same-sex partnerships—through, for instance, the extension of domestic partnership benefits—with the de jure recognition of marriage, through the actual laws governing the marriage contract.

domestic partnership   Relationship between an unmarried couple who share the financial responsibilities of a household. Although the term can be used to refer to unmarried heterosexual couples, it is most often used in discussions of same-sex couples to indicate a marriagelike relationship. Some states and cities have registries where same-sex couples can legally establish their domestic partnerships.

domestic partnership benefits   The economic benefits that would normally go to married couples—insurance, pension, and other financial benefits—extended to domestic partners. While partnership benefits may be extended to both heterosexual and homosexual couples, the term is most often used in discussions of same-sex couples, who are thereby allowed to enjoy the financial benefits of marriage if not the full legal recognition of that state.

Employment Non-Discrimination Act (ENDA)   A bill introduced to Congress in 1994 that would extend federal protection against employment discrimination under Title VII to discrimination on the basis of sexual orientation. As of this writing, the bill had not yet passed.

ex-gay movement   A movement that gained national attention in the late 1990s, as members of the Christian Right promoted Exodus International and other organizations that claimed to be able to "convert" homosexuals to heterosexuality through a combination of prayer, counseling, and group support. The ex-gay movement held out the possibility that gay people could stop engaging in homosexual activity and that some could even enter full-fledged heterosexual relationships, including marriage.

femme   A slang term meaning "feminine" or "the feminine one" that can be used to refer to either gay men or lesbians. In gay and lesbian relationships, gender roles are sometimes divided, with one partner being the "butch" and the other the "femme."

GMHC   Originally Gay Men's Health Crisis, the organization is now known by its initials to suggest a broader range of AIDS activism than the group's initial focus, which was on gay men with AIDS. GMHC was cofounded in August 1981, just months after the first AIDS cases were identified, by writer and activist Larry Kramer, who was soon expelled; its founding and subsequent history are the subject of Kramer's successful off-Broadway play *The Normal Heart.*

hate crimes   Criminal acts based primarily on prejudice against a particular group of people; the 1990 Hate Crime Statistics Act recognizes race, religion, national origin, and sexual orientation as categories of people against whom hate crimes might occur. In some states, hate crimes carry harsher penalties than other criminal acts.

heterosexism   Acts, words, or thoughts suggesting that heterosexuals are in any way superior to homosexuals; modeled on the terms *sexism* (commonly understood as the idea that men are superior to women) and *racism* (the idea that one race is superior to another).

HIV   The human immunodeficiency virus; generally accepted as the cause of AIDS in humans.

homoerotic   Having or expressing sexual feelings for people of the same sex.

homophile   A 1950s and 1960s term that literally means "lover of men"; it was used by early gay rights organizations to indicate those who supported "homosexual" men; thus, members of homophile organizations such as the Mattachine Society were not necessarily admitting to being homosexual.

homophobia   Literally, the irrational fear of homosexuals; used more widely to denote hatred for gay men and lesbians and the view that they are somehow inferior to heterosexuals.

Human Rights Campaign   The major national gay rights lobbying organization, which focuses on influencing Washington politics through seeking influence among politicians and attempting to elect gay or gay-friendly political leaders. The group and its leader, Elizabeth Birch, became controversial in the gay rights movement when it endorsed right wing New York senator Al D'Amato to reward him for some gay-friendly stands he had taken; many gay men and women perceived that his liberal opponent, Charles Schumer, was more generally supportive of gay people and their allies.

intersex   A term used to indicate people born "between genders," with hormonal and biological markers that indicate both male and female characteristics.

in the closet   Slang term for hiding one's gay or lesbian identity, feelings, or practices. A gay man or woman who is "in the closet" might have an active gay or lesbian life that he or she hides from others. The term also refers to people who are unaware of their own gay or lesbian feelings. This is also referred to as "closeted."

Knight Initiative Known officially as Proposition 22, a referendum sponsored by California state senator Pete Knight and subsequently approved by that state's voters to legally define marriage as being only between a man and a woman and require the state to deny recognition to same-sex marriages contracted in other states.

Mattachine Society The first gay rights group in the United States. It was founded by Harry Hay in 1950.

Moral Majority The name of a group once led by Reverend Jerry Falwell, now known as the Liberty Alliance. Falwell took the name from a remark of former President Richard Nixon, who claimed that there was a "silent majority" that did not agree with the more visible actions of radicals.

National Gay and Lesbian Task Force (NGLTF) Formerly known as the National Gay Task Force, one of the major national gay rights organizations. Its activities range from national lobbying and educational efforts to grassroots organizing and legal work.

outing A term made popular by gay journalist Michelangelo Signorile that means making someone's homosexuality public against the person's wishes. Outing was justified on the grounds that a public figure who could help other gay men and lesbians by revealing the truth had no right to hide this information, particularly if the person in question had opposed gay rights or made homophobic statements.

passing The attempt to be viewed as belonging to another, preferred category; the word may indicate gay people who pass as straight, Jews who pass as gentile, or people of color who pass as white. In some contexts, the word also refers to men or women, including transsexuals and transgender people who pass as people of the opposite sex.

postgay A term popularized by *Out* magazine, among others, meant to indicate that the time for gay rights activism is over and that gay people are now free to live their lives simply as human beings, not limited to the category of gay human beings.

queer A relatively new term used to indicate both homosexuals and heterosexuals who do not accept mainstream society's definitions of gender and sexuality. It became popular in the 1990s as the gay rights movement became both broader and more militant.

Queer Nation A militant branch of ACT UP that became popular during the early 1990s and was known for developing the term *queer* as a protest against the old categories of "homosexual" and "heterosexual." Rather than winning more rights within the existing system of gender and sexuality, Queer Nation wanted to challenge the system itself.

sadomasochism The term for a variety of sexual practices and relationships characterized by one dominant partner (a sadist, or in slang terms, the "top") and one submissive, or passive, other (a masochist, or in slang terms, the "bottom"). Sometimes sadomasochistic relationships involve the dominant partner inflicting physical or psychological pain on the submissive one; sometimes the relationship simply involves giving orders. Those who practice "S and M" stress that these are consensual relationships, wherein many provisions are made for the submissive partner to stop the pain or punishment at will.

separatism A theory, popular among many lesbian-feminists of the 1970s, that a persecuted group of people should live as separately as possible in its own community.

sexual minorities A catchall term for those whose sexual practices are unusual; generally used to refer to people who practice sadomasochism, as well as transvestites and transgender people, as opposed to "mainstream" gay men and lesbians (and heterosexuals).

sodomy A term used to indicate a number of sexual practices that laws in various states once considered illegal. While the term originally referred only to the sexual practice of a man inserting his penis into another man's anus, the legal use of the term varied widely. In some states it also referred to other homosexual acts, such as one man's penis making contact with another man's mouth. In other states it referred to any contact between penis and anus or penis and mouth, whether homosexual or heterosexual. Sodomy laws were also used to criminalize sexual acts among women, even though the original definition of the word could not be used that way. Since 2003, when the U.S. Supreme Court decision *Lawrence v. Texas* struck down laws against private, consensual, nonpaying sodomy between adults, the term is less important legally but it is still often used as synonymous with homosexual sex.

top A slang term used to refer to the dominant partner in a lesbian or gay relationship and/or to the dominant partner in a sadomasochistic relationship. It also refers to the insertive partner in specific sexual acts.

transgender A general term suggesting that a person has been born into a body of the "wrong" gender; that is, the person feels herself to be a woman but has been born into a man's body; or feels himself to be a man but has been born into a woman's body. Some transgender people choose to dress as the gender they feel they "really" are; others may choose to have an operation and/or take hormones to change to their "true" gender. Some transgender people identify as gay men or lesbians; others feel they are straight men or women born into the "wrong" bodies.

transsexual A person who has changed from one gender to another, usually by means of an operation and/or hormone treatments.

transvestite A person who dresses as a member of the opposite sex; although popular stereotypes suggest that transvestites are gay, people of any sexual orientation may be transvestites. Although some transvestites may feel that they are "really" of the opposite sex, many simply enjoy a permanent or temporary change of costume.

visitation rights (a)The right to visit one's child, often an issue when child custody is in dispute. Historically, lesbian mothers (and, less frequently, gay fathers) have seen their visitation rights restricted on the grounds of their homosexuality; for example, they might not be allowed to see their children alone or might be forbidden to see them in the presence of their lesbian or gay partners. **(b)** The right to visit another family member when that person is ill and unable to make his or her wishes known; a right automatically granted to married heterosexuals who wish to see their spouses but usually denied to gay men and women who wish to visit their partners.

PART II

GUIDE TO FURTHER RESEARCH

CHAPTER 7

HOW TO RESEARCH
GAY RIGHTS

One of the biggest difficulties confronted by the researcher of gay rights is the overwhelming amount of available material. As discussed earlier, the term *gay rights* can be used to refer to legal, political, cultural, social, and economic issues. Moreover, the gay rights movement has been moving, in the words of Evan Wolfson of Freedom to Marry, "at Internet speed," implying that researchers may be overwhelmed by the vast number of books, articles, magazines, web sites, and other sources of information on everything from Supreme Court decisions to commitment ceremonies.

Further complicating the problem is the uneven nature of the information: There is a great deal of information on some topics and very little on others. Some political, cultural, and legal arenas have been transformed at dizzying speed (even as this book was being prepared, for example, major developments were occurring regarding gay marriage), while others have changed very little. In still other cases, the developments themselves have been uneven or wildly contradictory: custody battles are still difficult for lesbian mothers, even as almost all states now allow gay men and lesbians to adopt; same-sex marriages have been legalized in Massachusetts even as new laws against gay marriage are passed.

How, then, can researchers proceed? Here are some general suggestions, followed by more specific advice about where to find material.

TIPS FOR RESEARCHING GAY RIGHTS

- Define the Topic as Specifically as Possible. Whether surfing the Internet, checking out a bookstore, exploring a library, or doing a database search, one is likely to run into an overwhelming amount of material even on an apparently narrowly defined topic. The more specifically a researcher has decided what aspects of gay rights are of interest and how much needs to be known, the easier it will be to find what he/she wants. For suggestions on particular

213

categories that can help define a topic, see the subheads used in the periodicals section of Chapter 8.

- Be Aware of the Key Historical Landmarks. As discussed in Chapter 3, much of the gay rights movement has proceeded in leaps and bounds, defined by certain key historical moments. Among the most important are the Stonewall uprising of 1969; the beginning of the antigay backlash in 1977; the beginning of the AIDS crisis in 1981; the founding of ACT UP in 1987; the election of President Clinton in 1992, which ushered in an era of major developments regarding gays in the military, gay marriage, and gay adoption; the accession of George W. Bush to the Presidency in 2000, which ushered in an era of White House hostility to gay rights; the U.S. Supreme Court decision of *Lawrence v. Kansas* in July 2003, striking down all sodomy laws in the United States; the Massachusetts Supreme Judicial Court decision in November 2003, ordering the state to begin allowing gay civil marriages by May 17, 2004; and the November 2004 presidential election, in which a president extremely opposed to gay rights was elected, and 11 amendments to state constitutions were passed banning gay marriage. Obviously, the landmarks are different for various issues—we have tried to suggest the most important turning points in Part I of this book—so the researcher must have key dates firmly in mind to evaluate the usefulness of any published source.

- Know the Sources. As we have also seen, there is no such thing as a monolithic "gay rights movement" or "anti–gay rights movement." Both supporters and opponents of gay rights have widely varying opinions; indeed, little agreement exists on what "gay rights" means. To some, it signifies sexual freedom; to others, it is defined by Supreme Court cases and lower court rulings; to still others, it refers to the growing political power of gay and gay-friendly politicians; to yet more others, it concerns such civil rights as adoption, child custody, marriage, employment, and housing. Thus the researcher looking for overviews or evaluations, or seeking commentators to help explain the significance of a particular event, has to be especially aware of a source's potential bias.

GETTING STARTED:
SOME HELPFUL SOURCES

BOOKS

This volume attempts to provide a comprehensive overview of the modern gay rights movement from 1969–2004. Another very useful overview, covering the period from 1900–1997, is *Becoming Visible: An Illustrated History of Lesbian and Gay Life in Twentieth-Century America*, by Molly McGarry and Fred Wasserman (New York: New York Public Library, Penguin Studio, 1998), which is based on an exhibit curated at the New York Public Library by Fred Wasserman, Molly McGarry, and Mimi Bowling. Drawing from the most extensive display of lesbian and gay history ever mounted in a museum or gallery space, the book covers gay history, politics, and culture. The book focuses on material concerning New York City but is probably the single best overview of the gay rights movement currently available.

Yet another helpful source is *Out for Good: The Struggle to Build a Gay Rights Movement in America*, by Dudley Clendinen and Adam Nagourney (Simon & Schuster, 1999). Beginning with the Stonewall uprising in 1969 and proceeding to the height of the AIDS crisis in 1988, *Out for Good* is a thoroughly detailed chronicle of political events and organizations, with extensive coverage of New York City, Los Angeles, and San Francisco and a great deal of information about other centers of lesbian and gay activity, such as Minneapolis, New Orleans, Atlanta, and Washington, D.C. *Out for Good* tends to focus on political and electoral events, offering profiles of people and organizations committed to working within the system; its information is far less comprehensive concerning radical politics, cultural activity, and developments in lesbian and gay theory. It also tends to cover gay men far more than lesbians. However, no other book includes such a wealth of information about the events of those two decades.

Witness to Revolution, The Advocate *Reports on Gay and Lesbian Politics, 1967–1999*, edited by Chris Bull (Alyson Books, 1999), is an anthology of major articles on gay rights from one of the nation's major national gay publications. Although this book is no substitute for an actual history, it does touch on many of the major issues of the past three decades, with particular focus on the gay conservatives who came out in the 1990s.

The books section of the following chapter includes information on a large number of books, but here, for your convenience, are some key historical and political texts (see individual listings in the following chapter for specific publication information):

- **Profiles of Key People and Events:** Martin Duberman's *Stonewall*; Kay Tobin and Randy Wicker's *The Gay Crusaders* (profiles of pre-Stonewall gay activists); Eric Marcus's *Making History* (a collection of oral histories); John D'Emilio's *Sexual Politics, Sexual Communities: The Making of a Homosexual Minority in the United States, 1940–1970*; Randy Shilts's *The Mayor of Castro Street: The Life and Times of Harvey Milk*.

- **Landmark Personal Accounts and Opinions:** Martin Duberman's *Cures: A Gay Man's Odyssey*; Robin Morgan's *Going Too Far: The Personal Chronicle of a Feminist*; Joan Nestle's *A Restricted Country*; Gore Vidal's *United States: Essays, 1952–1992*; Edmund White's *States of Desire: Travels in Gay America*.

- **Anthologies of Gay History:** Jonathan Ned Katz's *Gay American History: Lesbians and Gay Men in the U.S.A.*; Karla Jay and Allen Young's *Out of the Closets, Voices of Gay Liberation* (an anthology of the first post-Stonewall gay liberation writings in America, compiled in 1972); Mark Blasius and Shane Phelan's *We Are Everywhere, A Historical Sourcebook of Gay and Lesbian Politics* (including international material, with a focus on the United States, from 1754 to 1994).

- **Key Works of Lesbian Feminism:** Sidney Abbott and Barbara Love's *Sappho Was a Right-On Woman* (a 1972 exploration of lesbian issues); Del Martin and Phyllis Lynon's *lesbian/woman* (a cultural analysis); Kate Millett's *Sexual Politics: The Classic Analysis of the Interplay Between Man, Women, and Culture*; *Building Feminist Theory: Essays from* Quest, *a Feminist Quarterly*; Lillian Faderman's *Surpassing the Love of Men* (an analysis of early "romantic friendships" between women in 18th-, 19th-, and 20th-century America and Europe) and *To Believe in Women: What Lesbians Have Done for America—A History.*

- **Coverage of the AIDS Crisis:** Paul Monette's *Borrowed Time: An AIDS Memoir* and *Becoming a Man: Half a Life Story* (memoirs); Randy Shilts's *And the Band Played On* (a history of the crisis from the first appearance of the virus to the discovery of how it was spread); Larry Kramer's *Reports from the Holocaust: The Making of an AIDS Activist* (focusing on Kramer's key role in AIDS activism, 1981–1988).

- **Gay Urban Life:** Frances FitzGerald's *Cities on a Hill: A Journey Through Contemporary American Cultures*; George Chauncey's *Gay New York: Gender, Urban Culture, and the Making of the Gay Male World, 1890–1940*; Charles Kaiser's *The Gay Metropolis.*

- **Key Cultural Works:** Rita Mae Brown's *Rubyfruit Jungle* (a coming-of-age lesbian novel); Andrew Holleran's *Dancer from the Dance* (a portrait of pre-AIDS sexual liberation in New York City); Armistead Maupin's *Tales from the City* and *More Tales from the City* (a fictional chronicle of gay life in San Francisco throughout the 1970s and 1980s); Harvey Fierstein's *Torch Song Trilogy* (a Tony Award–winning play about 1970s gay life in New York—also available as a movie); Larry's Kramer's *The Normal Heart* (a play about the founding of Gay Men's Health Crisis at the beginning of the AIDS epidemic); Tony Kushner's *Angels in America* (a Pulitzer Prize–winning play about gay politics and the beginning of the AIDS crisis); Adrienne Rich's *The Dream of a Common Language: Poems, 1974–1978*; Judy Grahn's *The Work of a Common Woman* (a 1978 poetry collection); Rosa Guy's *Ruby* (a 1976 novel about a lesbian relationship in New York City's West Indian community); Audre Lorde's *Zami: A New Spelling of My Name* (a "biomythography" in which Lorde explores the interrelationships between her sexual and racial identities).

NEWSPAPERS

One excellent way to research gay rights is to pick a narrowly defined topic and do a search on a readily available database, such as Pro Quest, which is available in many public libraries. However, even a narrowly defined topic can yield an overwhelming plethora of articles. For researchers trying to grasp an issue quickly, it might be useful to focus on one or two major newspapers. The *New York Times* and the *San Francisco Chronicle* have the well-deserved reputations of never missing a major event related to gay rights; of the two, the *Chronicle* offers the most supportive coverage, as well as being readily available by database. The *Atlanta Journal-Constitution, Detroit News, Denver Post, Houston Chronicle, Los Angeles Times,* and *Washington Post* are also good sources for coverage, whereas the *Boston Globe's* coverage tends to be somewhat less exhaustive. The *Christian Science Monitor* offers a more skeptical view of the gay rights movement. The *Wall Street Journal's* coverage is the most critical, and that paper offers the most frequent expression of antigay opinion. The *Washington Times,* extremely conservative in its outlook, provides some of the nation's most comprehensive coverage of gay rights issues in its news pages, along with a wide variety of conservative and antigay opinions in its editorial page.

MAGAZINES

A second type of database is usually required for periodicals other than newspapers, particularly for scholarly journals and more specialized publications. For this book, the university database from Yale University, specifically its lesbian and gay abstracts section, was very helpful. Many universities have a similar database, although, as with Yale, they often require either an institutional affiliation or a fee. Scholarly journals that are particularly useful for researching lesbian and gay issues include the *Journal of Homosexuality,* the *Gay and Lesbian Review* (formerly the *Harvard Gay and Lesbian Review*), the *Gay and Lesbian Quarterly, Signs,* and *Choice.*

Specialized lesbian and gay periodicals are another key source of information. The best national sources of information are the weeklies the *Advocate* (which is based in Los Angeles) and the *Village Voice* (which is based in New York and is not specifically a gay/lesbian publication but has excellent coverage and analysis and is also available online). *Gay Community News,* based in Massachusetts, is inclusive but published irregularly and has better coverage of radical politics and more extensive information about lesbian issues than the *Advocate.* *Off our backs* is a national monthly with a radical feminist perspective that offers frequent coverage of lesbian issues. *Lesbian News* is a monthly magazine that includes news and political coverage along with a comprehensive look at culture and entertainment. *POZ* is a monthly magazine targeted toward the HIV/AIDS community. It is an excellent source for the latest information on treatment, activism, and legal cases involving HIV/AIDS. Naturally, though, articles from these sources will be skated toward a progay bias.

Other key gay publications are the *Washington* [D.C.] *Blade, LGNY* (New York), *L.A. Gay Times,* and *Bay Windows* (San Francisco). *Sojourner,* in the Boston/Cambridge area, is a feminist journal with extensive coverage of lesbian issues and culture. Other local lesbian and gay publications usually include coverage of national events and trends.

One useful way of following lesbian and gay issues is to look for the work of particular columnists and journalists known for their investigative reporting and/or analysis. Hard-hitting journalist Michelangelo Signorile won fame (some would call it notoriety) for "outing" nationally known gay figures in his weekly column for *Outweek* magazine, but his work also includes extensive coverage of the gay marriage issue, sexism among gay men, trends regarding safe-sex practices, and other cutting-edge issues in the gay community. Signorile is also the author of *Queer in America: Sex, Media and the Closets of Power* (New York: Random House, 1993) and *Life Outside, The Signorile Report on Gay Men: Sex, Drugs, Muscles, and the Passages of Life* (New York: HarperCollins, 1997).

Richard Goldstein, a columnist and editor at the *Village Voice*, offers wide-ranging cultural and political analysis on a variety of topics, including gay issues, as does his fellow reporter Alisa Solomon. Both Goldstein and Solomon write extensively for a number of other publications as well, including *The Nation*, a national political journal whose coverage of progressive politics includes frequent articles on gay rights. Doug Ireland is a writer and commentator who often writes about gay political issues.

Dan Savage writes "Savage Love," a nationally syndicated sexual advice column and is the author of *The Kid, An Adoption Story: How My Boyfriend and I Decided to Get Pregnant* and *Skipping Towards Gomorrah: The Seven Deadly Sins and the Pursuit of Happiness in America*. Elise Harris is a journalist who writes for *The Nation* and other publications.

Major cultural and political commentators include Tony Kushner, author of the Pulitzer Prize–winning play *Angels in America* and a frequent contributor to *The Nation;* Jonathan Rauch, writer for *Atlantic Monthly* and *National Journal*, who drew national attention with his *Gay Marriage: Why It Is Good for Gays, Good for Straights, and Good for America;* former *New Republic* editor Andrew Sullivan, whose conservative, Catholic perspective informs his books *Virtually Normal* and *Love Undetectable: Notes on Friendship, Sex, and Survival;* conservative writer Bruce Bawer, author of *A Place at the Table* (1993), a formulation of gay rights that stresses acceptance into mainstream society; and Gabriel Rotello, who won fame for his 1997 book, *Sexual Ecology: AIDS and the Destiny of Gay Men*, in which he argued that gay men needed to develop serially monogamous relationships to combat the spread of AIDS.

RESEARCH AND THE INTERNET

The Internet can also be a rich source of data. Again, researchers should be aware that they will encounter an overwhelming amount of information of widely varying quality if they simply enter "gay rights" or "gay legal rights" in a search engine (although this also can be a surprisingly effective way of finding good information quickly). Otherwise, there are two choices: to approach the issue from the "legal" side or approach it from the "gay rights" side.

An outstanding source of gay legal rights information on the Web is the web site maintained by Lambda Legal, a gay rights group at http://www.lambdalegal. org. The weekly magazine the *Advocate* maintains a web site with current news at http://www.advocate.org. The gay directory "gayscape," at http://www. gayscape.com, has a subcategory called "Pride," whose listings in turn include "gay rights," "activist groups," "anti-violence," "gays and lesbians in the military," and "gay, lesbian and bisexual youth."

A less user-friendly but still useful source is Queer Resources Directory, http://www.qrd.org, which has links to business, legal, and workplace issues. Information on court cases and legislation is also available through the web sites for the National Gay and Lesbian Task Force (http://www.thetaskforce.org), Human Rights Campaign (http://hrc.org), National Committee on Lesbian Rights (http://nclrights.org), and National Organization for Women (information on lesbian rights; http://now.org/now/issues/lgbi/index.html). (For more detailed information, see the bibliography.)

Some useful antigay web sites include http://www.weeklystandard.com, the web site of the conservative publication, the *Weekly Standard;* http://www.aclj.org, the web site for the American Center for Law and Justice, which brings a wide variety of lawsuits from a conservative perspective on gay rights, affirmative action, and other issues; http://www.reclaimamerica.com, sponsored by the Center for Reclaiming America, a self-described effort to mobilize Christians at the grassroots level to oppose gay rights as well as to promote creationism, oppose abortion and pornography, and protect religious liberties; http://www.familypolicy.net, sponsored by the Family Policy Network, a socially conservative Christian network committed to defending religious liberties and the traditional family. For antigay web sites focusing on opposition to gay marriage, see http://www.allianceformarriage.org and http://www.nogaymarriage.com, both of which offer news, analyses, and opportunities for activism to oppose gay marriage. The web sites for the anti–gay rights groups in Chapter 9 are also rich sources of information from this perspective.

Researchers looking for specific court cases and legislation can turn to one of the many free sources for legal information on the Web. Unfortunately, electronic law libraries—including Westlaw and Lexis-Nexis—all cost money to use, either via subscription or on a per-use basis, and they really are the only way to get comprehensive access to most court cases before 1990 with the exception of Supreme Court cases, which are available through http://www.findlaw.com. Findlaw.com also offers a comprehensive directory of various Internet legal resources, including a state-by-state guide, but many states do not offer online texts of court cases; many others go back only a few years or, at most, to 1990.

Another useful Internet resource is the Meta-Index for U.S. Legal Research, a service of Georgia State University's College of Law: http://gsulaw.gus.edu/metaindex. You can access Supreme Court cases, circuit court cases, federal legislation, and federal regulations, as well as find links to other online law resources.

Cornell Law School also offers its Legal Information Institute (http://law.cornell.edu), which makes available a variety of legal resources. For anything other than New York State law, however, researchers would do better to use one of the other sources.

Finally, for a wide range of information on international, federal, and state courts, Northwestern University offers government publications and maps at http://www.library.nwu.edu/govpub/resource/legal/courts.html.

Anti–Gay Rights Positions

Another way to track the gay rights movement is to follow the newsmakers and opinion-makers who oppose gay rights. Columnist and presidential candidate Pat Buchanan and journalist George Will offer conservative opinions in a variety of newspaper op-ed pages, as does Ann Coulter, a syndicated columnist. Buchanan regularly publishes in the *New York Post*, and Will frequently appears in the *Washington Post*. The following activists can be tracked in database searches of news stories or as authors of op-ed and opinion pieces: Jerry Falwell of the Liberty Alliance; Pat Robertson of the 700 Club; Gary Bauer of the Family Research Council and a presidential candidate in 2000; James Dobson of Focus on the Family; anti–gay-rights leader Phil Burress; Reverend Fred Phelps, leader of the antigay protests surrounding Matthew Shepard's death and around the funerals of people who died from AIDS complications. Many of the anti-gay rights organizations in Chapter 9 also maintain web sites with news, information, and analyses from an antigay perspective.

CHAPTER 8

ANNOTATED BIBLIOGRAPHY

The following bibliography contains three major sections: books, articles, and web sites.

The books section is by no means a comprehensive listing of all the books on this wide-ranging topic; rather, it is a selection of the most important and representative volumes that a beginning researcher might find useful. It includes those books considered "classics" as well as a broad sampling of key books on major topics in gay rights.

The articles were drawn primarily from daily newspapers around the United States, as well as from some specialized publications such as the *Nation*. The intention was to include a wide variety of newspapers so that researchers would have access to the spectrum of opinion across the nation and to focus primarily on sources that would be available in most libraries. Thus, for more specialized gay/lesbian sources and more scholarly periodical resources, the researcher is advised to consult the specialized periodicals described in the previous chapter.

Articles are organized according to the following topics: adoption, AIDS issues, ballot measures, civic organizations, court decisions, culture/media, custody of children, domestic partnerships, education, hate crimes, history/analysis of the progay movement, housing rights, immigration laws, international gay rights issues, marriage, military, politics, religion, sodomy laws, transgender issues, and workplace issues.

The web sites listed here likewise do not represent the virtual universe of available Internet resources. They do, however, constitute a good starting place for the beginning researcher, along with an assurance that with these listings, the researcher can easily keep up with major political and legal events in the ever-changing field of gay rights.

BOOKS

Adam, Barry D. *The Rise of a Gay and Lesbian Movement*. Boston: Twayne, 1987.
    Adam thoroughly reviews the early gay and lesbian rights movements in Germany and the United States along with the reactions they provoked among

the heterosexual majority. He also provides encapsulations of changes taking place in Canada, Mexico, and Europe.

Bawer, Bruce. *A Place at the Table: The Gay Individual in American Society.* New York: Touchstone Books, 1994. Bawer, a gay, conservative Christian, posits that the media-dominated gay centers of New York, Los Angeles, and San Francisco are out of touch with the kinds of lives most gay men are living in the heartland of the country. He believes these men constitute a virtual gay silent majority who have been silenced by the political and sexual radicals of the gay "elite." In his opinion, the excesses and self-destructiveness of gay culture must be addressed before the community has any hope of achieving real political equality.

Bawer, Bruce, ed. *Beyond Queer: Challenging Gay Left Orthodoxy.* New York: Free Press, 1996. Bawer gathers 38 articles from 17 writers, including himself, who attack the "queer establishment" and argue for a more moderate approach to lesbian and gay rights. The book is divided into six separate sections, each focusing on an area that Bawer considers crucial for defining gay issues outside of a radical discourse: the failures of the gay liberation movement since the Stonewall riot; gay relations with the right; social oppression of gays; the inadequacies of a gay identity based on countercultural values; gays and religion; and "Family Values," particularly gay marriage.

Berubé, Allan. *Coming Out under Fire: The History of Gay Men and Women in World War Two.* New York: Free Press, 1990. This is a comprehensive and scholarly study of the role played by lesbians and gay men in World War II, along with the military's policies and attitudes about homosexuality. It provides an excellent context for any discussion of the "don't ask, don't tell" controversy that has dominated gay political discourse in the 1990s.

Blasius, Mark, and Shane Phelan, eds. *We Are Everywhere: A Historical Sourcebook of Gay and Lesbian Politics.* New York: Routledge, 1997. Blasius and Phelan have compiled a volume of primary source material that will help both the academic historian as well as the common reader. Manuscripts range from 18th-century legal documents to contemporary essays and analyses. The book charts how life has changed for gay people as well as how gay people themselves have created change.

Boswell, John. *Same-Sex Unions in Premodern Europe.* New York: Vintage, 1995. In this landmark book, Boswell traces the history of same-sex marriages in the early Christian church throughout Europe and the Mediterranean world. He makes a very strong case that these unions existed and were even officially sanctioned. Boswell takes great pains to distinguish the sexual presumptions about marriage among our premodern ancestors from those held by our postmodern society.

Bryant, Anita. *The Anita Bryant Story: The Survival of Our Nation's Families and the Threat of Militant Homosexuality.* Old Tappan, N.J.: Revell, 1977. The Stonewall riots of 1969 may have signaled the "coming out" of the gay liberation movement, but Anita Bryant's campaign to overturn a gay rights ordinance in Dade County, Florida, marked the beginnings of the Religious Right backlash that continues to this day. It also proved that the gay community could effectively organize nationally to combat homophobia. Bryant tells her side of the story in her own words.

Bunch, Charlotte. *Passionate Politics.* New York: St. Martin's Press, 1986. A collection of essays by one of the leading theorists of the lesbian-feminist movement, this book includes an extensive section detailing Bunch's early experience and involvement in the gay and lesbian rights movement.

Chauncey, George. *Gay New York: Gender, Urban Culture, and the Making of the Gay Male World, 1890–1940.* New York: Basic Books, 1994. Chauncey has had much to do with altering perceptions about gay and lesbian history. In this book he reveals that the New York of the early 20th century had a thriving gay culture that, contrary to popular perception, was quite open about its existence and which supported clubs, restaurants, and bathhouses. The sexual suppression during the middle part of the century virtually erased this history. This book is a powerful reminder that cultural acceptance does not equal political empowerment.

———. *Making of a Modern Gay World: 1935–1975.* New York: Basic Books, 2004. Something of a sequel to *Gay New York*, this volume continues the historical narrative of Chauncey's first book by reconstructing the racially segregated and class-stratified African-American, Latino, and white gay male worlds and sexual cultures of postwar New York, analyzing the sources of postwar antipathy to homosexuality and reinterpreting the development of gay politics and the transformation of urban liberalism. He uses the changes in gay social organization, culture, and consciousness in the 1950s and 1960s to illuminate the broader changes in the concepts of urbanity, nationalism, and race.

Clendinen, Dudley, and Adam Nagourney. *Out for Good: The Struggle to Build a Gay Rights Movement.* New York: Simon & Schuster, 1999. This comprehensive look at the political, reformist wing of the modern gay rights movement is based on interviews with 330 gay rights activists directly involved in everything from the Stonewall riots of 1969 to ACT UP in 1987.

Comstock, Gary David. *Violence against Lesbians and Gay Men.* New York: Columbia University Press, 1991. Comstock examines the history of violence against gay men and lesbians. He then speculates, based on sociological evidence, about why adolescent and young adult males are most likely to commit these crimes.

Comstock, Gary David, and Susan E. Henking, eds. *Que(E)Rying Religion: A Critical Anthology.* New York: Continuum Publishing Group, 2000. Comstock and Henking have assembled a collection of essays that variously address the intersection of homosexuality and religion. A variety of religious traditions are included, and the writers, primarily academics, are not all gay, lesbian, or bisexual. Some of the topics covered include being Muslim and gay, religious responses to the AIDS crisis, and women partners in the New Testament. Most of the essays are scholarly, but a few offer personal reflections on the issue of sexuality and faith.

Crampton, Louis. *Homosexuality and Civilization*. Cambridge, Mass: Belknap Press, 2003. Crampton, an early pioneer of gay and lesbian studies, attempts the monumental task of chronicling the history of homosexuality in Europe and parts of Asia from ancient Greece to the 18th century. Historical epochs examined include classical Greece and Rome, Arab Spain, imperial China, and pre-Meiji Japan, as well as the reigns of such Western rulers as James I of England and Queen Christina of Sweden. However, Crampton's central focus is the persecution of homosexuals by religious authorities throughout Europe during the Middle Ages and Renaissance and the persistence of homoerotic imagery in the art of the period. His book also serves as a rebuke to the post-structuralist school of thought, which maintains that modern ideas of homosexual identity cannot be transposed to other historical periods.

Cruikshank, Margaret. *The Gay and Lesbian Liberation Movement*. New York: Routledge, Chapman & Hall, 1992. Cruikshank's book, part of the series "Revolutionary Thought/Radical Movements," divides the gay and lesbian movement into three distinct philosophical streams: a movement for sexual liberation, a civil rights movement, and an upsetting of hundreds of years of Western thought. She is particularly interested in the complex negotiations between gay men and lesbians.

D'Emilio, John. *Making Trouble*. New York: Routledge, Chapman & Hall, 1992. D'Emilio's book contains a collection of his essays on a wide variety of topics that affect the gay and lesbian community, from capitalism to higher learning and from sodomy statutes to effective strategies for building a movement.

———. *Sexual Politics, Sexual Communities: The Making of a Homosexual Minority in the United States, 1940–1970*. Chicago: University of Chicago Press, 1983. D'Emilio fills in the history of the gay and lesbian rights movement in the country before Stonewall. He presents an examination of such groups as the Mattachine Society and the Daughters of Bilitis, as well as other early "homophile" organizations.

———. *The World Turned: Essays on Gay History, Politics, and Culture*. Durham, N.C.: Duke University Press, 2002. D'Emilio is both a historian and the former head of the National Gay and Lesbian Task Force Public Policy Institute. In this collection of 16 essays he offers both personal remembrances of key events in his personal development as a gay man and analyses of major historical events and personages. Topics covered include Bayard Rustin, the openly gay organizer of Martin Luther King's March on Washington; Larry Kramer, the writer and AIDS activist; the legacy of radical gay and lesbian liberation; the scapegoating of gays and lesbians by the Christian Right; and the gay-gene controversy and debate over whether people are "born gay."

D'Emilio, John, William B. Turner, and Urvashi Vaid, eds. *Creating Change: Sexuality, Public Policy, and Civil Rights*. New York: St. Martin's Press, 2000. The editors divide the book into three main sections: gays' relationship to presidential politics and governmental institutions; the gay legislative agenda; and the building of a politically viable advocacy movement. Topics discussed include immigration law, gay Republicans, lesbian health care during the

Clinton administration, gay rights and the Supreme Court, gays in the military, marriage and domestic partnership, and federal AIDS policy. Taken together, the essays collected here illustrate the incremental nature of change inherent in the American political system, especially when viewed against the swifter social acceptance within mainstream media culture.

Duberman, Martin. *About Time: Exploring the Gay Past.* New York: Meridian, 1991. Duberman, one of the country's foremost gay historians and political theorists, collects many of his essays into this volume, as well as a selection of historical documents dating to the 19th century.

——. *Cures: A Gay Man's Odyssey, Tenth Anniversary Edition.* Boulder, Colo: Westview Press, 2002. Duberman's autobiographical account of his attempts to "cure" himself of his homosexuality through therapy, medical treatments, and faith healers. Duberman tells of the double life he led as a young professor at Princeton, passing as straight by day and going into the gay clubs of Trenton and New York by night, until he came out as a gay man around the time of Stonewall. For this edition, Duberman has written a new preface and an afterword, bringing the gay experience in America today up to date and discussing such issues as gay rights, same-sex marriage, gay scholarship, and AIDS.

——. *Midlife Queer: Autobiography of a Decade, 1971–1981.* Madison: University of Wisconsin Press, 1998. Duberman continues his examination of the gay rights movement with this examination of the urban gay culture of the post-Stonewall 1970s. He refracts this history through the multiple prisms of radical politics, fledgling gay studies programs, alternative psychiatric therapies, and the sexual social scene of the pre-AIDS generation.

——. *Stonewall.* New York: Dutton, 1993. Well-written account of the events of June 27 and 28, 1969, commonly referred to as the Stonewall riots. Duberman provides an excellent historical context for what is generally recognized as the birth of modern gay liberation by recounting the lives of six individuals who experienced the event.

Duberman, Martin, Martha Vicinus, and George Chauncey, Jr., eds. *Hidden from History; Reclaiming the Gay and Lesbian Past.* New York: New American Library, 1989. The three editors, all leading scholars in the field of gay and lesbian studies, have collected essays tracing the history of same-sex relationships and desire from preindustrial societies through the 19th century and into the postmodern era.

Eskridge, William N. *Gaylaw: Challenging the Apartheid of the Closet.* Cambridge, Mass: Harvard University Press: 2002. Defining "gaylaw" as the ongoing history of judicial regulations regarding gender and sexual nonconformity, Eskridge, a law professor at Yale University, provides an exhaustive chronicle of legal constraints upon sexual orientation and gender status. The book opens with an overview of the post–Civil War treatment of people who violated societal norms of gender or sexuality. Part 2 stresses why the legal perpetuation of "apartheid of the closet" demands reevaluation. He pays particular attention to the issues of marriage and military service, offering constitutional interpretations that support the full inclusion of gays and lesbians in both institutions.

Eskridge, William N., and Nan D. Hunter. *Sexuality, Gender and the Law.* 2nd edition. New York: Foundation Press, 2003. Part of the University Casebook Series designed for legal students, this book provides the tools for fast, easy, on-point research into legal precedents for cases involving sexuality and gender. It includes selected cases designed to illustrate the development of this body of law.

Federman, Lillian. *Naked in the Promised Land: A Memoir.* New York: Houghton Mifflin, 2003. One of the foremost scholars of lesbian history in the United States, Federman reveals in this memoir that her initial ambition was to be a movie star. The daughter of a mentally unbalanced immigrant mother, Federman thought she could "rescue" her mother from her Holocaust survivor's guilt by becoming famous. In pre–gay liberation Los Angeles, however, this was no easy task. After abandoning her Hollywood dreams, she worked her way through college as a burlesque stripper, eventually earning a Ph.D. and coming to terms with her sexuality.

———. *Odd Girls and Twilight Lovers: A History of Lesbian Life in Twentieth-Century America.* New York: Columbia University Press, 1991. Faderman tells the compelling story of lesbian life in the 20th century, from the "Boston marriages" of the early 1900s to the "lipstick lesbians" of today. Using journals, unpublished manuscripts, songs, news accounts, novels, medical literature, and numerous interviews, she relates an often surprising narrative of lesbian life.

———. *Surpassing the Love of Men: Romantic Friendship and Love Between Women from the Renaissance to the Present.* New York: Morrow, 1981. Springing from an examination of Emily Dickinson's passionate friendship and private correspondence with her sister-in-law, Sue Gilbert, Faderman's exploration of the history of female same-sex relationships in Western culture is a classic of lesbian-feminist scholarship.

———. *To Believe in Women: What Lesbians Have Done for America—A History.* New York: Houghton Mifflin, 1999. Faderman continues the work she began in *Surpassing the Love of Men*, chronicling the stories of the women who, while fighting for suffrage, higher education, and women's entrance into "male" professions, also "lived in committed relationships with other women."

Fricke, Aaron. *Reflections of a Rock Lobster: A Story about Growing Up Gay.* Boston: Alyson Publications, 1981. Fricke recounts the story of his legal battle to be allowed to take another boy to his senior prom.

Garner, Abigail. *Families Like Mine: Children of Gay Parents Tell It Like It Is.* New York: HarperCollins, 2004. Garner, who created the site FamiliesLikeMine. com, attempts to educate teens, young adults, and their families about non-traditional families by interweaving her experiences growing up with a gay father and straight mother with those of children who were raised by lesbian, gay, bisexual, or transgender parents. Garner raises issues about the messages passed on to children about what it means to be "well-adjusted"; the risks and advantages of coming out, for both parents and children; and the effects a "homohostile" world has on young people.

Gerstmann, Evan. *Same-Sex Marriage and the Constitution.* Cambridge: Cambridge University Press, 2003. Does the Constitution protect the right to same-sex marriage? Gerstmann examines the legal debate and asks whether, in a democratic society, the courts, rather than voters, should resolve the question. He argues that marriage was one of the first fundamental rights the Supreme Court acknowledged, and as such, gay marriage is an important response to the Constitution's promise of legal equality.

Gibson, Gifford Guy, with Mary Jo Risher. *By Her Own Admission: A Lesbian Mother's Fight to Keep Her Son.* Garden City, N.Y.: Doubleday, 1977. In 1976, a Texas jury declared Mary Jo Risher an "unfit mother" because she was a lesbian. Her son, Richard, was taken from her and awarded to her former husband. This book recounts the story of the long court battles surrounding that event.

Harris, Daniel. *The Rise and Fall of Gay Culture.* New York: Hyperion, 1997. In this collection of interconnected essays, Harris argues that the social gains gay men have won in the past 30 years have gradually robbed them of their unique cultural identity. Later essays include stinging critiques of more recent cultural phenomenon such as glossy gay magazines and AIDS memorabilia.

Hippler, Mike. *Matlovich: The Good Soldier.* Boston: Alyson Publications, 1989. This book chronicles the life and struggles of the first gay man to come out while still in the military. His five-year dispute with the air force would foreshadow much of the controversy that has dogged the armed services during the 1990s.

Hunter, Nan D., Courtney G. Joslin, and Sharon M. McGowan. *The Rights of Lesbians, Gay Men, Bisexuals, and Transgender People.* Carbondale: Southern Illinois University Press, 2004. One of the American Civil Liberty Union's handbooks on individual rights, this book is a complete review of the rights of LGBT citizens. Now in its fourth edition, it addresses legal issues regarding freedom of speech and association, employment, housing, the military, families and parenting, and HIV disease. New to this edition are two appendices that include contact information for national and regional LGBT legal groups, an overview of the legal system to explain some of the terms and concepts that appear throughout the book, and a summary of highlights of the law state by state.

Jay, Karla, and Allen Young. *After You're Out.* New York: Links Books, 1975. This collection offers several dozen personal essays describing the profound changes the early gay liberation movement made in individual lives. The book is divided into three main sections: "Identity and Lifestyles," "Survival in a Hostile World," and "Creating Community and Helping Ourselves."

———. *Out of the Closets.* New York: Douglas Books, 1972. This is one of the essential documents of the early radical culture that gave birth to the gay liberation movement. Topics covered include health care, the Cuban revolution, and sexual politics.

Katz, Jonathan. *Gay American History: Lesbian and Gay Men in the U.S.A.* New York: Thomas Y. Crowell, 1976. A scholarly compendium of almost 200 source documents chronicling homosexual practice in America from 1566 to the mid-1970s; the chapter "Resistance: 1859–1972" contains much material on the early gay rights movement.

————. *Love Stories: Sex Between Men Before Homosexuality.* Chicago: University of Chicago Press, 2003. Katz has uncovered evidence of male-to-male sexual and affectional relationships throughout the 19th century. Topics covered include Abraham Lincoln's decades-long intimate friendship with Joshua Speed; the relationship between the American consul to Scotland and a famous British transvestite; the existence of gay bars in lower Manhattan during this period; and erotic arrangements between American sailors during the Civil War and their "chickens." Katz also unearths clues pointing toward homosexual behavior in the biographies of writers Walt Whitman and Charles Warren Stoddard, mathematician James Mills Peirce, and philosopher Edward Carpenter.

Keen, Lisa, and Suzanne Goldberg. *Strangers to the Law: Gay People on Trial.* Ann Arbor: University of Michigan Press, 1998. Keen and Goldberg chronicle the background, strategies, proceedings, and arguments of the case against Colorado's Amendment 2 that became known as *Romer v. Evans.*

King, J. L. *On the Down Low: A Journey into the Lives of "Straight" Black Men Who Sleep with Men.* New York: Broadway Books, 2004. Part memoir, part psychological study, King's book looks at the lives and lifestyles of black men who sleep with other men but do not consider themselves to be gay. These men live "on the down low," or "DL," and their sexual activities have gained significant notice as the rate of HIV/AIDS infection in black women has skyrocketed through transmission via heterosexual sex. King cites the negative image many socially conservative black men have of homosexuality as an obstacle to those men being honest with their partners and themselves about who they are.

Kramer, Larry. *Reports from the Holocaust: The Story of an AIDS Activist.* New York: St. Martin's Press, 1989. Kramer is a cofounder of Gay Men's Health Crisis (now GMHC) and ACT UP (AIDS Coalition to Unleash Power); he is also the author of the controversial novel *Faggots* and the play *The Normal Heart.* In this book he has created a memoir of his frontline work in the battle against AIDS.

Leupp, Gary P. *Male Colors: The Construction of Homosexuality in Tokugawa Japan.* Berkeley: University of California Press, 1996. Leupp examines male-male sex in early modern Japan, where it was not only tolerated but celebrated, much as in ancient Athens. He finds an explanation for its unusual prevalence in social factors such as the absence of women from monasteries and their scarcity in samurai society and the cities, the culture surrounding Kabuki theater, and the world of male prostitutes.

Marcus, Eric. *Is It a Choice?—Revised Edition: Answers to 300 of the Most Frequently Asked Questions About Gays and Lesbian People.* San Francisco: Harper,

1999. In simple, straightforward language geared especially for teenage readers, Marcus offers insightful and sensitive answers to the most frequently asked questions regarding homosexuality. Topics covered include same-gender relationships, coming out, family roles, and politics. Questions answered range from "Do gay parents raise gay children?" to "If you think a friend is gay or lesbian, what should you say?"

————. *Making History: The Struggle for Gay and Lesbian Equal Rights, 1945–1990: An Oral History*. New York: Columbia University Press, 1992. Approximately 45 individuals, mostly gay and lesbian but some heterosexual, talk about the gay and lesbian rights movement, especially their own roles in regard to that movement.

McGarry, Molly, and Fred Wasserman. *Becoming Visible*. New York: Penguin Putnam, 1998. A pictorial history of gay and lesbian life in New York City that documents the landmark exhibit of the same name at the New York Public Library. The book illustrates the intersecting worlds of sex, politics, and cultural life that have created what is now generally thought of as the gay community.

Moats, David. *Civil Wars: Gay Marriage in America*. New York: Harcourt, 2004. Moats chronicles the battle over gay marriage in Vermont, which culminated in 2000 with the first state law allowing gay civil unions. Moats, who won a Pulitzer Prize for his editorials supporting the law, brings a balanced perspective and an urgency to the judicial and legislative drama. His goal is to answer the following question, "How did such a thing happen in Vermont?" The resulting book is as much a history of liberalism in that state as it is a replay of the matrimonial conflict. Included are transcripts of Vermont citizens' testimony before the legislature in support of the law.

Murray, Stephen O. *Latin American Male Homosexualities*. Albuquerque: University of New Mexico Press, 1995. This book explores the multiple viewpoints of gay men of Latino descent.

Murray, Stephen O., and Will Roscoe, eds. *Boy-Wives and Female Husbands: Studies of African Homosexualities*. New York: St. Martin's Press, 1998. Among the many myths created about Africa, the myth that homosexuality is absent or incidental is one of the oldest and most enduring. The editors challenge this misperception in the essays collected here, which date from the colonial period to the present and cover the major regions of black Africa. Evidence of same-sex marriages, cross-dressing, role reversal, and premarital peer homosexuality is presented within a context of many societies' politically motivated denial of the reality of same-sex desire.

Owens, Robert E. *Queer Kids: The Challenges and Promise for Lesbian, Gay, and Bisexual Youth*. Binghamton, N.Y.: Haworth Press, 1998. In this book Owens advocates for the concerns of gay teens. Observing what he considers to be the benign neglect of society at large in providing support and vital information for queer kids, Owens focuses on counselors, parents, and adolescents; discusses stereotypes and prejudices; and seeks to provide viable solutions to the challenges facing young people coming of age in a heterosexual-dominant culture. His book serves as an excellent reference guide to gay community resources across the United States and includes interviews with teen activists from across the country.

Phelan, Shane. *Sexual Strangers: Gays, Lesbians, and Dilemmas of Citizenship.* Philadelphia: Temple University Press, 2001. In this book, Phelan introduces the idea of the United States as a "heterosexual regime." She questions whether LGBT people can be seen as citizens in a cultural context that limits their political and social visibility, relegating them to the ambiguous category of "strangers" to full participation and acceptance. She urges the reader to embrace what she terms *strangeness* as a means of achieving inclusive citizenship for everyone.

Rauch, Jonathan. *Gay Marriage: Why It Is Good for Gays, Good for Straights, and Good for America.* New York: Times Books, 2004. Rauch offers a thoughtful, reasoned argument for the eventual integration of same-sex marriage into national life. He favors a gradual, state-by-state approach to advancing the cause of gay marriage throughout the United States, stressing that gay activists must give straight America time to adjust to the new reality. He argues that civil unions offer a "marriage-lite" version of wedded commitment that can only weaken the institution for both gays and straights, and that only full matrimonial rights and responsibilities can rescue gays and lesbians from a lifetime of perpetual adolescence.

Robson, Ruthann. *Sappho Goes to Law School: Fragments in Lesbian Legal Theory.* New York: Columbia University Press, 1998. Robson applies poststructural analysis, queer theory, and a feminism rooted in everyday concerns to a wide range of legal problems and possibilities facing the lesbian community. Topics explored include lesbians and criminal justice, same-sex marriage, and child custody cases. Beyond politics, Robson theorizes a radical overturn of Socratic pedagogy, the basis of much of Western thought processes, to be replaced by a system of learning based on Sapphic lyric models.

Roscoe, Will. *Changing Ones: Third and Fourth Genders in Native North America.* New York: St. Martin's Press, 2000. More than 150 American Indian tribes across America have members who engage in some form of gender identification beyond "male" and "female," known as *berdaches.* Roscoe's study reveals how integral these third and fourth genders, as well as same-sex marriage, have been to the tribes' societies, in contrast to the intolerance demonstrated by western Europe's Judeo-Christian culture. In indigenous North America, *berdaches* served as artists, medicine people, religious experts, and tribal leaders. Combining the fields of anthropology, sociology, queer theory, gay and lesbian studies, and gender studies, this book offers an alternative view of homosexuality than that of traditional psychoanalytic theory.

Rotello, Gabriel. *Sexual Ecology: AIDS and the Destiny of Gay Men.* New York: Dutton, 1997. Rotello's chronicle follows the growth of promiscuity among homosexual men through its promotion by bathhouse owners and the gay media. He views this cultural phenomenon as the biological precondition that allowed the AIDS virus to explode in the gay male population. He warns against a return to past sexual mistakes, as a generation comes of age who did not witness firsthand the devastation of AIDS. Rotello's book was highly controversial when first published and remains an interesting attempt to link scientific and sociological methodologies.

Roughgarden, Joan. *Evolution's Rainbow: Diversity, Gender, and Sexuality in Nature and People.* Berkeley: University of California Press, 2004. In this innovative celebration of diversity and individuality in animals and humans, evolutionary biologist (and transgender person) Joan Roughgarden challenges accepted wisdom about gender identity and sexual orientation. She presents examples of nonbinary gender and sexual behavior among hundreds of species of fish, birds, reptiles, and mammals, including primates, and posits that contemporary Darwinian sexual selection theory betrays a cultural bias against homosexuality. She also mounts a critique of the suppression of this information in traditional writing about biology and calls for educational improvement in the fields of biology, psychology, and medicine.

Russo, Vito. *The Celluloid Closet: Homosexuality in the Movies.* New York: Harper & Row, 1987. In this groundbreaking book, Russo deconstructs 70 years of Hollywood cinematic practice and representation. He unearths hitherto buried images of homosexuality and gender variance in Hollywood films from the 1920s to the present, thus tracing a history of how gay men and lesbians have been erased or demonized in movies and, indeed, in all of American culture.

Schulman, Sarah. *Stagestruck: Theater, AIDS, and the Marketing of Gay America.* Durham, N.C.: Duke University Press, 1998. Using her critical reaction to the Broadway hit *Rent,* which features gay and lesbian characters in a story about struggling artists in New York's East Village as a starting point, Schulman discusses how gay themes and characters are distorted when "alternative lifestyles" are offered up for consumption by American pop culture. Schulman's contention that the musical's creator Jonathan Larson stole plot elements from her novel dealing with a similar theme only adds fuel to her argument that the realities of LGBT life get simplified in these new contexts. She widens her critique to include discussions of such cultural products as the movie *Philadelphia* and the magazine for people living with HIV/AIDS, *Poz.*

Schulman, Sarah, and Urvashi Vaid. *My American History: Lesbian and Gay Life During the Reagan/Bush Years.* New York: Routledge, Chapman & Hall, 1994. A compilation of editorials, news articles, speeches, and book excerpts published in gay and feminist publications that chronicles the growth of the gay and lesbian coalition, ACT UP, and the Lesbian Avengers between 1981 and 1993. Included are examinations of early AIDS activism; battles against the Moral Majority and antigay violence; the dispute over gay and lesbian books in the New York City public schools; the growth of federal AIDS initiatives and funding; and the rise of basketball star Earvin "Magic" Johnson as the ideal AIDS poster boy. To some of the pieces Schulman appends brief commentaries that update the development of the issues discussed and that place them in greater perspective.

Sears, Alan, and Craig Osten. *The Homosexual Agenda: Exposing the Principal Threat to Religious Freedom Today.* Nashville: Broadman & Holman Press, 2003. The authors, members of the Alliance Defense Fund, offer an exposé of what they view as the real goals of the gay rights movement and its rising legal activism: The homosexual agenda has as its primary aim to "trump" the rights of all other groups, especially those of people of faith. In Sears and Osten's opinion, gay rights activists are pleading for tolerance, while at the same time attempting to silence anyone who disagrees with their position.

Shilts, Randy. *And the Band Played On: Politics, People, and the AIDS Epidemic.* New York: St. Martin's Press, 1987. In the first major book on AIDS, *San Francisco Chronicle* reporter Randy Shilts examines the making of an epidemic. His work is critical of the medical and scientific communities' initial response and particularly harsh on the Reagan Administration, but he also turns a similarly critical eye on the gay community. He wonders why gay men were so reluctant to mobilize as so many around them were dying. This book is indispensable for any discussion of the early days of the AIDS crisis.

———. *Conduct Unbecoming.* New York: St. Martin's Press, 1993. Shilts has written an accessible history of U.S. military policies regarding gays and lesbians in the armed forces. He focused particularly on the "don't ask, don't tell" controversy in the early days of the administration of President Clinton and the often contradictory positions held both by the military and its spokespeople.

———. *The Mayor of Castro Street: The Life and Times of Harvey Milk.* New York: St. Martin's Press, 1982. This is considered a classic of gay biography, written by one of America's best-known gay journalists. Milk was the first openly gay man in history to be elected to the city government of a major American city. He was subsequently assassinated, along with the city's pro-gay mayor, George Moscone, by a disgruntled fellow politician. Shilts contextualizes Milk's life within the immense social and political changes that were occurring in the United States in the 1970s.

Signorile, Michelangelo. *Queer in America: Sex, the Media, and the Closets of Power.* New York: Random House, 1993. In this memoir, the provocateur of "outing" discusses his history of publicly exposing the homosexuality of celebrities and government officials. Among the people that Signorile revealed as gay in his weekly magazine column were billionaire publisher Malcolm Forbes and assistant secretary of defense Pete Williams. Signorile defends outing as a powerful tool that eliminates the refuge of the closet for hypocritical enemies of gay rights, an argument that raises serious legal, ethical, and psychological issues.

Simpson, Ruth. *From the Closet to the Courts: The Lesbian Transition.* New York: Richard Seaver/Viking Press, 1976. A very personal view of the early years of the gay rights movement by a lesbian whose involvement in the movement began in 1969.

Smith, Barbara, ed. *Home Girls: A Black Feminist Anthology.* New York: Kitchen Table: Women of Color Press, 1983. Smith has collected writings from the country's leading African-American feminists, including many in the lesbian-feminist movement. Smith released an updated paperback edition of the book in October 1999.

Smith, Charles Michael. *Fighting Words: Personal Essays by Black Gay Men*. New York: Avon Books, 1999. Collecting almost 30 essays into one collection, Smith presents the range of issues African-American gay men face in the United States. Battling racism in the gay community and homophobia in the black community, these men explore with honesty the demands of often conflicting identities.

Sullivan, Andrew. *Virtually Normal: An Argument About Homosexuality*. New York: Knopf, 1995. From the standpoint of many activists in the gay rights movement, Sullivan has a decidedly conservative take on the issues facing the gay community. A practicing Catholic and onetime editor of the centrist magazine *New Republic*, Sullivan eschews radical "identity politics" and believes that winning marital rights is the key to gay people's dream of full participation in the political and cultural life of this country. This book is considered essential reading by gay rights advocates for any discussion of the same-sex marriage controversy that has dominated gay discourse in the 1990s.

Timmons, Stuart. *The Trouble with Harry Hay: Founder of the Gay Movement*. Boston: Alyson Publications, 1990. This biography of one of the most important figures of the early gay rights movement in the United States follows Hay's career from the 1950s to the 1980s.

Tobin, Kay, and Randy Wicker. *The Gay Crusaders*. New York: Paperback Library, 1972. The authors present biographical sketches of 15 men and women active in the early stages of the gay and lesbian rights movement.

Vaid, Urvashi. *Virtual Equality: The Mainstreaming of Gay and Lesbian Liberation*. New York: Anchor/Doubleday, 1995. The title of Vaid's book refers to her belief that the gay community has access to power but no real civil rights protection and has visibility while remaining vulnerable to discrimination and violence. Vaid challenges the gay community to face the forces that divide it and begin the work necessary to achieve genuine equality with the rest of America.

Warner, Michael. *The Trouble with Normal: Sex, Politics and the Ethics of Queer Life*. New York: Free Press, 1999. Warner adds a provocative view to the debate on gay marriage, suggesting that rather than trying to assimilate into the world of "normality," gay men and lesbians make common cause with other groups that are excluded from the definition of normality. He is particularly concerned about the tendency for gay men and lesbians to see marriage as a means to become "normal"; in Warner's view, marriage is inappropriate to the sexual relationships of many people, both gay and straight and is unethical in its arbitrary denial of rights to unmarried people.

White, Edmund. *States of Desire: Travels in Gay America*. New York: Simon & Schuster, 1991. In this collection of essays, noted gay novelist White interviews gay men living in towns, cities, and rural communities across the United States.

ARTICLES

ADOPTION

Basinger, Brian. "Court Upholds Ban on Gay Adoption: Florida's Law Gets OK from Appeals Court." *Florida Times-Union*, January 29, 2004, p. B1. A federal appeals court upholds a Florida law banning gays and lesbians from adopting children, saying that same-sex unions are an untested family structure.

———. "Florida Awaits Pivotal Gay Adoption Decision; Appeals Court Could Uphold or Strike Down State Ban on All Adoptions by Gays and Lesbians." *Florida Times-Union*, December 7, 2003, p. A8. Florida is the only state in the nation with an outright ban on gay and lesbian adoption, ruling out all homosexuals, regardless of whether they are single or in a relationship. Note: The 11th Circuit Court of Appeals ruled against the gay male couples in the suit.

Carey, Benedict. "Experts Dispute Bush on Gay-Adoption Issue." *New York Times*, January 29, 2005, p. A16. Some sociologists have disputed a remark made by President George W. Bush that a heterosexual family is ideal for raising children, saying there is no scientific evidence that children raised by gay couples do any worse than their peers raised in more traditional households.

Chiang, Harriet. "Adoption Procedure Used by Gays Upheld: State High Court Backs 2nd-Parent Method." *San Francisco Chronicle*, August 5, 2003, p. A1. In a 6-1 decision hailed as a major victory for gay rights, the California Supreme Court said state law allows second-parent adoptions, where a birth parent keeps a child while also agreeing to have it adopted by a second parent.

Crary, David. "60% of Adoption Agencies Take Gays' Applications." *Houston Chronicle*, October 29, 2003, p. 11. The majority of the nation's adoption agencies now accept applications from gays and lesbians, though resistance remains strong among many of those affiliated with a church.

Crowe, Robert. "'2nd-Parent' Option Provides Equal Rights: Adoption Law Applies to Unmarried Couples." *Houston Chronicle*, June 25, 2004, p. 34. Same-sex couples in Texas cannot adopt children together. However, the Texas Family Code does not prevent two unmarried people, regardless of sexual orientation, from adopting the same child. This practice of "second-parent" adoption is a way for many gay and lesbian couples to assure that both partners have full parental rights.

Fagan, Amy. "Oklahoma Abides by Out-of-State Adoptions by Gays." *Washington Times*, April 14, 2004, p. A7. Oklahoma's attorney general has decided that when a child is born in that state and adopted in another state by a same-sex couple, Oklahoma must recognize the adoption and list both partners as parents on the birth certificate.

———. "Same-Sex Adoption Negated in State: Oklahoma Law Reverses Ruling." *Washington Times*, May 7, 2004, p. A5. Oklahoma's governor has signed legislation overturning a ruling by the state's attorney general that Oklahoma must recognize both partners' names on a child's adoptive birth certificate when he or she is adopted by a same-sex couple.

Ford, Dave. "Faces of Adoption in the Bay Area: Forming and Finding Families." *San Francisco Chronicle*, February 17, 2002, p. E5. Profiles of several San Francisco–area same-sex couples and the unique issues they face as a gay or lesbian parenting unit.

Greenhouse, Linda. "Justices Refuse to Consider Law Banning Gay Adoption." *New York Times*, January 11, 2005, p. A14. The U.S. Supreme Court has refused to hear a challenge to a Florida law that prohibits gay men and lesbians from adopting children.

Hammer, David. "Arkansas to Appeal Gay Parent Ruling: A Judge Decided the State Couldn't Regulate 'Public Morality' with Its Ban on Fostering." *Houston Chronicle*, December 31, 2004, p. 9. Judge Timothy Fox has struck down an Arkansas state ban on placing foster children in any household with a gay member, ruling that the state agency enforcing the rule had overstepped its authority by trying to regulate "public morality."

Rankin, Bill. "Appeals Court Upholds Ban on Gay Adoptions: Judges' 6-6 Decision Keeps Controversial Florida Law in Place." *Atlanta Journal-Constitution*, July 22, 2004, p. A1. The federal appeals court in Atlanta has let stand a decision upholding Florida's law banning adoption of children by gays and lesbians. But Judge Stanley Birch, who wrote that initial ruling, issued an accompanying statement saying that he personally considered Florida's law to be misguided.

Villafranca, Armando. "Talton Won't Meet Gay Lobby: Activists Decry Lawmaker's Proposed Foster Care Limits." *Houston Chronicle*, April 10, 2003, p. 29. Representative Robert Talton has introduced a bill in the Texas legislature that would block gays and lesbians from becoming foster parents in that state. When activists came to his office to lobby him on the issue, he ordered state troopers to block their access.

White, Gayle, and Greta Lorge. "Vatican Condemns Same-Sex Unions: Statement Says Kids Suffer If Adopted by Gay Couples." *Atlanta Journal-Constitution*, August 1, 2003, p. B1. The Vatican releases a document asserting that allowing children to be adopted by gays and lesbians "would actually mean doing violence to these children."

AIDS Issues

Bone, James. "Cirque du Soleil in Row over HIV Sacking." *Times of London*, November 22, 2003, p. 22. The Montreal-based circus faces demonstrations after it fired HIV-positive acrobat Matthew Cusick, citing safety concerns for its other performers.

Boseley, Sarah. "Anger at US Ban on AIDS Scientists: Bangkok Conference Forced to Cancel Meetings and Retract Papers after Authors Stopped from Attending." *Guardian of London*, July 12, 2004, p. 2. The U.S. Department of Health and Human Services, headed by Secretary Tommy Thompson, has been accused of actively preventing some American researchers from participating in the most recent international AIDS conference. Secretary Thompson was openly booed at the last conference in Madrid in 2002, and his agency has drawn international criticism for its handling of the health crisis.

Davidow, Julie. "HIV Tests Taken Out of the Shadows: Rapid Response Kits Allow Agencies to Screen More At-Risk Gay Men." *Seattle Post-Intelligencer*, March 31, 2004, Issue 755, p. A1. Across the nation there are signs that HIV virus is once again on the rise among men who have sex with men. In response, AIDS activists are taking a new, rapid-response blood test to the places where gay men congregate.

———. "Sims Praises AIDS/HIV Manifesto but Prevention Plan Criticized for Limited Community Comment." *Seattle Post-Intelligencer*, October 16, 2003, p. B3. A Seattle community health task force issues a declaration calling HIV infection unacceptable and avoidable and emphasizing personal choice and responsibility as the path to halting rising AIDS transmission rates.

De Campos, Raquel Pontes. "AIDS: The Great Divide: Dispute over Generic Drugs Pits the World's Haves Against Have-Nots." *Seattle Times*, June 13, 2001, p. A3. Developing nations are in search of affordable AIDS medications, while some industrialized countries, although seeking to maintain a humanitarian face on the AIDS issue, want to protect the patent rights of their pharmaceutical companies.

Egelko, Bob. "AIDS Activists Charged with Stalking: Two Taken into Custody, Held on $500,000 Bail after Hearing." *San Francisco Chronicle*, November 29, 2001, p. A23. David Pasquarelli and Michael Petrelis have been arrested and charged with stalking and making terrorist threats against city health officials and staff members of the *San Francisco Chronicle*. The men were angered by reports in the paper about the rise in unsafe sex practices among Bay Area gay men.

Epstein, Edward. "House Set to OK AIDS Funding: Abortion Gag Rule Has Barred Some Programs Overseas." *San Francisco Chronicle*, March 17, 2003, p. A1. An agreement between the White House and Congress will allow money earmarked for AIDS prevention to go to international health agencies and clinics that provide family planning and abortion services. This despite a long-standing executive order barring such groups from receiving funding.

———. "Retired Drug Company Executive Named Global AIDS Czar." *San Francisco Chronicle*, July 3, 2003, p. A4. AIDS activists are highly critical of President Bush's nominee for the position of global AIDS coordinator. Randall Tobias is former chief executive officer of Eli Lilly & Company and a major Republican campaign contributor.

Goldberg, Robert. "Disease Control: AIDS Activists Should Learn from SARS." *Washington Times*, May 15, 2003, p. A19. Goldberg calls for AIDS to stop being viewed as a political or civil rights issue and instead to be treated only as a public health crisis that requires widespread mandatory screening.

Heredia, Christopher. "Dance of Death: Crystal Meth Fuels HIV." *San Francisco Chronicle*, May 4, 2003, p. A1. Gay men in California who use the illegal drug, speed, are twice as likely to be HIV-positive than those who don't use it. San Francisco AIDS activists and health professionals are up against a party culture that is helping spread the disease.

———. "Proposal for Reporting HIV Raises Confidentiality Worries: Social Security Digits Included in State's Plan." *San Francisco Chronicle*, May 16, 2001, p. A7. Faced with rising rates of infection among gay men in California, the state's health department wants to begin reporting HIV infections using the last four digits of patients' Social Security numbers. Activists counter this will discourage people from getting tested.

Jacobs, Andrew. "Crystal Meth Use by Gay Men Threatens to Reignite an Epidemic." *New York Times*, January 12, 2004, p. B1. Two-thirds of gay men testing positive for HIV at New York's health clinic for the LGBT community report that they were under the influence of crystal methamphetamine when they engaged in unsafe sex.

———. "Gays Debate Radical Steps to Curb Unsafe Sex." *New York Times*, February 15, 2005, p. A1. Gay activists and AIDS prevention workers are frustrated by those who continue to engage in unsafe sex, especially in light of a newly discovered virulent variant of AIDS, but differ on how best to promote public health without violating privacy rights.

Kalfrin, Valerie. "Gay Activist Faces Prostitution, HIV Charges." *Tampa Tribune*, March 25, 2004, p. 2. Mauricio Rosas, a well-known Florida AIDS activist, has been arrested for being a sex worker and for the criminal transmission of HIV. Under Florida law, whether Rosas practiced safe sex in his paid encounters is irrelevant.

Livermore, Lisa. "Activists Turn to United States and Hope." *St. Louis Post-Dispatch*, June 1, 2003, p. B4. As President George W. Bush attends the Group of Eight meeting in France, AIDS activists hope he can persuade allies to contribute to the fight against the disease. He has signed a bill contributing $15 billion in the fight against HIV worldwide.

Mallaby, Sebastian. "AIDS and Anti-Americanism: Activists Are Too Quick to Dismiss the Bush Administration's Efforts to Battle the Disease." *Star-Ledger*, July 20, 2004. p. 15. Mallaby criticizes the international AIDS activist community for its hostility to the George W. Bush administration's efforts to combat global AIDS. He cites research that has found abstinence/monogamy–only programs to be effective measures for cutting HIV infection rates.

Marech, Rona. "Cirque Settles with Fired Gymnast." *San Francisco Chronicle*, April 23, 2004, p. B7. Cirque du Soleil has agreed to one of the largest public settlements for an HIV-discrimination complaint mediated by the Equal Employment Opportunity Commission after it dismissed an HIV-positive performer.

Margasak, Larry. "Racy Advertisements Anger AIDS Activists, Lawmakers: Some Say the Ads Are Money Misspent." *Wisconsin State Journal,* September 10, 2001, p. A3. Provocative ads designed to publicize San Francisco AIDS prevention programs have come under fire from both AIDS activists and conservative members of Congress. The ads' creators defend them, saying they are effective.

McNeil, Donald G., Jr. "Views Mixed on U.S. Shift on Drugs for AIDS." *New York Times,* May 18, 2004, p. A9. The George W. Bush administration has decided it is willing to buy anti-AIDS cocktails that combine three drugs in one pill from low-cost generic manufacturers, who are now the only companies making 3-in-1 pills. Activists hail this move but are critical of the FDA's approval process.

Milbank, Dana. "Secret Service Ousts 7 Anti-Bush Hecklers." *Seattle Times,* September 11, 2004, p. A7. Activists from the Philadelphia chapter of the AIDS activist organization ACT UP were arrested at a campaign stop for President George W. Bush in suburban Pennsylvania.

Myller, Rolf. "AIDS Groups' Funding Reviewed." *Seattle Times,* August 19, 2002, p. A2. The Department of Health and Human Services is reviewing federal funding of more than a dozen prominent AIDS organizations whose members joined in a demonstration against Secretary Tommy Thompson at an international AIDS conference in Barcelona, Spain.

Nesmith, Jeff. "U.S. Cuts 28 CDC Experts at Forum." *Atlanta Journal-Constitution,* June 25, 2004, p. A13. Democratic members of Congress have charged the George W. Bush administration with forcing 28 researchers from the Centers for Disease Control and Prevention to cancel presentations at the international HIV/AIDS conference to be held in Bangkok.

Ness, Carol. "Activists Fight Barriers to Organ Transplants for HIV-Positive Patients." *San Francisco Chronicle,* December 30, 2001, p. A20. AIDS patients are living longer on improved pharmaceutical regimens; however, the opportunistic infections associated with the disease, as well as the drugs used to treat it, can damage organs. Activists are fighting to get HIV-positive patients onto transplant waiting lists.

Nichols, John. "Acting Up on the Floor: AIDS Protesters Infiltrate Youth Convention." *Capital Times,* September 2, 2004, p.7A. AIDS activists infiltrated a gathering of Young Republicans on the floor of Madison Square Garden in New York City during that party's national convention. According to ACT UP, the demonstration was to demand that the George W. Bush administration support cancellation of the global debt owed by poor countries, many of which are dealing with major outbreaks of the AIDS epidemic.

Price, Joyce Howard. "Waste, Fraud Seen in AIDS Programs." *Washington Times,* February 15, 2002, p. A10. Citizens Against Government Waste, a conservative government watchdog group, has issued a report highly critical of federal AIDS programs, especially those of a sexual nature, and are calling for appropriations to be reconsidered.

Rabin, Roni. "Researchers Link Web to Unsafe Gay Sex: 40% Men with Syphilis Say They Found Partners Through Internet, Study Finds." *Houston Chronicle*, July 31, 2003, p. 8. Researchers are concerned that the dramatic increase in syphilis in large cities in recent years is a harbinger of a new spike in HIV/AIDS cases. Activists are faced with the challenge of getting a prevention message out to gay men who are increasingly meeting sexual partners while sitting home alone.

Rofes, Eric. "A New Day Has Dawned: Did Activism or AIDS Get Gays out of the Closet?" *San Francisco Chronicle*, May 31, 2001, Section 4, p. A27. Twenty years after the first cases of AIDS were diagnosed in gay men, Rofes challenges the conventional wisdom that holds that gays and lesbians would still have no civil rights protections if it weren't for the epidemic.

Russell, Sabin. "S.F. Ban on AIDS Drug Ads Proposed: Dubious Message in Bus Shelters." *San Francisco Chronicle*, March 15, 2001, p. A17. AIDS activists want San Francisco to consider banning pharmaceutical ads from city bus shelters which, in their view, present the distorted picture that HIV infection is easily manageable through drug therapy.

Simmons, Deborah. "Condom-Mania: HIV/AIDS Activists Are Part of the Problem." *Washington Times*, December 5, 2003, p. A23. Simmons is highly critical of a new Washington, D.C., initiative that makes condoms readily available throughout the city, even at government offices. In her opinion, the only effective way to stop the spread of AIDS is through abstinence.

Singer, Rena. "Drug Firms Yield to Cry of the Poor: Yesterday, 39 Drug Companies Withdrew a Lawsuit to Bar South Africa from Importing Cheap Anti-AIDS Drugs." *Christian Science Monitor*, April 20, 2001, p. 1. Calling it a "moral victory," activists celebrate the end of a lawsuit brought by the major pharmaceutical companies against the government of South Africa. The drug companies sought to stop that country from importing cheap, generic AIDS drugs from India.

Tucker, Cynthia. "Blacks Flee Gays, Can't Flee AIDS." *Atlanta Journal-Constitution*, March 14, 2004, p. D8. Tucker views homophobia within the black mainstream community as contributing to rising rates of HIV infection among gay African-American men, as well as in heterosexual black women.

Villarosa, Linda. "AIDS Fears Grow for Black Women." *New York Times*, April 5, 2004, p. A1. Heterosexual African-American women accounted for a disproportionate amount of new HIV infections from 1999 to 2002. Part of this is attributable to the "down low" lifestyle of some black men who have sex with other men but do not identify as gay or bisexual.

Williams, Lance. "AIDS Quilt Caught up in Tempest: Its Creator Sues Owners, Saying Tour Plan Got Him Fired." *San Francisco Chronicle*, January 21, 2004, p. A1. Cleve Jones, the gay rights activist who created the AIDS Memorial Quilt, and the Atlanta nonprofit foundation that owns it are locked in a bitter dispute over how best to use the public artwork in the fight against AIDS during an election year.

Yee, Daniel. "AIDS Cases Are Making a Grim Comeback: Last Week, New Figures Showed That AIDS Diagnoses Increased for the First Time in 10 Years." *Wisconsin State Journal*, August 11, 2003, p. A1. The Centers for Disease Control and Prevention has released statistics showing that the number of people newly infected with AIDS has increased for the first time since the early '90s.

BALLOT MEASURES

Bettman, Marianna Brown. "Legal World Is Taking Big Steps for Gay Rights." *Cincinnati Post*, September 4, 2003, p. A17. Editorial from a former Ohio appelate judge calling for the repeal of Article XII of the Cincinnati city charter, which forbids granting homosexuals special consideration under the law.

Burress, Phil. "Charter Bans Special Rights for Gays." *Cincinnati Post*, September 17, 2003, p. A17. Burress, the president of the Cincinnati organization Citizens for Community Values, argues against repealing Article XII of that city's charter, which states that homosexuals are not entitled to any special legal protections.

Coolidge, Alexander. "Conservative Groups Urge P&G Boycott." *Cincinnati Post*, September 17, 2004, p. B9. Conservative Christian groups are targeting Procter & Gamble and urging consumers to boycott its detergent and toothpaste brands because the Cincinnati-based company supports a ballot measure repealing Article 12, a Cincinnati charter amendment that bars the city from enacting gay rights legislation.

Lowy, Joan. "Local Gay Rights Issue May Help John Kerry." *Cincinnati Post*, July 29, 2004, p. A12. Cincinnati-area political activists are predicting that a gay rights measure on the November ballot in that city has the potential to draw more gay and lesbian and young voters to the polls, thereby tipping Ohio's electoral votes in favor of Democratic presidential nominee John Kerry.

Osborne, Kevin. "City Voters Approve Issue 3." *Cincinnati Post*, November 3, 2004, p. A1. Cincinnati voters have approved by a 54 to 46 percent margin a repeal of an 11-year-old charter amendment that prohibited city officials from passing any laws aimed at protecting gay and lesbian people from housing or employment discrimination.

———. "Not Many Blasé in Gay Issue Battle." *Cincinnati Post*, September 18, 2004, p. A1. Article 12, a Cincinnati law passed in 1993 that prevents gay men and lesbians from seeking protection against discrimination, has cost that city millions of dollars in lost revenues over the subsequent decade. A measure to rescind the law is on the November ballot, sparking heated debate among supporters and opponents.

Parvaz, D. "Gays, Lesbians Await Tacoma Vote: Fourth Attempt to Ban Discrimination Expected to Pass." *Seattle Post-Intelligencer*, April 23, 2002, p. B1. For the second time, the Tacoma, Washington, city council is expected to vote to add sexual orientation to its list of categories protected from discrimination. The first time it tried to do so in 1989, the law was overturned by ballot measure.

Sloat, Bill. "Cincinnati Rewrites Ballot Issue in Effort to Save Gay-Rights Vote." *Cleveland Plain Dealer,* August 31, 2004, p. B3. Cincinnati officials have rewritten a voter initiative aimed at nullifying a section of the charter that blocks the city council from passing any laws that could be construed as bestowing special status on gays and lesbians. Opponents of the measure argued that the ballot wording was biased in favor of gay rights.

CIVIC ORGANIZATIONS

Duin, Julia. "Boy Scouts Fight Back: San Diego Park Case Heads to Court in Latest Gay-Rights Battle." *Washington Times,* March 7, 2004, p. A1. The city of San Diego is being sued to force it to evict the Boy Scouts of America from land it leases in the publically accessible Balboa Park. Duin profiles this and other cases from around the country where the organization is being challenged because of its stated opposition to homosexuality.

Hubbell, John M. "Gays Reaffirmed as Big Brothers, Sisters: Conservatives Call for Boycott, but Mentor Group Unconcerned." *San Francisco Chronicle,* August 16, 2002, p. A2. Unlike other charitable youth groups that rebuff gay and lesbian adults, Big Brothers Big Sisters of America has reaffirmed its commitment to including them as volunteers. Because of this, some Christian activists are calling for a boycott.

Richardson, Lynda. "Marching Out of Step, by Some Irish and Gay Norms." *Houston Chronicle,* March 7, 2003, p. B2. A profile of Brendan Fay, the Irishborn activist who has been battling for 12 years to open the New York City St. Patrick's Day parade to gays and lesbians.

COURT DECISIONS

Esther, John. "Death to Lesbians: How Sexual Orientation Affects the Sentencing of Women." *Lesbian News,* January 2004, Vol. 29:6, p. 38. Some activists claim that 80 percent of the women on death row are lesbians. Sexual orientation has often had a detrimental effect when it comes to the sentencing of members of the LGBT community as it has with any other marginalized group.

Landau, Joseph. "Misjudged." *New Republic,* February 16, 2004, Vol. 230:5, p. 16. Landau argues that, contrary to conservative fears, recent court cases related to the Supreme Court's *Lawrence v. Texas* decision demonstrate that the decision did not pave the way for substantial advances in gay rights.

Soraghan, Mike. "Activist Judges Difficult to Define." *Denver Post,* July 11, 2004, p. A1. As the debate on a gay marriage ban heats up, legal experts say the term *activist judge* is imprecise at best and, at worst, used by people who simply disagree with a given ruling. However the term is used, some conservatives are trying to impeach justices who rule favorably in gay rights cases.

Wallheimer, Brian. "2 Lawmakers Target Gay Marriage Proposal for Constitutional Ban: Would Require Statewide Vote." *St. Louis Post-Dispatch*, January 21, 2004, p. B1. In Illinois, two representatives, one Democrat and one Republican, introduce legislation that would amend the state's constitution to outlaw same-sex marriage.

CULTURE/MEDIA

Aaronovitch, David. "The Pilgrims Wouldn't Mind Gay Marriage." *Guardian of London*, March 2, 2004, p. 9. As Provincetown, site of both one of America's most famous gay communities and the original landing spot of the Pilgrims, gears up for a summer of same-sex weddings, a commentator from England points out that America's Puritan founders might not have looked that askance at recent developments in Massachusetts.

Addison, Kasi. "Homophobic Reggae Lyrics Spark Anger: Newark Festival Organizers Say Performers Have Been Asked Not to Sing Offensive Songs." *Newark Star-Ledger*, September 18, 2004, p. 22. The Gay and Lesbian Alliance Against Defamation has criticized the organizers of a reggae festival in New Jersey for including three artists on the program whose songs call for the hanging, shooting, and stabbing of homosexuals.

Bellafonte, Ginia. "A Gay Boomtown Is More Mainstream and Less the Cliché." *New York Times*, May 15, 2004, p. A1. An influx of gay men and lesbians has revitalized the city of Wilton Manors, Florida. The article includes a description of conditions in the city before gays and lesbians started to move there in 1997.

Binnie, Jon, and Beverley Skeggs. "Cosmopolitan Knowledge and the Production and Consumption of Sexualized Space: Manchester's Gay Village." *Sociological Review*, February 2004, Vol. 52:1, pp. 39–62. According to the authors, the logic of late capitalism offers opportunities for the incorporation of previously marginalized groups, while simultaneously dividing them at the same time. This cultural process is quantified through an examination of Manchester, England's gay neighborhood.

Byrd, A. Dean. "The Malleability of Homosexuality: A Debate Long Overdue." *Archives of Sexual Behavior*, October 2003, Vol. 32:5, pp. 423–426. Byrd comments on physician Robert L. Spitzer's research about the effectiveness of reparative therapy in sexual orientation. Dr. Spitzer's research seems to point in the direction that gay men and lesbians can become heterosexual.

Connor, Steve. "Fury at Study That Finds Homosexuals Can Be Cured." *Independent of London*, October 6, 2003, p.4. A study conducted by Robert Spitzer, a professor of psychiatry at Columbia University, that claims it may be possible to change a person's sexual orientation, has set off a firestorm of controversy.

Constable, Burt. "Let's Hope Time Cures My Regrettable Stupidity and Cruelty." *Arlington Heights Daily Herald*, July 8, 2003, p. 9. A straight columnist openly examines the roots of his own discomfort with the notion of gay male sexual relations.

Cooperman, Alan. "CBS, NBC Reject Religious Ads as 'Too Controversial': But the Church Says Networks Are Censoring Views." *Houston Chronicle*, December 2, 2004, p. 4. The CBS and NBC television networks have rejected an advertisement for the United Church of Christ that shows two bouncers turning away a gay couple outside a church. A memo from CBS rejecting the ad linked it to the current gay marriage debate and said that the network won't accept ads about current controversial issues.

Gebeloff, Robert, and Mary Jo Patterson. "Same-Sex Couples Mainstream into Suburbs, with Kids." *Newark Star-Ledger*, November 16, 2003, p. 1. An analysis of Census 2000 data shows that, from a demographic perspective, same-sex and mixed-sex couples are more similar than not, as gay and lesbian couples make the move out of their traditional urban neighborhoods into the suburbs.

Gittler, Juliana. "Survey Looks at Gay, Lesbian Consumers: Online Census Was Done to Create a Profile to Guide Advertisers." *Syracuse Post-Standard*, October 16, 2001, p. D9. In the largest survey of its kind, the 2001 Gay-Lesbian Consumer Online Census conducted by Syracuse University has helped to identify the purchasing habits of gays and lesbians nationwide.

Goodman, Tim. "Gays Run Gantlet of Humiliation: With a Few Exceptions." *San Francisco Chronicle*, August 1, 2003, p. D1. Goodman examines the phenomenon of gays and lesbians on reality television. After declining from its peak of TV representation in the late 90s, shows like *Queer Eye for the Straight Guy* and *Boy Meets Boy* represent a comeback for the community, but at what price?

Haslanger, Phil. "Spongebob Gets Flak for Siding with Respect, Tolerance, Diversity." *Madison Capital Times*, February 3, 2005, p. 9A. Haslanger examines comments made by James Dobson, founder of the anti–gay rights organization Focus on the Family, critical of a video distributed by the We Are Family Foundation that uses cartoon characters to promote cultural diversity to elementary-school children.

Heldenfels, R. D. "Television Marches Straight Ahead with More Gay Characters." *Akron Beacon Journal*, February 27, 2004, p. C3. Heldenfels suggests that the most powerful counterweight to President George W. Bush's proposed Constitutional amendment outlawing same-sex marriage may be the proliferation of gay and lesbian characters on television.

Heredia, Christopher. "Gays Searching for Ways to Help after Terror Attacks." *San Francisco Chronicle*, November 5, 2001, p. A8. Prohibitions against military service, donating blood, and receiving survivor benefits have left many gays and lesbians feeling alienated from the rest of the country in the post-9/11 era.

Hill, Craig A., and Jeannie D. DiClement. "Methodological Limitations Do Not Justify the Claim That Same-Sex Attraction Changed Through 'Reparative

Therapy.'" *Archives of Sexual Behavior,* October 2003, Vol. 32:5, pp. 440–443. Dissenting comments on physician Robert L. Spitzer's research about the effectiveness of reparative therapy in sexual orientation. Hill and DiClement see a role for religion in promoting the internalization of homophobia.

Jubera, Drew, David Wahlberg, and Kristina Torres. "Black Gays Find Welcome in City: But Many Feel Estranged from African-American Mainstream." *Atlanta Journal-Constitution,* February 22, 2004, p. A1. Atlanta has become a mecca for black gay men and lesbians from across the nation. However, many are finding little welcome among the city's black establishment churches and social institutions.

Kee, Lorraine. "'The L Word': Local Lesbians Are Looking In." *St. Louis Post-Dispatch,* February 22, 2004, p. E1. Lesbians in St. Louis react to the premiere of Showtime cable network: *The L Word,* the first show on television to focus exclusively on the lives of gay women.

Kotulak, Ronald. "Gay, Straight Brain Activity Is Different, Research Finds: But Experts Say Issue Needs Further Study." *Houston Chronicle,* November 30, 2003, p. 8. Researchers at the University of Chicago have confirmed that the hypothalamus, the sex center in the brain, functions differently in gay men than in heterosexual men.

Kristof, Nicholas D. "Gay at Birth?" *New York Times,* October 25, 2003, p. A19. Citing recent research in the field of neuroscience that points to sexual orientation as being at least in part genetically determined, Kristof points out that a principle of American society is that it does not discriminate against people on the basis of circumstances that they cannot choose.

Laurence, Charles. "Going Straight: New Research Published Last Week Has Found That Homosexuals and Lesbians Who Undergo Psychiatric Therapy Can Change Their Sexuality." *Sunday Telegraph,* October 12, 2003, p. 20. Dr. Robert Spitzer, professor of psychiatry at Columbia University, has published findings in the journal *Archives of Sexual Behaviour* concluding that gays and lesbians can change their sexual orientation. Laurence interviews some of the study's subjects.

Mathis, Derrick. "Gay Hip-Hop Comes Out." *Advocate,* May 13, 2003, Issue 889, pp. 44–49. Caushun, a 25-year-old ex-hairdresser and out gay man from Brooklyn, New York, has landed a major record deal on Baby Phat Records. Is a musical genre often associated with homophobic lyrics ready for this development?

Ostrow, Joanne. "Stereotype Tripping up Strides in Gay Shows." *Denver Post,* June 23, 2003, p. F1. In the six years since Ellen DeGeneres made broadcast history as the first openly homosexual star of a sitcom, gay and lesbian characters are everywhere on TV. Ostrow wonders, though, if the community has traded self-parody for exposure.

Paul, Noel C., and Kendra Nordin. "Gay Marriage Vote: Who Won and Lost; The Complexity of the Massachusetts Decision Symbolizes a Nation Locked in Marriage Ambivalence." *Christian Science Monitor,* March 31, 2004, p. 3. The authors view the vote by the Massachusetts legislature to pass a constitutional amendment that outlaws gay marriage while ensuring same-sex civil unions as indicative of the ambivalence felt by the entire nation for gay rights.

Paulson, Amanda. "Debate on Gay Unions Splits along Generations." *Christian Science Monitor,* July 7, 2003, p. 1. In a cultural climate where homosexuality has never been a taboo subject for current teens, recent polls suggest that young adults and older people view gay rights in starkly different terms.

Rice, Christopher. "A Kick in the Teeth." *Advocate,* April 13, 2004, Issue 912, p. 72. Rice opines that President George W. Bush's endorsement of a Constitutional amendment banning gay marriage has galvanized his previously apathetic, consumerist generation of gay men.

Rich, Frank. "A Gay Marriage War in the Making." *International Herald Tribune,* February 28, 2004, p. 8. Rich views the same-sex marriages taken place in San Francisco as part of an ongoing culture war whose outcome is historically inevitable.

Salamon, Julie. "Culture Wars Pull Buster into the Fray." *New York Times,* January 27, 2005, p. E1. PBS has pulled an episode of its popular children's series *Postcards from Buster* after Education Secretary Margaret Spelling denounced the show for including a segment on lesbian mothers.

Solis, Dianne. "More Firms Aiming Their Ads at Gays: Targeted Marketing Mines Lucrative Niche, Breaks Cultural Ground." *Seattle Times,* August 17, 2003, p. E8. More high-profile companies are pitching products and services directly to gay and lesbian consumers in the gay and mainstream media alike through advertising crafted specifically for the LGBT community.

Spitzer, Robert L. "Can Some Gay Men and Lesbians Change Their Sexual Orientation? 200 Participants Reporting a Change from Homosexual to Heterosexual Orientation." *Archives of Sexual Behavior,* October 2003, Vol. 32:5, pp. 403–418. This study tested the hypothesis that some individuals whose sexual orientation is predominantly homosexual can, with some form of reparative therapy, become predominantly heterosexual. The majority of participants gave reports of change in the past year.

Theis, Sandy. "Is Being Gay Something That Can Be Overcome?" *Cleveland Plain Dealer,* October 25, 2004, p. A1. While scientists still don't really know what causes someone to be homosexual, with the search for answers leading to the intersection of biology, psychology, and politics, a growing number of ex-gays counsel others to believe that homosexuality is a malady that can be cured through "reparative therapy."

CUSTODY OF CHILDREN

Finz, Stacy. "Estranged Lesbians Battle for Custody of Twins: Courts Must Decide If Egg Donor Should Have Parental Rights." *San Francisco Chronicle,* December 5, 2003, p. A1. A lesbian couple in California are embroiled in a custody fight over their fraternal twins. Both women are considered the children's biological mother since one donated her eggs to the other to carry to term. However, the courts so far have only recognized the birth mother.

Krueger, Curtis. "Gay Dads Get Daughters Plus Praise from Judge." *St. Petersburg Times*, September 9, 2004 p. 1A. Two young girls from Florida's foster-care system should be allowed to live permanently with the two gay men they call "Dad and Daddy," Circuit Judge Irene Sullivan has ruled. Because the two men had so dramatically transformed the troubled girls' lives, Sullivan also recommended that the state use them to train other foster parents.

Richardson, Valerie. "Court Raps Mom on Homophobic Leaflets; Case Affects Religious, Gay Rights." *Washington Times*, November 9, 2003, p. A4. Richardson reports on the legal case of Dr. Cheryl Clark, a born-again Christian embroiled in a child custody dispute with her lesbian ex-partner, Elsey McLeod. McLeod wants the court to prevent Dr. Clark from exposing their daughter to anything that can be construed as homophobic.

Sack, Kevin. "Judge's Ouster Sought after Antigay Remarks." *New York Times*, February 20, 2002, p. A15. Gay rights organizations are calling for the resignation of Chief Justice Roy Moore of the Alabama Supreme Court, who wrote in a child custody opinion that homosexuality was an "inherent evil against which children must be protected."

DOMESTIC PARTNERSHIPS

Baxter, Sarah. "Spread of Gay Schools Sparks Segregation Row." *Times of London*, August 3, 2003, p. 25. Report on the controversy surrounding New York City's plans to fully integrate the previously privately run and funded Harvey Milk High School for LGBT youths into the public school system.

Bell, Elizabeth, Ray Delgado, and Justino Aguila. "Many Say Verdict Was Just; S.F. Gay Community Looks Ahead to Partner's Wrongful-Death Suit." *San Francisco Chronicle*, March 22, 2002, p. A20. Marjorie Knoller and Robert Noel are found guilty in the mauling death of Diane Whipple, a lesbian. Whipple's surviving partner is attempting to sue the two for wrongful death; they claim she has no legal standing to do so since she was not Whipple's "spouse."

Bergman, Justin. "Gays Say Virginia Law Goes Too Far." *Cincinnati Post*, May 26, 2004, p. A5. An amendment to Virginia's 1997 Affirmation of Marriage Act, which prohibits gay marriages, extends that ban to civil unions and partnership contracts. Gay activists fear the law could be used to invalidate any contract between same-sex life partners.

Cain, Brad. "Oregon Republican to Push for Law Allowing Civil Unions." *Seattle Times*, November 22, 2004, p. B3. After voters in Oregon approve a constitutional amendment specifying that marriage could only be between one man and one woman, Republican state senator Ben Westlund is drafting legislation that would provide gay and lesbian couples some of the same rights bestowed upon married couples. Several members of his political party, however, are displeased with his actions.

Cobb, Victoria. "Virginians Still Believe in Traditional Marriage." *Virginian Pilot-Ledger Star,* May 24, 2004, p. B9. Cobb, director of legislative affairs for the Family Foundation of Virginia, defends the passage of the Marriage Affirmation Act in the Virginia state legislature. Gay activists are calling it the most restrictive antigay law in the nation.

Ehrhart, Earl. "Declaration of Independence: Governments Have No Right to Force Private Clubs to Change." *Atlanta Journal-Constitution,* January 4, 2005 p. A9. Ehrhart, a Georgia state representative, argues that Druid Hills Gulf Club has the constitutional right to exclude same-sex couples from its spousal benefits. And he announces his plan to introduce legislation that will forbid the state or any local government from imposing penalties on private social organizations engaged in lawful expression.

Egelko, Bob. "High Court Takes Gay-Rights Case on Club Bias." *San Francisco Chronicle,* June 10, 2004, p. B3. The California Supreme Court has agreed to decide whether California businesses can discriminate legally against same-sex couples. The case involves a lesbian couple, B. Birgit Koebke and Kendall French, who were denied a family membership by a San Diego country club.

Fisher, Janon. "Gays Sign Up for New Jersey Domestic Partner Status." *New York Times,* July 11, 2004, p. A33. For the first time in New Jersey, same-sex couples are able to register as domestic partners. Under a new law, qualifying couples are extended the right to visit sick partners in the hospital and may make legal and health-related decisions for them.

Gierach, Ryan. "Critics Saying Government's Survivor Benefits for Same-Sex Partners Not Enough." *Lesbian News,* August 2002, Vol. 28:1, p. 17. President George W. Bush has signed into law a measure that retroactively grants survivor benefits to the last listed beneficiary on the deceased's life insurance if the deceased left behind no spouse or children after 9/11. Gay activists are divided on how beneficial the legislation is.

Gootman, Elissa. "Judge Allows Suit in Death of Gay Mate." *New York Times,* April 16, 2003, p. D8. A New York judge rules that a gay man who joined his domestic partner in a civil union in Vermont has the right to file a wrongful death suit against St. Vincent's hospital in Manhattan. This is the first time a court outside of Vermont has ordered that a same-sex couple united in civil ceremonies there should be treated as spouses elsewhere.

———. "Seeing Families, Senator Calls for Changes in Sept. 11 Fund." *New York Times,* January 14, 2002, p. B2. New York Senator Hillary Clinton has called for changes in the plan to distribute financial compensation from the federal government to the victims of the September 11 terrorist attacks, including clarification of the status of any same-sex partners of those killed.

Hartlaub, Peter. "Lawyers Move to Dismiss Suit in Dog Mauling: Motions Call Civil Case Filed by Victim's Partner a 'Sham.'" *San Francisco Chronicle,* June 18, 2001, p. A13. Sharon Smith, the surviving lesbian partner of a woman who was mauled to death by two dogs, has sued the dogs' owners in San Francisco Superior Court, hoping to test California law that allows only legal heirs to file wrongful death cases.

Jacobs, Sonji. "Bill Thwarts Atlanta Ordinance: City Would Be Unable to Fine Club over Denial of Benefits to Gay Partners." *Atlanta Journal-Constitution*, March 18, 2005, p. A1. The Georgia state legislature has voted to block Atlanta's attempt to penalize private organizations that do not offer gay and lesbian couples the same benefits as married couples.

Lamb, David. "Virginia Limits on Gays Stir Debate." *Seattle Times*, June 21, 2004, p. A8. A new Virginian law that reaffirms the state's ban on same-sex marriage could also negate powers of attorney, wills, leases, child custody arrangements, joint bank accounts, and health insurance granted by companies that recognize domestic partnerships.

Liptak, Adam. "Montana Universities Must Offer Health Insurance to Gay Employees' Partners, Court Rules." *New York Times*, December 31, 2004, p. A18. The Montana state supreme court has ruled that the state's public universities must provide their gay employees with insurance coverage for their domestic partners. Observers note that it is the first time that any state high court has ruled that a state has a constitutional obligation to provide health-care benefits for domestic partners.

———. "Golf Club Files Suit over Fine: Druid Hills Targets City's Human Rights Ordinance." *Atlanta Journal-Constitution*, January 1, 2005, p. C1. Druid Hills Golf Club has filed suit against Atlanta, seeking to block the city from fining the club for not treating partners of gay members the same as spouses of married members. The club also is seeking to have the city's human rights ordinance thrown out for violating the state constitution, since a recently passed amendment prevents any homosexual union from receiving the same recognition as marriage.

———. "Mayor Fines Druid Hills Club over Gay Policy." *Atlanta Journal-Constitution*, December 28, 2004, p. A1. Atlanta Mayor Shirley Franklin has fined Druid Hills Golf Club $500 a day—up to a maximum of $90,000—because it denies spousal benefits to partners of gay members of the private club. Franklin's decision marks the first time the city has levied a fine under its human rights ordinance.

Marech, Rona. "Gays Cautious about New Partners Law: Some Opt out, Fearing Legal or Financial Troubles." *San Francisco Chronicle*, September 20, 2004, p. A1. California's new domestic partner legislation, which extends state marriage rights and responsibilities to same-sex partners goes into effect on January 1, 2005. However, some of the state's gay and lesbian couples are dissolving their existing partnerships or choosing not to register because they fear that under the new law their public benefits could be reduced.

Messina, Debbie. "Gays Unite Against New Law: Scared as Never Before, Many Prepare to Speak out as Never Before." *Virginian Pilot*, June 29, 2004, p. B1. A law enacted by the Virginian state legislature that would invalidate many legal arrangements entered into by gay and lesbian couples has spurred many previously apolitical homosexual citizens into community activism.

———. "State's New Laws Take Effect Today: More Restrictive Measure Meets with Protests." *Virginian Pilot*, July 1, 2004, p. A1. Calling it the most restrictive antigay law in the nation, gay rights protestors staged rallies decrying Virginia's House Bill 751 on the day it went into effect. The bill invalidates most legal contracts that gay and lesbian couples enter into to construct marriage-like arrangements.

Reinert, Patty. "Gay Rights Battle Not Just about Marriage; State-Backed Civil Unions a Major Step." *Houston Chronicle*, March 8, 2004, p. 1. Even if a Constitutional amendment banning same-sex marriage is passed, now that Texas's sodomy law has been overturned the state is more likely to enact domestic partnership legislation.

Romney, Lee. "New Calif. Law Boosts Domestic Partners' Rights, Responsibilities." *Seattle Times*, January 2, 2005. p. A4. Due to a 2003 law that goes into effect January 1, California's registered domestic partners now enjoy hundreds of state rights and responsibilities formerly granted only to married spouses. In order to end their partnerships, registered partners will now be required to divorce, and all property will be split equally between partners, as it is for married heterosexual couples.

Salladay, Robert, and Tanya Schevitz. "Davis Signs Partner Benefit Bill: Business Groups Say It Will Make It Harder to Operate in the State." *San Francisco Chronicle*, October 13, 2003, p. A1. Just before leaving office, California governor Gray Davis signs into law a measure that would require most businesses with state contracts of more than $100,000 to begin offering domestic partnership benefits if they also extend those benefits to married couples.

Schuppe, Jonathan "N.J. Senate Approves Domestic Partners Bill: Governor Promises to Enact Legal Rights for Same-Sex Couples." *Newark Star-Ledger*, January 9, 2004, p. 1. The New Jersey state senate passes one of the strongest gay rights bills in the country, granting same-sex couples many of the same financial and legal benefits as married couples.

Tagami, Ty. "Partner Benefits Disputed/Backers and Foes of Gay Marriage Ban Spar over Impact on Couples' Coverage." *Atlanta Journal-Constitution*, April 3, 2004, p. A1. Advocates for gay rights worry that an amendment to the Georgia state constitution to ban same-sex marriage could roll back domestic partner benefits available through some private employers and local governments.

Walsh, Rebecca. "Utah House Adopts Third Statement Against Gay Marriage." *Salt Lake Tribune*, February 20, 2004, p. A5. Utah legislators pass the "Marriage Recognition Policy," which will bar state agencies from recognizing gay unions performed in other states and deny same-sex couples inheritance rights, medical powers of attorney, and child custody.

Washington, April M. "A Double Standard: City's Benefits Policy for Gay Couples Lacks Parity, Experts Say." *Rocky Mountain News*, September 1, 2004, p. 5A. City of Denver gay and lesbian employees face major barriers when trying to gain health insurance for their partners. Unlike their married co-workers, homosexuals must fill out an affidavit and respond to a host of questions that some say are intrusive and demeaning.

Wetzstein, Cheryl. "Lesbians' 'Divorce' in Iowa Targeted: Only Vermont Can Act, Foes of Judge Claim." *Washington Times*, January 1, 2004, p. A4. Claiming the judge has no jurisdiction to end something that doesn't legally exist in Iowa, a group of state lawmakers and a conservative group are pursuing legal action against a state district judge who issued a ruling to two Iowa lesbians terminating their Vermont civil union.

EDUCATION

Archibald, George. "Changing Minds: Former Gays Meet Resistance at NEA Convention." *Washington Times*, July 27, 2004, p. A2. Members of the Ex-Gay Educators Caucus were met with open hostility at the National Education Association's convention in Washington, D.C., when they tried to distribute literature that claimed sexual orientation could be changed. The group is composed of teachers who identify as former gay men and lesbians.

———. "'How to Be Gay' Course Draws Fire at Michigan: Professor Calls It a Class on Culture." *Washington Times*, August 18, 2003, p. A1. Professor David M. Halperin has ignited a controversy at the University of Michigan after announcing his course offering, How to be Gay: Male Homosexuality and Initiation. Family values activists are calling for public funding of the course to be cut.

———. "NEA Groups Protest Award to Gay Studies Activist." *Washington Times*, July 3, 2004, p. A04. The leaders of the National Education Association (NEA) Republican Educators Caucus and NEA Ex-Gay Educators Caucus are formally protesting plans to give Kevin Jennings of the Gay Lesbian Straight Education Network a human rights award at the union's annual dinner.

Avalos-Lavimodiere, Valerie. "Gay-Sensitivity Training Challenged: Group Vows to Represent Visalia Unified Students, Teachers Who Refuse to Go." *Fresno Bee*, August 25, 2002, p. A1. The Pacific Justice Institute, a conservative nonprofit organization, vows to represent any student or teacher in the Visalia Unified School District in California who objects to attending what it calls "pro-gay training." The district is under court order to provide sensitivity training on antigay harassment.

Bellantoni, Christina. "'Gay-Straight' Clubs in Schools Anger Foes." *Washington Times*, November 18, 2004, p. B1. Family groups and state lawmakers in Virginia, Maryland, and Washington, D.C., say gay-straight student alliance clubs in the region—some operating at middle schools—promote homosexuality and encourage teens to be sexually active.

Carlson, Coralie. "Supreme Court Tackles Debate over Mandatory Student Fees: University of Wisconsin Students Say the First Amendment Protects Them from Having to Subsidize Groups They Oppose." *Minneapolis Star Tribune*, November 10, 1999, p. 5A. The Supreme Court hears a case brought by a group of conservative Christian students at the University of Wisconsin who claim they are forced to subsidize student groups with whom they disagree, including the school's gay campus center.

Dionne, E. J., Jr. "Recruiting Ban on the Military Is Shortsighted." *Investor's Business Daily*, December 6, 2004 p. A19. Dionne argues that a federal appeals court ruling that colleges can bar military recruiters from their campuses to protest the "don't ask, don't tell" policy without losing federal funding is ultimately bad for the United States. His reasoning is based not on support for the military's policy but rather his concern that not enough students from elite universities are entering the armed forces, creating a dangerous estrangement between the armed services and America's professional class.

Egelko, Bob. "Web Porn Filters Go to High Court: Case to Decide Whether Use in Libraries Violates Freedom of Speech." *San Francisco Chronicle*, March 5, 2003, p. A5. The Supreme Court hears arguments in a case concerning whether the federal government can compel local libraries to install computer software designed to filter pornography. The software often ends up filtering out content related to gay and lesbian issues.

Erickson, Doug. "Gay-Straight Alliances Catch on in Middle Schools" *Wisconsin State Journal*, January 18, 2004, p. A1. While gay-straight alliances have been around for a decade in Wisconsin high schools, the trend now is to start them at middle schools. Supporters say they lead to acceptance of diversity and less harassment; opponents say they promote homosexuality.

Ewing, Vanessa Lynn, Arthur A. Stukas, Jr., and Sheehan, Eugene P. "Student Prejudice Against Gay Male and Lesbian Lecturers." *Journal of Sociology*, October 2003, Vol. 143:5, pp. 569–580. The authors examine whether gay men and lesbians are evaluated more negatively than individuals of unspecified sexual orientation when attributional ambiguity surrounds evaluations.

Fernandes, Deirdre. "Debate over Gay Students Persists Despite Survey Change: Elimination of Questions about Slurs Against Gays Shifts Focus to School Board." *Winston-Salem Journal*, February 13, 2003, p. A1. The Winston-Salem/Forsyth County school board has decided to remove a set of questions about discrimination against gays and lesbians from a systemwide survey after protests by community groups and some members of the board.

Fernandez, Jennifer. "Guilford Schools Policy Fights Discrimination in Classrooms: Some Gay-Rights Leaders Say the Policy Hasn't Made a Difference Yet." *Piedmont News & Record*, March 20, 2004, p. B1. Fernandez examines one school district in North Carolina after it implements a policy designed to shield gay and lesbian students from harassment. Discrimination has not declined, but activists are optimistic that in time it will.

Fischler, Marcelle S. "Gays Enjoy the Night at a Prom of Their Own." *New York Times*, June 17, 2001, p. 1. Long Island Gay and Lesbian Youth has sponsored the first ever prom for LGBT youths in suburbia at the Island Hills Golf and Country Club in Sayville, New York. Two hundred and twenty young people from the New York metropolitan area attended the event.

Greenhouse, Linda. "Court Upholds Law to Make Libraries Use Internet Filters." *New York Times*, June 24, 2003, p. A1. The Supreme Court, in a 6-3 decision, upholds the federal Children's Internet Protection Act, which would withhold funding to any library that fails to install pornography filters on computers. Critics charge the filters often screen out non-pornographic material, particularly that related to gay and lesbian issues.

Gay Rights

————. "No Student Veto for Campus Fees." *New York Times*, March 23, 2000, p. A1. In a 9-0 decision in *Board of Regents v. Southworth*, the Supreme Court rules that public universities can collect student activity fees even from students who object to particular activities. The case involved conservative Christian students at the University of Wisconsin.

Heredia, Christopher. "Young People Are More Confident Than Ever about Standing up for Their Sexuality." *San Francisco Chronicle*, June 23, 2000, p. 3. With the formation of gay student support groups at high schools across the country, many LGBT students are coming out at a younger age.

Hernandez, Duran. "Inner Srength Came Only after Trial by Fire." *Fresno Bee*, August 17, 2002, p. B7. One California gay teen shares his story of how his life changed for the better after helping to form a gay-straight student alliance at his high school.

Holmes, Erin. "Play Stirs Controversy at Schools: Some Parents Say Story about Gay Man's Killing Is Inappropriate for School." *Arlington Heights Daily Herald*, October 23, 2003, p. 1. Parents of some students at two Illinois high schools are protesting the schools' staging of *The Laramie Project*, a play by Moìses Kaufman about the events surrounding the murder of gay college student Matthew Shepard.

Hughes, Jim. "Teens Sue in Favor of Gay/Straight Alliance: Springs District Forbids Meeting at Palmer High." *Denver Post*, December 14, 2003, p. A29. A group of Colorado Springs high school students has filed a lawsuit in federal court alleging that the Palmer High School Gay/Straight Alliance, unlike other clubs, has been barred from holding meetings on school property.

Irvin, Nat. "Bad Idea: Gay School Sends Wrong Message." *Winston-Salem Journal*, September 14, 2003, p. A19. Irvin, an African-American who attended segregated schools as a child, suggests that creating a separate educational environment for LGBT teenagers is not to their advantage.

Kershaw, Sarah. "Gay Students Force New Look at U.S. College Traditions." *New York Times*, November 27, 2004, p. A12. Universities and high schools across the United States, moved in part by protests from gay students, are re-examining the ritual of crowning homecoming kings and queens, titles that often reward student achievement and occasionally come with substantial scholarships.

Kleinknect, William. "Gay Group Takes Stand for Equality at School: Student's Lawsuit Leaves Seton Hall in Legal Tangle." *Newark Star-Ledger*, November 15, 2004, p. 13. Anthony Romeo, a gay sociology major at the Roman Catholic–affiliated Seton Hall University in South Orange, New Jersey, has filed a lawsuit against the school after it denied official recognition to a gay student group.

Kropf, Schuyler. "Gays Want DeMint to Apologize." *Charleston Post and Courier*, October 5, 2004, p. B1. Several gay rights organizations are demanding an apology from Republican U.S. Senate candidate Jim DeMint, who said during a campaign appearance that known homosexuals should not get teaching jobs in South Carolina's schools.

Lewin, Tamar. "Battle on Gay Pride Shirts Leads to Suit Against School." *New York Times*, November 24, 2004, p. A18. The American Civil Liberties Union has filed suit against a Missouri high school that twice admonished gay student Brad Mathewson for wearing T-shirts bearing gay pride messages. The suit charges that the school violated Matthewson's Constitutional right to free expression.

Lindsay, Jay. "College Tries to Ease Way for Gays, Lesbians: Aid for Students Whose Parents Cut Them Off." *Seattle Times*, September 9, 2001, p. A6. Bridgewater State College in Massachusetts has instituted a new scholarship for gay and lesbian students whose parents cut them off financially when they learn of their children's homosexuality. It is believed to be the first of its kind.

Liptak, Adam. "Colleges Can Bar Army Recruiters." *New York Times*, November 30, 2004, p. A1. A three-judge panel of the U.S. Court of Appeals for the Third Circuit, in Philadelphia, has ruled that educational institutions have a First Amendment right to keep military recruiters off their campuses to protest the Defense Department policy of excluding gays from military service.

Lott, Tim. "Schools with the Wrong Lessons." *Evening Standard*, July 31, 2003, p. 13. Lott, a British commentator, decries the formation of the Harvey Milk High School in New York City. He sees it as part of a disturbing educational trend on both sides of the Atlantic to segregate children based on perceived difference. He fears this denies common humanity and lays up a deep reservoir of potential conflict.

Macdonald, Mary. "Rule Aimed at Gay Clubs Would Make All Students Get Approval." *Atlanta Journal-Constitution.* March 18, 2005, p. D1. A proposal before the Georgia Board of Education would require any student who wants to take part in school-related clubs or after-school activities to obtain written permission from his or her parents. Gay activists fear the new rule would dissuade closeted teens from joining gay-straight alliances.

Martin, Betty L. "Bellaire High Gay-Straight Club Promotes Self Tolerance, Not Sex." *Houston Chronicle*, May 1, 2003, p. 1. Teen activists struggle to get the message to their communities that student gay/straight alliances are not about promoting sexual relations between members, but rather about creating a safe space where they can figure out who they are.

Matus, Ron. "Campus Asks If Gay Rights and Religion Can Coexist." *St. Petersburg Times*, November 29, 2004, p. 1B. Gay and lesbian students at the University of North Florida have filed complaints about harassment from straight peers, while criticizing administrators for being too slow to respond. However, tensions became too great to ignore after the student body president refused to give the gay student group money for a benefit drag show, saying that his Christianity forbade him from supporting cross-dressing.

McLemee, Scott. "A Queer Notion of History." *Chronicle of Higher Education*, September 12, 2003, Vol. 50:3, pp. A14–17. In the Supreme Court ruling overturning sodomy laws, the works of several prominent gay and lesbian historians were cited in the majority opinion. It's been a long process for this particular area of historical inquiry to attain academic respectability.

Mooney, John. "Texas' Textbook Battle Could Be Felt in Jersey." *Newark Star-Ledger*, November 14, 2004, p. 25. The Texas school board has asked that all references to marriage in the four textbooks it is considering purchasing for students define marriage as between a man and woman and remove gender-neutral references—such as "partners"—that could include same-sex relationships. Since publishers are reluctant to create separate versions of the same book, the request could affect curriculum across the country.

Murphy, Kevin. "UW Student Fee System Upheld by Fed Appeals Court: Shabaz's Decision Overturned." *Capital Times*, October 2, 2002, p. 2A. The U.S. Court of Appeals for the Seventh Circuit overturns the decision of District Judge John Shabaz, who ruled that the University of Wisconsin's fee system violated students' First Amendment rights because it was not "viewpoint neutral," a standard applied by the U.S. Supreme Court when it reviewed the case.

Nathans, Aaron. "Shabaz Rules UW Fees Unfair: Groups' Funding Not Viewpoint Neutral." *Capital Times*, December 8, 2000, p. 1A. Despite its 9-0 victory in the U.S. Supreme Court, Judge John Shabaz has ruled that the University of Wisconsin may not compel students to pay for ideological or political organizations they disagree with—until it complies with the Court's "viewpoint neutral" standard.

Pohlig, Colleen. "When Parents Are Gay, Kids' Reactions Vary." *Seattle Times*, August 9, 2001, p. B1. Pohlig asks: How do you tell your peers your parents are gay when the school halls hum with gay-bashing? More and more children are facing this dilemma as the number of same-sex parenting households increases.

Tseng, Nin-Hai. *Florida Times Union*. "Mom Challenges Ruling on Yearbook Tuxedo Pose." February 23, 2005, p. B1. Kelli Davis, a senior at Fleming Island High School in Florida and an open lesbian, chose to be photographed in a tuxedo for her class photo rather than the traditional off-the-shoulder wrap dress. In response, her principal, Sam Ward, removed her photo from the class yearbook.

Wall, Lucas. "Advocate for Gay Club Thrust into the Spotlight." *Houston Chronicle*, March 19, 2003, p. 28. Profile of Marla Dukler, a Texas high school student who filed a suit against Klein Independent School District for violating the free speech rights of students who wanted to meet on school grounds to discuss gay rights and tolerance.

———. "Gay Club 'A Matter of Law': Klein Officials Say They Had to Approve Group." *Houston Chronicle*, March 6, 2003, p. 21. Klein Independent School District officials in Texas say they had no choice under federal law but to approve a gay-straight alliance club at Klein High School after students there sued, claiming their free speech rights were being violated.

Winerip, Michael. "Tolerance and Hypocrisy on Gay-Straight Clubs." *New York Times*, January 29, 2003, p. B10. Report from the rural South on the spread of gay/straight student alliances at high schools throughout the region. School officials are often caught between federal mandates to provide equal time for all extracurricular student interests and conservative religious groups.

Wright, Ellen. "Louisiana School Punishes Seven-Year-Old Boy for Talking about His Lesbian Moms." *Lesbian News*, January 2004, vol. 29:6, p. 12. After honestly answering a classmate's questions about his family, seven-year-old Marcus McLaurin was berated by his teacher in front of his classmates and sent to a behavioral clinic at his elementary school.

Zoepf, Katherine. "Trying to Make His Special Students Feel Ordinary." *New York Times*, September 12, 2003, p. B2. A profile of Bill Salzman, the new principal of New York City's Harvey Milk High School, the nation's first publicly financed school for gay, lesbian, and transgender students.

HATE CRIMES

Antlfinger, Carrie. "Gay Advocacy Groups Decry the Use of 'Gay Panic' Defense." *Wisconsin State Journal*, February 2, 2005, p. A1. Gary Hirte, a 19-year-old who has confessed to killing a 37-year-old gay man, Glen Kopitske, is on trial to determine if he was insane when the crime was committed; Hirte claimed that sexual contact with the victim sent him into an uncontrollable rage.

Carter, Barry. "Newark Vigil Remembers Lesbian Teen: Slain Girl's Friends and Family Gather along with Gay-Rights Activists." *Newark Star-Ledger*, May 12, 2004, p. 29. Sakia Gunn was killed waiting for a bus with friends after rebuffing the advances of Richard McCullough. He allegedly attacked her after learning she was a lesbian and later became one of the first New Jerseyans indicted in a bias-related homicide.

Castro, Hector. "Seattle Man Recovering from Hate Crime Attack Spurs Gay Community." *Seattle Post-Intelligencer*, July 10, 2004, p. B1. The gay community in Seattle, a city known for its tolerance, has been shaken by the vicious slashing and beating of a gay man, Micah Painter. Included with the article are the FBI's statistics for hate crimes against homosexuals for 2002.

Chin, Abigail. "Businesses with Gay Clienteles Vandalized." *Denver Post*, November 7, 2004, p. C1. There have been at least eight instances of vandalism against gay-oriented businesses during 2004 in Denver, owners say. Four other times, vandals targeted a gay and lesbian community center. Members of the gay community there say the incidence of property crimes against gay businesses is on the rise.

Cloud, John. "The New Face of Gay Power." *Time*, October 13, 2003, Vol. 162:15, pp. 52–57. Five years after the murder of Matthew Shepard, gays and straights in Wyoming are still learning to live with each other. One of the results of this tragedy was the formation of the Republican Unity Coalition, a gay-straight alliance.

Del Medico, Jennifer, and Bev McCarron. "Schools Grapple with Gay Bashing: Beating at Hillsborough High Draws Attention to Efforts to Promote Tolerance." *Newark Star-Ledger*, May 13, 2002, p. 15. Scott Lipich, a New Jersey teen, was beaten by four classmates in his high school's cafeteria in front of 600 other students. The attack has galvanized school officials throughout the state to take action to stop bias crimes against students.

Estrada, Heron Marquez. "An 'Exorcism' Does Damage to Cathedral: A Dispute About Gay Rights in Church Leaves a Stain." *Minneapolis Star Tribune*, November 24, 2004, p. 1B. Members of a religious group, Catholics Against Sacrilege, who oppose openly gay and lesbian congregants from receiving communion in their church, are suspected of sprinkling salt and oil around the Cathedral of St. Paul in St. Paul, Minnesota. Authorities consider the action vandalism and intend to prosecute those responsible under hate crime legislation.

Fagan, Amy. "Fast Track on Hate-Crime Bill Draws Senate GOP Outcry." *Washington Times*, June 11, 2002, p. A4. A bill sponsored by Senator Edward M. Kennedy of Massachusetts would expand the federal definition of hate crimes to include those motivated by a person's sex, sexual orientation, or disability and greatly broaden the federal government's ability to investigate and prosecute them.

Ingold, John. "Anti-Gay Missives Spark Probe: FBI Seeks Source of Threatening Fliers Distributed in Denver Area." *Denver Post*, March 30, 2004, p. B1. The Federal Bureau of Investigation has begun looking into dozens of antigay fliers mailed to members of the Denver-area gay community and gay rights supporters over the past four years, some of which have included death threats.

Lee, Felicia R. "ABC News Revisits Student's Killing, and Angers Some Gays." *New York Times*, November 26, 2004, p. A33. The Gay and Lesbian Alliance Against Defamation is protesting an investigative report on the ABC newsmagazine *20/20* that reexamines the circumstances surrounding the murder of Matthew Shepard in Laramie, Wyoming. Shepard's convicted killer, Aaron J. McKinney, now says that the crime wasn't motivated by antigay hatred but rather a crystal methamphetamine–fueled robbery gone bad.

Liptak, Adam. "Ex-Inmate's Suit Offers View into Sexual Slavery in Prisons." *New York Times*, October 16, 2004, p. A1. A federal appeals court has allowed a civil rights lawsuit filed by an incarcerated gay man against the state of Texas to go to trial. Roderick Johnson contends that prison officials failed to protect him against systemic rape from other prisoners. The ruling is the first to acknowledge the equal protection rights of homosexuals sexually abused in prison.

Lochhead, Carolyn. "Senate OKs Bill Including Gays as Hate Crime Victims." *San Francisco Chronicle*, June 16, 2004, p. A5. A measure to expand the federal definition of hate crimes to include sexual orientation, a long-standing priority of lesbians and gays, has passed the Senate with the most number of votes since activists began pressuring Congress to broaden the statute. However, the bill has never yet emerged from conference committee to become law.

Marech, Rona. "Gay Activists Mark a Grim Anniversary: Brutal 1998 Slaying Left Legacy of Pain and Hope in Laramie." *San Francisco Chronicle*, October 7, 2004, p. B1. Activists in the Marriage Caravan Express, a cross-country bus ride designed to raise awareness of marriage inequality, stop in Laramie, Wyoming, for a rally on the sixth anniversary of the murder of gay college student Matthew Shepard.

Scott, Jeffry. "Killing of Gay Teen Shakes Alabamians: Critics Say Hate Crime Law Should Be Expanded to Include Homosexuals." *Atlanta Journal-Constitution*, August 9, 2004, p. A1. Openly gay teenager Scotty Weaver was killed July 18 in Bay Minette, Alabama, when he returned home from working the night shift as a cook. Investigators believe the three people who lived with him were the attackers. His death has prompted calls for Alabama to extend hate crimes protection to gay men and lesbians.

Seymour, Add, Jr. "Morehouse Gays Gain Supporters: Groups Want Protection Put in Student Handbook." *Atlanta Journal-Constitution*, November 23, 2002, p. F5. Following the baseball bat beating of a student, a gay student organization and a national legal rights group are demanding Morehouse College officials add to the school's student handbook the specific prohibition of anti-gay discrimination and violence.

Wakelin, Anna, and Karen M. Long. "Effects of Victim Gender and Sexuality on Attributions of Blame to Rape Victims." *Sex Roles*, November 2003, Vol. 49:9/10, pp. 477–488. Research suggests that homosexual male rape victims receive more blame than heterosexual victims. This study shows that when participants were asked to assign blame for an imaginary crime, the character of gay male victims was seen to be a stronger contributory factor than it was for other victims.

Warren, Beth. "Seminar to Take On 'Gay Panic' Defense." *Atlanta Journal-Constitution*. February 24, 2005, p. C6. The Atlanta Police Department, the FBI, and hate-crime researchers are offering the first national symposium to inform prosecutors of ways to defeat the so-called gay panic defense, wherein defendants in gay bashings and murders argue that sexual advances from the victim drove them to commit the crime.

HISTORY/ANALYSIS OF THE GAY RIGHTS MOVEMENT

Aguilera, Elizabeth, and David Olinger. "Gay Marriage Enjoyed Brief Honeymoon in Colo. in '75." *Denver Post*, February 17, 2004, p. A1. In the midst of the San Francisco marriage controversy, not many remember that Boulder, Colorado, was actually the first jurisdiction to issue gay marriage licenses almost 30 years ago.

Deggans, Eric. "Similar Struggles? Gay Rights and Civil Rights." *St. Petersburg Times*, January 18, 2004, p. 1P. Conservative gay rights supporter argues against New Jersey Supreme Court ruling against Boy Scouts of America, which retroactively expelled a former Eagle Scout for being openly gay. Writer argues against the ruling on First Amendment grounds. Can the struggle for gay rights be compared to black people's classic civil rights struggle? Deggans examines the historical parallels and current divisions between the two movements.

Gay Rights

Kornblum, Janet. "Lesbian Activists Blaze Trail for Half Century." *USA Today*, March 4, 2004, p. 6D. A profile of Del Martin and Phyllis Lyon, longtime gay rights activists. They helped found the first lesbian organization in the nation, Daughters of Bilitis, and were the first couple to be married in San Francisco.

Lewin, Tamar. "The Gay Rights Movement, Settled Down." *New York Times*, February 29, 2004, Week in Review, p. 5. What does it mean that gay rights activists, once the standard-bearers for sexual freedom, are now preoccupied with homosexual marriage—and fighting President George W. Bush's plans for a Constitutional amendment to outlaw it?

Lombardi-Nash, Michael. "1904: The First Lesbian Feminist Speaks." *Gay & Lesbian Review Worldwide*, May/June 2004, Vol. 11:3, p. 31. Focuses on the first known lesbian activist, Anna Rüling, and includes a description of a speech she gave in 1904 before the Scientific Humanitarian Committee, the first gay organization in world history.

Manly, Howard. "Gay vs. Civil Rights Fight Misses Point." *Boston Herald*, March 9, 2004, p. 27. While agreeing that the gay rights cause and the traditional African-American civil rights movement are not equivalent, Manly views the dispute between the two groups as diverting political energy away from the underlying principles shared by both.

Martin, Jonathan. "From Fear to Dignity: 2 Gay Men, 2 Journeys." *Seattle Times*, June 29, 2003, p. A1. Profiles of two Seattle-area gay men, 35 years apart in age. The two men have very different relationships to the "closet" based on their individual pre- and post-Stonewall experiences.

May, Meredith. "City Hall Slayings: 25 Years Later; From Milk's Times to Our Times." *San Francisco Chronicle*, November 27, 2003, p. A1. On the 25th anniversary of the assassination of Harvey Milk, the first openly homosexual elected official in the United States, May surveys the huge gains made by gays and lesbians since his death.

Meadow, James B. "Elver Barker Courageously Worked for Gay Rights." *Rocky Mountain News*, September 9, 2004, p. 13B. This obituary of one of the founders of the gay rights movement in the Rocky Mountains region tells how Barker became an activist in the 1950s after being fired from his job at the Alameda County, California, welfare office for being homosexual.

Rich, Frank. "Angels, Reagan, and AIDS in America." *New York Times*, November 16, 2003, Arts and Leisure, p. 1. On the occasion of the premiere of the film adaptation of Tony Kushner's Pulitzer Prize–winning play, *Angels in America*, the *New York Times'* chief cultural critic examines the failings of the Reagan administration to address the AIDS crisis of the mid-1980s.

Turner, Allan. "Museum on a Mission to Save Local Gay History: Collection Shows Long Fight to Gain Rights in Houston." *Houston Chronicle*, August 24, 2004, p. 1. Volunteers for the fledgling Gulf Coast Archive and Museum of Gay, Lesbian, Bisexual and Transgender History are working to preserve the history of the gay rights movement and gay culture in the coastal region of Texas.

Williams, Alvin. "Distinctions Drawn." *Washington Times*, April 13, 2004, p. A12. Williams, the president of Black America's Political Action Committee, editorializes against drawing comparisons between the historic civil rights struggles of African Americans and today's gay rights movement.

HOUSING RIGHTS

Mansnerus, Laura. "Court Revives Lesbians' Suit over Housing." *New York Times*, July 3, 2001, p. B1. New York's highest court has reinstated a lawsuit challenging Yeshiva University's policy of excluding same-sex couples from university housing, The court ruled that the two women could sue the school under New York City's human rights law.

IMMIGRATION LAWS

Crary, David. "U.S. Immigration Laws Not Friendly to Gay Couples: They Aren't Treated Same as Straight Counterparts." *Seattle Times*, November 24, 2003, p. A10. When a binational couple is heterosexual, the foreigner can immigrate to America as a fiancé or spouse. Not so with gay and lesbian couples—even if they have had legal same-sex marriages in the Netherlands or Canada.

Egelko, Bob. "Gay Group Appeals Asylum Ruling: Guadalajara Police Beat Mexican Man." *San Francisco Chronicle*, October 27, 2004, p.B3. Lambda Legal has challenged an immigration judge's decision that a gay Mexican man, who fled his country after being beaten and threatened by police, is not entitled to political asylum because his sexual orientation is not obvious, and he could avoid harm by pretending to be straight.

Marech, Rona. "Same-Sex Couples Flock to Gay-Friendly Canada." *San Francisco Chronicle*, March 9, 2004, p. A1. Ever since Canada's immigration law was changed in 2002 to recognize same-sex partners for immigration purposes, a growing number of gay and lesbian couples have migrated there—especially couples in which one partner is a U.S. citizen and one is not.

Symington, Denis. "Kicked out of America." *Advocate*, February 3, 2004, Issue 907, p. 9. Symington recounts his personal experiences with American immigration law. He and his partner of nine years, a native of Russia, now live in London because his partner's visa application was denied by U.S. authorities.

INTERNATIONAL GAY RIGHTS ISSUES

Althaus, Dudley. "Probe of Editor's Death Plagued by Criticisms." *Houston Chronicle*, April 3, 2004, p. 1. A gay male couple, one of whom is a U.S. citizen, has been charged in the murder of prominent Mexican journalist Roberto Mora. Police claim Mora was killed in a fit of jealous rage; gay activists counter that the real killers are drug traffickers and that the police targeted the men because they are gay.

Arie, Sophie, and Gaby Hinsliff. "Parting Shot: Italian Bows Out in Euro Gay Row." *London Observer*, October 31, 2004, p. 2. A constitutional crisis in the European Union was averted after Rocco Buttiglione, an Italian nominee to the European Commission whose antigay views had made him a target of intense public criticism, withdrew his candidacy for Commissioner of Justice. In that position, Buttiglione would have been responsible for enforcing European antidiscrimination laws.

Bowes, Gemma. "Call for Travel Boycott as Zanzibar Bans Gays." *Observer*, April 25, 2004, p. A1. A gay rights group is calling for travelers to boycott the East African island after its parliament passed a law that calls for people in same-sex relationships to be jailed for up to 25 years.

Bradley, John R. "Queer Sheik." *New Republic*, March 15, 2004, Vol. 230:9, pp. 11–13. Traditionally, self-identified gays and lesbians who openly displayed their sexual preferences lived in mortal fear in Saudi Arabia, but with the forced return of many Saudis from the United States, attitudes toward homosexuality are becoming more tolerant.

Burleigh, James. "Leading Gay Activist Murdered in Jamaica." *Independent of London*, June 10, 2004, p. 28. The mutilated body of Jamaica's best-known gay rights activist, Brian Williamson, has been found at his home in Kingston, and the island's sole gay advocacy group is calling it a possible hate crime.

Byrnes, Brian. "Wary of Past Abuses, Argentine Capital Approves Gay Rights." *Christian Science Monitor*, July 14, 2003, p. 7. Buenos Aires becomes the first city in Latin America to allow civil unions for same-sex partners. Byrnes suggests that the new law reflects that country's present commitment to civil rights following the military dictatorship of the early 1980s.

Deputy, Paul Waugh. "Posters Advertising 'Romantic' Holidays Are Banned from the Tube for Bias Against Gays." *Independent of London*, September 29, 2003, p. 2. A leisure company that bans gays and lesbians from its Caribbean resorts has been forced to remove ads promoting its vacation packages from the London Underground.

Hari, Johann. "At Last the UN Recognises the Need for Gay Rights." *Independent of London*, April 25, 2003, p. 17. Hari documents several incidents from around the world where the human rights of gay men and lesbians were suppressed—most notably in Egypt, where 50 men were tried for "debauchery" after attending a party on a boat—and calls upon the U.N. Commission on Human Rights to pass a draft resolution establishing sexual orientation as a protected class.

Helfer, Laurence R. "U.S. Trails the World on Gay Rights, Basic Liberties." *International Herald Tribune*, June 19, 2003, p. 8. The author, a professor at Loyola Law School, contends that despite recent gains, the United States still lags far behind many other nations when it comes to civil rights for gays and lesbians.

Henley, Jon. "Court Annuls France's First Gay Marriage: Couple Vow to 'Fight to the End' as Issue Causes Political Storm." *Guardian of London*, July 28, 2004, p. 14. A court in Bordeaux has ruled that the marriage of Stephane Chapin and Bertrand Charpentier was not valid because "the traditional function of a marriage is commonly considered to be the founding of a family." The decision confirmed the hostility of France's conservative government toward the notion of same-sex marriage.

———. "French Mayor Announces Plan to Conduct First Gay Wedding." *Guardian of London*, April 24, 2004, p. 14. Noel Mamere, the Green Party mayor of a Bordeaux suburb, has said he will conduct what would be France's first gay wedding ceremony in the name of equal rights for homosexuals.

Hurst, Greg. "Lords Finally Vote to Scrap Section 28." *Times of London*, July 11, 2003, p. 15. The House of Lords in the British parliament votes to overturn Section 28, the controversial law that forbids the teaching of anything related to homosexuality in the English school system.

Lutyens, Dominic. "The Gay Team." *Observer of London*, October 26, 2003, p. 29. Profiles of 20 prominent British gays and lesbians from all fields of endeavor. The last 10 years has seen an explosion of visibility for the gay community in the United Kingdom.

Orr, Deborah. "So Many Equal Rights, yet Still So Little Equality: Gay Teenagers May Have More Rights Than Before, but in a Practical Sense the Victory Is Hollow." *Independent of London*, November 25, 2003, p. 17. As Queen Elizabeth prepares to announce a bill that would confer the same rights to same-sex couples as married couples, Orr examines the terrain of gay rights in Britain, from transsexual rights to those of gay teenagers.

Predrag, S. "Muslim Countries Block UN Resolution in LGBT Human Rights." *Lesbian News*, June 2003, Vol. 28:11, p. 18. Five Muslim countries—Egypt, Libya, Malaysia, Pakistan, and Saudi Arabia—have blocked the adoption of a United Nations resolution that would protect the human rights of gays, lesbians, bisexuals, and transsexuals.

Robertson-Textor, Marisa. "A One-Man Gay Rights Movement." *Advocate*, March 2, 2004, Issue 909, p. 26. Report on the campaign to free openly gay journalist and political activist Ruslan Shapirov, who was sentenced to 5.5 years in prison on charges of homosexual behavior in his native Uzbekistan after writing articles critical of the government.

Ross, Peter. "First Among Equals." *Glasgow Sunday Herald*, October 31, 2004, p. 18. A profile of international gay rights activist Peter Tatchell. Over his activist career, Tatchell has protested everything from homophobia in the Anglican Church in Britain to Robert Mugabe's campaign against homosexuality in Zimbabwe and the antigay reggae culture in Jamaica.

Seabrook, Jeremy "It's Not Natural: The Developing World's Homophobia Is a Legacy of Colonial Rule." *Guardian of London* July 3, 2004, p. 21. Seabrook maintains that antigay attitudes and laws in the Caribbean, Africa, and Asia didn't arise out of their native cultures but rather from Victorian anxieties about homosocial relationships that were imposed by their European conquerors.

Soulas, Delphine. "France Ready to Change Civil Pact: Set to Sidestep Debate on Gay 'Marriage.'" *Washington Times*, December 12, 2004, p. A8. France's Pacte Civil de Solidarité, a law designed to give same-sex couples many of the social, legal, and financial benefits of marriage, has proven to be a success, outside of the gay community as well as in it. Approximately 60 percent of the couples cohabitating under the law are heterosexual, so their new legal status has sparked a fundamental change in the way French society is organized.

Sterling, Toby. "Europe Goes for Civil Unions." *Capital Times*, March 5, 2004, p. 1A. As the gay marriage debate rages in the United States, in the Netherlands after three years of legal sanction, same-sex unions have ceased to be controversial.

Swarns, Rachel L. "Gays Respond Quickly to Killings in Cape Town." *New York Times*, February 4, 2003, p. A44. In Cape Town, South Africa, nine gay men are murdered at a massage parlor. They are believed to have been executed by men who entered the establishment looking for two male prostitutes who were involved in a drug deal.

Taylor, Diane. "Women: 'If You're Gay in Jamaica, You're Dead.'" *Guardian of London*, August 2, 2004, p. 6. Some human rights organizations have categorized Jamaica as one of the most homophobic countries in the world. Violence and prejudice against gay men there has garnered international attention, but Jamaican lesbians also face an often hostile social environment. This article asserts that their stories have been ignored.

Walker, Jonathan. "Anger at UN Gay Rights Delay." *Birmingham Post*, April 30, 2003, p. 5. A coalition between the Vatican and Muslim nations successfully stalled a UN resolution that would expand the organization's definition of discrimination to include that based on sexual orientation.

Wiseman, Paul. "Same-Sex Marriage Spurs Few Political Ripples in Taiwan." *Seattle Times*, February 27, 2004, p. A10. As Taiwan moves toward becoming the first Asian nation to legalize some form of gay marriage, surprisingly little political opposition has emerged to counter this development.

MARRIAGE

Albrecht, Brian. "Issue 1 Conflicts with Domestic Abuse Law, Judge Says." *Cleveland Plain Dealer*, March 24, 2005, p. A1. Judge Stuart Friedman has ruled that an amendment to the Ohio state constitution that denied legal recognition to unmarried and gay couples has rendered part of the state's domestic violence law unconstitutional since the law expressly recognizes the relationship between an unmarried offender and victim.

Allison, Wes. "Activists Think Timing Could Set Gays Back." *St. Petersburg Times*, February 25, 2004, p. 1A. Interviews with gay activists who disagree that the movement should be focusing on marriage. They view issues such as discrimination in housing and employment to be much more urgent.

Badertscher, Nancy. "Vote Elicits Glee, Gloom: Lawmakers Say Fight Has Not Ended." *Atlanta Journal-Constitution*, April 1, 2004, p. A12. Interviews with Georgia state legislators who supported and opposed the proposed state constitutional amendment barring same-sex marriage.

Beardsley, Elisabeth J. "Legislators Seek Civil Compromise." *Boston Herald*, February 11, 2004, p. 4. Lawmakers in the Massachusetts legislature weigh several options as they respond to the state's highest court ruling that mandates same-sex marriage licenses be issued beginning May 17.

Bellafante, Ginia. "In an Ohio Town, Same-Sex Marriage Ban Brings Tensions to Surface." *New York Times*, November 13, 2004, p. A10. After Ohio voters approve an amendment to their state constitution to outlaw same-sex marriage, gay and lesbian residents of Granville, Ohio, say the success of the anti–gay marriage amendment exposed biases in their town that were stronger than they suspected.

Belluck, Pam. "Decision Limits Gays: Massachusetts to Bar Couples Ineligible in Their Own States." *International Herald Tribune*, April 1, 2004, p. 5. After refusing to ask for a stay in the Massachusetts gay marriage ruling, the state's attorney general, Thomas Reilly, offers Governor Mitt Romney a way to prevent out-of-state, same-sex couples from flooding local marriage registrars.

———. "Governor of Massachusetts Seeks to Delay Same-Sex Marriages." *New York Times*, April 16, 2004, p. A1. With only one month before same-sex marriages are to become legal in Massachusetts, Governor, Mitt Romney makes a last-ditch effort to keep them from taking place until at least 2006.

———. "Maybe Same-Sex Marriage Didn't Make the Difference." *New York Times*, November 7, 2004, p. WK5. Political observers, both pro-gay and antigay, are debating what impact, if any, the gay marriage controversy had on President Bush's reelection victory.

———. "Romney Won't Let Gay Outsiders Wed in Massachusetts." *New York Times*, April 25, 2004, p. A1. Governor Mitt Romney announces that same-sex couples visiting Massachusetts will not be granted marriage licenses, citing a 90-year-old law that forbids nonresidents of Massachusetts from marrying in that state if the union would be void in their home state.

———. "Setback Is Dealt to Gay Marriage." *New York Times*, March 30, 2004, p. A1. The Massachusetts legislature approves a state constitutional amendment that would ban gay marriage and create same-sex civil unions instead.

———. "Town Set to Defy Governor on Same-Sex Marriage Issue." *New York Times*, May 11, 2004, p. A16. In defiance of Governor Mitt Romney, the Cape Cod town of Provincetown has voted to issue marriage licenses to out-of-state, same-sex couples even if they have no intention of moving to Massachusetts.

Belluck, Pam, David D. Kirkpatric, Kate Zezina, Tom Marshall, and Michael Levenson. "Hundreds of Same-Sex Couples Wed in Massachusetts." *New York Times*, May 18, 2004, p. A1. On May 17, 2004, Massachusetts became the first state in the United States to allow same-sex marriages. Report includes accounts of weddings across the state, as well as last-minute efforts to stop them.

Benedetti, Frank. "The Right to Live as a 'True American': One Gay Man Simply Wants What Most Other People Take for Granted." *Winston-Salem Journal*, August 13, 2003, p. A9. Benedetti, a gay man in a long-term relationship, responds to a reader who wondered what gays and lesbians want, elucidating a succinct list of demands.

Gay Rights

Bhatt, Sanjay. "Judge Backs Gay Marriage: State High-Court Fight Next." *Seattle Times*, August 5, 2004, p. A1. King County (Washington State) superior court judge William Downing has ruled that denying gay men and lesbians the right to marry is a violation of their rights to due process, thereby ruling the state's Defense of Marriage law unconstitutional. However, he stopped short of ordering officials to begin issuing marriage licenses because the state's supreme court still must weigh in on the matter.

Black, Eric. "The Gay Divide: Why Same-Sex Marriage Is Separating Minnesotans." *Minneapolis Star Tribune*, March 21, 2004, p. 1A. Examines the deep cultural divisions, even in a traditionally liberal state like Minnesota, between pro– and anti–same-sex marriage activists, which underlie the Constitutional amendment debate.

Blanchard, Mark. "Court Picks Tied to Gay Agenda: Top Bench to Consider Same-Sex 'Marriage' Legality." *Washington Times*, August 31, 2004, p. A13. Opposition parties are accusing Canadian prime minister Paul Martin of packing that nation's Supreme Court with gay rights supporters. Courts in three of Canada's provinces have legalized homosexual marriage in their jurisdictions, and the highest court must now decide whether to extend these rulings to include the entire country.

Block, Sandra. "Gay Couples Enter Golden Years with More Risk." *USA Today*, May 17, 2004, p. 1B. Older gay couples face a much greater risk of spending the end of their lives in poverty because they are ineligible for a host of federal protections, ranging from Social Security survivor benefits to estate tax exemptions.

Blumner, Robyn E. "What Happened to Live and Let Live?" *St. Petersburg Times*, February 15, 2004, p. 7P. Blumner believes that American society will one day come to view laws against gay marriage the same way it does laws against miscegenation and cites other current situations where marriages that are illegal in some states but not in others are still recognized by all.

———. "Why Gay Marriage Is Good for Conservatism." *St. Petersburg Times*, May 23, 2004, p. 7P. Jonathan Rauch, author of *Gay Marriage*, argues that, contrary to the views of many on the right, the advent of same-sex legal unions is a victory for conservative values in America.

Booth-Nadav, Stephen, and Phil Campbell. "Gender No Bar to 'Sacred' Marriages." *Rocky Mountain News*, December 1, 2003, p. 38A. A rabbi and minister argue that the spiritual quality of any affectional union should be evaluated by the ways in which its partners treat each other, not by their gender, and therefore there is no legitimate religious basis for outlawing same-sex marriage.

Brink, Graham. "Same-Sex Marriage Lawsuit Long Shot, Legal Experts Say." *St. Petersburg Times*, July 26, 2004, p. 1A. Paula Schoenwether and Nancy Wilson have filed a federal lawsuit in Tampa asking a judge to force the state of Florida and the federal government to legally recognize the marriage they entered into in the state of Massachusetts. However, legal observers doubt they will succeed.

Browning, Don, and Elizabeth Marquardt. "A Marriage Made in History?" *New York Times*, March 9, 2004, p. A25. Browning and Marquardt argue that both sides of the marriage debate are using faulty logic: Those opposed to gay marriage have no real proof that it harms society and those for it are mischaracterizing the history of the institution.

Bumiller, Elisabeth. "Bush Backs Ban in Constitution on Gay Marriage." *New York Times*, February 25, 2004, p. A1. Saying the union of a man and a woman is "the most fundamental institution of civilization," President George W. Bush declares his support for an amendment to the Constitution that would ban same-sex marriage.

Caldwell, Christopher. "Vows." *New York Times Book Review*, April 11, 2004, p. 10. Review of Jonathan Rauch's book *Gay: Why It Is Good for Gays, Good for Straights, and Good for America*. Rauch argues that marriage will require gays to trade in a libertine lifestyle for a respectable bourgeois one, something he views positively.

Campbell, Colin. "Gay Pair Seeks Canada's First Same-Sex Divorce." *New York Times*, July 22, 2004, p. A4. Two Toronto women who were among the first same-sex couples to marry in Canada are now seeking what may be the first Canadian same-sex divorce. The two women married on June 18, 2003, after a 10-year relationship and separated five days later.

Carr, Howie. "Fitchburg's Silver-Tongued Solon Our Last Best Hope." *Boston Herald*, April 21, 2004, p. 16. Carr, a Boston-area radio talk-show host, lauds the efforts of state legislative representative Emile Goguen to have the justices of the Massachusetts Supreme Judicial Court removed for ruling in favor of gay marriage.

———. "Time to Make SJC Judges Pay for Indecent Proposal." *Boston Herald*, February 6, 2004, p. 5. Carr advocates the direct election of Massachusetts superior court justices after that state's supreme court orders it to begin issuing same-sex marriage licenses.

Chapman, Dan. "Gay Union Pioneers Send Ripples South: Canadians Who Wed Expect Wave of Acceptance to Sweep across United States." *Atlanta Journal-Constitution*, March 4, 2004, p. A1. Throughout the Western Hemisphere, only the Canadian provinces of Ontario and British Columbia legally sanction same-sex marriages. Chapman examines the impact of this, legally, culturally and economically, both north and south of the border.

Chiang, Harriet. "After the Wedding Bells, Gays Face Maze of Legal Obstacles." *San Francisco Chronicle*, April 26, 2004, p. A1. The state of California now must find a way to deal with the more than 4,000 same-sex couples who received marriage licenses in San Francisco and consider themselves legally wed. But are they?

———. "The Battle over Same-Sex Marriage: Suits Challenging State Law Get OK." *San Francisco Chronicle*, April 2, 2004, p. B3. San Francisco superior court judge James Warren gave the green light for two lawsuits that challenge California laws defining marriage as between a man and a woman to go to trial, thereby putting the state's contentious marriage issue on the fast track to resolution.

————. "S.F. Sues over Legality of Same-Sex Marriages: City Asks Judge to Rule That State's Ban Is Discriminatory, Unconstitutional." *San Francisco Chronicle*, February 20, 2004, p. A19. San Francisco officials sue the state of California on the grounds that laws defining marriage as between a man and woman, particularly Proposition 22, illegally discriminate against gays and lesbians.

Chiang, Harriet, and John Wildermuth. "Governor Demands End to Gay Marriages: Lockyer Told to Act Against S.F.'s Same-Sex Licenses." *San Francisco Chronicle*, February 21, 2004, p. A1. After a state superior court judge in San Francisco refuses to halt the gay marriages taking place there, California governor Arnold Schwarzenegger orders his attorney general to find some legal way to block them.

Chilstrom, Herbert. "Many People of Faith Reject Banning of Same-Sex Unions." *Capital Times*, December 4, 2004, p. 9A. As Wisconsin debates a proposed amendment to its constitution outlawing same-sex marriage, Chilstrom, the retired presiding bishop of the American Lutheran Church, reminds readers that there exists a spectrum of opinions within Christianity about the validity of homosexual relationships. He concludes that, regardless of one's personal feelings about such relationships, discrimination against gay and lesbian couples is morally wrong.

Clemetson, Lynette. "Both Sides Court Black Churches in the Battle over Gay Marriage." *New York Times*, March 1, 2004, p. A1. Both gay rights activists and religious conservatives are lobbying for support from African-American religious leaders. While many of the leading civil rights organizations have come out strongly in favor of gay marriage, individual black churches are far more ambivalent on the matter.

Cloud, John. "How Oregon Eloped." *Time*, May 17, 2004, Vol. 163, Issue 20, p. 56. Oregon circuit judge Frank Bearden has ruled for the first time in U.S. history that a state must accept and register marriages of same-sex couples and given the legislature 90 days to develop laws that would protect gay couples' rights.

Cohen, Tom. "1st Legal Gay Marriage Takes Place in Canada: Court Overturns Ban; Government Can Appeal." *Seattle Times*, June 11, 2003, p. A1. Two Canadian men are married in the country's first legal same-sex wedding just hours after an Ontario appeals court ruled that Canada's ban on homosexual marriage was unconstitutional.

Coile, Zachary. "GOP Argues Gay Marriage Could Cost U.S. Billions: Dems Say Same-Sex Couples Pay Taxes, Deserve Benefits." *San Francisco Chronicle*, May 14, 2004, Vol 29:39, p. A4. House Republicans arguing in favor of a Constitutional amendment banning same-sex marriage voice a new argument against granting gay and lesbian couples full marriage rights: the costs to the federal government.

Cooper, Michael. "Hevesi Extends Pension Rights To Gay Spouses." *New York Times*, October 14, 2004, p. B1. New York State Comptroller Alan G. Hevesi has ruled that the state's pension system will treat gay couples with Canadian wedding licenses the same way it treats other married couples. The decision means that gay couples married in Canada and working for the state of New York would be entitled to automatic cost-of-living increases and accidental death benefits for survivors.

Crampton, Thomas. "Asbury Park Halts Gay-Marriage Applications, Sending Issue to Courts." *New York Times*, March 11, 2004, p. B5. After a warning from New Jersey's attorney general, the City of Asbury Park stops accepting applications for marriage licenses from same-sex couples, but the city council also votes to sue the state over the issue.

———. "Ministers Who Officiated at Same-Sex Marriages Go to Court." *New York Times*, March 23, 2004, p. B5. Two Unitarian ministers who performed wedding ceremonies for gay and lesbian couples in New Paltz, New York, face charges of multiple counts of solemnizing marriages without a license.

———. "Using the Courts to Wage a War on Gay Marriage." *New York Times*, May 9, 2004, p. A14. The Liberty Counsel, a conservative activist organization, has adopted many of the legal tactics normally associated with liberal and progressive groups like the ACLU or NAACP in its nationwide fight against same-sex marriage.

Dao, James. "Flush with Victory, Grass-Roots Crusader Against Same-Sex Marriage Thinks Big." *New York Times*, November 26,2004, p. A28. A profile of Phil Burress, head of the Cincinnati-based Citizens for Community Values. Burress is one of the architects of a nationwide church-based strategy to outlaw same-sex marriage.

———. "Ohio Legislature Votes to Ban Same-Sex Unions." *New York Times*, February 4, 2004, p. A12. The Ohio legislature gives final approval to one of the most sweeping bans on same-sex unions in the country, which also would bar state agencies from giving benefits to both gay and heterosexual domestic partners.

———. "State Action Is Pursued on Same-Sex Marriage." *New York Times*, February 27, 2004, p. A24. As same-sex marriage actions spread across the nation, state legislatures begin the process of amending their constitutions to forbid it.

Dart, Bob. "'Outing' of Gay Capitol Aides Adds Twist to Same-Sex Marriage Fight." *Atlanta Journal-Constitution*, July 14, 2004, p. A1. In a controversy reminiscent of the days of AIDS activism in the late '80s, gay rights advocates are divided over the "outing" of homosexual staffers of lawmakers who support the proposed Constitutional amendment to outlaw same-sex marriage.

Davis, Clive. "Gay Marriage Debate." *Washington Times*, April 18, 2004, p. B8. Davis places the same-sex marriage debate within the larger historical context of the institution's gradual removal from what he argues is its primary function—procreation.

Deans, Bob. "Bush: Ban Gay Marriage—An Amendment Is Needed, the President Says, but He Doesn't Preclude Civil Unions." *Atlanta Journal-Constitution*, February 25, 2004, p. A1. Saying same-sex weddings threaten "the most fundamental institution of civilization," President George W. Bush calls for a

Constitutional amendment to supersede court rulings in favor of marriage rights for gays and lesbians.

Deggans, Eric. "'Too Much, Too Soon': Why Should They Have to Wait?" *St. Petersburg Times,* November 13, 2004, p. 16A. Deggans criticizes mainstream Democrats willing to abandon the cause of same-sex marriage in the face of the its crushing defeat in 11 states in the 2004 election. Deggans, an African-American man married to a white woman, wonders what would have happened if the electorate had been asked to vote on mixed-race marriages in 1968 when the Supreme Court struck down miscegenation laws.

Dinan, Stephen. "House to Debate Court Stripping: Bill Targets Gay 'Marriage' Activism." *Washington Times,* July 22, 2004 p. A8. Representative John Hostettler has introduced the Marriage Protection Act to the House of Representatives. The law would forbid federal courts from ruling on the constitutionality of the 1996 Defense of Marriage Act, which says no state can be forced to recognize a same-sex marriage solemnized in another state.

Duchschere, Kevin. "Is Gay Marriage a Civil-Rights Issue? Five Black Leaders Say It's Not Same." *Minneapolis Star Tribune,* March 26, 2004, p. 1B. A group of Twin Cities black religious leaders that supports a state constitutional amendment defining marriage as between a man and a woman maintain there is no parallel between the African-American struggle to win civil rights and the campaign for gay marriage.

Duin, Julia. "Diocese to Bar Same-Sex 'Marriage': Episcopal Ban in Massachusetts." *Washington Times,* May 14, 2004, p. A1. In a surprise move, Massachusetts Episcopal bishop Thomas Shaw, a liberal supporter of gay marriage, has banned clergy in this diocese from solemnizing same-sex "marriages' when they become legal in the state.

———. "Evangelicals Prefer That States Outlaw Gay 'Marriage': Constitutional Ban Draws Less Support in Poll." *Washington Times,* April 14, 2004, p. A3. Evangelical Christians, estimated at 32 percent of the American population, want gay marriage outlawed—but by state legislatures, not through a Constitutional amendment.

Egelko, Bob. "Gays Argue for 'Marriage Equality': Court Briefs Charge State Ban Based on 'Archaic Stereotypes.'" *San Francisco Chronicle,* September 3, 2004, p. A1. A dozen gay and lesbian couples and the City of San Francisco have launched a legal attack on California's ban on same-sex marriage, arguing that the law enshrines bigotry, discriminates arbitrarily, and violates a Constitutional right to marry one's chosen partner.

———. "Judge Strikes Down Ban on Same-Sex Marriage." *San Francisco Chronicle,* March 15, 2005, p. A1. Superior Court judge Richard Kramer has ruled that California's ban on same-sex marriage is unconstitutional, comparing it to archaic laws that once blocked interracial marriage or promoted "separate but equal" segregation.

———. "Same-Sex Marriage Foes Win Right to Proceed with Suits: Ruling Allows Groups to Defend State Law Barring Gay Nuptials." *San Francisco Chronicle,* September 17, 2004, p. B3. The California Supreme Court has ruled that two organizations supporting the state's opposite sex–only marriage law could proceed with their lawsuits challenging San Francisco mayor Gavin Newsom's authorization of marriage licenses to same-sex couples. The groups are concerned that California attorney general Bill Lockyer, a supporter of gay rights, will not defend the law with enough vigor.

———. "Top State Court Voids S.F.'s Gay Marriages: A Mayor Overruled." *San Francisco Chronicle*, August 13, 2004, p. A1. California's highest court unanimously struck down San Francisco's attempt to legalize same-sex marriages. The court stated that Mayor Gavin Newsom had illegally defied the state law that defines marriage as a union between a man and a woman.

Emerson, Bo. "The Longest Race for Karla Drenner: Lawmaker and Marathoner Presses on, Despite Defeat on Gay Marriage Amendment." *Atlanta Journal-Constitution*, November 21, 2004, p. A1. A profile of Georgia state representative Karla Drenner, the first openly gay legislator in the South, who led the failed fight in her state against a constitutional amendment banning same-sex marriage.

Fagan, Amy. "An Early Test for Same-Sex 'Marriage': Floridian Rejects Go-Slow Approach." *Washington Times*, August 12, 2004, p. A1. Lawyer Ellis Rubin is countering the strategy of most national gay rights organizations by pushing ahead with challenges to Florida's heterosexual-only marriage laws. He has filed a federal lawsuit on behalf of a lesbian couple who want Florida to recognize their Canadian marriage.

———. "Federal DOMA Upheld as Constitutional: Lesbian's Challenge to '96 Law Rebuffed in Washington State." *Washington Times*, August 22, 2004, p. A2. A federal judge in Washington State has upheld the federal Defense of Marriage Act as Constitutional, marking the first time a federal court has ruled on the 1996 law, which defines marriage as the union between a man and a woman.

Fischer, Howard, and Patty Machelor. "Mass. Ruling May Help 2 Ariz. Men." *Arizona Daily Star*, February 5, 2004, p. A11. The ruling by the Massachusetts Supreme Judicial Court sanctioning same-sex marriage has emboldened plaintiffs in similar cases across the nation. Here is a report on an Arizona gay couple's efforts to have their partnership legally recognized.

Florio, Gwen. "Issue Shifts from the Bedroom to the Altar: Gay-Marriage Debate Moves to Mainstream." *Denver Post*, July 13, 2003, p. A1. Examines reactions to the gay marriage controversy and the Supreme Court sodomy ruling among citizens in Colorado.

Foderaro, Lisa W. "Taking a Stand Where Church and State Collide." *New York Times*, July 23, 2004, p. B2. A profile of Reverend Dawn Sangrey, a Unitarian minister charged with officiating over marriages that lacked proper licenses when she married several same-sex couples in New Paltz, New York. The charges against her were later dismissed.

Freeman-Jones, Harry. "Same-Sex Marriage Pioneer Sees No Turning Back." *Syracuse Post-Standard*, April 16, 2004, p. A9. Freeman-Jones looks back at his own marriage in 1973, one of the first public gay wedding ceremonies in the

United States, and finds that the arguments and language of those who opposed him and his partner then haven't changed much in 30 years.

Glaberson, William, and Jim Rutenberg. "City to Appeal Move Backing Gay Marriage." *New York Times*, February 6, 2005, p. A1. A day after a judge in Manhattan issued the first New York state court ruling in support of gay marriage, Mayor Michael R. Bloomberg said New York City would appeal the decision.

Goldstein, Richard. "Civil Unions: The Radical Choice." *Advocate*, February 3, 2004, Issue 907, p. 72. Leftist commentator Goldstein argues that civil unions are a radical alternative to the conservative choice of same-sex marriage because they offer more flexibility and divorce civil benefits from institutionalized coupledom.

Gordon, Rachel. "Newsom's Plan for Same-Sex Marriages: Mayor Wants to License Gay and Lesbian Couples." *San Francisco Chronicle*, February 11, 2004, p. A1. San Francisco mayor Gavin Newsom announces plans to begin issuing marriage licenses to same-sex couples in defiance of state law.

Greenhouse, Linda. "Supreme Court Paved Way for Marriage Ruling with Sodomy Law Decision." *New York Times*, November 19, 2003, p. A24. Greenhouse posits that in its sodomy ruling the Supreme Court crafted a strikingly inclusive decision that both apologized for the past and anchored gay rights firmly in the tradition of human rights. This in turn prepared the legal terrain for the Massachusetts ruling mandating same-sex marriage in that state.

Griffith, Victoria. "Children May Hold Key to Gay Marriage: Court Cites Minors' Rights as Reason for Letting Gays Marry." *Financial Times*, November 29, 2003, p. 8. With an estimated nine million U.S. children being raised by gay and lesbian parents, gay rights activists argue that they should not be unfairly penalized because of their parents' sexual orientation.

Grow, Doug. "Gay-Marriage Pioneers, Again: After Fading from Public View, Minnesota Couple Files New Suit." *Minneapolis Star Tribune*, May 20, 2004, p. 2B. Jack Baker and Michael McConnell, a Minnesota couple who first attempted to legally marry in 1971, have filed suit against the IRS, claiming that it has violated their right to due process by refusing to allow them to file a joint tax return.

Gumbel, Andrew. "The Anti-Bohemian, Establishment Man Who Has Defied the White House on Gay Rights: Gavin Newsom, Mayor of San Francisco." *Independent of London*, March 1, 2004, p. 29. An interview with the mayor who chose to defy California state law by authorizing his city clerk to issue marriage licences to same-sex couples.

Gunderson, Julie. "Same-Sex 'Marriage' in the Quad." *Washington Times*, August 8, 2004 p. B5. Gunderson, a senior at St. Olaf's College in Minnesota, a Lutheran school, argues that young people are more tolerant of same-sex marriage than their parents because the current higher education teaching system has abandoned any ethical arguments based on morals.

Haga, Chuck. "A Mother's Love Prompts Vigil at Rally Opposing Gay Marriage." *Minneapolis Star Tribune*, April 2, 2004, p. 1B. Profile of Janelle

Holmvig, heterosexual woman living in Minneapolis, who's become an activist in the effort to legalize same-sex marriage.

Hanley, Robert, and Laura Mansnerus. "Asbury Park Deputy Mayor Officiates at a Gay Marriage." *New York Times*, March 9, 2004, p. B5. The gay marriage movement spreads to New Jersey as the city clerk's office issues marriage licenses to a same-sex couples, and the deputy mayor performs the ceremony.

Hays, Matthew. "Blame Canada." *Advocate*, July 22, 2003, Issue 894, pp. 26–30. Eleven months before gay marriage became legal in Massachusetts, gays and lesbians were able to legally wed in the Canadian province of Ontario.

———. "Dodging the Altar." *Advocate*, May 11, 2004, Issue 914, p. 36. Canadian same-sex couples have not been rushing to the altar after gay marriage became legal in Ontario. Access to universal health care and statutes concerning common law spouses are part of the reason.

Heath, Michael. "Gay Marriage Affirmed; State Court Casts a 'Queer' Eye Toward Wedded Equality." *Syracuse Post-Standard*, November 21, 2003, p. A11. Heath, a minister and psychotherapist, locates the opposition to same-sex marriage in an anxiety with and ignorance about gay and lesbian sexuality.

Herel, Suzanne. "Court Halts Gay Vows; 29-Day Drama: S.F. Unleashed a 'Gay-Marriage Tsunami.'" *San Francisco Chronicle*, March 12, 2004, p. A1. In the wake of the California Supreme Court halting San Francisco's marriage license experiment, Herel recaps the often dramatic 29-day period of same-sex weddings in the city.

Hohler, Bob, and Jayson T. Blair. "O'Donnell Inspires Other Artists: Gays, Lesbians No Longer Limited to Backing up Straights' Ceremonies." *Boston Globe*, February 28, 2004, p. A11. In the wake of comedian Rosie O'Donnell's highly publicized wedding to her female partner in San Francisco, other prominent gay and lesbian celebrities comment on the events taking place there.

Houck, Jeanne. "Group to Fight K.Y. Marriage Ban." *Cincinnati Post*, April 19, 2004, p. A8. Gay rights group organizes to defeat an amendment to the Kentucky state constitution that would outlaw gay marriage.

Hulse, Carl. "On Same-Sex Marriage, Foes Often Seem to Talk Past Each Other." *International Herald Tribune*, March 31, 2004, p. 6. Hulse listens to both sides in the fight over the proposed Constitutional amendment to prohibit gay marriage in the United States, finding that it seems the debate is about everything except whether the government should recognize the marriage of two people of the same sex.

———. "Senate Hears Testimony on a Gay Marriage Amendment." *New York Times*, March 4, 2004, p. A26. The Senate Judiciary Subcommittee on the Constitution hears from activists and scholars both in favor of and in opposition to a Constitutional amendment outlawing same-sex marriage.

Ingram, David. "Bill Acts to Brace Law on Wedlock: GOP State Senator Files to Amend N.C.'s Ban on Gay Unions." *Winston-Salem Journal*, May 13, 2004, p. A1. The North Carolina senate's top Republican, Senator James Forrester, has filed a bill to amend the state constitution, which would ban civil marriage and all other legal unions between two people of the same sex.

Jacobs, Andrew. "Judge in New Jersey Hears Arguments on Gay Marriage." *New York Times*, June 28, 2003, p. B4. In a state known for its liberal judicial establishment, large numbers of gay and lesbian families, and moderate electorate, seven same-sex couples file suit demanding the same marital rights as straight couples.

Jacobs, Sonji. "Gay Marriage Ban Headed to Court." *Atlanta Journal-Constitution.* November 3, 2004, p. EX14. Georgia residents overwhelmingly vote, by a margin of 77 percent to 23 percent, to amend their state's constitution and ban same-sex marriage. They join citizens in 10 other states who approved similar amendments on November 2. Gay rights activists vow to challenge the constitutionality of the measure in court.

———. "Gay Marriage Ban Nixed in Louisiana." *Atlanta Journal-Constitution*, October 6, 2004, p. A1. Louisiana judge William Morvant has tossed out a constitutional amendment that the state's voters approved in September to ban same-sex marriage. The judge ruled that the amendment was invalid because it pertains not only to same-sex marriage but also to civil unions, therefore violating the state's single-subject rule.

———. "Marriage Measure Challenged: Suit Charges Amendment Is Unlawful." *Atlanta Journal-Constitution*, November 10, 2004, p. B1. The American Civil Liberties Union and Lambda Legal have filed suit in Georgia to block that state's constitutional amendment banning same-sex marriage from going into effect. The organizations argue that it violates Georgia's single-subject rule because it addresses civil unions in addition to marriage.

Janolsky, Michael. "Social Conservatives Criticize Cheney on Same-Sex Marriage." *New York Times*, August 26, 2004, p. A25. Vice President Dick Cheney, whose daughter Mary is an out lesbian, has publicly expressed his opposition to a proposed Constitutional amendment banning same-sex marriage. Contrary to the George W. Bush administration's position, Cheney believes the matter should be left to each state to decide.

Johnson, Kirk. "A Lightning Rod on Gay Marriage, and Her Split Town." *New York Times*, March 11, 2004, p. A14. Profile of Representative Marilyn Musgrave from Greeley, Colorado, the sponsor of a proposed amendment to the U.S. Constitution that would ban same-sex marriage.

Keane, Thomas M., Jr. "Romney Obsesses over Gay Weddings." *Boston Herald*, April 28, 2004, p. 31. Keane takes Massachusetts govenor Mitt Romney to task for this "frenzied" efforts to find a way around his state's supreme judicial court ruling on gay marriage.

Kemper, Bob. "Gay Republicans Turn Against Bush: Marriage-Ban Proposal Angers Groups." *Seattle Times*, March 3, 2004, p. A4. Two of the largest Republican gay rights groups, Log Cabin Republicans and the Republican Unity Coalition, who helped deliver one million votes to President George W. Bush in 2000, announce plans to organize against his anti–gay marriage stance.

Kim, Eun-Kyung. "Gay Marriage Would Make Their Families Official, Kids Say: They Say Recognition for Parents Is Overdue." *St. Louis Post-Dispatch*,

April 7, 2004, p. A1. Kim profiles several children of same-sex couples who welcome the prospect of gay marriage as an opportunity to finally feel like they are recognized as being part of a family.

Kinsley, Michael. "A New Proposal: End Marriage; At Least, Get Government Out of It." *Minneapolis Star Tribune*, July 14, 2003, p. 13A. Kinsley calls for the complete privatization of marriage by ending the institution of government-sanctioned coupling as we now know it.

Kirkpatrick, David D. "Backers of Gay Marriage Ban Find Tepid Response in Pews." *New York Times*, May 16, 2004, p. A1. An alliance of conservative Christians was threatening a churchgoer revolt unless President George W. Bush championed an amendment banning same-sex marriage, but members say they have been surprised and disappointed by what they call a tepid response from the pews.

———. "Gay Marriage Opponents Keep Low Profile for Now." *New York Times*, May 17, 2004, p. A16. The main opponents of same-sex marriage in Massachusetts, most of them conservative Christians, said they planned to keep quiet and stay out of the way as gay people began celebrating their first marriages.

———. "Rally Against Gay Marriage Draws Thousands to Capital." *New York Times*, Oct 16, 2004, p. A12. Tens of thousands of conservative Christians gather on the Mall in Washington, D.C., for a demonstration against same-sex marriage that doubled as a rally to turn out conservative Christian voters on Election Day.

Koppelman, Andrew, and Steven Lubet. "The Marriage Amendment Mistake: Ban on Gay Unions Would Deny Power Reserved to States." *Newark Star-Ledger*, February 11, 2004, Vol. 3:11, pp. 122–125 ff. The writers editorialize against the proposed same-sex marriage amendment on the grounds that it would undermine the integrity of the Constitution by upsetting the balance between the states and the federal government.

Kramer, Staci D. "Same-Sex Marriage Takes a Hit: Missouri Vote Defining Marriage as Between a Man and a Woman May Boost Other State Drives." *Christian Science Monitor*, August 5, 2004, p. 1. Missouri has amended its constitution to forbid same-sex marriage. Seventy percent of voters approved a ballot measure declaring marriage to "only exist between a man and a woman."

Krauss, Clifford. "Canadian Leaders Agree to Propose Gay Marriage Law." *New York Times*, June 18, 2003, p. A1. The Canadian cabinet approves a new national policy to open marriage to gay couples, paving the way for Canada to become the third country to allow same-sex unions.

Kurtz, Howard. "Same-Sex Marriage Difficult Territory for Nation's Media: Critics Say Coverage of Controversy Has Been out of Context, Too Political." *Houston Chronicle*, March 7, 2004, p. 17. Kurtz dissects the media's spin on the San Francisco marriage controversy and finds a decidedly liberal bias in the coverage that ignores context.

Kurtz, Stanley. "Gay Priests and Gay Marriage." *Nation*, June 3, 2002, Vol. 54:10, pp. 33–36. Kurtz draws parallels between the Catholic Church's sexual abuse scandal and the gay marriage controversy. He argues that the monogamous ethos of traditional marriage would be subverted by homosexual promiscuity since gay priests weren't able to maintain sexual restraint, despite their religious vows.

Larini, Rudy. "As Trend Grows, Activists Seek Same-Sex Weddings in N.J.: Gay Advocacy Groups Draw Parallel to Anti–Jim Crow Efforts at Dawn of Civil Rights Era." *Newark Star-Ledger,* March 5, 2004, p. 1. Gay rights advocates in New Jersey are keeping a close watch on the same-sex marriages occurring across the country, hoping the ceremonies raise public awareness of the issue while their own legal challenge wends its way through the court system.

Lelchuk, Ilene. "Son of Gay Marriage Foe Weds in San Francisco: Sen. Knight Wrote State Law Banning Same-Sex Unions." *San Francisco Chronicle*, March 10, 2004, p. A12. David Knight, son of state senator William "Pete" Knight, the author of the California ballot measure that banned same-sex marriage, weds his partner of 10 years in a ceremony at San Francisco City Hall.

Lewis, Neil A. "Bush Seeking Means to Block Gay Marriage: White House Puts Lawyers on the Case." *International Herald Tribune*, August 1, 2003, p. 4. In his first public comments regarding homosexuals since the Supreme Court's sodomy decision, President George W. Bush, while reminding the nation that we are all sinners, states his conviction that marriage should remain between one man and one woman.

Liptak, Adam. "Caution in Court for Gay Rights Groups."*New York Times*, November 12, 2004, p. A16. Fearful that aggressive action could backfire and generate public hostility, some gay rights groups plan to limit the scope of their legal challenges to the constitutional amendments banning gay marriage that were passed by 11 states on November 2.

———. "Law on Interracial Unions Illuminates Debate on Gays." *International Herald Tribune*, March 18, 2004, p. 8. President George W. Bush's assertion that the Constitution's full faith and credit clause would require other states to recognize same-sex marriages solemnized in Massachusetts is challenged by legal scholars citing past antimiscegenation laws.

———. "A Troubled 'Marriage.'" *New York Times*, April 1, 2004, p. A26. Liptak dissects the Massachusetts Supreme Judicial Court ruling sanctioning same-sex marriage and finds the arguments on both sides largely hinge on the language used to describe the benefits granted to gay couples.

Lochhead, Carolyn. "Annie Has 2 Moms—and They Sued the State." *San Francisco Chronicle*, May 17, 2004, p. A11. Profile of Julie and Hillary Goodridge, the lesbian couple from Boston who were the lead plaintiffs in the Massachusetts case that established same-sex marriage in that state.

———. "Lawyer's Gay Rights Strategy—Patience While Public Adjusts." *San Francisco Chronicle*, May 24, 2004, p. A1. An interview with Mary Bonauto, the lead attorney for Gay and Lesbian Advocates and Defenders, who successfully argued the gay marriage case before the Massachusetts Supreme Court. She urges caution among activists to give mainstream America a chance to adjust to the new gay marriage reality.

————. "Massachusetts Court Allows Gay Marriage; Bush Says He'll Fight for Constitutional Ban on Unions." *San Francisco Chronicle*, November 19, 2003, p. A1. The Massachusetts Supreme Judicial Court rules 4–3 that gays and lesbians have a right to full civil marriage, igniting a ferocious political battle over one of the most controversial social issues in contemporary America.

————. "Pivotal Day for Gay Marriage in U.S. Nears: Massachusetts Move to Legalize Weddings May Intensify Backlash in Other States." *San Francisco Chronicle*, May 2, 2004, p. A1. On May 17, 2004, for the first time in U.S. history, a state will begin granting marriage licenses to homosexuals, but the new Massachusetts reality has set off a ferocious backlash across the country.

————. "Same-Sex Marriage Foe Assails Constitutional Ban; Barr Says Issue Should Be Decided by States." *San Francisco Chronicle*, March 31, 2004, p. A4. In testimony before the House Judiciary Committee, former Georgia representative Bob Barr, author of the 1996 Defense of Marriage Act, while still opposing gay same-sex marriage, vigorously argued against a Constitutional amendment on the matter.

————. "Same-Sex Marriage Momentum Stuns Both Its Backers and Foes." *San Francisco Chronicle*, March 5, 2004, p. A19. President George W. Bush's pledge in his State of the Union address in late January 2004 to defend traditional marriage has touched off a reaction that is rippling across the country. An issue that was considered too radical to even be seriously discussed a year prior is now dominating political discourse.

Lochhead, Carolyn. "Senate Kills Gay Marriage Ban: Activists Hail Defeat of Constitutional Amendment—Backers Vow to Try Again." *San Francisco Chronicle*, July 15, 2004 p. A1. Calling it the "biggest win in the history of the lesbian and gay civil rights movement," activists celebrated the defeat in the U.S. Senate of a proposed Constitutional amendment that would have limited marriage to one man and one woman. Supporters of the measure vowed to introduce legislation into the House of Representatives later that year.

Lueck, Thomas J. "Police Charge New Paltz Mayor for Marrying Same-Sex Couples." *New York Times*, March 3, 2004, p. B4. The mayor of New Paltz, New York, Jason West, is charged with solemnizing a marriage without a license, a misdemeanor under New York state law.

Lyons, Tom. "Turning Straight a Rarity, so Preach Gay Civil Unions as Next Best Thing." *Sarasota Herald-Tribune*, August 3, 2003, p. BS1. Lyons argues that since most homosexuals can't be expected to become straight, the best way to ensure the containment of diseases like AIDS is to encourage gays to enter into monogamous relationships through civil unions.

Martin, Jonathan. "Gay-Marriage Foes in Oregon to Seek Injunction Today." *Seattle Times*, March 5, 2004, p. C3. A newly formed group called the Defense of Marriage Coalition announced plans to file a court injunction today against Multnomah County, Oregon, which has issued 786 marriage licenses (as of the date of this article) since announcing it would accept applications from same-sex couples.

Massachusetts Supreme Court. "Excerpts from Ruling on Gay Marriage." *New York Times*, February 5, 2004, p. A27. Excerpts from the 4-3 opinion in *Goodridge vs. Department of Public Health*, which mandates that the state of Massachusetts may not offer civil unions as an acceptable alternative to same-sex marriage.

Marech, Rona. "Top Court in Canada OKs Gay Marriage: Lawmakers Sought Ruling Before Introducing Bill." *San Francisco Chronicle*, December 10, 2004, p. A1. In a landmark decision, Canada's Supreme Court has ruled that the Canadian government can legally extend marriage rights to same-sex couples, paving the way for nationwide legislation that would allow same-sex couples to marry in every province.

McCall, William. "Oregon High Court Pondering Complex Issue: Gay Marriage." *Seattle Times*, December 16, 2004, p. B1. The Oregon Supreme Court must decide if more than 3,000 marriage licenses issued to same-sex couples in Multnomah County during 2004 are still valid after Oregon citizens voted to amend the state constitution to forbid same-sex marriages.

Miller, Sara B. "The Judge on the Front Lines of Culture War; Massachusetts' Top Justice Made History, and Drew Fury, with Tuesday's Ruling on Gay Marriage." *Christian Science Monitor*, November 21, 2003, p. 1. Profile of the chief justice of the Massachusetts Supreme Judicial Court, South African–born Margaret Marshall. She is the author of the landmark opinion that same-sex couples are entitled to wed.

Mitchell, Shawn. "'Civil' Conflict Proposal Subverts Marriage and Its Foundations and Hurts Children." *Rocky Mountain News*, January 10, 2004, p. 12C. Mitchell opposes same-sex marriage for two reasons: the first is that a gay union deprives children of role modeling by both a mother and a father, and the second is that it undermines the social and legal underpinnings of the institution for others.

Mulkern, Anne C. "Canada Offers Preview of Gay-Marriage Impacts."*Denver Post*, July 4, 2004, p. A1. At the time this article was published, three Canadian provinces—Ontario, Quebec, and Vancouver—had legalized same-sex marriage, and the Canadian government was considering doing the same. Although one-half of Canadians oppose gay marriage, the same percentage as in the United States, the issue has proven far less volatile in Canada than in the United States.

———. "Gay-Marriage Ban Fails: Procedural Vote Scraps Measure."*Denver Post*, July 15, 2004, p. A1. A proposal to end debate on a proposed Constitutional amendment to ban same-sex marriage and proceed to an up-or-down vote on its merits failed to garner enough support in the U.S. Senate, killing its chances in that body for the current session.

Murphy, Dean E., and Christine Hauser. "California Supreme Court Voids San Francisco's Gay Marriages." *International Herald Tribune*, August 13, 2004, p. 5. In a sharp setback for gay rights groups, the California Supreme Court has ruled that more than 4,000 same-sex marriage licenses issued in San Francisco in February 2004 were "void and of no legal effect." The lawsuit seeking to block the licenses was brought by the state's attorney general and a conservative Christian group.

Murphy, Dean E. "Court in California Hears Gay Marriage Arguments." *New York Times*, December 23, 2004, p. A14. Judge Richard A. Kramer heard opening arguments in a civil case brought by the City of San Francisco and more than a dozen same-sex couples seeking to overturn a California law defining marriage as between one man and one woman. Defending the law are state attorney general Bill Lockyer and several Christian and conservative organizations.

———. "San Francisco Forced to Halt Gay Marriages." *New York Times*, March 12, 2004, p. A1. The California Supreme Court orders the City of San Francisco to stop issuing marriage licenses to same-sex couples.

———. "San Francisco Married 4,037 Same-Sex Pairs from 46 States." *New York Times*, March 18, 2004, p. A26. A demographic analysis of the data gathered by the San Francisco city government from gay men and lesbians applying for marriage licences there supports national trends for same-sex couples.

———. "San Francisco Sees Tide Shift in the Battle over Marriage." *New York Times*, March 13, 2004, p. A12. Reaction to the California Supreme Court ruling that the City of San Francisco must desist in issuing same-sex marriage licenses.

———. "Schwarzenegger Backs Off His Stance Against Gay Marriage." *New York Times*, March 3, 2004, p. A12. The Hollywood movie star and popular governor of California publically declares that the citizens of the state would have his complete support if they decided to amend the family code to allow for same-sex marriage.

O'Brien, Kevin. "Majority Should Speak Up: Opponents of Same-Sex Marriage Must Be Willing to Say 'We Think It's Wrong, and We're Not Going to Condone It.'" *Cleveland Plain Dealer*, March 10, 2004, p. B9. O'Brien sees the foes of gay marriage up against powerful liberal forces in the media and judiciary that are determined to desensitize the American citizenry to what he deems a "perversion."

Paul, Noel C. "Massachusetts as Gay Wedding Capital: Massachusetts' Move Will Ricochet across Nation as Out-of-Staters Take Licenses Home." *Christian Science Monitor*, May 17, 2004, p. 1. Hundreds of gay and lesbian couples are expected to apply at Massachusetts's town and city halls for marriage licenses, and couples from California to New York will be among those exchanging vows. As they return home, they are expected to challenge local laws.

Peter, Jennifer. "Boston at Center of Gay Marriage Furor: Thousands Express Support, Opposition to Proposed Ban." *Houston Chronicle*, February 11, 2004, p. 3. Gay rights activists, conservative leaders, and media from around the globe converge on the Massachusetts Statehouse as lawmakers take up a constitutional amendment to ban gay marriage.

Pollitt, Katha. "Adam and Steve—Together at Last." *Nation*, December 15, 2003, Vol. 277:20, p. 9. Pollit explains her supportive stance on the decision of the Massachusetts Supreme Court to declare that gay marriage is a constitutional right. She examines several contrary arguments and finds them all lacking.

Pople, Laura, and John Tomicki. "Debating Same-Sex Marriage." *Newark Star-Ledger*, April 27, 2003, p. 1. In an e-mail exchange, Pople, the president of the New Jersey Gay & Lesbian Coalition, and Tomicki, the executive director of the conservative League of American Families, debate the moral and legal issues surrounding gay marriage.

———. "Same-Sex Newlyweds Are Trickling in for Divorces." *Wisconsin State Journal*, December 11, 2004, p. A6. Less than seven months after same-sex couples began to wed legally in Massachusetts, the state is seeing its first gay divorces. Opponents to gay marriage point to the divorces as proof that gay and lesbian couples are incapable of sustaining committed relationships, while gay marriage advocates say the rate of divorce is no greater than that of heterosexual couples.

Preusch, Matthew. "Oregon County, With Portland, Offers Same-Sex Marriages." *New York Times*, March 4, 2004, p. A26. Oregon's most populous county begins issuing marriage licenses to same-sex couples, becoming a flashpoint in the national debate over gay marriage.

———. "Oregonians Look to One Suit to Settle Gay Marriage Issue." *New York Times*, March 25, 2004, p. A16. The American Civil Liberties Union files suit in Portland, Oregon, on behalf of nine same-sex couples contending that Oregon's law limiting marriage to a man and woman violates the state constitution.

Rauch, Jonathan. "Imperfect Unions." *New York Times*, August 15, 2004, p. WK11. Gay conservative Jonathan Rauch comments on New Jersey governor James McGreevey's decision to resign his office after publicly declaring his homosexuality and acknowledging an extramarital affair with another man. In Rauch's view, the situation is further proof of the need to allow gay men and lesbians to enter into same-sex marriages, saying that otherwise they will continue to engage in immature and irresponsible actions, as McGreevey did.

Reinert, Patty. "Top Court Rejects Gay Marriage Challenge: Massachusetts' Law That Allows Same-Sex Unions Remains Intact." *Houston Chronicle*, November 30, 2004. p.1. The U.S. Supreme Court has rejected a challenge to Massachusetts's gay marriage law, leaving intact a state court ruling that has led to thousands of weddings for same-sex couples and a national debate on the issue. The case was filed by the Liberty Counsel, a Florida-based group that opposes gay rights.

Rosen, Jeffrey. "Yawn." *New Republic*, May 3, 2004, Vol. 230:16, p. 18. Rosen argues that May 17, 2004, when same-sex couples gained the right to marry in Massachusetts, did not mark the beginning of a major political or legal shift in the United States and that activists are better served politically by seeking change through legislatures rather than the courts.

Rowe, Claudia. "Matt Coles, Director of the ACLU's Lesbian and Gay Rights Project." *Seattle Post-Intelligencer*, July 14, 2004, p. B1. In an interview, Coles, who heads the American Civil Liberties Union (ACLU) unit challenging heterosexual-only state marriage laws, analyzes the waning congressional support for the federal gay marriage amendment and discusses the fight to change Washington State's marriage laws.

————. "Ministers to Protest Gay Marriages: Conservative Group to Back Lawsuit Aimed at Ending City Recognition." *Seattle Post-Intelligencer*, March 11, 2004, p. B1. Report on civil protest in support of a lawsuit planned by the American Family Association to block Seattle mayor Greg Nickels' directive to honor same-sex marriages officiated in other jurisdictions.

————. "Oregon County Defies State on Gay Marriage: Officials Continue to Issue Same-Sex Wedding Licenses." *Seattle Post-Intelligencer*, March 16, 2004, p. A1. Multnomah County commissioners have refused to stop issuing marriage licenses to same-sex couples on the grounds that the Oregon state constitution forbids discrimination against any class of people.

Rubenstein, William B. "Hiding Behind the Constitution." *New York Times*, March 20, 2004, p. A13. Rubenstein posits that both Republicans and Democrats are avoiding the main issue of the gay marriage debate by seeking refuge in the abstractions of the Constitution, framing the debate as one about separation of powers and federalism.

Ruiz, Rosanna. "Anti-Gay Policies Blasted: Black Same-Sex Couples Could Be Doubly Harmed, Report Concludes." *Houston Chronicle*, October 7, 2004, p. 1. A report released jointly by the National Gay and Lesbian Task Force and the National Black Justice Coalition concludes that African-American same-sex couples would be disproportionately harmed by anti–gay marriage policies because they are already at a disadvantage in terms of income and housing compared to black heterosexual couples.

Sanchez, Rene. "Gay Unions Go Before Calif. Court." *Washington Post*, May 26, 2004, A3. California's Supreme Court has expressed serious doubts that San Francisco city officials had the right to issue marriage licenses to nearly 4,000 gay and lesbian couples earlier this year in defiance of state law.

Santora, Marc. "Spitzer's Opinion Mixed on Status of Gay Marriage." *New York Times*, March 4, 2004, p. A1. New York attorney general Eliot Spitzer issues a legal opinion that New York must recognize same-sex marriages performed in other states, but that state law does not permit such ceremonies inside the state itself.

Santora, Marc, and Thomas Crampton. "Same-Sex Weddings in Upstate Village Test New York Law." *New York Times*, February 28, 2004, p. A1. Reports on the performance of marriage ceremonies for gay men and lesbians in the village of New Paltz, New York. Governor George Pataki has ordered Attorney General Eliot Spitzer to stop the weddings, but Spitzer has refused.

Scagliotti, John. "Straight, Not Narrow." *Nation*, May 31, 2004, vol. 278:21, p. 6. Scagliotti argues that same-sex marriage is a defining issue for straight progressives, as well as for gays. He views conservatives as manipulating the idea of a heterosexual majority to drive American politics to the Right.

Schreiner, Bruce. "Group Delivers Message on Gay Marriage." *Kentucky Post*, April 12, 2004, p. A9. Report on protests in the Kentucky state capital of

Frankfort led by Kent Ostrander of the Family Foundation in favor of an amendment to the state constitution banning gay marriage.

Schwanberg, Robert. "Appeals Court Hears Gay-Marriage Case: Suit Pits Rights of Same-Sex Couples Against the 'Specter' of Polygamy." *Newark Star-Ledger*, December 8, 2004, p. 15. In a case that could make New Jersey the second state to allow people of the same sex to marry, three appellate division judges heard arguments in a case seeking to overturn that state's refusal to permit gay marriages.

Seelye, Katharine Q., and Janet Elder. "Strong Support Is Found for Ban on Gay Marriage." *New York Times*, December 21, 2003, p. A1. A New York Times/CBS News poll finds that 55 percent of Americans support a Constitutional amendment that would limit the right of marriage to a man and woman.

Silvestrini, Elaine. "Appeals Dropped on Gay Marriage." *Tampa Tribune*, January 26, 2005, p.1. A U.S. District Court in Florida has ruled that the state does not have to recognize the marriages of two lesbian couples in Massachusetts and Canada.

Smith, Bill. "Backers Cite Values, God in Rural Vote." *St. Louis Post-Dispatch*, August 8, 2004, p. B1. A measure on the Missouri ballot to amend the state constitution to outlaw gay marriage garnered 70 percent of the vote, mostly from the state's rural counties. Religious conservatives from those areas explain why they voted for the amendment.

Spencer, Carrie. "Ohio Backs Gay-Marriage Ban." *Cincinnati Post*, November 3, 2004, p. A11. Ohioans approve by a margin of 62 percent to 38 percent a measure to amend their state's constitution to ban same-sex marriages. The amendment goes beyond outlawing homosexual marriage to prohibit state and local governments from granting legal recognition to unmarried couples of either sex.

Sprengelmeyer, M.E. "Gay Marriage Ban Fails; Musgrave's Amendment Falls Short in House Vote." *Rocky Mountain News*, October 1, 2004, p. 4A. Backers of Colorado congresswoman Marilyn Musgrave's proposed Marriage Protection Amendment—a law that would enshrine a ban against same-sex marriage in the U.S. Constitution—fall far short of the two-thirds vote in the House of Representatives needed to pass a Constitutional amendment.

St. Clair, Stacy. "Gay Rights Protest Closes Marriage License Bureau." *Arlington Heights Daily Herald*, May 18, 2004, p. 13. Chanting "Marry us, or marry no one," gay rights activists stage a sit-in at the Cook County, Illinois, marriage license bureau, shutting it down on the same day gay marriage became legal in Massachusetts.

Steinhauer, Jennifer. "Law Dept. Backs Barring Marriage Licenses for Gays." *New York Times*, March 4, 2004, p. B6. In the city with the largest gay and lesbian population in the country, the New York municipal law department has instructed the city clerk that same-sex couples should be denied marriage licenses.

Sullivan, Andrew. "Why the M Word Matters to Me." *Time*, February 16, 2004, Vol. 163:7, p. 104. Conservative gay commentator Sullivan presents his views on the importance of marriage to gay couples and states his belief that marriage will allow homosexuals to feel pride for themselves and their partner in society.

Szaniszlo, Marie. "Some Say Showing Is Offensive." *Boston Herald*, March 29, 2004, p. 4. In the midst of the state's gay marriage debate, the Massachusetts Catholic Conference produces a video entitled "Same-Sex Unions: Truth and Consequences" that claims civil unions would discriminate against the poor.

Tanner, Robert. "Attorneys General Wrestle with Gay Marriage." *Cincinnati Post*, March 5, 2004, p. A6. As municipalities across the nation engage in civil disobedience by issuing marriage licenses to same-sex couples, the chief law enforcers in each state are faced with tough decisions about how to proceed.

Tavernise, Sabrina. "New York Judge Opens a Window to Gay Marriage." *New York Times*, February 5, 2005, p. A1. New York State judge Doris Ling-Cohan has ruled that a state law effectively denying gay couples the right to marry violated the state constitution, a decision that raised the possibility that New York City would begin issuing marriage licenses to same-sex couples.

Tharpe, Jim. "Face-Off Moves to Capitol: Gay Marriage Ban Proposal Draws Activists on Both Sides of the Issue to Rallies Downtown." *Atlanta Journal-Constitution*, March 1, 2004, p. A1. Amid pro– and anti–gay marriage rallies on the Georgia Capitol steps, legislators vote on an amendment to the state constitution that would establish marriage as only between one man and one woman.

———. "Gay Marriage Ban Amendment Passes: Georgia Voters to Decide Issue in November." *Atlanta Journal-Constitution*, April 1, 2004, p. A1. The Georgia House of Representatives narrowly endorses a referendum that would put before Georgia voters an amendment to the state constitution outlawing same-sex marriage.

Theis, Sandy, and Barb Galbincea. "Heights Officials, Colleges Take 'Sue Me' Stance on Marriage Law." *Cleveland Plain Dealer*, December 2, 2004, p. A1. As Ohio's new constitutional amendment banning any legal arrangements granting same-sex couples marriage rights goes into effect, local municipalities and public colleges have announced their intentions to continue to offer domestic partnership benefits. Supporters of the new law say they will take the institutions to court to stop them from offering the benefits.

Tucker, Cynthia. "Bible Verses Used as 'Bible Versus.'" *Atlanta Journal-Constitution*, November 7, 2004, p. D8. Tucker reminds readers that slavery advocates in the 19th century used biblical passages to justify that institution's continued existence as she criticizes the black community's support for anti–gay marriage amendments.

———. "It's Easy as Sin to Target Gays." *Atlanta Journal-Constitution*, April 4, 2004, p. D6. Tucker has harsh words for black ministers in Georgia who have publicly advocated that the state legislature pass a constitutional amendment that would ban same-sex marriage in that state.

Turnbull, Lornet, Keith Ervin, and Bob Young. "Marriage Licenses Denied; Gays Take County to Court; Sims Is Both Defendant, Supporter; Nickels Acts to Recognize Unions." *Seattle Times*, March 9, 2004, p. A1. Six same-sex couples file suit to challenge Washington State's Defense of Marriage Act, and the mayor of Seattle, Greg Nickels, issues an executive order recognizing gay unions of city employees who marry elsewhere.

Von Sternberg, Bob. "Foes of Gay Marriage Press for More Bans." *Minneapolis Star Tribune*. December 26, 2004, p. 14A. After voters in 11 states vote overwhelmingly to prohibit same-sex marriage, opponents of the concept are pushing ahead to enact bans in as many as 15 more states in 2006. Victories in all of these elections would make anti–gay marriage amendments the law in more than half of the states in the nation.

Walters, Steven, and Stacy Forster. "Wisconsin Assembly Votes to Block Same-Sex Marriage." *Milwaukee Journal Sentinel*, March 5, 2004, p. E4. After a marathon 14-hour session, the Wisconsin State Assembly overwhelmingly endorses a state constitutional amendment to ban gay marriages. The measure is expected to easily pass the state senate.

Weinkopf, Chris. "California's State of the Union: Traditional Family Is 'Rational Basis.'" *Los Angeles Daily News*, March 20, 2005, p. V1. Weinkopf argues that marriage is not a civil right, like voting, but rather a combination of subsidy and coercion designed to encourage a behavior—the formation of monogamous, procreative unions.

Wetzstein, Cheryl. "Gay 'Marriage' Licenses Halted; Both Sides Claim Victory in Oregon Judge's Ruling." *Washington Times*, April 21, 2004, p. A4. Judge Frank Bearden has halted Multnomah County, Oregon, officials from issuing more gay marriage licenses, but has ruled that Oregon must recognize the 3,000 licenses already granted to same-sex couples.

———. "Gay 'Marriage' Ruling Contested: Foes Sue, Say Massachusetts Court Lacks Authority." *Washington Times*, April 28, 2004, p. A4. A bipartisan group of Massachusetts lawmakers file a lawsuit challenging the authority of the state's highest court to legalize same-sex marriage; they ask that the supreme court extend its stay of the decision past the May 17 deadline.

Williams, Beth. "Gays Study Canadian Ruling on Marriage." *Wisconsin State Journal*, July 6, 2003, p. A1. Some same-sex couples in Wisconsin have crossed the U.S.-Canadian border to get married in Ontario. But legislators in the state say there is no way the marriages will be legally recognized once the partners return to the States.

Wright, Erik Olin. "Civil Union, Not Marriage, Licenses Needed." *Capital Times*, March 17, 2004, p. 9A. Wright proposed a solution to the conflict between religious conviction and civil justice: The state should stop issuing marriage licenses altogether and replace them with civil union licenses for all couples. Religious institutions are then free to "marry" whomever they want.

Wright, Jeff. "Marriage Measure Hits Home in Oregon." *Eugene Register-Guard*, September 6, 2004, p. A1. Oregon is one of 12 states where voters will weigh in on "defense of marriage" amendments in November 2004. Because polls show Oregon voters equally divided on whether or not to support the ballot measure, both pro– and anti–gay rights national organizations are pouring money into the state in an effort to sway the electorate.

Wolfe, Dan. "Gay Marriage Amendment: Put Sacred Institution Beyond Courts' Reach." *Atlanta Journal-Constitution*, November 1, 2004, p. A13. Wolfe, a conservative Christian, asserts that marriage is neither defined nor bestowed by government but rather is the creation of civilization and God. He advocates passage of the amendment to Georgia's state's constitution that would ban same-sex marriage.

Wooten, Jim. "Marriage Is Amendment's Only Subject." *Atlanta Journal-Constitution*, November 16, 2004, p. A15. Georgia recently passed a constitutional amendment outlawing same-sex marriages and any legal arrangements that confer marriage-like rights on same-sex unions. Wooten argues that challenges to the amendment are based on fallacious reasoning. Gay marriage proponents say the amendment violates Georgia's law against having multiple subjects in the same amendment—in this case, both marriage and domestic partnership—but Wooten argues the second part of the amendment merely refines the definition of marriage.

Yardley, William. "Move Is Made in Connecticut Courts to Legalize Gay Marriage." *New York Times*, August 26, 2004, p. B5. A gay rights group that won a Massachusetts case legalizing gay marriage has announced a similar suit in Connecticut. Seven couples are plaintiffs in the suit, which cites several recent pieces of legislation expanding the rights of Connecticut same-sex couples as their reason for seeking full marriage protections there.

York, Amanda. "Critics See Problems in Gay Marriage Ban." *Kentucky Post*, October 26, 2004, p. A8. The amendment that writes a prohibition against gay marriage into the state constitution could pose problems for straight people in Kentucky, say legal experts who oppose the measure. The amendment declares that any legal status similar to marriage is invalid for unmarried people.

Zernike, Kate. "Groups Vow Not to Let Losses Dash Gay Rights." *New York Times*, November 14, 2004, p. A30. In the wake of election-day victories in 11 states for anti–gay marriage amendments, activists gathered at a conference of the National Gay and Lesbian Task Force to strategize about how to proceed within what many view as a hostile climate for gay civil rights.

MILITARY

Biederman, Patricia Ward. "For Gays, Secrecy in Love, War." *L. A. Times*, April 17, 2003, p. A1. Examines the unique burden of the partners of gay and lesbian military personnel during wartime.

Blume, Robyn E. "'Don't Ask, Don't Tell' Rules Don't Make Sense." *St. Petersburg Times*, April 27, 2003, p. 1D. Blumner asks which is more important: defeating terrorism or maintaining discrimination against gays and lesbians in the armed services? She believes maintaining present polices will only hurt the war effort.

Dillon, Sam. "Law Schools Seek to Regain Ability to Bar Military Recruiters." *New York Times*, September 20, 2003, p. A14. The Solomon amendment, passed by Congress in 1995, denies federal funding to any college or university that bars military recruiters from its campus. Now a coalition of law schools is suing the federal government, claiming the law violates their First Amendment right to academic freedom.

Egelko, Bob. "Gay and Lesbian Republicans Sue over 'Don't Ask, Don't Tell.'" *San Francisco Chronicle*, October 13, 2004, p. A3. Log Cabin Republicans, a gay conservative political group, have filed a lawsuit in Lost Angeles challenging the "don't ask, don't tell" policy, which prohibits gays and lesbians from serving openly in the armed forces. The suit contends that previous rulings upholding the 1993 policy have been undermined by recent U.S. Supreme Court rulings on gay rights.

Feagler, Dick. "Military Lets Go of Gays Who Keep Us Safe." *Cleveland Plain Dealer*, February 27, 2005, p. H1. Feagler contrasts the actions of the U.S. Department of Defense, which has spent $200 million to ferret out suspected gay and lesbian troops, with the British Royal Navy, which recently announced an aggressive recruitment campaign within the gay community to enlist new sailors.

Files, John. "Military Appeals Court Reverses Heterosexual Sodomy Conviction." *New York Times*, December 13, 2004, p. A24. A military appeals court has overturned the conviction of a soldier for heterosexual sodomy in a decision that legal scholars and advocates for gay rights say may have broader implications for gay men and lesbians serving in the armed forces. The court based its ruling in part on the Supreme Court decision in *Lawrence v. Texas*, which declared unconstitutional a Texas statute that outlawed sodomy.

———. "Military Said to Oust 10,000 Gays." *International Herald Tribune*, March 25, 2004, p. 4. According to a report by the Servicemembers Legal Defense Network, in the decade since President Bill Clinton and Congress adopted a policy allowing gays to serve in the armed forces as long as they kept their sexual orientation secret, thousands have been discharged on the grounds of failure to do so.

———. "Number of Gays Discharged from Services Drops Again." *New York Times*, February 13, 2005, p. A33. According to Pentagon statistics, the number of men and women discharged from the military because they were discovered to be gay has fallen for the third year in a row, for a decrease of 50 percent since the terrorist attacks on September 11, 2001.

———. "Rules on Gays Exact a Cost in Recruiting, a Study Finds." *New York Times*, February 24, 2005, p. A21. The military has spent more than $200 million to recruit and train personnel to replace troops discharged in the last decade for being openly gay, a new congressional study has found.

Frank, Nathaniel. "Why We Need Gays in the Military." *New York Times*, November 28, 2003, p. A43. On the 10th anniversary of President Clinton's signing of the "don't ask, don't tell" policy into law, Frank presents several reasons why it's in the best interests of the military and the nation for gay men and lesbians to be able to openly serve.

Heredia, Christopher. "Army Discharges 6 Gay Foreign Language Students: Monterey Institute Follows Pentagon Policy Despite Shortage of Speakers of Arabic." *San Francisco Chronicle*, November 15, 2002, p. A2. In a move that crystallized for many gay activists the drawbacks of the Pentagon's "don't ask, don't tell" policy, a group of army linguists studying Middle Eastern languages at the Defense Language Institute have been discharged for being gay.

Martz, Ron. "Difficult Decision for Gay Soldier: Atlantan Among 770 Discharged Last Year." *Atlanta Journal-Constitution*, June 23, 2004, p. A3. Martz profiles Sergeant Brian Muller, a veteran of the Bosnia and Afghanistan missions, who was discharged from the army after disclosing his homosexuality to his commanding officer.

Marquis, Christopher. "Gay Partners, Too, Are Separated by War, and by Their Need for Secrecy." *New York Times*, April 18, 2003, p. B39. Profiles gay couples who served in the Iraq war but have to hide their reunions when they return to the United States because of the "don't ask, don't tell" policy in the Department of Defense.

Neff, Lisa. "Gay in the Navy." *Advocate*, March 30, 2004, Issue 911, p. 32. Offers a look at conditions for openly gay men and women in the U.S. Armed Forces in 2004. In Iraq, they are serving alongside the British armed forces, which lifted its ban on gay military service members in January 2000.

Pitts, Leonard, Jr. "Don't Be Shocked, but There Are Many Gays among Us." *Houston Chronicle*, January 5, 2004, p. 2. Pitts humorously draws parallels between the social anxiety that prevents gay men from officially serving in the military and the cold war paranoia represented by movies such as *Invasion of the Body Snatchers*.

———. "The Military Fears Gays More Than It Fears Osama." *Seattle Times*, November 24, 2002, p. C2. Despite advertising its need for Arabic speakers in the face of the war on terrorism, the military has discharged several linguists studying that language because they are gay.

Smith, Angela D. "Lesbian Hopes Lawsuit Gets Her Back into Army." *Seattle Times*, December 26, 2004, p. B2. A profile of Jennifer McGinn, one of 12 gay and lesbian plaintiffs in a federal lawsuit who are challenging their expulsion from the military because of their sexual orientation. The plaintiffs are basing their lawsuit on the Supreme Court's 2003 decision in *Lawrence v. Texas* that the Fourteenth Amendment guarantees gay people the right to privacy when engaged in consensual intimate relationships.

Stern, Seth. "Law Schools Revolt over Pentagon Recruitment on Campus: Some Have Filed Suit Against the Military in Protest of What They See as Discrimination Towards Gays in the Service." *Christian Science Monitor*, November 6, 2003, p. 2. Some of America's most prestigious law schools are embroiled in a conflict with the Pentagon over its "don't ask, don't tell" policy. The Defense Department wants its military recruiters to have full access to campuses; the schools counter this would violate their antidiscrimination policies.

Uyttebrouck, Olivier. "Probe Wanted into School Military Recruitment Ban." *Albuquerque Journal*, September 28, 2001, p. A1. A state legislator has asked for an investigation into a policy that bars military law recruiters from the University of New Mexico School of Law because of the Defense Departments policy of "don't ask, don't tell."

Zuckerbrod, Nancy. "'Don't Ask, Don't Tell' Dismissals Reach Lowest Level Since '95: Group Attributes Decline to U.S. Wars." *Houston Chronicle*, March 24, 2004, p. 4. According to the Servicemembers Legal Defense Network, the number of gays dismissed from the military under the Pentagon's "don't ask, don't tell" policy has dropped to its lowest level in nine years.

POLITICS

Bancroft, Colette. "Activism Comes Out." *St. Petersburg Times*, March 22, 2004, p. 1E. Profile of Nadine Smith, the first openly lesbian African American to run for civic office in Florida and the head of Equality Florida, the largest gay rights organization in the state.

Beaumont, Peter. "Gay Community Fears New Era of Intolerance: Equality Campaigners Are in Despair at the Rise of the Homophobic Right." *London Observer*, November 7, 2004, p. 17. After 11 states voted strongly against gay marriage and civil unions and elected antigay Republicans to legislative offices, some gay rights advocates are describing the current climate for gay issues as the worst since the Stonewall riots of 1969.

Boyer, Dave. "Rights for Gays Issue in Senate." *Washington Times*, January 29, 2002, p. 8. Senate Democrats have called attention to the deaths of homosexuals on September 11 to promote the passage of a workplace antidiscrimination bill (ENDA) and hate crime legislation.

Broder, John M. "Groups Debate Slower Strategy on Gay Rights." *New York Times*, December 9, 2004, p. A1. Leaders of the gay rights movement are embroiled in a bitter and increasingly public debate over whether they should moderate their goals after 11 states approved constitutional amendments prohibiting same-sex marriages.

Bumiller, Elisabeth. "On Gay Marriage, Bush May Have Said All He's Going To." *New York Times*, March 1, 2004, p. A13. President George W. Bush is caught between opposing forces within his own party over the gay marriage issue: evangelicals who want a ban against same-sex marriage enshrined in the Constitution and more moderate Republicans, including himself, who believe it is a matter for states to decide.

Byrd, Rudolph P., and Nathan McCall. "New Birth Missionary Baptist March: King's Vision Ignored in Hate Crusade." *Atlanta Journal-Constitution*, December 19, 2004, p. D9. After thousands join Bishop Eddie Long and Rev. Bernice King, daughter of Martin Luther King, in a march in Atlanta for traditional family values and against civil rights for gays and lesbians, Byrd and McCall offer the opinion that Long's moral agenda could actually endanger the lives of black people.

Clemetson, Lynette. "Proposed Marriage Ban Splits Washington's Gays." *New York Times*, July 25, 2004, p. A17. The election-year fight over an amendment to the U.S. Constitution has left many gay Republicans in Washington, D.C., stunned and fearful—of other gay people. They claim to be facing increasingly hostile confrontations about their work with conservatives from gay liberals with whom they socialize in the city's clubs and restaurants.

Collins, Michael. "Debate Turning into Farce." *Cincinnati Post*, August 9, 2003, p. A10. Collins ridicules some of the extreme statements made in oposition to gay marriage and the overturning of Texas's sodomy law.

Cook, Rhonda. "Marriage Bout Spurs Gays: Referendum Prompts New Interest in Election." *Atlanta Journal-Constitution*, July 14, 2004, p. B3. In Georgia several openly gay and lesbian candidates are running for state legislature in the November 2004 election. They say the effort to amend that state's constitution to ban same-sex marriage is what convinced them to throw their hats into the political ring.

Dewan, Shaila K. "Pataki Signs Law Protecting Rights of Gays." *New York Times*, December 18, 2002, p. A1. Thirty-one years after the first gay rights bill was introduced into the New York state legislature, Governor George E. Pataki signs into law a bill extending civil rights protections to gays and lesbians in the state.

Diamant, Jeff. "Issue Helps Bush with Blacks: Churchgoers Taking Second Look Due to His Stance on Gay Marriage." *Houston Chronicle*, August 8, 2004, p. 16. In the 2000 election, President George W. Bush received only 8 percent of the African-American vote. Because of his firm opposition to gay marriage, however, more black voters are seriously considering support for him in the 2004 race.

Driscoll, James. "New Gay Political Strategies: Better Results Call for Better Leadership." *Washington Times*, November 18, 2004, p. A21. Driscoll, a member of the Republic gay rights group Log Cabin Republicans, argues that the push for gay marriage in 2004 was a colossal mistake. He identifies four areas he believes the gay rights movement would do better to focus on: the military, the elimination of the "glass ceiling" for gay people in the business world, the election of openly gay politicians, and civil unions.

Epstein, Edward. "Bush's Gay Nominees Draw Little Opposition: S.F. Appointee Sails Through." *San Francisco Chronicle*, December 29, 2002, p. A1. President George W. Bush has nominated six openly gay men for positions in his administration, and the nominations have been approved with comparatively little opposition, in contrast to President Clinton's efforts to appoint an openly gay man to an ambassador position.

Fagan, Amy. "Gay Rights Group Taps Conservatives: Foes of Marriage Amendment Used in Campaign." *Washington Times*, April 26, 2004, p. A4. Report on the Human Rights Campaign, the largest gay rights organization in the nation, and its strategy to defeat the proposed Federal Marriage Amendment by taking advantage of the division among Republicans over the issue.

Frank, Thomas. "Failure Is Not an Option, It's Mandatory." *New York Times*, July 16, 2004, p. A21. Frank examines the debate in the U. S. Senate over the Constitutional marriage amendment and concludes that the measure's defeat was as much a victory for its supporters as its opponents. In his opinion this skirmish in the "culture war" was designed to allow Republicans to paint themselves as "populist."

Gadoua, Renee K. "Debate over Gay Marriage Heats up as States, Courts Consider Legalization." *Syracuse Post-Standard*, August 10, 2003, p. A1. Gadoua identifies six key events driving the change in social and political status for gay men and lesbians: Ontario's legalization of same-sex marriage, the U.S. Supreme Court sodomy ruling, the Massachusetts marriage ruling, President George W. Bush's proposed Constitutional amendment, openly gay Gene Robinson's election as an Episcopal bishop, and the Vatican's call to Catholic politicians to oppose gay marriage.

Goldenberg, Suzanne. "Gay in the USA: Could It Be That America Is Waking up to Homosexuality?" *Guardian of London* July 15, 2003, p. 6. A British view of the sweeping cultural and legal changes occurring on the American political landscape as a result of the gay rights movement and the resulting conservative response.

Goodman, Ellen. "This Is No Time to Retreat on Gay Rights." *St Louis Post-Dispatch*. December 18, 2004, p. 38. In the wake of the anti–gay marriage amendment victories, Goodman asks whether the gay rights movement should wait for mainstream society to become more comfortable with the prospects of change; or whether people only become more comfortable after changes have already occurred.

Goodstein, Laurie, and David D. Kirkpatrick. "Conservative Group Amplifies Voice of Protestant Orthodoxy." *New York Times*, May 22, 2004, p. A1. A conservative group in Richmond, Virginia, is planning to split the Episcopal Church along liberal and orthodox lines over the ordination of openly gay bishop, Gene Robinson.

Hulse, Carl. "Republican Lawmakers Back Senator in Gay Dispute." *New York Times*, April 30, 2003, p. A22. Congressional colleagues dismiss calls from gay rights groups to strip Senator Rick Santorum of his party leadership position after critical remarks he made about homosexuality.

Jordan, Lara Jakes. "Homosexuality Viewed as Threat: Acting upon 'Orientations' Endangers American Family, Pennsylvania Republican Says." *Seattle Times*, April 23, 2003, p. A6. Senator Rick Santorum draws fire from gay rights groups after he gives an interview to the Associated Press about the Supreme Court sodomy case, stating his belief that homosexual acts are a threat to the American family.

Keane, Thomas M., Jr. "Catholics May Opt to Set Own Course." *Boston Herald*, August 6, 2003, p. 26. Catholic politicians such as Democratic presidential nominee, John Kerry, have been put into an untenable position by a recent Vatican pronouncement that they are morally obligated to oppose same-sex marriage. Keane wonders which they'll choose: political conscience or the large U.S. Catholic vote.

Kennedy, Susan P. "Blinded by the Cause of Same-Sex Marriage." *San Francisco Chronicle*, November 21, 2004, p. B5. Kennedy, an openly lesbian public official, takes her fellow gay progressives to task for criticizing California senator Dianne Feinstein's assertion that the push for gay marriage hurt the Democratic party in the 2004 elections. She asserts that gay rights activists should accept the truth in Feinstein's statements and find ways to work within the reality of an antigay backlash.

Kershaw, Sarah, and Judith Berck. "Adversaries on Gay Rights Vow State-by-State Fight." *New York Times*, July 6, 2003, p. A8. Spurred on by the Supreme Court's landmark ruling decriminalizing gay sexual conduct, both sides in the debate over gay rights are vowing an intense state-by-state fight over deeply polarizing questions.

Kirkpatrick, David D. "Cheney Daughter's Political Role Disappoints Some Gay Activists." *New York Times*, August 30, 2004, p. P1. Mary Cheney, the openly lesbian daughter of Vice President Dick Cheney, serves as one of her father's chief campaign advisers. Her role in helping to reelect an administration that is viewed by many gay rights activists as hostile to their concerns has been controversial. Her father's public disavowal of a proposed Constitutional amendment banning same-sex marriage has further complicated matters.

———. "Gay Activists in the G.O.P. Withhold Endorsement." *New York Times*, September 8, 2004, p. A19. The board of Log Cabin Republicans, the largest group for gay men and lesbians in the party, has voted overwhelming against endorsing President Bush for reelection because of his support for a proposed Constitutional amendment banning same-sex marriage.

———. "Gay Marriage Becomes a Swing Issue with Pull." *New York Times*, August 14, 2004, p. A7. Supporters and opponents of same-sex marriage are calling the California Supreme Court decision nullifying San Francisco's marriage licenses a prelude to bigger battles at the ballot box. Both social conservatives and gay rights groups say the debate is becoming increasingly intertwined with the presidential election.

———. "Warily, a Religious Leader Lifts His Voice in Politics." *New York Times*, May 13, 2004, p. A22. A profile of James C. Dobson, the child psychologist and founder of Focus on the Family, who is widely regarded as one of the nation's most influential evangelical leaders. He is taking a more active role in politics in response to the gay marriage controversy.

Kocieniewski, David, and John Holl. "Lawyers Say Ex-McGreevey Aide Is Not Gay and Never Agreed to Intimate Contact." *New York Times*, August 15, 2004, p. A35 New Jersey governor Jim McGreevey resigned his position after revealing that he had an extramarital affair with Golan Cipel, the Israeli national whom he had hired to a top state office. Cipel's lawyers claim, however, that the relationship was not consensual and that McGreevey was sexually harassing his employee.

Lewis, Bob. "Lawmaker to Quit after Allegation He Is Gay." *Seattle Times*, August 31, 2004, p. A8. Representative Edward Shrock has announced that he will not seek a third term in Congress after assertions on a web log that he is gay. Shrock, who is married, voted for legislation to ban gay marriage.

Littwin, Mike. "Gay Bashing Gets No Free Ride on the Hill This Year." *Rocky Mountain News*, April 27, 2004, p. 7A. Littwin celebrates the defeat of several proposed antigay measures in the Colorado legislature, including one that would have forbid teachers in that state from ever mentioning homosexuality in the classroom.

Lowe, Peggy. "Coors, Brewery Part Company on Gay Rights: Activists Appreciate Corporation's Efforts, but Can't Back Pete." *Rocky Mountain News*, June 26, 2004, p. 4A. Coors Brewing Company is a major underwriter of Denver's annual gay and lesbian pride celebration and has a reputation as one of the most gay-friendly employers in Colorado. However, the company's chief officer, Pete Coors, is running for political office on an anti–gay rights platform.

———. "Web Site Takes on Cheneys: Group Seeks to Shame VP into Backing Daughter's Gay Rights." *Rocky Mountain News*, March 6, 2004, p. 21A. Equality Campaign Inc., a national civil rights group working to defeat the Constitutional amendment against same-sex marriage, has created the Internet site DearMary.com designed to put pressure on Vice President Dick Cheney's openly lesbian daughter Mary.

Mansnerus, Laura. "McGreevey Steps Down after Disclosing a Gay Affair." *New York Times*, August 13, 2004 p. A1. Governor James McGreevey of New Jersey has announced his pending resignation at a news conference where he also revealed that he is gay. He becomes the first governor in American history to publicly disclose his homosexuality.

Marech, Rona. "Activists Consider Ethics, Efficacy of Outing." *San Francisco Chronicle*, November 14, 2004, p. A1. U.S. District Judge Nancy Gertner rules that identifying an individual as gay or lesbian does not constitute slander. In response, some activists turn to the tactic of "outing" to expose closeted government employees who, in these activists' opinion, work against the interests of the gay community.

Mason, Julie. "President Puts Lid on Santorum Flap: Controversy Causes Awkward Moments." *Houston Chronicle*, April 27, 2003, p. 8. After refusing comment for several days, President George W. Bush publicly comes to the defense of Pennsylvania Republican senator Rick Santorum for his remarks comparing homosexuality to incest, bigamy, polygamy, and adultery.

May, Meredith. "Backlash Against Gay Rights: Too Much Too Fast Has Spurred Intolerance, Poll Suggests." *San Francisco Chronicle*, July 30, 2003, p. A3. Nationwide polls reveal a dramatic shift away from support for gay rights after the Supreme Court strikes down Texas's sodomy law.

Moore, Dirk. "A Privileged Lesbian Aids an Anti-Gay Administration." *Roanoke Times*, October 21, 2004, p. B9. Presidential candidate John Kerry mentions the homosexuality of Vice President Dick Cheney's daughter, Mary, during a debate with President George W. Bush and controversy ensues. Moore criticizes Mary Cheney's involvement with an administration that is, in his eyes, homophobic.

Moscoso, Eunice. "Most Latinos Back Gay Marriage Bans: Catholic Roots Shape Support of Traditional Family, Polls Say." *Atlanta Journal-Constitution*, March 25, 2004, p. A5. A national survey and polls in different regions show that support for gay marriage and homosexual behavior in general is lower among Hispanics than whites; however, gay rights activists maintain that the reality is more complicated.

Nagourney, Adam. "A Thorny Issue for 2004 Race." *New York Times*, November 19, 2003, p. A1. The Massachusetts gay marriage ruling creates political challenges for both Democrats and Republicans as the two parties gear up for the 2004 presidential election.

Olvera, Javier Erik. "Girding the Gay Vote: Collaborative Effort under Way to Elect Friendly Candidates." *Rocky Mountain News*, July 5, 2004, p. 12A. An intense campaign to entice gay rights supporters to vote in the November 2004 election is under way in Colorado. The goal is to galvanize enough voters to defeat candidates who do not support gay and lesbian issues such as antidiscrimination laws and same-sex marriage.

Powell, Michael. "Activists: Something Lost in Fight for Gay Marriage." *Washington Post*, March 31, 2004, p. A3. The feminists and gay rights theorists who critique the national campaign for marriage from the Left are the voices less often heard in this battle. Here, several longtime activists express their concerns about what is being lost as the movement focuses on attaining this traditional marker of middle class status.

Rainey, James, and Susannah Rosenblatt. "Cheneys Fume over Kerry's Remarks: An 'Angry' Vice President, Wife Lash Out at Rival's Mention of Gay Daughter." *Houston Chronicle*, October 15, 2004, p. 10. Democratic presidential candidate John Kerry faced blistering criticism after he mentioned the homosexuality of Vice President Dick Cheney's daughter, Mary, during a debate against President George W. Bush. Kerry was responding to a question posed by the debate monitor, who asked whether the two candidates believed homosexuality was a choice.

Reid, Tim. "Lesbian Daughter Puts Cheney in Fix over Gay Marriage." *Times of London*, March 6, 2004, p. 20. Vice President Dick Cheney's daughter is openly gay. Homosexual rights activists accuse him of being hypocritical for supporting an amendment to the U.S. Constitution that would bar same-sex marriages.

Rutledge, Mike. "Gay Rights Law OK'd: Commissioners' Vote Unanimous." *Kentucky Post*, April 30, 2003, p. K1. Covington, Kentucky, city commissioners pass a new law banning discrimination based on age, sexual orientation, marital status, and parental status. It affects employment, housing, and public accommodations, such as hotels and restaurants.

Safire, William. "The Lowest Blow." *New York Times*, October 18, 2004, p. A17. Safire argues that the Kerry/Edwards campaign violated the privacy of Vice

President Dick Cheney's family when its two candidates referred to Mary Cheney's lesbianism during both a presidential and a vice presidential debate. He views the statements as "smarmy" attempts to discredit Cheney in the eyes of conservative voters.

Sandalow, Marc. "Bans on State Ballots Could Benefit Bush: Conservatives Would Gain Most from Get-Out-the-Vote Campaign." *San Francisco Chronicle*, May 17, 2004, p. A11. With as many as 14 states placing same-sex marriage bans on their ballot this November, some strategists believe hundreds of thousands of conservative voters who might otherwise have stayed home will show up at the polls and vote for George W. Bush.

Slackman, Michael, and Andrew Jacobs. "Sex, Ambition and the Politics of the Closet: A Double Life." *New York Times*, August 15, 2004, p. A33. Slackman and Jacobs profile New Jersey governor Jim McGreevey. McGreevey recently announced his resignation after publicly declaring his homosexuality.

Smith, Dane. "Gays, Lesbians Could Lose State Protections: Bill Has Good Chance, Backers Say." *Minneapolis Star Tribune*, February 7, 2003, p. 1B. A bill to remove protections for gays and lesbians from Minnesota's human rights law has been introduced in the House. Supporters say that they are concerned that the current legislation has led to the promotion of homosexuality in schools.

Stolberg, Sheryl Gay. "'Vocal Gay Republicans Upsetting Conservatives." *New York Times*, June 1, 2003, p. A26. For the first time, administration officials in a Republican White House have met with the gay political group, Log Cabin Republicans. But conservatives are warning President George W. Bush that there will be repercussions if he courts the homosexual vote.

Thomas, Ralph. "Senate Republicans Kill Anti-Discrimination Bill." *Seattle Times*, March 6, 2004, p. B6. Conservatives in the Washington state legislature have defeated a bill that would extend antidiscrimination protection to gays and lesbians in that state. Activists have been trying to get the legislation passed for the last 30 years.

Tu, Janet I. "Gay-Rights Debate Painted in Myriad Shades of Gray." *Seattle Times*, July 6, 2003, p. A1. The media tends to focus on those taking extreme positions in the gay rights debate; however, a fuller range of nuances and ambivalence are felt not just by the broad middle but by those at either end of the political spectrum.

Von Drehle, David. "Addicted to the Judiciary: Liberals Have Left Themselves Vulnerable at the Polls by Relying Too Much on the Courts." *Newark Star-Ledger*, November 22, 2004, p. 19. Von Drehle contends that recent battles over gay marriage, both in courts and at the ballot box, demonstrate that the liberal wing of American politics is more adept at persuading like-minded judges than it is at persuading undecided voters. He argues that real progress on issues like gay rights won't be achieved until liberals learn how to reach out to voters.

Von Sternberg, Bob. "Climate Has Changed on Gay-Rights Issues: What Seems to Be a Sudden Burst in Recent Weeks of Events Affecting Gay-Related Issues Has Been Long in the Making." *Minneapolis Star Tribune*, August 10, 2003, p. 1A. An in-depth examination of the "Big Fat Gay Summer" of 2003, when the entire country experienced an explosion in the amount of attention paid to issues surrounding the gay rights movement.

———. "Legal Battle of Same-Sex Marriage Far from Over." *Minneapolis Star Tribune*, June 28, 2003, p. 9A. Advocates for gay rights worry that a backlash from the Supreme Court's decision in the Texas sodomy case could slow the recent progress in civil rights for homosexuals.

Wetzstein, Cheryl. "Frank Touts 'Gay Agenda': Brings 'Marriage' to Convention." *Washington Times*, July 30, 2004, p. A15. In remarks before the Democratic National Convention in Boston, Representative Barney Frank, an openly gay Democratic congressman from Massachusetts, said that gay and lesbian members of his party want more than marriage rights; they also want equal access to the military, jobs, and schools without fear of being persecuted for being homosexual.

White, Gayle. "GOP Gays Mull Dilemma over Bush: They Like President, Hate Marriage Ban He Backs." *Atlanta Journal-Constitution*, April 18, 2004, p. A4. As the Log Cabin Republicans, an organization for gays in that party, gather for their annual convention, members debate how much support to show President George W. Bush in the 2004 election campaign.

Williams, Sarah T. "Coming Out in Droves to Protest: Gays, Lesbians and Supporters Rallied to Urge Legislators to Turn Down a Bill That Would Cut Sexual Orientation out of the State Human Rights Law." *Minneapolis Star Tribune*, March 7, 2003, p. 1B. Protestors speak out against a proposal before the Minnesota legislature to remove "gay and lesbian" as a protected category from the state's Human Rights Act.

Woodward, Calvin. "Republicans Approve Firm Plank in Platform against Gay Unions." *St. Louis Post-Dispatch*, August 26, 2004, p. A6. A panel made up largely of conservative delegates to the Republican National Convention has approved wording for a party platform calling for a Constitutional amendment that would ban same-sex marriage and opposing legal recognition of gay civil unions.

Younge, Gary. "Gay Is the New Black: The Gay Rights Issue Has Been a Ticking Timebomb for the Bush Government. And Now It Looks about to Explode." *Guardian of London*, June 16, 2003, p. 13. Examines the way issues involving race are "coded," while issues of homosexuality are often openly derided in conservative political discourse. The implications of this for the 2004 presidential election is discussed.

RELIGION

Allen, Martha Sawyer. "A State of Belief: Most Would Reject Gay Clergy." *Minneapolis Star Tribune*, December 26, 2003, p. 1A. A poll conducted in Minnesota, a state with a sizable gay community and liberal leanings, reveals that a majority of respondents would not accept openly gay clergy and do not feel same-sex couples should have the same rights as married straight couples.

Banerjee, Neela. "United Methodists Move to Defrock Lesbian." *New York Times*, December 3, 2004, p. A18. In the second ecclesiastical trial of a gay Methodist minister in less than a year, a jury of 13 clergy members in eastern Pennsylvania convicts fellow pastor Irene Elizabeth Stroud of violating a church law against homosexuals in the ministry by living in a lesbian relationship and orders her defrocked.

Banerjee, Neela, and Brian Lavery. "Anglican Leaders Seek Move to Avoid a Schism." *New York Times*, February 25, 2005, p. A14. The Episcopal Church and the Anglican Church of Canada have been asked to withdraw their representatives temporarily from a key governing body of the Anglican communion over the American church's consecration of an openly gay man as a bishop and both churches' blessing of same-sex unions.

Day, Elizabeth. "Anglicans Tell U.S. Church to 'Repent' over Gay Bishop." *London Telegraph*. September 26, 2004, p. 9. A commission of archbishops from the worldwide Anglican Communion has demanded a formal apology from the American Episcopal Church for consecrating openly gay Gene Robinson as bishop of New Hampshire. It has also recommended that the American church be excommunicated if Robinson does not resign his post.

Diamant, Jeff. "A Catholic Paper on Gay Marriage Ban: Bishops Will Help Faithful Understand Policy Against Same-Sex Unions." *Newark Star-Ledger*, November 12, 2003, p. 6. The United States Conference of Catholic Bishops issues a document entitled "Questions and Answers about Marriage and Same-Sex Unions," which outlines church opposition to gay and lesbian marriage.

———. "Anglican Church Scolds Episcopals for Gay Consecration." *Newark Star-Ledger*, October 19, 2004, p. 1. A report by the Anglican Communion's Lambeth Commission has recommended that the U.S. Episcopal Church should express regret for the turmoil that resulted from consecrating an openly gay bishop last year and should not appoint any other bishops "living in a same-gender union" until a new church consensus emerges. The document also advises Episcopal bishops to stop letting priests bless same-sex unions.

Duin, Julia. "Gay Issues Slowly Erode Episcopal Membership: Windsor Report Seen as an Ineffectual Response." *Washington Times*, November 27, 2004, p. A1. Disappointed that the international Anglican Communion has failed to punish the American Episcopal Church over the ordination of openly gay Gene Robinson as archbishop of New Hampshire, several dioceses have chosen to break away from the church.

———. "Silenced Priest Warns of Gay Crisis: Catholic Bishops in Annual Meeting." *Washington Times*, November 15, 2004, p. A1. Rev. James Haley of the Diocese of Arlington, Virginia, claims that at the root of the sex-abuse scandal in the Catholic Church are groups of homosexual clerics, not solely pedophiles, who control who gets admitted to seminaries, which men get nominated for bishop, and which priests get desirable parishes.

Flynn, Eileen E. "Austin Jews Join in Gay Union Debate: Ceremony Underscores Split in Conservative Judaism." *Austin American-Statesman*, November

22, 2004, p. A1. As the Conservative branch of Judaism struggles to define its stance on gay marriage and clergy, some worry that division could cause a schism in the movement. Some Conservative Jews point to passages in the Torah which they say clearly forbid homosexuality, while others contend that these passages are open to interpretation.

Gallagher, John. "The Shame of Father Shanley." *Advocate*, July 23, 2002, Issue 868, pp. 36–41. Father Paul Shanley appeared to be a pioneer for gay liberation in the 1970s, but it seems that he abused his position as a Roman Catholic priest to have sex with boys, adolescents, and young men confused about their sexuality.

Goodstein, Laurie. "Bishop Would Deny Rite for Defiant Catholic Voters." *New York Times*, May 14, 2004, p. A16. The Roman Catholic bishop of Colorado Springs has issued a pastoral letter saying that Catholics in the United States should not receive communion if they vote for politicians who defy church teaching by supporting issues such as same-sex marriage.

———. "Conservative Methodists Propose Schism over Gay Rights." *New York Times*, May 7, 2004, p. A20. Conservative members of the Methodist Church have proposed that the denomination dissolve itself and split into separate churches over the issue of homosexuality at its quadrennial general conference.

———. "Episcopal Bishops Suspend Naming Any New Ones." *New York Times*, March 17, 2005, p. A24. Bishops of the Episcopal Church of the United States, under pressure from leaders of the international Anglican Communion not to approve any more openly gay bishops, have decided not to approve any new bishops at all for a year.

———. "Gay Episcopal Bishop Sees Glint of Hope in Church Report." *New York Times*, October 21, 2004, p. A18. Bishop V. Gene Robinson responds to an Anglican commission report critical of his investiture by the Episcopal Church as archbishop of New Hampshire. Robinson sees the potential for gradual acceptance of gay rights in the document and views it as a positive step that will allow his church to move toward healing the rift caused by his elevation to bishop.

———. "Homosexuality in Priesthood Is under Increasing Scrutiny." *New York Times*, April 19, 2002, p. A1. Is there a closeted culture of homosexuality in the priesthood, and if it does exist, is it connected to the sex abuse problem? Experts insist that there is little connection between pedophilia and homosexuality.

———. "Two Studies Cite Child Sex Abuse by 4% of Priests." *New York Times*, February 27, 2004, p. A1. Two studies have found that the Roman Catholic Church suffered an epidemic of child sexual abuse by priests over the last 52 years. More than 80 percent of the abuse at issue was of a homosexual nature.

Guthrie, Julian. "Dismay and Disgust at Vatican in S.F.'s Castro: Many Hailed Recent Advances in Gay Rights." *San Francisco Chronicle*, August 1, 2003, p. A21. Gauges the responses of people in San Francisco's historically gay neighborhood to the Catholic Church's official proclamation against gay and lesbian unions of any kind.

Gay Rights

Kristof, Nicholas D. "Hug an Evangelical." *New York Times*, April 24, 2004, p. A1. Kristof argues that if liberals expect tolerance from conservative Christians over gay marriage, they should extend the same courtesy to evangelicals.

Lampman, Jane. "A Church Split on Gay Inclusion: Episcopalians Vote in Coming Days over Blessing Same-Sex Unions." *Christian Science Monitor*, July 28, 2003, p. 1. The issues of gay marriage and ordination threaten to tear apart the Episcopal Church in America and the Anglican Communion worldwide.

McKinney, Matt. "Church Censured for Gay Pride Support: Archdiocese Orders St. Joan of Arc to Remove Materials from Its Web Site." *Minneapolis Star Tribune*, October 28, 2004, p. 1B. A Catholic church in Minneapolis known for its progressive stands on social issues has been ordered by the Vatican and the Archdiocese of St. Paul and Minneapolis to remove gay pride material from its Web site and stop allowing unordained guests to speak during Mass.

Murphy, Dean E. "Gay Marriage Licenses Create a Quandary for the Clergy." *New York Times*, March 6, 2004, p. A7. By getting married with a license from the City of San Francisco in a church or synagogue, many couples are hoping to chip away at opposition to same-sex marriages among religious people and thereby advance the broader goals of the gay rights movement.

Price, Joyce Howard. "Christians Face Hearing in Felonies at Gay Rights Event." *Washington Times*, January 11, 2005, p. A3. Four Christian activists from the evangelical organization Repent America have been arraigned in Philadelphia on felony charges for disrupting a gay block party, Outfest, held each year in that city.

Torkelson, Jean. "Bishop Seeks Harmony over Gay Rights with Release of Report: O'Neill Asks Episcopalians to Try to 'Work Together.'" *Rocky Mountain News*, September 1, 2004, p. 6A. Colorado Episcopal Bishop Rob O'Neill has issued a diocesan report asking advocates of gay rights in the church to minimize their efforts until the national church addresses the issue. At the same time O'Neill's report calls for the development of an "ethics of human sexuality" that would include gays and lesbians.

———. "Rift over Same-Sex Ceremonies Frays Colorado Episcopal Diocese: Clergy Exchange Volleys as Church Weighs Gay Rights." *Rocky Mountain News*, July 10, 2004, p. 3A. A private same-sex ceremony between two Episcopalian women has escalated into accusations of perjury against retired Colorado bishop, Jerry Winterrowd, who had privately crafted guidelines for such ceremonies while publicly testifying that he hadn't done so. The controversy in the Colorado diocese is viewed as microcosm of the larger debate over same-sex marriage in American society.

Tubbs, Sharon. "Do Gays Have a Prayer in Churches?" *St. Petersburg Times*, February 8, 2004, p. 1E. Overview of the history of the complex relationship between gay men and lesbians and mainstream Christian churches in the United States. Tubbs surveys 10 major denominations to quantify their current positions on homosexuals and homosexuality.

Vara, Richard. "Baptists Urge 'Way Out' for Gays: Convention Focuses on Plans to Target Homosexual Lifestyle." *Houston Chronicle*, June 18, 2003, p. 3. The Southern Baptist Convention, a Christian denomination known for its hard-line stance on homosexuality, announces the launching of "The Way Out," a ministry designed to convince gays and lesbians to give up their "destructive lifestyle."

Vegh, Steven G. "Some Groups Offering Gays Opportunities for 'Recovery.'" *Virginian Pilot*, September 14, 2004, p. A1. As the current debate continues over whether same-sex marriage should be allowed, some ministries within the evangelical Christian community, such as Sought Out in Virginia, contend that a homosexual orientation can be changed.

SODOMY LAWS

Bookman, Jay. "Gay Rights Ruling: 'Scalia Constitution' Is Scary." *Atlanta Constitution*, June 30, 2003, p. A11. Bookman views Justice Antonin Scalia's dissent in the Supreme Court's Texas sodomy decision as indicative of how civil rights in general could erode were Scalia to become chief justice.

Frank, Jon. "Man Gets 6 Months for Soliciting Sex in Restroom, Intends to Appeal." *Virginian Pilot-Ledger Star*, February 18, 2004, p. B4. A Virginia Beach man, Joel D. Singson, is appealing his conviction of soliciting public sex on the grounds that after the Supreme Court has invalidated all sodomy laws, what he was doing was no longer criminal.

Gilreath, Shannon. "State Law Should Reflect High Court Ruling." *Winston-Salem Journal*, July 5, 2003, p. A11. Editorial calling for the North Carolina legislature to repeal that state's sodomy law in the wake of the Supreme Court Texas decision as a symbolic recognition of the civil rights of gays and lesbians.

Greenhouse, Linda. "A Conservative Court Endorses Gay Rights: In 6-to-3 Split, Justices Say Texas Law Is Demeaning to Lives of Homosexuals." *International Herald Tribune*, June 30, 2003, p. 5. In a landmark ruling, the U.S. Supreme Court overturned the Texas sodomy statute, and by extension all remaining laws of its ilk, and issued a de facto apology for the 1986 *Bowers v. Hardwick* decision.

Lewis, Jason. "The Supreme Court Continues to Assault Self-Government." *Minneapolis Star Tribune*, July 6, 2003, p. 2A. Lewis views the Supreme Court sodomy decision as one more step in the erosion of the concept of federalism and an assault on self-government that supplants the will of the people as exercised through elected legislatures.

Lochhead, Carolyn. "Gay Rights Affirmed in Historic Ruling; 6-3 Decision: Supreme Court Throws Out Sodomy Law." *San Francisco Chronicle*, June 27, 2003, p. A1. In the case of *Lawrence v. Texas*, the U.S. Supreme Court declares that state's sodomy statute to be unconstitutional on the grounds that homosexual persons have the right to organize their private sexual relationships however they choose without the fear of state punishment. Justice Sandra Day O'Connor sides with the majority, but on the basis of equal protection.

———. "High Court Ruling Likely to Usher in New Era for Gays: Decision's Logic to Have Impact on Other Rights." *San Francisco Chronicle*, June 29, 2003, p. A4. The Supreme Court decision in *Lawrence v. Texas* declaring all sodomy statutes unconstitutional has wide-ranging implications. While groundbreaking, some are asking what took the Court so long.

Reinert, Patty, and Armando Villafranca. "Court's Decision Viewed as Step Toward Equal Treatment for Gays." *Houston Chronicle*, June 28, 2003, p. 3. Examines reactions among activists on both the right and left to the Supreme Court's sodomy decision. The ruling has had an immediate legal impact as the Court sends back a case to Kansas involving the statutory rape conviction of a teenager for having sex with a younger boy.

TRANSGENDER ISSUES

Associated Press. "School Board in California Defies Bias Law: Millions in Aid Are at Risk." *St. Louis Post-Dispatch*, April 4, 2004, p. A11. A school district in Orange County, California, is risking the loss of millions in state aid for refusing to update its antidiscrimination policy so as to protect transgender students. School officials say the state mandate promotes homosexuality.

Canedy, Dana. "Sex Change Complicates Battle over Child Custody." *New York Times*, February 18, 2002, p. A12. Examines the case of Michael Kantaras and his wife, Linda, who are embroiled in a divorce and custody battle over their two children. Ms. Kantaras contends their marriage and his adoption of her children were never valid because Mr. Kantaras was born a biological female and later underwent a sex change.

Evans, Arthur. "Paying for Transgender Surgery: San Francisco Has More Pressing Needs." *San Francisco Chronicle*, April 29, 2001, p. D8. Evans, a long-time gay activist, is opposed to proposed legislation that would require the City of San Francisco to pay for sex-change operations for any eligible city employee who wants one.

Gorlick, Adam. "Gender Barrier Lowered at Women's College: Smith Recognizes Transgender Students." *Houston Chronicle*, June 25, 2003, p. 22. The student body at the all-female Smith College have voted to replace the pronouns "she" and "her" with "the student" in the student constitution to cover people who are transgender.

Jacobs, Jennifer. "Making a Change: A Transgender Person Talks about the Challenges of Making the Transition from Male to Female." *Syracuse Post-Standard*, March 25, 2004, p. E1. A profile of Frances Fisher, a male-to-female transsexual living in a small city in central New York State. It's taken two-and-a-half years to legally change her name, and she's now preparing for the surgery that will finally make her female.

Marech, Rona. "Transgender Youth Gaining Acceptance: More Schools Are Honoring Students' Gender Identity." *San Francisco Chronicle*, November 26, 2004, p. B1. A growing number of young people are openly questioning their gender in high school and even middle school, and as they do, educators are increasingly facing questions about such sensitive matters as bathroom usage and name changes, as well as finding ways to protect these students from harassment and physical violence.

Martin, Mark. "Davis Signs Ban on Bias Against Transgenders: Leno Bill Makes State 4th in U.S. to Provide Them with Protected Status." *San Francisco Chronicle*, August 5, 2003, p. A12. California governor Gray Davis has signed legislation making it illegal for landlords and businesses in that state to discriminate against any person whose gender identity differs from their biological sex.

O'Hare, Peggy. "Silicone Suspected in 3rd Death: Injections Used to Enhance Body." *Houston Chronicle*, August 21, 2003, p. 21. Investigators are alarmed that many in the transgender community are not heeding warnings about the dangers of body-enhancement techniques, such as silicone injections, after a third Houston-area transgender woman dies from the procedure.

O'Hare, Peggy, Leigh Hopper, and Dale Lezon. "Deaths Spotlight Silicone Shots: Direct Injection Used in Transgender Community, Police Say." *Houston Chronicle*, August 9, 2003, p. 27. A male-to-female Houston transsexual has been arrested for aggravated assault after administering illegal silicone injections to another transsexual who later died. The injections are sought by men who want a sex change, but cannot afford the surgery.

Rice, Harvey. "A Same-Sex Marriage Case Poses a Legal Puzzle: Court May Not Grant Transgender Man's Request to Void Union." *Houston Chronicle*, February 18, 2004, p. 21. A lawsuit seeking to end the marriage of two women, one of whom was born male, could require a Houston judge to recognize a same-sex union. Linda Gail Carter, born James H. Murphey, is seeking to void her marriage to Constance Gonzales.

Stacy, Mitch. "Transsexual Dad Wins Custody Fight: Experts, Advocates Call Ruling Groundbreaking." *Seattle Times*, February 22, 2003, p. A6. Circuit judge Gerald O'Brien has granted custody of two children to female-to-male transsexual Michael Kantaras and ruled that Kantaras is a man under Florida law. The law, the judge said, "provides that marriage shall take place between one man and one woman. It does not provide when such status of being a man or woman shall be determined."

WORKPLACE ISSUES

Basch, Mark. "CSX Corp. Revises Its Anti-Bias Policy: Words 'Sexual Orientation' Added." *Florida Times-Union*, December 23, 2003, p. F1. Amid a campaign by New York City pension funds to push Fortune 500 companies to adopt employment policies of antidiscrimination against gays and lesbians, the Jacksonville-based rail transportation company does just that.

Broyles, Vernadette Ramirez. "Faith-Based Groups Left Open to Suits." *Atlanta Journal-Constitution*, July 23, 2003, p. A13. Broyles, the public policy counsel for a national faith-based nonprofit called "We Care America," argues that the United Methodist Children's Home of North Georgia should not be forced to hire gay and lesbian employees.

Coile, Zachary. "Ashcroft Bars Gay Pride Event at Justice Dept." *San Francisco Chronicle*, June 7, 2003, p. A3. Saying that President George W. Bush has not officially declared June Gay Pride Month, U.S. attorney general John Ashcroft has refused to allow gay and lesbian Justice Department employees to hold their annual event.

Cummins, H. J. "New State Marriage Laws Raise Benefits Concerns." *Minneapolis Star Tribune*, November 5, 2004, p. 1D. After 11 states approved constitutional bans on gay marriages, national employer groups said the bans could be used to challenge domestic partner benefits offered by private employers for same-sex couples. However, other experts point out that federal law prevents states from dictating to an employer the terms of its benefits.

Egelko, Bob. "Federal Court Setback for Gay Rights: Workplace Harassment Isn't Illegal, Judges Say." *San Francisco Chronicle*, March 30, 2001, p. A9. In a case involving a gay man who worked as a butler at the MGM Grand Hotel in Las Vegas, a federal judicial panel has ruled that while workplace harassment of gays and lesbians because of their sexual orientation is "appalling," it does not violate federal law.

Freed, Gwendolyn. "Gays and Lesbians Report Friendlier Workplaces." *Minneapolis Star Tribune*, October 2, 2003, p. 1D. According to a national survey released on the eve of Out & Equal Workplace Advocates' Workplace Summit, attitudes are warming toward LGBT people in the workplace; however, people still report having been fired for their sexuality.

Holl, John. "With Two Men Out, McGreevey Steps up to the Plate and Saves the Day." *New York Times*, August 27, 2004, p. B6. Two employees of a baseball stadium in Atlantic City, New Jersey, were fired after publicly making jokes about Governor James McGreevey, who recently came out as a gay man. When the governor heard about the incident, he urged that the men be reinstated.

Joyce, Amy. "In the Past Decade, More Businesses Have Added Policies to Protect Gay Employees, Advocates Say: A Report Card on Gender Policies." *Houston Chronicle*, November 7, 2004, p. 6. A growing number of corporations are expanding the reach of protections against discrimination related to sexual identity by including protections for gender identity as well as sexual orientation.

Joyner, Tammy. "Home Depot to Add Same-Sex Benefits." *Atlanta Journal-Constitution*, September 3, 2004, p. F1. After being criticized for offering pet insurance to its employees while not extending benefits to same-sex partners, Fortune 500 corporation Home Depot has announced its intention to include same-sex domestic partners in its health plan.

Kershaw, Sarah. "Wal-Mart Sets a New Policy That Protects Gay Workers." *New York Times*, July 2, 2003, p. A1. Wal-Mart Stores, the largest private employer in the United States and one generally associated with conservative cultural values, has expanded its antidiscrimination policy to protect gay and lesbian employees.

Kleinknect, William. "Ex-Officer Awarded $2.8M in Harassment Case." *Newark Star-Ledger*, November 16, 2004, p. 57. Karen Caggiano, a former Essex County, New Jersey, sheriff's officer who claimed she was harassed on the job because she is a lesbian—and received little relief from her superiors when she complained—has been awarded monetary damages by a jury.

Lichtblau, Eric. "Justice Dept. Draws Heavy Criticism over Cancellation of Gay Rights Event." *New York Times*, June 7, 2003, p. A12. In a move that has implications for the right of federal employees to associate on government property outside of official working time, Attorney General John Ashcroft has canceled the Justice Department's annual event to observe Gay Pride Month.

Marshall, Samantha. "Rosier Outlook for Gays in NYC." *Crain's New York Business*, February 2, 2004, Vol. 20:5, p. 1. New York City companies have taken the lead during the past year in creating a workplace that's more welcoming to gay employees, including writing policies to protect the rights of gays and introducing domestic partner benefits.

Moore, John. "Kaiser Exhibits Double Standard in Protecting 'Image.'" *Denver Post*, April 6, 2003, p. F5. Stuart Sanks, a Denver-area actor employed by the heath-care corporation Kaiser Permanente in its Educational Theater Program, has been forbidden by the company from accepting a role in a production of *Bent*. The play is about gay victims of the Nazi Holocaust

Morgan, Christopher, and Jonathon Carr-Brown. "Churches Will Get Right to Sack Gays." *Times of London*, June 1, 2003, p. 11. In a move that has implications for U.S.-based churches, the British government has decided to grant religious organizations the legal right to exclude gay and lesbian people from employment, the first time such discrimination has been codified in English law.

Munday, Dave. "Gay Workers Fear for Their Jobs: Nondiscrimination Policies Still Scarce." *Charleston Post and Courier*, April 4, 2004, p. E1. In most states, there is no law against firing a gay or lesbian worker because of sexual orientation. As the nation debates same-sex marriage, gays and lesbians say they have a more basic concern: keeping their jobs.

Pondel, Evan. "More Companies Offer Benefits to Same-Sex Couples, but Others Won't Till It's Required by Law." *Los Angeles Daily News*, August 29, 2004, p. B1. Approximately 40 percent of Fortune 500 companies offered health benefits to gay couples at the end of 2003, according to the Human Rights Campaign Foundation. While the trend is toward extending health benefits to domestic partners of employees, many companies are still reluctant to do so.

Saulny, Susan. "Ex-Employee Says Helmsley Abused Him." *New York Times*, January 15, 2003, p. B3. Charles Bell, a former employee of Leona Helmsley, has filed suit against her, claiming she conducted a "vicious, antigay attack campaign" against him and fired him as the general manager of her Park Lane Hotel because he was gay.

Seper, Jerry. "Gays' 'Protected-Class' Status Doubted: Counsel Suspends Enforcement of Harassment Caims During Study." *Washington Times*, March 22, 2004, p. A3. The Office of Special Counsel, which protects government employees from workplace discrimination, has suspended enforcement of harassment claims based on sexual orientation, pending an analysis of whether federal law covers homosexuals.

Thompson, Lynn. "Gays Protected in Public Workforce." *Seattle Times*, July 19, 2002, p. B2. A Washington State appeals court has ruled that firing a public employee on the basis of sexual orientation violates the U.S. Constitution's guarantee of equal protection. The case involved a lesbian employed at a county hospital.

WEB SITES

ACT UP: AIDS Coalition to Unleash Power. Available Online. URL: http://www.actupny.org. Downloaded on May 15, 2004. The web site is for the New York branch of ACT UP, the AIDS Coalition to Unleash Power. A current issues index on the home page offers the latest information on AIDS activism, while a listing of crucial links offers further data on AIDS treatment, research, and politics. The site also provides a wide variety of documents and essays on ACT UP's history and current activities.

Alliance for Marriage. Available Online. URL: http://www.allianceformarriage.org. Downloaded on October 10, 2004. The web site for the Alliance for Marriage, a nonprofit research and education group devoted to promoting traditional marriage in America, with a particular emphasis on married fatherhood. The site offers continually updated news and information on efforts to enshrine traditional definitions of marriage in law, as well as analysis and perspectives on marriage-related issues.

American Center for Law and Justice. Available Online. URL: http://www.aclj.org. Downloaded on October 10, 2004. The web site for the American Center for Law and Justice (ACLJ), a conservative legal group set up to provide a right-wing counterpart to the liberal American Civil Liberties Union (ACLU). The ACLJ brings a wide range of suits on conservative issues, opposing gay rights, affirmative action, and what it sees as other liberal causes. Its web site has a wide range of analyses, press releases, and news stories on the lawsuits it initiates as well as related issues.

The Data Lounge. Available Online. URL: http://www.datalounge.com. Downloaded on May 15, 2004. An online magazine that offers continuously updated political analysis and news, with a focus on gay rights. The home page offers a link called "news" that allows researchers to get past and current Data Lounge articles on AIDS, antigay initiatives, antigay violence, culture and the media, education, family and child care, gay origins, gay vote, government and sodomy laws, health, marriage and domestic partnerships, military service, perspectives in Africa, religion, sexual expression, workplace issues, and bias laws and initiatives. An excellent way to get a quick snapshot of the latest developments on any issue.

Family Policy Network. Available Online. URL: http://www.familypolicy.net. Downloaded on October 10, 2004. The web site for the Family Policy Network, a group that aims to mobilize Christians at the grassroots level in support of the traditional family and religious liberties, with a particular opposition to gay rights. Hate crimes, gay marriage, and other gay rights issues are included in its news coverage and analyses.

Gayscape.com—The Gay Internet. Available Online. URL: http://www. gayscape.com. Downloaded on May 15, 2004. A gay directory. The subcategory called "Pride" includes listings for gay rights; activist groups; antiviolence; gays and lesbians in the military; and gay, lesbian, and bisexual youths.

Human Rights Campaign Web Site. Available Online. URL: http://www. hrc.org. Downloaded on May 15, 2004. The web site of the Human Rights Campaign (HRC), the major national gay rights lobbying group. In addition to offering information on the HRC and its current activities, the home page offers current news stories and links to information on HIV/AIDS, workplace, antigay/hate, marriage, lesbian health, and transgender issues, as well as specific information on the HRC's major legislative efforts, such as efforts to defeat the Federal Marriage Amendment and pass the Permanent Partners' Immigration Act. A link to "Coming Out Resources" provides a resource guide on that issue, as well as a listing of various national organizations and a suggested bibliography linked to an online bookstore.

LAMBDA: GLBT Community Services Web Site. Available Online. URL: http://www.lambda.org. Downloaded on May 15, 2004. A nonprofit gay/lesbian/bisexual/transgender agency based in El Paso, Texas. This excellent, youth-oriented web site provides information on a wide range of issues, including hate crimes, domestic violence among gay/lesbian families, health issues, and a special section on "youth OUTreach."

LAMBDA Legal Web Site. Available Online. URL: http://www.lambdalegal. org. Downloaded on May 15, 2004. The web site for the LAMBDA Legal Defense and Education Fund, the oldest and largest U.S. group working for the civil rights of lesbians, gay men, bisexuals, the transgender, and people with HIV/AIDS. The site offers news of LAMBDA's latest cases.

National Center for Lesbian Rights Home Page. Available Online. URL: http://www.nclrights.org. Downloaded on May 15, 2004. The web site for the National Committee on Lesbian Rights. The home page offers links to information on recent decisions and legal cases that affect lesbian rights.

National Gay and Lesbian Task Force Online. Available Online. URL: http://www.thetaskforce.org. Downloaded on May 15, 2004. The web site for the National Gay and Lesbian Task Force, one of the major U.S. gay political organizations. Researchers can find news and legislative updates in this comprehensive online newsletter, as well as reports on recent state legislative actions and links to downloadable publications on a variety of topics, including a report on federal and state marriage benefits, a guide to making homeless shelters safe for transgender people, and a report on education policy and GLBT youths.

No Gay Marriage. Available Online. URL: http://www.nogaymarriage.com. Downloaded on October 10, 2004. Sponsored by the American Family Organization, this web site includes a directory of and links to a wide range of web sites offering anti–gay marriage news, analyses, and opportunities for activism.

NOW and Lesbian Rights. Available Online. URL: http://www.now.org/issues/lgbi/index.html. Downloaded on May 15, 2004. Lesbian rights page on the web site of the National Organization for Women (NOW). The site offers information on lesbian rights actions that NOW is involved in, as well as information on current key issues.

Oasis Magazine. Available Online. URL: http://www.oasismag.com. Downloaded on May 29, 2004. A self-described "online Webzine written by, about and for queer and questioning youth." Includes links to online journals, poetry, members' forums, and news. Recent forums included discussions of gay marriage in Massachusetts and what to do when you have a crush on a straight boy.

OutProud Available Online. URL: http://www.outproud.org. Downloaded on May 15, 2004. The web site for Outproud, the National Coalition of Gay, Lesbian, Bisexual, & Transgender Youth. The web site offers youth-oriented resources on a wide variety of topics, with a focus on coming out.

Queer Resources Directory. Available Online. URL: http://www.qrd.org. Downloaded on May 15, 2004. The web site of the Queer Resources Directory offers a wide range of topics, including national and international information. Organizations, directories, and newsletters can also be accessed.

Reclaim America. Available Online. URL: http://www.reclaimamerica.org. Downloaded on October 10, 2004. The web site of the Center to Reclaim America, founded in 1996 to mobilize Christians on a number of conservative issues, including opposition to gay rights. Information on gay adoption, hate crimes bills, gay marriage, and other gay rights issues can be found on the site, along with an online bookstore and other resources for analysis and activism.

CHAPTER 9

ORGANIZATIONS AND AGENCIES

This chapter lists all of the major organizations concerning gay rights, including both those groups who favor gay rights and those who oppose them. The chapter begins with a listing of the major pro–gay rights groups—the national organizations set up to promote the legal, political, and cultural rights of lesbians and gay men. It goes on to list lesbian and gay groups that focus on legal issues, lesbian and gay youth groups, and some other significant gay rights groups, particularly those representing lesbians and gay men of color. The final section of this chapter includes a listing of the major national anti–gay rights groups.

PRO–GAY RIGHTS GROUPS

MAJOR NATIONAL GAY AND LESBIAN ORGANIZATIONS

AIDS Coalition to Unleash Power (ACT UP)—New York
332 Bleecker Street, Suite G5
New York, NY 10014
Phone: (212) 966-4873
E-mail: actupny@panix.com
URL: http://www.actupny.org
Engages in AIDS activism; has some access to research. Although this listing is New York City–specific, the New York chapter maintains information sources relevant to all other chapters.

American Civil Liberties Union (ACLU)
Lesbian and Gay Rights Project/ AIDS Project

125 Broad Street, 18th Floor
New York, NY 10004-2400
Phone: (212) 549-2568
Fax: (212) 549-2650
URL: http://www.aclu.org/Lesbian
GayRights/LesbianGayRights
Main.cfm
Researches legal issues and represents cases related to civil rights issues, including gay rights.

Gay and Lesbian Alliance Against Defamation (GLAAD)
5455 Wilshire Boulevard, #1500
Los Angeles, CA 90036
Phone: (323) 933-2240
Fax: (323) 933-2241

248 West 35th Street, 8th Floor
New York, NY 10001
Phone: (212) 629-3322
Fax: (212) 629-3225

URL: http://www.glaad.org
Promotes accurate portrayals of lesbians and gay men in the media and popular culture.

Gay Men's Health Crisis (GMHC)
The Tisch Building
119 West 24th Street
New York, NY 10011
Phone: (212) 367-1000
Hotline: (212) 807-6655, (800)
    AIDS-NYC or (800) 243-7692
E-mail: hotline@gmhc.org
URL: http://www.gmhc.org
An AIDS activist organization whose mission statement is, "to provide compassionate care to people with AIDS; educate to keep people healthy; and advocate for fair and effective public politics." The Lesbian AIDS Project, located at the same address, can be reached by calling (212) 367-1335.

Human Rights Campaign (HRC)
1640 Rhode Island Avenue NW
Washington, D.C. 20036
Phone: (202) 628-4160,
    (800) 777-4723
TTY: (202) 628-1572
Fax: (202) 347-5723
E-mail: hrc@hrc.org
URL: http://www.hrc.org
Lobbies Congress; engages in political action, grassroots organizing; prepares research reports on a wide variety of gay rights issues; and offers political support to gay and gay-friendly candidates.

Lambda Legal
National Headquarters:
120 Wall Street

Suite 1500
New York, NY 10005-3904
Phone: (212) 809-8585
Fax: (212) 809-0055

Western Regional Office:
3325 Wilshire Boulevard
Suite 1300
Los Angeles, CA 90010-1729
Phone: (213) 382-7600
Fax: (213) 351-6050

Midwest Regional Office:
11 East Adams
Suite 1008
Chicago, IL 60603-6303
Phone: (312) 663-4413
Fax: (312) 663-4307

Southern Regional Office:
1447 Peachtree Street NE
Suite 1004
Atlanta, GA 30309-3027
Phone: (404) 897-1880
Fax: (404) 897-1884

South Central Regional Office:
3500 Oak Lawn Avenue
Suite 500
Dallas, TX 75219-6722
Phone: (214) 219-8585
Fax: (214) 219-4455
URL: http://www.lambdalegal.org
Does legal research and takes cases; also has an AIDS project. It is a key source of information on gay legal issues, including marriage and civil unions, adoption, employment, and civil liberties.

National Gay and Lesbian Task Force (NGLTF)
1325 Massachusetts Avenue NW
Suite 600
Washington, DC 20005

Phone: (202) 393-5177
Fax: (202) 393-2241
TTY: (202) 393-2284
E-mail: ngltf@ngltf.org
URL:http://www.thetaskforce.
  org

Lobbying, political action, grassroots organizing, legal research, and training for political action. Its network of state organizations is currently focusing on identifying voters in order to become more successful in statewide referendum on gay civil rights and gay marriage.

**Parents, Families and Friends
  of Lesbians and Gays
  (PFLAG)**
1726 M Street NW
Suite 400
Washington, DC 20036
Phone: (202) 467-8180
Fax: (202) 467-8194
E-mail: publications@pflag.org
URL: http://www.pflag.org

Activist group representing gay-friendly straight people. Its offers opportunities for activism, support groups, news and information, and suggestions for dealing with gay and lesbian family members.

**Senior Action in a Gay
  Environment (SAGE)**
305 Seventh Avenue, 16th Floor
New York, NY 10001
Phone: (212) 741-2247
Fax: (212) 366-1947
E-mail: sageusa@aol.com
URL: http://www.sageusa.org

Activist group for gay senior citizens, offering both support groups and opportunities for political action.

OTHER GAY AND LESBIAN LEGAL PROJECTS

**Gay & Lesbian Advocates &
  Defenders (GLAD)**
30 Winter Street
Suite 800
Boston, MA 02108
Phone: (617)426-1350
E-mail: gladlaw@glad.org
URL: http://www.glad.org

GLAD litigates for gay men, lesbians, and HIV-positive people of all orientations throughout the New England region, including the states of Maine, New Hampshire, Vermont, Massachusetts, Connecticut, and Rhode Island. GLAD has successfully argued cases involving gay marriage, the Boy Scouts, sodomy, prisoners' rights, public accommodation, and domestic violence, among others.

**National Center for Lesbian
  Rights (NCLR)**
870 Market Street
Suite 750
Phone: (415) 392-6257
Fax: (415) 392-8442
E-mail: info@nclrights.org
URL: http://www.nclrights.org

NCLR is a national legal resource center with a primary commitment to advancing the rights and safety of lesbians and their families through litigation, public policy advocacy, free legal advice, and public education. Some of the organization's current efforts include the Sports Project, which assists athletics professionals who may be experiencing antigay harassment; the Elder Law Project, which provides affordable legal assistance to LGBT persons over the age of 60; and helping to draft the Permanent Partners Immigration Act.

National Lesbian and Gay Law
Association (NLGLA)
200 East Lexington Street
Suite 1511
Baltimore, MD 21202
Phone: (508) 982-8290
Fax: (410) 244-0775
E-mail: info@nlgla.org
URL: http://www.nlgla.org
NLGLA is a national association of lawyers, judges and other legal professionals, law students, community activists, and LGBT legal organizations. NLGLA sponsors an annual conference, Lavender Law, as well as job fairs and yearly awards that recognize leaders in the field of gay rights litigation.

ORGANIZATIONS THAT FOCUS ON LESBIAN AND GAY YOUTHS

Center Kids and Youth
Enrichment Services (YES)
Lesbian and Gay Community
Services Center
208 West 13th Street
New York, NY 10011
Phone: (212) 620-7310
Fax: (212) 924-2657
E-mail: gaycenter@gaycenter.org
URL: http://www.gaycenter.org
Both of these organizations are affiliated with the New York Lesbian and Gay Community Services Center. Center Kids offers the children of LGBT parents a supportive space in which to meet peers with similar families. Center Kids also offers support programs for LGBT people consid-

ering biological or adoptive parenting and sponsors a preschool-age playgroup. YES offers free and confidential support services, leadership training, discussion groups, creative arts workshops, and social activities to LGBT youths between the ages of 13 and 21.

Gay, Lesbian, and Straight
Educational Network (GLSEN)
121 West 27th Street
Suite 804
New York, NY 10001
Phone: (212) 727-0135
Fax: (212) 727-0254
E-mail: glsen@glsen.org
URL: http://www.glsen.org
GLSEN works to eliminate bullying and harassment of LGBT students by fostering the creation of gay-straight student alliances in school districts throughout the nation. The organization also seeks to educate all students about gay and lesbian historical and cultural issues by sponsoring Lesbian, Gay, and Bisexual History Month every October.

Hetrick-Martin Institute (HMI)
2 Astor Place
New York, NY 10003
Phone: (212) 674-2400
Fax: (212) 674-8650
TTY: (212) 674-8695
E-mail: info@hmi.org
URL: http://www.hmi.org
HMI provides social support and programming for at-risk LGBT youths ages 12 to 21. Its programs include the Harvey Milk High School, the first public high school expressly for LGBT students; the After-School Services Department, a drop-in program offering hot meals, activities, classes, and performances; and the

Supportive Services Department, which counsels young people on issues around sexuality, coming out to parents and friends, and HIV, as well as providing referrals to social services agencies for clients coping with homelessness, abuse, addiction, and neglect.

**National Youth Advocacy
  Coalition (NYAC)**
1638 R Street NW
Suite 300
Washington, DC 20009
Phone: (202) 319-7596,
  (800) 541-6922
Fax: (202) 319-7365
TTY: (202) 319-9513
E-mail: nyac@nyacyouth.org
URL: http://www.nyacyouth.org
NYAC is a social justice organization that advocates for and with LGBT young people in an effort to end discrimination against these youths and ensure their physical and emotional well-being. It sponsors an annual National Youth Summit as well as regional meetings and provides health and sexuality workshops to educate young people about safe sex, HIV prevention, and drug abuse. In 1999 it launched a Racial and Economic Justice Initiative, which focuses on finding effective advocacy strategies for young people dealing with issues of race and class in addition to sexuality.

OTHER POSSIBLE SOURCES FOR PRO–GAY RIGHTS INFORMATION

AIDS Action
1906 Sunderland Place NW
Washington, DC 20036
Phone: (202) 530-8030

Fax: (202) 530-8031
http://www.aidsaction.org
AIDS Action is a national organization dedicated to the development, analysis, cultivation, and encouragement of policies and programs to respond to the HIV epidemic. It is divided into two branches: The AIDS Action Foundation develops and disseminates educational materials on public policy and healthcare programs, the demographic impact of HIV, and medical research; the AIDS Action Council advocates for legislation and social policies and programs for HIV prevention, treatment, and care.

AIDS.ORG
7985 Santa Monica Boulevard #99
West Hollywood, CA 90046
Phone: (323) 656-6036
URL: http://www.aids.org
The mission of AIDS.ORG is to help prevent HIV infections and improve the lives of those affected by HIV or AIDS by providing education on its web site. *AIDS Treatment News*, an online periodical about health and activism issues for the HIV-positive community, and facts sheets on HIV can be downloaded from the site. AIDS.ORG is currently developing programs to combat HIV/AIDS in young people and in Africa.

**American Foundation for AIDS
  Research (amFAR)**
120 Wall Street, 13th Floor
New York, NY 10005-3908
Phone: (212) 806-1600
Fax: (212) 806-1601

1828 L Street NW, #802
Washington, DC 20036-5104

Phone: (202) 331-8600,
    (800) 39-AMFAR or
    (800) 392-6327
Fax: (202) 331-8606
URL: http://www.amfar.org
AMFAR provides monetary support
in the form of grants for AIDS research and HIV/AIDS prevention
and treatment education programs. It
also advocates for the civil rights of
people infected with HIV and for the
establishment of effective public policy to stop the spread of the disease.

**Association of Gay and Lesbian
    Psychiatrists (AGLP)**
4514 Chester Avenue
Philadelphia, PA 19143
Phone: (215) 222-2800
URL: http://www.aglp.org
AGLP advocates for a greater understanding of GLBT mental health issues among psychiatric medical
professionals. It publishes a quarterly
newsletter, as well as the *Journal of
Gay and Lesbian Psychotherapy*; con-
ducts seminars and discussion groups
at the annual meeting of the American Psychiatric Association; and provides mental health referrals for
GBLT patients.

**Center for Lesbian and Gay
    Studies (CLAGS)**
The Graduate Center
City University of New York
365 Fifth Avenue, Room 7115
New York, NY 10016
Phone: (212) 817-1955
E-mail: clags@gc.cuny.edu
**URL: http://web.gc.cuny.edu/
    clags/who.htm**
CLAGS is dedicated to the study of
the political, social, and cultural his-
tory of lesbian and gay lives and insti-

tutions, as well as historical figures
and social forces opposed to gay
rights. CLAGS sponsors scholarly
conferences and lectures on various
aspects of GLBT life and culture;
provides fellowships to scholars of
lesbian and gay studies; and publishes
books of interest to students of gay
and lesbian history.

**Committee on Lesbian, Gay, and
    Bisexual Concerns (LGBC)**
**American Psychological
    Association**
Public Interest Directorate
750 First Street NE
Washington, DC 20002-4242
Phone: (202) 336-6050
E-mail: publicinterest@apa.org
URL: http://www.apa.org
LGBC is a project of the American
Psychological Association. It crafts
policy statements designed to pro-
mote the human rights of LGBT
people both in the United States and
internationally. Through its Healthy
Lesbian, Gay, and Bisexual Students
Project, it develops workshops for
educators so that they can recognize
and prevent risks to the health of
LGBT youths, such as drug abuse,
suicide, violence, and unsafe sexual
behavior.

**Gay and Lesbian Medical
    Association (GLMA)**
459 Fulton Street
Suite 107
San Francisco, California 94102
Phone: (415) 255-4547
**Referrals Hotline: (415) 255-4547
    x312**
Fax: (415) 255-4784
E-mail: info@glma.org
URL: http://www.glma.org

GLMA is national organization dedicated to improving health care for LGBT patients and protecting the rights of LGBT physicians and other health-care professionals. It sponsors conferences and seminars for LGBT physicians and students; provides a health-care referral service; administers the Lesbian Health Fund, which provides grants to researchers studying health issues of special interest to lesbians; and publishes the *Journal of the Gay and Lesbian Medical Association.*

Gay Asian Pacific Support
Network (GAPSN)
P.O. Box 461104
Los Angeles, CA 90046-1104
Phone: (213) 368-6488
E-mail: gapsn@gapsn.org
URL: http://www.gapsn.org
GAPSN sponsors discussion groups and socials at which gay and bisexual Asian Pacific Islander (API) men can meet, network, voice concerns, and foster self-empowerment. GAPSN advocates on behalf of its members in both the gay and API communities. Because many of its members are immigrants, GAPSN also provides members access to immigration services.

International Gay and Lesbian
Human Rights Commission
(IGLHRC)
350 Fifth Avenue, 34th Floor
New York, NY 10118
Phone: (212) 216-1814
Fax: (212) 216-1876
URL: http://www.iglhrc.org
IGLHRC works to advance the human rights of LGBT and HIV-positive people around the world through advocacy, documentation, coalition building, public education, and technical assistance.

LLEGÓ
The National Latina/o Lesbian,
Gay, Bisexual, and Transgender
Organization
1420 K Street
Suite 400
Washington, DC 20005
Phone: (888) 633-8320
Fax: (202) 408-8478
URL: http:www.llego.org
LLEGÓ is a national organization that represent Latina/o LGBT communities and addresses their needs regarding an array of social issues ranging from civil rights and social justice to health and human services. Its programs include Acción LLEGO, which seeks to advance civil and health-care rights for Latino LGBT people; Horizontes, which trains gay and bisexual Latino men to be community leaders in the fight against HIV; and Proyecto Fénix, which aims to educate Latino/a LGBT young people on the dangers of tobacco consumption.

National Education Association
Gay, Lesbian, Bisexual, and
Transgender Caucus
(NEA/GLBTC)
URL: http://www.nea-glc.org
NEA/GLBTC works to inform state education associations and the National Education Association (a national teacher's union) on sexual orientation issues and how they affect both teachers and students, and promotes nondiscriminatory policies toward LGBT people. To help achieve this goal, it has published a guide on

gay and lesbian issues for school employees.

National Minority AIDS Council (NMAC)
1931 13th Street NW
Washington, DC 20009
Phone: (202) 483-6622
Fax: (202) 483-1135
E-mail: info@nmac.org
URL: http://www.nmac.org
NMAC fosters leadership within the African-American, Latino, Asian, and Native American communities to address issues involving HIV/AIDS. It works to increase the participation of people of color in policy-making bodies and promotes programs to serve the needs of minority populations affected by the AIDS epidemic. In addition, it provides training to AIDS health-care organizations to help them create effective treatment services in minority communities.

Trikone
P.O. Box 14161
San Francisco, CA 94114
Phone: (415) 487-8778
E-mail: trikone@trikone.org
URL: http://www.trikone.org
Trikone is an advocacy and social organization for LGBT people of South Asian decent. It publishes a triannual magazine, *Trikone*, that features articles on South Asian culture, the immigrant experience, and political activism.

ANTI-GAY RIGHTS GROUPS

American Family Association (AFA)
P.O. Drawer 2440

Tupelo, MS 38803
Phone: (662)844-5036
Fax: (662) 842-7798
URL: http://www.afa.net
Founded by Reverend Donald E. Wildmon, the AFA sponsors many boycotts of TV shows it considers offensive and is concerned about a wide range of issues but with a special focus on homosexuality, which it considers a threat to the traditional family and to traditional morality.

Christian Broadcasting Network (CBN)
977 Centerville Turnkpike
Virginia Beach, VA 23463
Phone: (757) 226-7000
URL: http://www.cbn.com
Founded by Reverend Pat Robertson, CBN sponsors *The 700 Club* TV show and is active in a wide range of issues, including opposition to gay rights and same-sex marriage.

Concerned Women for America
1015 15th Street NW
Suite 1100
Washington, DC 20005
Phone: (202) 488-7000
Fax: (202) 488-0806
URL: http://www.cwfa.org
Describing itself as the largest public policy women's organization, Concerned Women for America is dedicated to bringing biblical principles to all levels of public policy, a mission that it interprets as including opposition to gay rights and same-sex marriage.

Faith and Action in the Nation's Capital
109 Second Street NE
Washington, DC 20002-7303

Phone: (202) 546-8429
Fax: (202) 546-6864
E-mail: info@faithandaction.org
URL: http://www.faithandaction.
  org
A Christian outreach group dedicated to bringing Christian principles into public policy, Faith and Action has a mission that the group interprets as including opposition to gay rights and same-sex marriage.

Family Research Council (FRC)
801 G Street NW
Washington, DC 20001
Phone: (202) 393-2100
Fax: (202) 393-2134
URL: http://www.frc.org
Founded by Gary Bauer to research and lobby on family issues, the FRC's motto is "Family, Faith, and Freedom."

Traditional Values Coalition
(TVC)
139 C Street SE
Washington, DC 20003
Phone: (202) 547-8570
Fax: (202) 546-6403

100 S. Anaheim Boulevard
Suite 350
Anaheim, CA 92805
Phone: (714) 520-0300
Fax: (714) 520-9602

URL: http://www.tvc.org
This site includes a number of useful links to news stories and is an excellent way to keep up with daily events from a conservative perspective.

PART III

APPENDICES

APPENDIX A

EXCERPTS FROM COURT DECISIONS

SUPREME COURT

BOWERS V. HARDWICK, 106 S. CT. 2841 (1986)

This landmark Supreme Court decision upheld the constitutionality of Georgia's sodomy law—and, by extension, affirmed the rights of individual states to outlaw sodomy. For background on this case, see Chapter 2. Justice Byron White wrote the majority opinion, joined by Chief Justice Warren Burger and Justices Lewis Powell, William Rehnquist, and Sandra Day O'Connor. Justice Harry Blackmun wrote a dissenting opinion, joined by Justices Brennan, Marshall, and John Paul Stevens. Following is White's majority opinion.

This case does not require a judgment on whether laws against sodomy between consenting adults in general, or between homosexuals in particular, are wise or desirable. It raises no question about the right or propriety of state legislative decisions to repeal their laws that criminalize homosexual sodomy, or of state-court decisions invalidating those laws on state constitutional grounds. The issue presented is whether the Federal Constitution confers a fundamental right upon homosexuals to engage in sodomy and hence invalidates the laws of the many States that still make such conduct illegal and have done so for a very long time. The case also calls for some judgment about the limits of the Court's role in carrying out its constitutional mandate. . . .

Accepting the decisions in [other] cases and the . . . description of them, we think it evident that none of the rights announced in those cases bears any resemblance to the claimed constitutional right of homosexuals to engage in acts of sodomy that is asserted in this case. No connection between family, marriage, or procreation on the one hand and homosexual activity on the other has been demonstrated, either by the Court of Appeals or by respondent. Moreover, any claim that these cases nevertheless stand for the proposition that any kind of private sexual conduct between consenting adults is constitutionally insulated from state proscription is unsupportable. . . .

Gay Rights

Precedent aside, however, respondent would have us announce, as the Court of Appeals did, a fundamental right to engage in homosexual sodomy. This we are quite unwilling to do. It is true that despite the language of the Due Process Clauses of the Fifth and Fourteenth Amendments, which appears to focus only on the processes by which life, liberty, or property is taken, the cases are legion in which those Clauses have been interpreted to have substantive content, subsuming rights that to a great extent are immune from federal or state regulation or proscription. Among such cases are those recognizing rights that have little or no textual support in the constitutional language. . . .

Striving to assure itself and the public that announcing rights not readily identifiable in the Constitution's text involves much more than the imposition of the Justices' own choice of values on the States and the Federal Government, the Court has sought to identify the nature of the rights qualifying for heightened judicial protection. In *Palko v. Connecticut*, 326 (1937), it was said that this category includes those fundamental liberties that are "implicit in the concept of ordered liberty," such that "neither liberty nor justice would exist if [they] were sacrificed." A different description of fundamental liberties appeared in *Moore v. East Cleveland*, (1977), where they are characterized as those liberties that are "deeply rooted in this Nation's history and tradition." See also *Griswold v. Connecticut*.

It is obvious to us that neither of these formulations would extend a fundamental right to homosexuals to engage in acts of consensual sodomy. Proscriptions against that conduct have ancient roots. See generally Survey on the Constitutional Right to Privacy in the Context of Homosexual Activity, 40 U. Miami L. Rev. 521, 525 (1986). Sodomy was a criminal offense at common law and was forbidden by the laws of the original 13 States when they ratified the Bill of Rights. In 1868, when the Fourteenth Amendment was ratified, all but 5 of the 37 States in the Union had criminal sodomy laws. In fact, until 1961, all 50 States outlawed sodomy, and today, 24 States and the District of Columbia continue to provide criminal penalties for sodomy performed in private and between consenting adults. . . . Against this background, to claim that a right to engage in such conduct is "deeply rooted in this Nation's history and tradition" or "implicit in the concept of ordered liberty" is, at best, facetious. . . .

Respondent, however, asserts that the result should be different where the homosexual conduct occurs in the privacy of the home. He relies on *Stanley v. Georgia*, (1969), where the Court held that the First Amendment prevents conviction for possessing and reading obscene material in the privacy of one's home: "If the First Amendment means anything, it means that a State has no business telling a man, sitting alone in his house, what books he may read or what films he may watch.". . .

Stanley did protect conduct that would not have been protected outside the home, and it partially prevented the enforcement of state obscenity laws; but the decision was firmly grounded in the First Amendment. The right pressed upon us here has no similar support in the text of the Constitution, and it does not qualify for recognition under the prevailing principles for construing the Fourteenth Amendment. Its limits are also difficult to discern. Plainly enough, otherwise illegal conduct is not always immunized whenever it occurs in the home. Victimless crimes, such as the possession and use of illegal drugs, do not escape the law where they are committed at home. Stanley itself recognized that its holding offered no protection for the possession in the home of drugs, firearms, or stolen goods. . . . And if respondent's submission is limited to the voluntary sexual conduct between consenting adults, it would be difficult, except by fiat, to limit the claimed right to homosexual conduct while leaving exposed to prosecution adultery, incest, and other sexual crimes even though they are committed in the home. We are unwilling to start down that road.

Even if the conduct at issue here is not a fundamental right, respondent asserts that there must be a rational basis for the law and that there is none in this case other than the presumed belief of a majority of the electorate in Georgia that homosexual sodomy is immoral and unacceptable. This is said to be an inadequate rationale to support the law. The law, however, is constantly based on notions of morality, and if all laws representing essentially moral choices are to be invalidated under the Due Process Clause, the courts will be very busy indeed. Even respondent makes no such claim, but insists that majority sentiments about the morality of homosexuality should be declared inadequate. We do not agree, and are unpersuaded that the sodomy laws of some 25 States should be invalidated on this basis.

ROMER V. EVANS, 517 U.S. 620 (1996)

This decision found that Colorado's Amendment 2 was unconstitutional. Amendment 2 prevented Colorado local governments from passing laws banning discrimination on the basis of sexual orientation. Justice Kennedy wrote the majority opinion, joined by John Paul Stevens, Sandra Day O'Connor, David Ruth Bader, Anthony M. Ginsburg, and Stephen Breyer, with Justice Antonin Scalia filing a dissenting opinion, joined by Chief Justice William Rehnquist and Justice Clarence Thomas. For more background on Romer v. Evans, see Chapter 2.

Majority Opinion

[The opinion begins by defining Amendment 2 as the statewide law that would repeal certain local antidiscrimination laws.]

Yet Amendment 2, in explicit terms, does more than repeal or rescind these provisions. It prohibits all legislative, executive or judicial action at any level of state or local government designed to protect the named class, a class we shall refer to as homosexual persons or gays and lesbians. The amendment reads:

> *"No Protected Status Based on Homosexual, Lesbian, or Bisexual Orientation. Neither the State of Colorado, through any of its branches or departments, nor any of its agencies, political subdivisions, municipalities or school districts, shall enact,*

adopt or enforce any statute, regulation, ordinance or policy whereby homosexual, lesbian or bisexual orientation, conduct, practices or relationships shall constitute or otherwise be the basis of or entitle any person or class of persons to have or claim any minority status, quota preferences, protected status or claim of discrimination. This Section of the Constitution shall be in all respects self-executing."

Soon after Amendment 2 was adopted, this litigation to declare its invalidity and enjoin its enforcement was commenced in the District Court for the City and County of Denver. Among the plaintiffs . . . were homosexual persons, some of them government employees. They alleged that enforcement of Amendment 2 would subject them to immediate and substantial risk of discrimination on the basis of their sexual orientation. Other plaintiffs . . . included the three municipalities whose ordinances we have cited and certain other governmental entities which had acted earlier to protect homosexuals from discrimination but would be prevented by Amendment 2 from continuing to do so. . . .

The State's principal argument in defense of Amendment 2 is that it puts gays and lesbians in the same position as all other persons. So, the State says, the measure does no more than deny homosexuals special rights. This reading of the amendment's language is implausible. . . .

Homosexuals, by state decree, are put in a solitary class with respect to transactions and relations in both the private and governmental spheres. The amendment withdraws from homosexuals, but no others, specific legal protection from the injuries caused by discrimination, and it forbids reinstatement of these laws and policies.

The change that Amendment 2 works in the legal status of gays and lesbians in the private sphere is far-reaching, both on its own terms and when considered in light of the structure and operation of modern anti-discrimination laws. . . .

Amendment 2 bars homosexuals from securing protection against the injuries that . . . public-accommodations laws address. That in itself is a severe consequence, but there is more. Amendment 2, in addition, nullifies specific legal protections for this targeted class in all transactions in housing, sale of real estate, insurance, health and welfare services, private education, and employment. . . .

Not confined to the private sphere, Amendment 2 also operates to repeal and forbid all laws or policies providing specific protection for gays or lesbians from discrimination by every level of Colorado government. . . .

Amendment 2's reach may not be limited to specific laws passed for the benefit of gays and lesbians. It is a fair, if not necessary, inference from the broad language of the amendment that it deprives gays and lesbians even of the protection of general laws and policies that prohibit arbitrary discrimination in governmental and private settings. . . . At some point in the systematic administration of [existing anti-discrimination] laws, an official must determine whether homosexuality is an arbitrary and thus forbidden basis for decision. Yet a decision to that effect would itself amount to a policy prohibiting discrimination on the basis of homosexuality, and so would appear to be no more valid under Amendment 2 than the specific prohibitions against discrimination the state court held invalid. . . .

In any event, even if, as we doubt, homosexuals could find some safe harbor in laws of general application, we cannot accept the view that Amendment 2's prohibition on specific legal protections does no more than deprive homosexuals of special rights. To the contrary, the amendment imposes a special disability upon those persons alone. Homosexuals are forbidden the safeguards that others enjoy or may seek without constraint. They can obtain specific protection against discrimination only by enlisting the citizenry of Colorado to amend the state constitution or perhaps, on the State's view, by trying to pass helpful laws of general applicability. This is so no matter how local or discrete the harm, no matter how public and widespread the injury. We find nothing special in the protections Amendment 2 withholds. These are protections taken for granted by most people either because they already have them or do not need them; these are protections against exclusion from an almost limitless number of transactions and endeavors that constitute ordinary civic life in a free society. . . .

We cannot say that Amendment 2 is directed to any identifiable legitimate purpose or discrete objective. It is a status-based enactment divorced from any factual context from which we could discern a relationship to legitimate state interests; it is a classification of persons undertaken for its own sake, something the Equal Protection Clause does not permit. "[C]lass legislation . . . [is] obnoxious to the prohibitions of the Fourteenth Amendment. . . ." Civil Rights Cases, 109 U.S., at 24.

We must conclude that Amendment 2 classifies homosexuals not to further a proper legislative end but to make them unequal to everyone else. This Colorado cannot do. A State cannot so deem a class of persons a stranger to its laws. Amendment 2 violates the Equal Protection Clause, and the judgment of the Supreme Court of Colorado is affirmed.

It is so ordered.

Minority Opinion

[The dissenting opinion argues that homosexuals are just another political class: they have the right to argue for special protection, and the public has the right to deny them that protection. For more detail on the dissenting opinion, see Chapter 2.]

The Court's opinion contains grim, disapproving hints that Coloradans have been guilty of "animus" or "animosity" toward homosexuality, as though that has been established as Unamerican. Of course it is our moral heritage that one should not hate any human being or class of human beings. But I had thought that one could consider certain conduct reprehensible—murder, for example, or polygamy, or cruelty to animals—and could exhibit even "animus" toward such conduct. Surely that is the only sort of "animus" at issue here: moral disapproval of homosexual conduct, the same sort of moral disapproval that produced the centuries-old criminal laws that we held constitutional in *Bowers*. The Colorado amendment does not, to speak entirely precisely, prohibit giving favored status to people who are homosexuals; they can be favored for many reasons—for example, because they are senior citizens or members of racial minorities. But it prohibits giving them favored status because of their homosexual conduct—that is, it prohibits favored status for homosexuality.

But though Coloradans are, as I say, entitled to be hostile toward homosexual conduct, the fact is that the degree of hostility reflected by Amendment 2 is the smallest conceivable. The Court's portrayal of Coloradans as a society fallen victim to pointless, hate-filled "gay-bashing" is so false as to be comical. Colorado not only is one of the 25 States that have repealed their antisodomy laws, but was among the first to do so. . . . But the society that eliminates criminal punishment for homosexual acts does not necessarily abandon the view that homosexuality is morally wrong and socially harmful; often, abolition simply reflects the view that enforcement of such criminal laws involves unseemly intrusion into the intimate lives of citizens. . . .

There is a problem, however, which arises when criminal sanction of homosexuality is eliminated but moral and social disapprobation of homosexuality is meant to be retained. The Court cannot be unaware of that problem; it is evident in many cities of the country, and occasionally bubbles to the surface of the news, in heated political disputes over such matters as the introduction into local schools of books teaching that homosexuality is an optional and fully acceptable "alternate life style." The problem (a problem, that is, for those who wish to retain social disapprobation of homosexuality) is that, because those who engage in homosexual conduct tend to reside in disproportionate numbers in certain communities; . . . have high disposable income, . . . and of course care about homosexual-rights issues much more ardently than the public at large, they possess political power much greater than their numbers, both locally and statewide. Quite understandably, they devote this political power to achieving not merely a grudging social toleration, but full social acceptance, of homosexuality. . . .

That is where Amendment 2 came in. It sought to counter both the geographic concentration and the disproportionate political power of homosexuals by (1) resolving the controversy at the statewide level, and (2) making the election a single-issue contest for both sides. It put directly, to all the citizens of the State, the question: Should homosexuality be given special protection? They answered no. The Court today asserts that this most democratic of procedures is unconstitutional. Lacking any cases to establish that facially absurd proposition, it simply asserts that it must be unconstitutional, because it has never happened before.

LAWRENCE *ET AL. V.* TEXAS, 123 S. CT. 2472 (2003)

Responding to a reported weapons disturbance in a private residence, Houston police entered petitioner Lawrence's apartment and saw him and another adult man, petitioner Garner, engaging in a private, consensual sexual act. Petitioners were arrested and con-

victed of deviate sexual intercourse in violation of a Texas statute forbidding two persons of the same sex to engage in certain intimate sexual conduct. In affirming, the State Court of Appeals held, inter alia, *that the statue was not unconstitutional under the Due Process Clause of the Fourteenth Amendment. The court considered* Bowers v. Hardwick, . . . *controlling on that point.*

Held: The Texas statute making it a crime for two persons of the same sex to engage in certain intimate sexual conduct violates the Due Process Clause. Pp. 3–18.

(a) Resolution of this case depends on whether petitioners were free as adults to engage in private conduct in the exercise of their liberty under the Due Process Clause. For this inquiry the Court deems it necessary to reconsider its *Bowers* holding. The *Bowers* Court's initial substantive statement—"The issue presented is whether the Federal Constitution confers a fundamental right upon homosexuals to engage in sodomy . . . ,"— discloses the Court's failure to appreciate the extent of the liberty at stake. To say that the issue in *Bowers* was simply the right to engage in certain sexual conduct demeans the claim the individual put forward, just as it would demean a married couple were it said that marriage is just about the right to have sexual intercourse. Although the laws involved in *Bowers* and here purport to do not more than prohibit a particular sexual act, their penalties and purposes have more far-reaching consequences, touching upon the most private human conduct, sexual behavior, and in the most private of places, the home. They seek to control a personal relationship that, whether or not entitled to formal recognition in the law, is within the liberty of persons to choose without being punished as criminals. The liberty protected by the Constitution allows homosexual persons the right to choose to enter upon relationships in the confines of their homes and their own private lives and still retain their dignity as free persons. . . .

(b) Having misapprehended the liberty claim presented to it, the *Bowers* Court stated that proscriptions against sodomy have ancient roots . . . It should be noted, however, that there is no longstanding history in this country of laws directed at homosexual conduct as a distinct matter. Early American sodomy laws were not directed at homosexuals as such but instead sought to prohibit nonprocreative sexual activity more generally, whether between men and women or men and men. Moreover, early sodomy laws seem not to have been enforced against consenting adults acting in private. Instead, sodomy prosecutions often involved predatory acts against those who could not or did not consent: relations between men and minor girls or boys, between adults involving force, between adults implicating disparity in status, or between men and animals. The longstanding criminal prohibition of homosexual sodomy upon which *Bowers* placed such reliance is as consistent with a general condemnation of nonprocreative sex as it is with an established tradition of prosecuting acts because of their homosexual character. Far from possessing "ancient roots," *ibid.*, American laws targeting same-sex couples did not develop until the last third of the 20th century. Even now, only nine States have singled out same-sex relations for criminal prosecution. Thus, the historical grounds relied upon in *Bowers* are more complex than the majority opinion and the concurring opinion by Chief Justice Burger there indicated. They are not without doubt and, at the very least, are overstated. The *Bowers* Court was, of course, making the broader point that for centuries there have been powerful voices to condemn homosexual conduct as immoral, but this Court's obligation is to define the liberty of all, not to mandate its own moral code, *Planned Parenthood of Southeastern Pa. v. Casey*, . . . The Nation's laws and traditions in the past half century are most relevant here. They show an emerging awareness that liberty gives substantial protection to adult persons in deciding how to conduct their private lives in matters pertaining to sex. . . .

(c) *Bowers'* deficiencies became even more apparent in the years following its announcement. The 25 States with laws prohibiting the conduct referenced in *Bowers* are reduced now to 13, of which 4 enforce their laws only against homosexual conduct. In those States, including Texas, that still proscribe sodomy (whether for same-sex or heterosexual conduct), there is a pattern of nonenforcement with respect to consenting adults acting in private. . . . —which confirmed that the Due Process Clause protects personal decisions relating to marriage, procreation, contraception, family relationships, child rearing, and education—and *Romer* v. Evans, . . . which struck down class-based legislation directed at homosexuals—cast *Bowers'* holding into even more doubt. The stigma the Texas criminal statute imposes, moreover, is not trivial. Although the offense is but a minor misdemeanor, it remains a criminal offense with all that imports for the dignity of the persons charged, including notation of convictions on their records and on job application forms, and registration as sex offenders under state law. Where a case's foundations have sustained serious erosion, criticism from other sources is of greater significance. In the United States, criticism of *Bowers* has been substantial and continuing, disapproving of its reasoning in all respects, not just as to its historical assumptions. And, to the extent *Bowers* relied on values shared with a wider civilization, the case's reasoning and holding have been rejected by the European Court of Human Rights, and that other nations have taken action consistent with an affirmation of the protected right of homosexual adults to engage in intimate, consensual conduct. There has been no showing that in this country the governmental interest in circumscribing personal choice is somehow more legitimate or urgent. *Stare decisis* is not an inexorable command. . . . *Bowers'* holding has not induced detrimental reliance of the sort that could counsel against overturning it once there are compelling reasons to do so. . . . *Bowers* causes uncertainty, for the precedents before and after it contradict its central holding. . . .

(d) *Bowers'* rationale does not withstand careful analysis. In his dissenting opinion in *Bowers Justice Stevens* concluded that (1) the fact a State's governing majority has traditionally viewed a particular practice as immoral is not a sufficient reason for upholding a law prohibiting the practice, and (2) individual decisions concerning the intimacies of physical relationships, even when not intended to produce offspring, are a form of "liberty" protected by due process. That analysis should have controlled *Bowers*, and it controls here. *Bowers* was not correct when it was decided, is not correct today, and is hereby overruled. This case does not involve minors, persons who might be injured or coerced, those who might not easily refuse consent, or public conduct or prostitution. It does involve two adults who, with full and mutual consent, engaged in sexual practices common to a homosexual lifestyle. Petitioners' right to liberty under the Due Process Clause gives them the full right to engage in private conduct without government intervention. . . . The Texas statute furthers no legitimate state interest which can justify its intrusion into the individual's personal and private life. . . .

41 S. W. 3d 349, reversed and remanded.

Kennedy, J., delivered the opinion of the Court, in which *Stevens, Souter, Ginsburg*, and *Breyer, JJ.*, joined. *O'Connor, J.*, filed an opinion concurring in the judgment. *Scalia, J.*, filed a dissenting opinion, in which *Rehnquist, C. J.*, and *Thomas, J.*, joined. *Thomas, J.*, filed a dissenting opinion.

Justice O'Connor, concurring in the judgment.

The Court today overrules *Bowers* v. *Hardwick*, 478 U. S. 186 (1986). I joined *Bowers*, and do not join the Court in overruling it. Nevertheless, I agree with the Court that Texas' statute banning same-sex sodomy is unconstitutional. . . . Rather than relying on the substantive component of the Fourteenth Amendment's Due Process Clause, as the Court does, I base my conclusion on the Fourteenth Amendment's Equal Protection Clause.

The Equal Protection Clause of the Fourteenth Amendment "is essentially a direction that all persons similarly situated should be treated alike." . . . Under our rational basis standard of review, "legislation is presumed to be valid and will be sustained if the classification drawn by the statute is rationally related to a legitimate state interest. . . .

Laws such as economic or tax legislation that are scrutinized under rational basis review normally pass constitutional muster, since "the Constitution presumes that even improvident decisions will eventually be rectified by the democratic processes." . . . We have consistently held, however, that some objectives, such as "a bare . . . desire to harm a politically unpopular group," are not legitimate state interests. . . . When a law exhibits such a desire to harm a politically unpopular group, we have applied a more searching form of rational basis review to strike down such laws under the Equal Protection Clause.

We have been most likely to apply rational basis review to hold a law unconstitutional under the Equal Protection Clause where, as here, the challenged legislation inhibits personal relationships. In *Department of Agriculture* v. *Moreno*, for example, we held that a law preventing those households containing an individual unrelated to any other member of the household from receiving food stamps violated equal protection because the purpose of the law was to "'discriminate against hippies.'", . . . The asserted governmental interest in preventing food stamp fraud was not deemed sufficient to satisfy rational basis review . . . In *Eisenstadt* v. *Baird*, 405 U. S. 438, 447–455 (1972), we refused to sanction a law that discriminated between married and unmarried persons by prohibiting the distribution of contraceptives to single persons. Likewise, in *Cleburne* v. *Cleburne Living Center, supra*, we held that it was irrational for a State to require a home for the mentally disabled to obtain a special use permit when other residences—like fraternity houses and apartment buildings—did not have to obtain such a permit. And in *Romer* v. *Evans*, we disallowed a state statute that "impos[ed] a broad and undifferentiated disability on a single named group"— specifically, homosexuals. 517 U. S., at 632. . . .

The statute at issue here makes sodomy a crime only if a person "engages in deviate sexual intercourse with another individual of the same sex." Tex. Penal Code Ann. §21.06(a) (2003). Sodomy between opposite-sex partners, however, is not a crime in Texas. That is, Texas treats the same conduct differently based solely on the participants. Those harmed by this law are people who have a same-sex sexual orientation and thus are more likely to engage in behavior prohibited by §21.06.

The Texas statute makes homosexuals unequal in the eyes of the law by making particular conduct—and only that conduct—subject to criminal sanction. It appears that prosecutions under Texas' sodomy law are rare . . . and in all probability will not be, enforced against private consensual conduct between adults"). This case shows, however, that prosecutions under §21.06 *do* occur. And while the penalty imposed on petitioners in this case was relatively minor, the consequences of conviction are not. As the Court notes, see *ante*, at 15, petitioners' convictions, if upheld, would disqualify them from or restrict their ability to engage in a variety of professions, including medicine, athletic training, and interior design . . . Indeed, were petitioners to move to one of four States, their convictions would require them to register as sex offenders to local law enforcement. . . .

And the effect of Texas' sodomy law is not just limited to the threat of prosecution or consequence of conviction. Texas' sodomy law brands all homosexuals as criminals, thereby making it more difficult for homosexuals to be treated in the same manner as everyone else. Indeed, Texas itself has previously acknowledged the collateral effects of the law, stipulating in a prior challenge to this action that the law "legally sanctions discrimination against [homosexuals] in a variety of ways unrelated to the criminal law," including in the areas of "employment, family issues, and housing.". . .

Texas attempts to justify its law, and the effects of the law, by arguing that the statute satisfies rational basis review because it furthers the legitimate governmental interest of the promotion of morality. In *Bowers*, we held that a state law criminalizing sodomy as applied to homosexual couples did not violate substantive due process. We rejected the argument that no rational basis existed to justify the law, pointing to the government's interest in promoting morality . . . The only question in front of the Court in *Bowers* was whether the substantive component of the Due Process Clause protected a right to engage in homosexual sodomy. . . . *Bowers* did not hold that moral disapproval of a group is a rational basis under the Equal Protection Clause to criminalize homosexual sodomy when heterosexual sodomy is not punished.

This case raises a different issue than *Bowers:* whether, under the Equal Protection Clause, moral disapproval is a legitimate state interest to justify by itself a statute that bans homosexual sodomy, but not heterosexual sodomy. It is not. Moral disapproval of this group, like a bare desire to harm the group, is an interest that is insufficient to satisfy rational basis review under the Equal Protection Clause. . . . Indeed, we have never held that moral disapproval, without any other asserted state interest, is a sufficient rationale under the Equal Protection Clause to justify a law that discriminates among groups of persons.

Moral disapproval of a group cannot be a legitimate governmental interest under the Equal Protection Clause because legal classifications must not be "drawn for the purpose of disadvantaging the group burdened by the law." . . . Texas' invocation of moral disapproval as a legitimate state interest proves nothing more than Texas' desire to criminalize homosexual sodomy. But the Equal Protection Clause prevents a State from creating "a classification of persons undertaken for its own sake." . . . And because Texas so rarely enforces its sodomy law as applied to private, consensual acts, the law serves more as a statement of dislike and disapproval against homosexuals than as a tool to stop criminal behavior. The Texas sodomy law "raise[s] the inevitable inference that the disadvantage imposed is born of animosity toward the class of persons affected.". . .

Texas argues, however, that the sodomy law does not discriminate against homosexual persons. Instead, the State maintains that the law discriminates only against homosexual conduct. While it is true that the law applies only to conduct, the conduct targeted by this law is conduct that is closely correlated with being homosexual. Under such circumstances, Texas' sodomy law is targeted at more than conduct. It is instead directed toward gay persons as a class. "After all, there can hardly be more palpable discrimination against a class than making the conduct that defines the class criminal." *Id.*, at 641 (*Scalia, J.*, dissenting) (internal quotation marks omitted). When a State makes homosexual conduct criminal, and not "deviate sexual intercourse" committed by persons of different sexes, "that declaration in and of itself is an invitation to subject homosexual persons to discrimination both in the public and in the private spheres." *Ante*, at 14.

Indeed, Texas law confirms that the sodomy statute is directed toward homosexuals as a class. In Texas, calling a person a homosexual is slander *per se* because the word "homosexual" "impute[s] the commission of a crime." . . . The State has admitted that because of the sodomy law, *being* homosexual carries the presumption of being a criminal . . . See *State* v. *Morales*, 826 S. W. 2d, at 202–203 ("[T]he statute brands lesbians and gay men as criminals and thereby legally sanctions discrimination against them in a variety of ways unrelated to the criminal law"). Texas' sodomy law therefore results in discrimination against homosexuals as a class in an array of areas outside the criminal law. See *ibid*. In *Romer* v. *Evans*, we refused to sanction a law that singled out homosexuals "for disfavored legal status." 517 U. S., at 633. The same is true here. The Equal Protection Clause "'neither knows nor tolerates classes among citizens.'" *Id.*, at 623 (quoting *Plessy* v. *Ferguson*, 163 U. S. 537, 559 (1896) (Harlan, J. dissenting)).

A State can of course assign certain consequences to a violation of its criminal law. But the State cannot single out one identifiable class of citizens for punishment that does not apply to everyone else, with moral disapproval as the only asserted state interest for the law. The Texas sodomy statute subjects homosexuals to "a lifelong penalty and stigma. A legislative classification that threatens the creation of an underclass . . . cannot be reconciled with" the Equal Protection Clause. . . .

Whether a sodomy law that is neutral both in effect and application, . . . would violate the substantive component of the Due Process Clause is an issue that need not be decided today. I am confident, however, that so long as the Equal Protection Clause requires a sodomy law to apply equally to the private consensual conduct of homosexuals and heterosexuals alike, such a law would not long stand in our democratic society. In the words of Justice Jackson:

> *"The framers of the Constitution knew, and we should not forget today, that there is no more effective practical guaranty against arbitrary and unreasonable government than to require that the principles of law which officials would impose upon a minority be imposed generally. Conversely, nothing opens the door to arbitrary action so effectively as to allow those officials to pick and choose only a few to whom they will apply legislation and thus to escape the political retribution that might be visited upon them if larger numbers were affected."* Railway Express Agency, *Inc. v.* New York, *336 U. S. 106, 112–113 (1949) (concurring opinion).*

That this law as applied to private, consensual conduct is unconstitutional under the Equal Protection Clause does not mean that other laws distinguishing between heterosexuals and homosexuals would similarly fail under rational basis review. Texas cannot assert any legitimate state interest here, such as national security or preserving the traditional institution of marriage. Unlike the moral disapproval of same-sex relations—the asserted state interest in this case—other reasons exist to promote the institution of marriage beyond mere moral disapproval of an excluded group.

A law branding one class of persons as criminal solely based on the State's moral disapproval of that class and the conduct associated with that class runs contrary to the values of the Constitution and the Equal Protection Clause, under any standard of review. I therefore concur in the Court's judgment that Texas' sodomy law banning "deviate sexual intercourse" between consenting adults of the same sex, but not between consenting adults of different sexes, is unconstitutional.

Minority Opinion

Justice Scalia, with whom *The Chief Justice* and *Justice Thomas* join, dissenting.

[*Justice Scalia begins by explaining his objections to overturning the previous decision,* Bowers v. Hardwick.]

. . . *Bowers* held, first, that criminal prohibitions of homosexual sodomy are not subject to heightened scrutiny because they do not implicate a "fundamental right" under the Due Process Clause . . . Noting that "[p]roscriptions against that conduct have ancient roots," *id.*, at 192, that "[s]odomy was a criminal offense at common law and was forbidden by the laws of the original 13 States when they ratified the Bill of Rights," *ibid.*, and that many States had retained their bans on sodomy . . . , *Bowers* concluded that a right to engage in homosexual sodomy was not "'deeply rooted in this Nation's history and tradition.'". . .

The Court today does not overrule this holding. Not once does it describe homosexual sodomy as a "fundamental right" or a "fundamental liberty interest," nor does it subject the Texas statute to strict scrutiny. Instead, having failed to establish that the right to homosexual sodomy is "'deeply rooted in this Nation's history and tradition,'" the Court concludes that the application of Texas's statute to petitioners' conduct fails the rational-basis test, and overrules *Bowers'* holding to the contrary, see *id.*, at 196. "The Texas statute furthers no legitimate state interest which can justify its intrusion into the personal and private life of the individual." *Ante*, at 18. . . .

I turn now to the ground on which the Court squarely rests its holding: the contention that there is no rational basis for the law here under attack. This proposition is so out of accord with our jurisprudence—indeed, with the jurisprudence of *any* society we know—that it requires little discussion.

The Texas statute undeniably seeks to further the belief of its citizens that certain forms of sexual behavior are "immoral and unacceptable," *Bowers*, *supra*, at 196—the same interest furthered by criminal laws against fornication, bigamy, adultery, adult incest, bestiality, and obscenity. *Bowers* held that this *was* a legitimate state interest. The Court today reaches the opposite conclusion. The Texas statute, it says, "furthers *no legitimate state interest* which can justify its intrusion into the personal and private life of the individual," *ante*, at 18 (emphasis added). The Court embraces instead *Justice Stevens'* declaration in his *Bowers* dissent, that "the fact that the governing majority in a State has traditionally viewed a particular practice as immoral is not a sufficient reason for upholding a law prohibiting the practice," *ante*, at 17. This effectively decrees the end of all morals legislation. If, as the Court asserts, the promotion of majoritarian sexual morality is not even a *legitimate* state interest, none of the abovementioned laws can survive rational-basis review. . . .

Finally, I turn to petitioners' equal-protection challenge, which no Member of the Court save *Justice O'Connor, ante,* at 1 (opinion concurring in judgment), embraces: On its face §21.06(a) applies equally to all persons. Men and women, heterosexuals and homosexuals, are all subject to its prohibition of deviate sexual intercourse with someone of the same sex. To be sure, §21.06 does distinguish between the sexes insofar as concerns the partner with whom the sexual acts are performed: men can violate the law only with other men, and women only with other women. But this cannot itself be a denial of equal protection, since it is precisely the same distinction regarding partner that is drawn in state laws prohibiting marriage with someone of the same sex while permitting marriage with someone of the opposite sex.

The objection is made, however, that the antimiscegenation laws invalidated in *Loving* v. *Virginia* . . . , similarly were applicable to whites and blacks alike, and only distinguished between the races insofar as the *partner* was concerned. In *Loving,* however, we correctly applied heightened scrutiny, rather than the usual rational-basis review, because the Virginia statute was "designed to maintain White Supremacy." . . . A racially discriminatory purpose is always sufficient to subject a law to strict scrutiny, even a facially neutral law that makes no mention of race. . . . No purpose to discriminate against men or women as a class can be gleaned from the Texas law, so rational-basis review applies. That review is readily satisfied here by the same rational basis that satisfied it in *Bowers*—society's belief that certain forms of sexual behavior are "immoral and unacceptable," . . . This is the same justification that supports many other laws regulating sexual behavior that make a distinction based upon the identity of the partner—for example, laws against adultery, fornication, and adult incest, and laws refusing to recognize homosexual marriage.

Justice O'Connor argues that the discrimination in this law which must be justified is not its discrimination with regard to the sex of the partner but its discrimination with regard to the sexual proclivity of the principal actor.

> *"While it is true that the law applies only to conduct, the conduct targeted by this law is conduct that is closely correlated with being homosexual. Under such circumstances, Texas' sodomy law is targeted at more than conduct. It is instead directed toward gay persons as a class."* Ante, *at 5.*

Of course the same could be said of any law. A law against public nudity targets "the conduct that is closely correlated with being a nudist," and hence "is targeted at more than conduct"; it is "directed toward nudists as a class." But be that as it may. Even if the Texas law *does* deny equal protection to "homosexuals as a class," that denial *still* does not need to be justified by anything more than a rational basis, which our cases show is satisfied by the enforcement of traditional notions of sexual morality.

Justice O'Connor simply decrees application of "a more searching form of rational basis review" to the Texas statute. *Ante,* at 2. The cases she cites do not recognize such a standard, and reach their conclusions only after finding, as required by conventional rational-basis analysis, that no conceivable legitimate state interest supports the classification at issue. . . . Nor does *Justice O'Connor* explain precisely what her "more searching form" of rational-basis review consists of. It must at least mean, however, that laws exhibiting "'a . . . desire to harm a politically unpopular group,'" *ante*, at 2, are invalid *even though* there may be a conceivable rational basis to support them.

This reasoning leaves on pretty shaky grounds state laws limiting marriage to opposite-sex couples. *Justice O'Connor* seeks to preserve them by the conclusory statement that "preserving the traditional institution of marriage" is a legitimate state interest. *Ante*, at 7. But "preserving the traditional institution of marriage" is just a kinder way of describing the State's *moral disapproval* of same-sex couples. Texas's interest in §21.06 could be recast in similarly euphemistic terms: "preserving the traditional sexual mores of our society." In the jurisprudence *Justice O'Connor* has seemingly created, judges can validate laws by characterizing them as "preserving the traditions of society" (good); or invalidate them by characterizing them as "expressing moral disapproval" (bad).

Today's opinion is the product of a Court, which is the product of a law-profession culture, that has largely signed on to the so-called homosexual agenda, by which I mean the agenda promoted by some homosexual activists directed at eliminating the moral opprobrium that has traditionally attached to homosexual conduct. I noted in an earlier opinion the fact that the American Association of Law Schools (to which any reputable law school *must* seek to belong) excludes from membership any school that refuses to ban from its job-interview facilities a law firm (no matter how small) that does not wish to hire as a prospective partner a person who openly engages in homosexual conduct. . . .

One of the most revealing statements in today's opinion is the Court's grim warning that the criminalization of homosexual conduct is "an invitation to subject homosexual persons to discrimination both in the public and in the private spheres." *Ante*, at 14. It is clear from this that the Court has taken sides in the culture war, departing from its role of assuring, as neutral observer, that the democratic rules of engagement are observed. Many Americans do not want persons who openly engage in homosexual conduct as partners in their business, as scoutmasters for their children, as teachers in their children's schools, or as boarders in their home. They view this as protecting themselves and their families from a lifestyle that they believe to be immoral and destructive. The Court views it as "discrimination" which it is the function of our judgments to deter. So imbued is the Court with the law profession's anti-anti-homosexual culture, that it is seemingly unaware that the attitudes of that culture are not obviously "mainstream"; that in most States what the Court calls "discrimination" against those who engage in homosexual acts is perfectly legal; that proposals to ban such "discrimination" under Title VII have repeatedly been rejected by Congress, see Employment Non-Discrimination Act of 1994, S. 2238, 103d Cong., 2d Sess. (1994); Civil Rights Amendments, H. R. 5452, 94th Cong., 1st Sess. (1975); that in some cases such "discrimination" is *mandated* by federal statute, see 10 U. S. C. §654(b)(1) (mandating discharge from the armed forces of any service member who engages in or intends to engage in homosexual acts); and that in some cases such "discrimination" is a constitutional right, see *Boy Scouts of America* v. *Dale*, 530 U. S. 640 (2000).

Let me be clear that I have nothing against homosexuals, or any other group, promoting their agenda through normal democratic means. Social perceptions of sexual and other morality change over time, and every group has the right to persuade its fellow citizens that its view of such matters is the best. That homosexuals have achieved some success in that enterprise is attested to by the fact that Texas is one of the few remaining States that criminalize private, consensual homosexual acts. But persuading one's fellow citizens is one thing, and imposing one's views in absence of democratic majority will is something else. I would no more *require* a State to criminalize homosexual acts—or, for that matter, display *any* moral disapproval of them—than I would *forbid* it to do so. What Texas has chosen to do is well within the range of traditional democratic action, and its hand should not be stayed through the invention of a brand-new "constitutional right" by a Court that is impatient of democratic change. It is indeed true that "later generations can see that laws once thought necessary and proper in fact serve only to oppress," *ante*, at 18; and when that happens, later generations can repeal those laws. But it is the premise of our system that those judgments are to be made by the people, and not imposed by a governing caste that knows best.

One of the benefits of leaving regulation of this matter to the people rather than to the courts is that the people, unlike judges, need not carry things to their logical conclusion. The people may feel that their disapproval of homosexual conduct is strong enough to disallow homosexual marriage, but not strong enough to criminalize private homosexual acts—and may legislate accordingly. The Court today pretends that it possesses a similar freedom of action, so that that we need not fear judicial imposition of homosexual marriage, as has recently occurred in Canada (in a decision that the Canadian Government has chosen not to appeal). . . . At the end of its opinion—after having laid waste the foundations of our rational-basis jurisprudence—the Court says that the present case "does not involve whether the government must give formal recognition to any relationship that homosexual persons seek to enter." *Ante*, at 17. Do not believe it. More illuminating than this bald, unreasoned disclaimer is the progression of thought displayed by an earlier passage in the Court's opinion, which notes the constitutional protections afforded to "personal decisions relating to *marriage*, procreation, contraception, family relationships, child rearing, and education," and then declares that "[p]ersons in a homosexual relationship may seek autonomy for these purposes, just as heterosexual persons do." *Ante*, at 13 (emphasis added). Today's opinion dismantles the structure of constitutional law that has permitted a distinction to be made between heterosexual and homosexual unions, insofar as formal recognition in marriage is concerned. If moral disapprobation of homosexual conduct is "no legitimate state interest" for purposes of proscribing that conduct, *ante*, at 18; and if, as the Court coos (casting aside all pretense of neutrality), "[w]hen sexuality finds overt expression in intimate conduct with another person, the conduct can be but one element in a personal bond that is more enduring," *ante*, at 6; what justification could there possibly be for denying the benefits of marriage to homosexual couples exercising "[t]he liberty protected by the Constitution," *ibid.?* Surely not the encouragement of procreation, since the sterile and the elderly are allowed to marry. This case "does not involve" the issue of homosexual marriage only if one entertains the belief that principle and logic have nothing to do with the decisions of this Court. Many will hope that, as the Court comfortingly assures us, this is so.

The matters appropriate for this Court's resolution are only three: Texas's prohibition of sodomy neither infringes a "fundamental right" (which the Court does not dispute), nor is unsupported by a rational relation to what the Constitution considers a legitimate state interest, nor denies the equal protection of the laws. I dissent.

STATE COURT

NORTON V. MACY, 417 F.2D. 1161 (1969)

When a National Aeronautics and Space Administration (NASA) employee was arrested for soliciting another man, he was fired from his job. The employee sued to regain his job, and the U.S. Court of Appeals eventually upheld his suit, ruling that federal employees could not be fired for "immoral behaviors" that did not affect their work performance. As the court described it:

Appellant's dismissal grew out of his arrest for a traffic violation. In the early morning of October 22, 1963, he was driving his car in the vicinity of Lafayette Square. He pulled over to the curb, picked up one Madison Monroe Procter, drove him once around the Square, and dropped him off at the starting point. The two men then drove off in separate cars. Two Morals Squad officers, having observed this sequence of events, gave chase, traveling at speeds of up to 45 miles per hour. In the parking lot of appellant's Southwest Washington apartment building, Procter told the police that appellant had felt his leg during their brief circuit of Lafayette Square and then invited him to appellant's apartment for a drink. The officers arrested both men and took them "to the Morals Office to issue a traffic violation notice."

. . . Meanwhile, pursuant to an arrangement, the head of the Morals Squad telephoned NASA Security Chief Fugler, who arrived on the scene at 3:00 A.M. in time to hear the last of the interrogation. . . .

[Subsequently] NASA concluded that appellant did in fact make a homosexual advance on October 22, and that this act amounted to "immoral, indecent, and disgraceful conduct." It also determined that, on the basis of his own admissions to Fugler, even as subsequently clarified, appellant possesses "traits of character and personality which render [him] unsuitable for further Government employment." A Civil Service Appeals Examiner and the Board of Appeals and Review upheld these conclusions. . . .

[The Court then outlines the two bases on which appellant's discharge could be justified.]

We are not prepared to say that the [Civil Service] Commission could not reasonably find appellant's homosexual advance to be "immoral," "indecent," or "notoriously disgraceful" under dominant conventional norms. But the notion that it could be an appropriate function of the federal bureaucracy to enforce the majority's conventional codes of conduct in the private lives of its employees is at war with elementary concepts of liberty, privacy, and diversity. And whatever we may think of the Government's qualifications to act *in loco parentis* in this way, the statute precludes it from discharging protected employees except for a reason related to the efficiency of the service. Accordingly, a finding that an employee had done something immoral or indecent could support a dismissal without further inquiry only if all immoral or indecent acts of any employee have some ascertainable deleterious effect on the efficiency of the service. The range of conduct which might be said to affront prevailing mores is so broad and varied that we can hardly arrive at any such conclusion without reference to specific conduct. Thus, we think the sufficiency of the charges against appellant must be evaluated in terms of the effects on the service of what in particular he has done or has been shown to be likely to do. . . .

[or, failing this test]

. . . appellee is now obliged to rely solely on this possibility of embarrassment to the agency to justify appellant's dismissal. . . .

[the Court then concludes that]

Lest there be any doubt, we emphasize that we do not hold that homosexual conduct may never be cause for dismissal of a protected federal employee. Nor do we even conclude that potential embarrassment from an employee's private conduct may in no circumstances affect the efficiency of the service. What we do say is that, if the statute is to have any force, an agency cannot support a dismissal as promoting of the efficiency of the service merely by turning its head and crying "shame."

Since we conclude that appellant's discharge cannot be sustained on the grounds relied on by the Commission, the judgment of the District Court may be Reversed.

GAY STUDENTS ORGANIZATION OF THE UNIVERSITY OF NEW HAMPSHIRE V. BONNER, 367 F. SUPP. 1088 (1974)

A group of gay students at the University of New Hampshire sued the university for equal access to facilities that would have been allowed to nongay students—a plea that was upheld in 1974 by the New Hampshire Supreme Court. As the court found:

This civil rights action arises out of the denial by the University of New Hampshire officials of the right of the Gay Students Organization (hereinafter GSO), a homosexual organization, to hold "social functions.". . .

The GSO was organized and officially recognized as a student organization in May of 1973. The normal recognition procedure was followed. . . . On November 9, 1973, the GSO sponsored a dance on campus. This function was held without incident. . . . After the dance, there was criticism by the Governor of New Hampshire, who complained to the University about the propriety of allowing such a "spectacle.". . .

Thereafter, the GSO asked for permission to sponsor an on-campus play on December 7, 1973, and to have a social function following the play. The GSO was granted the right to put on the play, but permission for a social function following the play was denied. . . .

The play was presented on December 7th as scheduled. Although the play itself caused little comment, there was some reaction to "Fag Rag Five" and "Fag Rag VI," two "extremist homosexual" publications which were distributed sometime during the evening. . . .

After the play, the Governor of New Hampshire wrote an open letter to the Board of Trustees, wherein he stated:

> *Therefore, after very careful consideration, I must inform you the trustees and administration that indecency and moral filth will no longer be allowed on our campuses.*
>
> *Either you take firm, fair and positive action to rid your campuses of socially abhorrent activities or I, as governor, will stand solidly against the expenditure of one more cent of taxpayers' money for your institutions. . . .*

Shortly thereafter, on December 17, 1973, Dr. Bonner, President of the University, issued a public statement which condemned the distribution of the Fag Rag literature, ordered an "immediate investigation" to establish responsibility for the distribution, and declared:

> *. . . I have ordered that the current Trustee ban on GSO social functions be interpreted more strictly by administrative authorities than had been the case before December 7, 1973.*

[The Court's summary of its findings concludes that:]

In essence, this case is quite simple. The First Amendment guarantees all individuals, including university students, the right to organize and associate "to further their personal beliefs." . . . Absent the attendance of well-defined circumstances, a university must recognize any bona fide student organization and grant to that organization the rights and privileges which normally flow from such recognition. . . . From this, it follows that the GSO has the same right to be recognized, to use campus facilities, and to hold functions, social or otherwise, as every other organization on the University of New Hampshire campus.

University officials must understand that *[quoting from a previous case:]*

mere disagreement . . . with the group's philosophy affords no reason to deny it recognition. . . . The [University], acting here as the instrumentality of the State, may not restrict speech or association simply because it finds the views expressed by any group to be abhorrent. . . .

For the foregoing reasons, the defendants are herewith enjoined from prohibiting or restricting the sponsorship of social functions or use of University facilities for such functions by the Gay Students Organization. Defendants are further enjoined from treating the Gay Students Organization differently than other University study organizations.

So ordered.

FRICKE V. LYNCH, 491 F. SUPP. 381 (1980)

Aaron Fricke wanted to take a male date to his high school senior prom—and when the school said he could not, Fricke sued. Eventually, a U.S. District Court ruled that same-sex couples had to be allowed to attend a high school senior reception:

This year, during or after an assembly in April in which senior class events were discussed, Aaron Fricke, a senior at Cumberland High School, decided that he wanted to attend the senior reception with a male companion. . . .

Aaron asked principal Lynch for permission to bring a male escort, which Lynch denied. . . . Lynch gave Aaron written reasons for his action; his prime reason was the fear that a disruption would occur and Aaron or, especially, Paul [his intended companion] would be hurt. He indicated in court that he would allow Aaron to bring a male escort if there were no threat of violence. . . .

After considerable thought and research, I [the judge] have concluded that even a legitimate interest in school discipline does not outweigh a student's right to peacefully express his views in an appropriate time, place, and manner. To rule otherwise would completely subvert free speech in the schools by granting other students a "heckler's veto," allowing them to decide—through prohibited and violent methods—what speech will be heard. The first amendment does not tolerate mob rule by unruly school children.

This conclusion is bolstered by the fact that any disturbance here, however great, would not interfere with the main business of school—education. No classes or school work would be affected; at the very worst an optional social event, conducted by the students for their own enjoyment, would be marred. In such a context, the school does have an obligation to take reasonable measures to protect and foster free speech, not to stand helpless before unauthorized student violence.

Appendix A

BRASCHI V. STAHL ASSOCIATES CO., 74 N.Y.2D 201, 544, N.Y.S. 2D 784, 543 N.R. 2ND 49 (1989)

When Miguel Braschi's life partner died, Braschi was in danger of being evicted from his rent-controlled apartment because only his partner's name was on the lease. A married widow or widower would have had the legal right to stay in the apartment—and Braschi sued for the same right. In 1989, the New York Court of Appeals ruled that unmarried domestic partners have the same housing rights available to married couples:

Appellant, Miguel Braschi, was living with Leslie Blanchard in a rent-controlled apartment located at 405 East 54th Street from the summer of 1975 until Blanchard's death in September of 1986. In November of 1986, respondent, Stahl Associates Company, the owner of the apartment building, served a Notice to Cure on appellant contending that he was a mere licensee with no right to occupy the apartment since only Blanchard was the tenant of record. In December of 1986 respondent served appellant with a Notice to Terminate, informing appellant that he had one month to vacate the apartment and that, if the apartment was not vacated, respondent would commence summary proceedings to evict him. . . .

[The Court then summarizes the history of the New York State housing law.]

Contrary to all of these arguments, we conclude that the term family, as used in 9 NYCRR §2204.6(d), should not be rigidly restricted to those people who have formalized their relationship by obtaining, for instance, a marriage certificate or an adoption order. The intended protection against sudden eviction should not rest on fictitious legal distinctions or genetic history, but instead should find its foundation in the reality of family life. In the context of eviction, a more realistic, and certainly equally valid, view of a family includes two adult lifetime partners whose relationship is long-term and characterized by an emotional and financial commitment and interdependence. This view comports both with our society's traditional concept of "family" and with the expectations of individuals who live in such nuclear units. . . .

[In reaching its final decision, the Court concludes that:]

Appellant and Blanchard lived together as permanent life partners for more than ten years. They regarded one another, and were regarded by friends and family, as spouses. The two men's families were aware of the nature of the relationship, and they regularly visited each other's families and attended family functions together, as a couple. Even today, appellant continues to maintain a relationship with Blanchard's niece, who considers him an uncle.

  In addition to their interwoven social lives, appellant clearly considered the apartment his home. He lists the apartment as his address on his driver's license and passport, and receives all his mail at the apartment address. Moreover, appellant's tenancy was known to the building's superintendent and doormen, who viewed the two men as a couple.

Financially, the two men shared all obligations including a household budget. The two were authorized signatories of three safe deposit boxes, they maintained joint checking and savings accounts, and joint credit cards. In fact, rent was often paid with a check from their joint checking account. Additionally, Blanchard executed a power of attorney in appellant's favor so that appellant could make necessary decisions—financial, medical and personal—for him during his illness. Finally, appellant was the named beneficiary of Blanchard's life insurance policy, as well as the primary legatee and co-executor of Blanchard's estate. Hence, a court examining these facts could reasonably conclude that these men were much more than mere roommates.

[Based on the Court's decision in this case, the New York State Housing Agency announced a new and broader definition of family that includes unmarried same-sex couples.]

IN THE MATTER OF ALISON D. (ANONYMOUS) V. VIRGINIA M. (ANONYMOUS), 77 N.Y. 2D 651, 572, N.E. 2D 27, 569 N.Y.S. 2D 586 (1991)

This case concerned a lesbian couple that had separated. At issue was the question of whether the nonbiological parent had visitation rights with the child that they had raised together. The court decision describes the facts of the case, goes on to give the minority opinion, which would deny the nonbiological parent any visitation rights whatsoever, and then gives the dissenting opinion by Judge Judith Kaye, who argued for the nonbiological parent's right to visit the child she had helped to raise.

Decision

At issue in this case is whether plaintiff, a biological stranger to a child who is properly in the custody of his biological mother, has standing to seek visitation with the child under Domestic Relations Law § 70. Plaintiff relies on both her established relationship with the child and her alleged agreement with the biological mother to support her claim that she has standing. We agree with the Appellate Division that, although plaintiff apparently nurtured a close and loving relationship with the child, she is not a parent within the meaning of Domestic Relations Law § 70. Accordingly, we affirm.

I

Petitioner Alison D. and respondent Virginia M. established a relationship in September 1977 and began living together in March 1978. In March 1980, they decided to have a child and agreed that respondent would be artificially inseminated. Together, they planned for the conception and birth of the child and agreed to share jointly all rights and responsibilities of child-rearing. In July 1981, respondent gave birth to a baby boy, A.D.M., who was given petitioner's last name as his middle name and respondent's last name became his last name. Respondent shared in all birthing expenses and, after A.D.M.'s birth, continued to provide for his support. During A.D.M.'s first two years, petitioner and respondent jointly cared for and made decisions regarding the child.

In November 1983, when the child was 2 years and 4 months old, petitioner and respondent terminated their relationship and petitioner moved out of the home they jointly owned. Petitioner and respondent agreed to a visitation schedule whereby petitioner continued to see the child a few times a week. Petitioner also agreed to continue to pay one-half of the mortgage and major household expenses. By this time, the child had referred to both respondent and petitioner as "mommy". Petitioner's visitation with the child continued until 1986, at which time respondent bought out petitioner's interest in the house and then began to restrict petitioner's visitation with the child. In 1987 petitioner moved to Ireland to pursue career opportunities, but continued her attempts to communicate with the child. Thereafter, respondent terminated all contact between respondent and the child, returning all of petitioner's gifts and letters. No dispute exists that respondent is a fit parent. Petitioner commenced this proceeding seeking visitation rights pursuant to Domestic Relations Law § 70.

Supreme Court dismissed the proceeding concluding that petitioner is not a parent under Domestic Relations Law § 70 and, given the concession that respondent is a fit parent, petitioner is not entitled to seek visitation pursuant to section 70. The Appellate Division affirmed, with one justice dissenting, and granted leave to appeal to our court. . . .

II

Petitioner concedes that she is not the child's "parent"; that is, she is not the biological mother of the child nor is she a legal parent by virtue of an adoption. Rather she claims to have acted as a "de facto" parent or that she should be viewed as a parent "by estoppel". Therefore, she claims she has standing to seek visitation rights. These claims, however, are insufficient under section 70. Traditionally, in this State it is the child's mother and father who, assuming fitness, have the right to the care and custody of their child, even in situations where the nonparent has exercised some control over the child with the parents' consent. . . . To allow the courts to award visitation—a limited form of custody—to a third person would necessarily impair the parents' right to custody and control. Petitioner concedes that respondent is a fit parent. Therefore she has no right to petition the court to displace the choice made by this fit parent in deciding what is in the child's best interests. . . .

While one may dispute in an individual case whether it would be beneficial to a child to have continued contact with a nonparent, the Legislature did not in section 70 give such nonparent the opportunity to compel a fit parent to allow them to do so. . . .

Accordingly, the order of the Appellate Division should be affirmed, with costs.

Judge Kaye's Dissenting Opinion

The Court's decision, fixing biology as the key to visitation rights, has impact far beyond this particular controversy, one that may affect a wide spectrum of relationships—including those of long-time heterosexual stepparents, "common law" and non-heterosexual partners such as involved here, and even participants in scientific reproduction procedures. Estimates that more than 15.5 million children do not live with two biological parents, and that as many as eight to ten million children are born into families with a gay or lesbian parent, suggest just how widespread the impact may be. . . .

But the impact of today's decision falls hardest on the children of those relationships, limiting their opportunity to maintain bonds that may be crucial to their development. The majority's retreat from the courts' proper role—its tightening of rules that should in visitation petitions, above all, retain the capacity to take the children's interests into account—compels this dissent. . . .

Most significantly, Virginia M. agrees that, after long cohabitation with Alison D. and before A.D.M.'s conception, it was "explicitly planned that the child would be theirs to raise together." It is also uncontested that the two shared "financial and emotional preparations" for the birth, and that for several years Alison D. actually filled the role of co-parent to A.D.M., both tangibly and intangibly. In all, a parent-child relationship—encouraged or at least condoned by Virginia M.—apparently existed between A.D.M. and Alison D. during the first six years of the child's life.

While acknowledging that relationship, the Court nonetheless proclaims powerlessness to consider the child's interest at all, because the word "parent" in the statute imposes an absolute barrier to Alison D.'s petition for visitation. That same conclusion would follow, as the Appellate Division dissenter noted, were the co-parenting relationship one of ten or more years, and irrespective of how close or deep the emotional ties might be between petitioner and child, or how devastating isolation might be to the child. I cannot agree that such a result is mandated by section 70, or any other law. . . .

CITY OF DALLAS AND MACK VINES V. MICA ENGLAND, 846 S.W. 2D 957 (TEX. 1993)

Mica England, a lesbian, was refused the right to apply for a job with the Dallas police force on the grounds that the state's sodomy laws made lesbianism illegal. As a result, the Texas Court of Appeals ruled that the state's sodomy laws were unconstitutional:

Mica England, appellee, sued the State of Texas, the City of Dallas, and Mack Vines, challenging the constitutionality of the Texas statute criminalizing private sexual relations between consenting adults of the same sex, Tex. Penal Code Ann. §21.06 (West 1989), and seeking to enjoin the Dallas Police Department's policy of not hiring lesbians and gay men because they violate this criminal statute. . . . The trial court now held the statute unconstitutional and enjoined the City of Dallas and its police chief both from enforcing the statute and from denying employment in the police department to lesbians and gay men solely because they violate the statute. . . .

Background

England applied for a position with the Dallas Police Department in 1989. She was invited to interview for the position and, when asked about her sexual orientation, she responded truthfully that she was a lesbian. The interviewer then informed England that under the police department's hiring policy her homosexuality made her ineligible for employment. England sued the police department, Vines (the police chief under whose tenure she was denied employment) and the State, challenging the constitutionality of the hiring policy and the criminal statute underlying the hiring policy. She also sought injunctive relief, damages, and attorney's fees. . . .

After granting the State's plea to the jurisdiction, the trial court granted partial summary judgment, declaring section 21.06 of the Penal Code unconstitutional, and enjoining the police department and its police chief from enforcing the statute and from denying employment in the police department based solely on an applicant's admission of violating section 21.06 or of being homosexual. . . .

The State as sovereign is immune from suit absent its consent. E.g., *Missouri Pac. R.R. v. Brownsville Navigation Dist.*, 453 S.W.2D 812, 813 (Tex. 1970). However, actions of a state official that are unconstitutional, illegal, wrongful, or beyond statutory authority are not immunized by government immunity and a suit seeking relief from the official's conduct is not one against the state. . . .

Conclusion

We affirm the trial court's judgment in all respects.

BAEHR, ET AL. V. LEWIN, 93, C.D.O.S. 3657

In this famous Hawaii case, a group of same-sex couples filed suit demanding the right to engage in same-sex marriages. The Hawaii Supreme Court ruled that the state constitution did not guarantee this right, while also pointing out that the state's ban on same-sex marriage might be illegal, because it violated the state's constitutional protection against discrimination on the basis of sex. The court decision remained pending while the state legislature revised the state constitution to make the court case moot. Following is an excerpt from the original court decision:

Background

On May 1, 1991, the plaintiffs filed a complaint for injunctive and declaratory relief in the Circuit Court of the First Circuit, State of Hawaii, seeking, *inter alia:* (1) a declaration that Hawaii Revised Statutes (HRS) §572-1 (1985)—the section of the Hawaii Marriage Law enumerating the requisites of [a] valid marriage contract [sic]—is unconstitutional insofar as it is construed and applied by the DOH [Department of Health] to justify refusing to issue a marriage license on the *sole* basis that the applicant couple is of the same sex; and (2) preliminary and permanent injunctions prohibiting the future withholding of marriage licenses on that sole basis.

[The Court then reviews the facts of the case, namely that three same-sex couples (the "applicant couples") filed applications for marriage licenses, but were denied by the DOH even though they qualified for such licenses on all criteria except that they were of the same sex. The Court then summarizes the defendant's arguments, essentially that there is no protection for same-sex marriages in Hawaii under either the state or federal constitution. The Court responds first to this point:]

Applying the foregoing standards to the present case, we do not believe that a right to same-sex marriage is so rooted in the traditions and collective conscience of our people that failure to recognize it would violate the fundamental principles of liberty and justice that lie at the base of our civil and political institutions. Neither do we believe that a right to same-sex marriage is implicit in the concept of ordered liberty, such that neither liberty nor justice would exist if it were sacrificed. Accordingly, we hold that the applicant couples do not have a fundamental constitutional right to same-sex marriage arising out of the right to privacy or otherwise.

[The Court then opens a new line of discussion, one that was never raised by the applicants themselves.]

Our holding, however, does not leave the applicant couples without a potential remedy in this case. As we will discuss below, the applicant couples are free to press their equal protection claim. If they are successful, the State of Hawaii will no longer be permitted to refuse marriage licenses to couples merely on the basis that they are of the same sex. But there is no fundamental right to marriage for same-sex couples under Article I, section 6 of the Hawaii Constitution.

[The Court then outlines reasons that the applicant couple may have good cause to continue pressing their case:]

The applicant couples correctly contend that the DOH's refusal to allow them to marry on the basis that they are members of the same sex deprives them of access to a multiplicity of rights and benefits that are contingent upon that status. Although it is unnecessary in this opinion to engage in an encyclopedic recitation of all of them, a number of the most salient marital rights and benefits are worthy of note. They include (1) a variety of state income tax advantages, including deductions, credits, rates, exemptions, and estimates, under HRS chapter 235 (1985 and Supp. 1992); (2) public assistance from and exemptions relating to the Department of Human Services under HRS chapter 346 (1985 and Supp. 1992); (3) control, division, acquisition, and disposition of community property under HRS chapter 510 (1985); (4) rights relating to dower, courtesy, and inheritance under HRS chapter 533 (1985 and Supp. 1992); (5) rights to notice, protection, benefits and inheritance under the Uniform Probate Code, HRS chapter 560 (1985 and Supp. 1992); (6) award of child custody and support payments in divorce proceedings under HRS 571 (1985 and Supp. 1992); (7) the right to spousal support pursuant to HRS §572-24 (1985); (8) the right to enter into premarital agreements under HRS chapter 572D (Supp. 1992); (9) the right to change of name pursuant to HRS §574-5(a)(3) (Supp. 1992); (10) the right to file a nonsupport action under HRS chapter 575 (1985 and Supp. 1992); (11) post-divorce rights relating to support and property division under HRS chapter 580 (1985 and Supp. 1992); (12) the benefit of the spousal privilege and confidential marital communications pursuant to Rule 505 of the Hawaii Rules of Evidence (1985); (13) the benefit of the exemption of real property from attachment or execution under HRS chapter 651 (1985); and (14) the right to bring a wrongful death action under HRS chapter 651 663 (1985 and Supp. 1992). For present purpose, it is not disputed that the applicant couples would be entitled to all of these marital rights and benefits, but for the fact that they are denied access to the state-conferred legal status of marriage.

[The Court then outlines the basis for a different challenge to same-sex marriages in Hawaii:]

The equal protection clauses of the United States and Hawaii Constitutions are not mirror images of one another. The fourteenth amendment to the United States Constitution somewhat concisely provides, in relevant part, that a state may not "deny to any person within its jurisdiction the equal protection of the laws." Hawaii's counterpart is more elaborate. Article I, section 5 of the Hawaii Constitution provides in relevant part that "no person shall . . . be denied the equal protection of the laws, *nor be denied the enjoyment of the person's civil rights or be discriminated against in the exercise thereof because of* race, religion, *sex*, or ancestry." (Emphasis added.) Thus, by plain language, the Hawaii Constitution prohibits its state-sanctioned discrimination against any person in the exercise of his or her civil rights on the basis of sex.

[Finally, the Court renders its conclusion and decision.]

Because, for the reasons stated in this opinion, one circuit court erroneously granted Lewin's [Director of DOH] motion for judgment on the pleadings and dismissed the plaintiff's complaint, we vacate the circuit court's order and judgment and remand this matter for further proceedings consistent with this opinion. On remand, in accordance with the "strict scrutiny" standard, the burden will rest on Lewin to overcome the presumption that HRS §572-1 [the state marriage license law] is unconstitutional by demonstrating that it furthers compelling state interests and is narrowly drawn to avoid unnecessary abridgments of constitutional rights.

APPENDIX B

EXCERPTS FROM STATEMENTS OF GOVERNMENT POLICY AND LEGISLATION

Policy on Homosexual Conduct in the Armed Forces

The following is a summary of the policy in force during most of President Bill Clinton's time in office, taken from a Secretary of Defense Memorandum of July 19, 1993, outlining the policy known as "don't ask, don't tell."

The Department of Defense has long held that, as a general rule, homosexuality is incompatible with military service because it interferes with the factors critical to combat effectiveness, including unit morale, unit cohesion and individual privacy. Nevertheless, the Department of Defense also recognizes that individuals with a homosexual orientation have served with distinction in the armed services of the United States.

Therefore, it is the policy of the Department of Defense to judge the suitability of persons to serve in the armed forces on the basis of their conduct. Homosexual conduct will be grounds for separation from the military services. Sexual orientation is considered a personal and private matter, and homosexual orientation is not a bar to service entry or to continued service unless manifested by homosexual conduct. . . .

POLICY GUIDELINES ON HOMOSEXUAL CONDUCT IN THE ARMED FORCES

Summary of Policy

Accession Policy Applicants for military service will no longer be asked or required to reveal if they are homosexual or bisexual, but applicants will be informed of the conduct that is proscribed for members of the armed forces, including homosexual conduct.

Discharge Policy Sexual orientation will not be a bar to service unless manifested by homosexual conduct. The military will discharge members who engage in homosexual conduct, which is defined as a homosexual act, a statement that the member is homosexual or bisexual, or a marriage or attempted marriage to someone of the same gender.

Investigation Policy No investigations or inquiries will be conducted solely to determine a service member's sexual orientation. Commanders will initiate inquiries or investigations when there is credible information that a basis for discharge or disciplinary action exists. Sexual orientation, absent credible information that a crime has been committed, will not be the subject of a criminal investigation. An allegation or statement by another that a service member is a homosexual, alone, is not grounds for either a criminal investigation or a commander's inquiry.

HATE CRIME STATISTICS ACT

The only existing federal legislation that explicitly makes gay men and lesbians a protected group is the Hate Crime Statistics Act of 1993. However, the act is specifically restricted to gathering statistics. Following is its complete text:

That
(a) this Act may be cited as the 'Hate Crime Statistics Act.'
(b)(1) Under the authority of section 534 of title 28, United States Code [this section] the Attorney General shall acquire data, for the calendar year 1990 and each of the succeeding 4 calendar years, about crimes that manifest evidence of prejudice based on race, religion, sexual orientation, or ethnicity, including where appropriate the crimes of murder, non-negligent manslaughter; forcible rape; aggravated assault, simple assault, intimidation; arson; and destruction, damage or vandalism of property.

(2) The Attorney General shall establish guidelines for the collection of such data including the necessary evidence and criteria that must be present for a finding of manifest prejudice and procedures for carrying out the purposes of this section.

(3) Nothing in this section creates a cause of action or a right to bring an action, including an action based on discrimination due to sexual orientation. As used in this section, the term "sexual orientation" means consensual homosexuality or heterosexuality. This subsection does not limit any existing cause of action or right to bring an action, including any action under the Administrative Procedure Act or the All Writs Act.

(4) Data acquired under this section shall be used only for research or statistical purposes and may not contain any information that may reveal the identity of an individual victim of a crime.

(5) The Attorney General shall publish an annual summary of the data acquired under this section.

(c) There are authorized to be appropriated such sums as may be necessary to carry out the provisions of this section through fiscal year 1994. Sec. 2.

(a) Congress finds that —

(1) the American family life is the foundation of American Society,

(2) Federal policy should encourage the well-being, financial security, and health of the American family,

(3) schools should not de-emphasize the critical value of American family life.

(b) Nothing in this Act [this note] shall be construed, nor shall any funds appropriated to carry out the purpose of the Act [this note] be used, to promote or encourage homosexuality.

DEFENSE OF MARRIAGE ACT (DOMA)

This act was passed by Congress in 1996 to preclude states from legalizing same-sex marriage, as Hawaii seemed poised to do. Due to the "Full Faith and Credit" clause of the U.S. Constitution, states are generally required to acknowledge contracts made in other states. DOMA—whose constitutionality has never been tested—would excuse states from recognizing same-sex marriages performed in other states.

No State, territory, or possession of the United States, or Indian tribe, shall be required to give effect to any public act, record, or judicial proceeding of any other State, territory, possession or tribe respecting a relationship between persons of the same sex that is treated as a marriage under the laws of such other State, territory, possession, or tribe, or a right or claim arising from such relationship.

INDEX

Locators in **boldface** indicate main topics. Locators followed by *c* indicate chronology entries. Locators followed by *b* indicate biographical entries. Locators followed by *g* indicate glossary entries.

Index

349

Index

Index

Index

Index

Index